Soil Fauna Assemblages

Global to Local Scales

This volume provides a modern introduction to the soil fauna and its contributions to ecosystem function, the mechanisms that structure soil fauna assemblages from local to global scales, and the potential impacts of global change on soil fauna assemblages. Written as an accessible primer, this book is a high-level overview of current knowledge rather than a detailed tome of all existing information, with emphasis placed on key findings and general patterns. It focusses on the soil fauna but contextualises these assemblages in relation to the microbial assemblages belowground and the vegetation aboveground.

It is clear that our knowledge of soil fauna assemblages is ever increasing, but there is still a lot to discover. Key areas of research are highlighted, with particular reference to the future of soil fauna assemblages.

UFFE N. NIELSEN is Senior Lecturer at Hawkesbury Institute for the Environment, Western Sydney University, Australia. He is broadly interested in the biogeography and community ecology of soil biota and how belowground assemblages influence ecosystem functioning, particularly in the light of global changes. He has extensive experience with soil fauna assemblages across a broad range of natural and managed ecosystems exploring the diversity and distribution of soil fauna under contemporary and global change scenarios. He has a particular interest in Antarctic ecosystems, and his research has brought him to various sites in continental and maritime Antarctica.

ECOLOGY, BIODIVERSITY, AND CONSERVATION

Series Editors
Michael Usher   *University of Stirling, and formerly Scottish Natural Heritage*
Denis Saunders   *Formerly CSIRO Division of Sustainable Ecosystems, Canberra*
Robert Peet   *University of North Carolina, Chapel Hill*
Andrew Dobson   *Princeton University*

Editorial Board
Paul Adam   *University of New South Wales, Australia*
H. J. B. Birks   *University of Bergen, Norway*
Lena Gustafsson   *Swedish University of Agricultural Science*
Jeff McNeely   *International Union for the Conservation of Nature*
R. T. Paine   *University of Washington*
David Richardson   *University of Stellenbosch*
Jeremy Wilson   *Royal Society for the Protection of Birds*

The world's biological diversity faces unprecedented threats. The urgent challenge facing the concerned biologist is to understand ecological processes well enough to maintain their functioning in the face of the pressures resulting from human population growth. Those concerned with the conservation of biodiversity and with restoration also need to be acquainted with the political, social, historical, economic, and legal frameworks within which ecological and conservation practice must be developed. The new *Ecology, Biodiversity, and Conservation* series will present balanced, comprehensive, up-to-date, and critical reviews of selected topics within the sciences of ecology and conservation biology, both botanical and zoological, and both 'pure' and 'applied'. It is aimed at advanced final-year undergraduates, graduate students, researchers, and university teachers, as well as ecologists and conservationists in industry, government, and the voluntary sectors. The series encompasses a wide range of approaches and scales (spatial, temporal, and taxonomic), including quantitative, theoretical, population, community, ecosystem, landscape, historical, experimental, behavioural, and evolutionary studies. The emphasis is on science related to the real world of plants and animals rather than on purely theoretical abstractions and mathematical models. Books in this series will, wherever possible, consider issues from a broad perspective. Some books will challenge existing paradigms and present new ecological concepts, empirical or theoretical models, and testable hypotheses. Other books will explore new approaches and present syntheses on topics of ecological importance.

Ecology and Control of Introduced Plants
Judith H. Myers and Dawn Bazely

Invertebrate Conservation and Agricultural Ecosystems
T. R. New

Risks and Decisions for Conservation and Environmental Management
Mark Burgman

Ecology of Populations
Esa Ranta, Per Lundberg, and Veijo Kaitala

Nonequilibrium Ecology
Klaus Rohde

The Ecology of Phytoplankton
C. S. Reynolds

Systematic Conservation Planning
Chris Margules and Sahotra Sarkar

Large-Scale Landscape Experiments: Lessons from Tumut
David B. Lindenmayer

Assessing the Conservation Value of Freshwaters: An International Perspective
Philip J. Boon and Catherine M. Pringle

Insect Species Conservation
T. R. New

Bird Conservation and Agriculture
Jeremy D. Wilson, Andrew D. Evans, and Philip V. Grice

Cave Biology: Life in Darkness
Aldemaro Romero

Biodiversity in Environmental Assessment: Enhancing Ecosystem Services for Human Well-being
Roel Slootweg, Asha Rajvanshi, Vinod B. Mathur, and Arend Kolhoff

Mapping Species Distributions: Spatial Inference and Prediction
Janet Franklin

Decline and Recovery of the Island Fox: A Case Study for Population Recovery
Timothy J. Coonan, Catherin A. Schwemm, and David K. Garcelon

Ecosystem Functioning
Kurt Jax

Spatio-Temporal Heterogeneity: Concepts and Analyses
Pierre R. L. Dutilleul

Parasites in Ecological Communities: From Interactions to Ecosystems
Melanie J. Hatcher and Alison M. Dunn

Zoo Conservation Biology
John E. Fa, Stephan M. Funk, and Donnamarie O'Connell

Marine Protected Areas: A Multidisciplinary Approach
Joachim Claudet

Biodiversity in Dead Wood
Jogeir N. Stokland, Juha Siitonen, and Bengt Gunnar Jonsson

Landslide Ecology
Lawrence R. Walker and Aaron B. Shiels

Nature's Wealth: The Economics of Ecosystem Services and Poverty
Pieter J. H. van Beukering, Elissaios Papyrakis, Jetske Bouma, and Roy Brouwer

Birds and Climate Change: Impacts and Conservation Responses
James W. Pearce-Higgins and Rhys E. Green

Marine Ecosystems: Human Impacts on Biodiversity, Functioning and Services
Tasman P. Crowe and Christopher L. J. Frid

Wood Ant Ecology and Conservation
Jenni A. Stockan and Elva J. H. Robinson

Detecting and Responding to Alien Plant Incursions
John R. Wilson, F. Dane Panetta, and Cory Lindgren

Conserving Africa's Mega-Diversity in the Anthropocene: The Hluhluwe-iMfolozi Park Story
Joris P. G. M. Cromsigt, Sally Archibald, and Norman Owen-Smith

National Park Science: A Century of Research in South Africa
Jane Carruthers

Plant Conservation Science and Practice: The Role of Botanic Gardens
Stephen Blackmore and Sara Oldfield

Habitat Suitability and Distribution Models: With Applications in R
Antoine Guisan, Wilfried Thuiller, and Niklaus E. Zimmermann

Ecology and Conservation of Forest Birds
Grzegorz Mikusiński, Jean-Michel Roberge, and Robert J. Fuller

Species Conservation: Lessons from Islands
Jamieson A. Copsey, Simon A. Black, Jim J. Groombridge, and Carl G. Jones

Soil Fauna Assemblages: Global to Local Scales
Uffe N. Nielsen

Soil Fauna Assemblages

Global to Local Scales

UFFE N. NIELSEN
Western Sydney University

CAMBRIDGE
UNIVERSITY PRESS

University Printing House, Cambridge CB2 8BS, United Kingdom

One Liberty Plaza, 20th Floor, New York, NY 10006, USA

477 Williamstown Road, Port Melbourne, VIC 3207, Australia

314–321, 3rd Floor, Plot 3, Splendor Forum, Jasola District Centre, New Delhi – 110025, India

79 Anson Road, #06-04/06, Singapore 079906

Cambridge University Press is part of the University of Cambridge.

It furthers the University's mission by disseminating knowledge in the pursuit of education, learning, and research at the highest international levels of excellence.

www.cambridge.org
Information on this title: www.cambridge.org/9781107191488
DOI: 10.1017/9781108123518

© Uffe N. Nielsen 2019

This publication is in copyright. Subject to statutory exception and to the provisions of relevant collective licensing agreements, no reproduction of any part may take place without the written permission of Cambridge University Press.

First published 2019

A catalogue record for this publication is available from the British Library.

ISBN 978-1-107-19148-8 Hardback

ISBN 978-1-316-64210-8 Paperback

Cambridge University Press has no responsibility for the persistence or accuracy of URLs for external or third-party internet websites referred to in this publication and does not guarantee that any content on such websites is, or will remain, accurate or appropriate.

Contents

Preface		*page* xi
1	**Soil and Its Fauna**	**1**
	1.1 A Brief History of Soil Fauna Ecology As a Field of Research	4
	1.2 Soil As a Habitat	9
	1.3 The Major Players	14
	1.4 Summary	41
2	**Functional Roles of Soil Fauna**	**42**
	2.1 Ecosystem Functioning	43
	2.2 Aboveground–Belowground Linkages	74
	2.3 Plant–Soil Feedbacks	78
	2.4 Soil Biodiversity and Ecosystem Functioning	80
	2.5 Summary	85
3	**Approaches to Studying Soil Fauna and Its Functional Roles**	**86**
	3.1 Quantifying Soil Fauna	87
	3.2 Diversity, Distribution, and Phylogeny	94
	3.3 Soil Fauna Functional Traits	97
	3.4 Contributions to Ecosystem Processes	101
	3.5 Soil Fauna As Bioindicators	110
	3.6 Statistical Tools	114
	3.7 Summary	119
4	**Soil Fauna Biogeography and Macroecology**	**121**
	4.1 Biogeographical Patterns	122
	4.2 Species-Area Relationship	135
	4.3 Distance-Decay Relationships	137
	4.4 Latitudinal Gradients	139
	4.5 Altitudinal Gradients	144

viii · Contents

	4.6	Regional versus Local Species Richness	148
	4.7	Distribution of Rare versus Abundant Species	149
	4.8	Summary	150
5	**Soil Fauna Assemblages at Fine Scales to Landscapes**		**152**
	5.1	Landscape to Continental Scales	152
	5.2	Ecosystem Scales	160
	5.3	Fine-Scale Patterns of Biodiversity	175
	5.4	Summary	190
6	**Anthropogenic Impacts on Soil Fauna Assemblages**		**192**
	6.1	Management Practices	193
	6.2	Fertilisation and Nitrogen Deposition	203
	6.3	Agrochemicals and Other Pollutants	206
	6.4	Impacts of Invasive Species	210
	6.5	Summary	220
7	**Climate Change Impacts on Soil Fauna**		**221**
	7.1	Elevated CO_2	222
	7.2	Warming	226
	7.3	Altered Rainfall Regimes	233
	7.4	Elevated O_3	239
	7.5	Global Change Interactions	241
	7.6	Summary	245
8	**Soil Fauna Assemblage Succession and Restoration**		**246**
	8.1	Successional Patterns of Soil Fauna Assemblage Structure	247
	8.2	Belowground Effects of Restoration Practices	254
	8.3	Potential for Soil Fauna to Aid Remediation of Degraded Sites	260
	8.4	Implications for Ecosystem Resistance and Resilience	265
	8.5	Summary	266

9	**The Future of Soil Fauna Assemblages**	**268**
	9.1 The Future of Soil Fauna Assemblages	270
	9.2 Managing Soil Fauna Biodiversity	272
	9.3 Harnessing Soil Biodiversity for Sustainable Land Use and Human Well-Being	278
	9.4 Critical Knowledge Gaps and Research Directions	284
	9.5 Summary	290
	Bibliography	291
	Index	351

Preface

Ecologists have long been fascinated by the diversity of life in soil (e.g. Anderson 1975, Bardgett 2002, Nielsen et al. 2010b), but the intricate nature of soils and small size of the organisms therein have made progress slow compared with other terrestrial ecosystems. Still, our knowledge of the ecology of soil fauna has been accumulating relatively rapidly over the past few decades, particularly due to an increased recognition of their role in ecosystem functioning and service provisioning, improved sensitivity of analytical equipment, and the application of molecular tools. It is thus well established that soil fauna assemblages are abundant and highly diverse, representing a broad range of life history strategies and feeding types, and that this fauna plays an essential role in ecosystem functionality, plant community dynamics, and even human health (e.g. Nielsen et al. 2015b, Wall et al. 2015). Determining how the diversity and composition of soil fauna communities influence ecosystem functioning, particularly in the light of global change, is one of the key research questions in contemporary soil ecology. Answering this question, however, requires a basic and robust understanding of soil fauna assemblages.

It is becoming increasingly clear that many soil invertebrates (including the unicellular protists) are not cosmopolitan, and that most taxa have restricted distributions and show distinct biogeographical patterns (e.g. Bates et al. 2013, Decaëns 2010, Nielsen et al. 2014, Wu et al. 2011a). The work by Decaëns (2010) in particular shows that it is possible to define macroecological patterns of belowground communities. His work confirms that many types of soil fauna show altitudinal, latitudinal, or area gradients in the same way as described for aboveground organisms, but that different mechanisms may structure aboveground and belowground assemblages at smaller scales. This builds on conceptual frameworks such as the one presented by Ettema and Wardle (2002) that illustrates the mechanisms that govern soil fauna diversity and assemblage structure at scales ranging from very fine spatial scales to regional scales. Such syntheses of knowledge and development of conceptual frameworks are highly important for progressing soil fauna ecology as a field.

This book is intended to provide an overview, rather than a detailed account of all studies, of patterns of soil fauna assemblage structure through time and space at local to global scales, with an explicit consideration of global change impacts and potential implications for ecosystem functioning. Our knowledge of soil fauna assemblages has accumulated rapidly over the past few decades, but there have been few attempts to unify and consolidate this knowledge to date. Although there is still much to learn, it thus appears timely to synthesise the knowledge we do have to take stock of what we currently know about soil fauna assemblages at local to global scales and the mechanisms that govern these, identify and describe biogeographical and macroecological patterns, and assess how soil fauna assemblage structure might be influenced by global change. This will broadly make it possible to provide evidence-based recommendations for more sustainable land management regimes harnessing the benefits of soil fauna and for conservation of soil faunal biodiversity. It will also help us identify key knowledge gaps and future research directions. The inclusion of global changes will be a critical component of the book given that a substantial part of Earth's terrestrial ecosystems has already been impacted by human activities. The book considers soil fauna very broadly, ranging from the oft-overlooked unicellular Protista to the abundant and diverse nematodes and microarthropods and the larger multicellular organisms such as earthworms, ants, and termites that act as ecosystem engineers. Protista will be included because they are an essential part of the soil food web, and although generally considered microbial given their single-celled nature, they are rarely considered in assessments of microbial assemblages which generally focus solely on archaeal, bacterial, and fungal components. A basic understanding of soil fauna ecology and its contribution to ecosystems is fundamental to appreciate the value of studying soil fauna assemblages; hence, the first couple of chapters will be dedicated to this topic. The book will not discuss in detail assemblage patterns of vertebrates and organisms that only spend part of their life history in soils (e.g. many insect larvae pupate in soils), but their role in Earth's ecosystems will be highlighted where relevant.

The book can be broadly divided into four virtual sections that address specific aims. First, Chapters 1 through 3 aim to provide the reader with a broad introduction to the soil fauna (Chapter 1), its functional roles in ecosystems (Chapter 2), and how soil fauna and its functional roles can be studied, with a particular focus on recent technological developments (Chapter 3). These chapters thus provide a strong foundation for contextualising the rest of the book. Second, Chapters 4 and 5 present an overview of our current understanding of patterns and drivers of soil fauna species distribution and assemblage structure and composition at global to local scales. These chapters will thus cover topics ranging from soil fauna biogeography and macroecology (Chapter 4) to patterns of assemblage structure at landscape scales to fine scales (Chapter 5). This should provide the reader with a robust understanding of why soil fauna assemblages look the way they do and a strong fundament for predicting the future state of soil fauna assemblages. Third, Chapters 6 through 8 will cover global change impacts, with Chapter 6 mostly focusing on direct impact (i.e. land use, management practices, invasive species) while Chapter 7 will focus on climate change impacts. Chapter 8 is focused on ecological restoration, which aims to restore ecosystems following global change impacts. I have included succession in this chapter because ecological restoration practices fundamentally rely on the process of succession to restore ecosystems. Finally, Chapter 9 will synthesise this information and look to the future of soil fauna assemblages. A particular focus will be given to the potential benefits we can gain from better management of soil fauna assemblages in natural and human-influenced ecosystems.

Finally, I would like to thank all of the people who have been involved directly or indirectly in making this book a reality. First, I would like to acknowledge Michael B. Usher, Dominic Lewis, and Cambridge University Press for their invitation to write this book and their support throughout the process. Without their encouragement I would not have taken on a project of this size to begin with. Second, I would like to thank all the people who have taken their time to provide feedback on drafts of one or more chapters, including Stef Bokhorst, Tancredi Caruso, David Coleman, Stefan Geisen, Patricia Gilarte, Christian Mulder, Casper Quist, Heikki Setälä, and Diana Wall. Their constructive feedback has been crucial to produce the final version of the book. Several people, including Byron J. Adams, Steven Chown, Stefan Geisen, Hans Petter Leinaas, Michael Plewka, Johan Six, and Kenneth Tinnesen, have also been kind enough to share their photos, which has made for a more visually pleasing book. Finally, I would like to thank my family and friends for understanding my dedication to research, long hours in the office and at home, and accepting my 'mental absence' while working on the book. Special gratitude goes to my partner, Ashley King, for her encouragement and support throughout the process, and for interpreting my crude sketches into professional diagrams.

To the reader – I hope you enjoy this book and that it will spur or increase your interest in the soil fauna, both in and of itself, and because of its importance to our ecosystems.

1 · *Soil and Its Fauna*

Soils provide the foundation of human existence, with most of contemporary food, fuel, and fibre production being soil based, and the delivery of these goods is critical to human prosperity. The realisation that the future of the human population depends on healthy soils is by no means recent, dating back as far as work by Aristotle and later Charles Darwin. Wallwork (1976) formalised it when he wrote that '[i]t is now recognized that an ecological approach, through conservation, is the only way Man can exploit his natural resources without endangering their potential for future generations.' While this critical role of soils to human populations has long been recognised, our understanding of what makes soil function is still developing. Briefly described, it is now widely recognised that soil formation is a time-consuming process that depends on parent material, climate, topography, time, and the biota including soil fauna (Jenny 1941), and that a range of factors, both abiotic and biotic, governs ecosystem functioning (Bardgett 2005). In essence, the plants aboveground capture carbon (C) from the air through photosynthesis, which fuels the ecosystem, using nutrients and water retrieved from the soil to produce organic matter. A large part of the organic matter produced by plants ends up in the soil through plant root production, the release of root exudates or through allocation of C to microbial symbionts, or via deposits of leaf and woody material or animal faecal matter following herbivory. The microorganisms and fauna inhabiting the soil then recycle the plant-derived organic matter. The soil microbes can be considered the true 'engine' of the soils, governing most soil processes and accounting for some 80%–95% of all heterotrophic soil respiration, but direct and indirect interactions with the soil fauna have large implications for soil functioning. Indeed, the presence of certain species of soil fauna can fundamentally modify ecosystem structure and functioning.

The soil fauna, the lead character of this book, thus forms an essential component of the soil food web that is intimately linked to ecosystem functioning through both direct and indirect effects, ultimately influencing humans through the delivery of ecosystem services. A robust understanding of the current distribution of soil fauna, its contributions to ecosystem functioning, and responses to global changes is therefore critical to make informed predictions about the future state of our ecosystems and improved land use management. The soil fauna is also interesting to study in and of itself because of the astonishing diversity and abundance found belowground. Indeed, the recognition of this diversity of life found in soils prompted the popular phrase 'the poor man's rainforest' coined by Usher et al. (1979). It is now well established that our soils are teeming with life, representing a broad array of morphologies and life history strategies (Giller 1996; Figure 1.1), and that this biota is itself a critical component of what we term 'soil' (Jenny 1941). Indeed, a conservative estimate is that more than 360,000 species, approximately a quarter of all hitherto described living species, are soil or litter dwellers (Decaëns et al. 2006). This fauna can be broadly divided into 'full-time' and 'part-time' soil inhabitants, with the latter including many soil-dwelling insect larvae, mound-building insects, and vertebrates (Wolters 2001). However, strictly speaking we can define 'true' soil fauna as that which occupies and forages in soils or in the litter layer at least during part of its life cycle. This definition excludes many larger vertebrates that construct tunnels or colonies in soil but forage on vegetation or animals aboveground. This book will focus on the fauna that spends most, if not all, of its life in close association with soils, but the interactions with and impacts of other soil occupants will be discussed where pertinent to the understanding of soil fauna contributions to ecosystem functioning, distribution, or assemblage composition.

The diversity of soil fauna has long captured the attention of soil ecologists (Anderson 1975, Macfadyen 1962), particularly the question of what mechanisms allow so many species to co-exist within the soil matrix and how their activities influence our ecosystems. There are, however, still many unanswered questions relating to the biology, ecology, and biochemistry of soils prompting several prominent researchers to label soils as 'a biotic frontier' (André et al. 1994, Hågvar 1998). Our understanding of soil ecology is increasing at a rapid rate, but there is still a great need for new investigators in the field, and there are likely many significant novel insights yet to come. Indeed, the development of novel techniques, more sensitive equipment, and new analytical approaches hold great promise for substantial developments in the field of soil ecology, including a stronger characterisation of soil fauna assemblages and their contributions to ecosystem function. Despite the acknowledgement

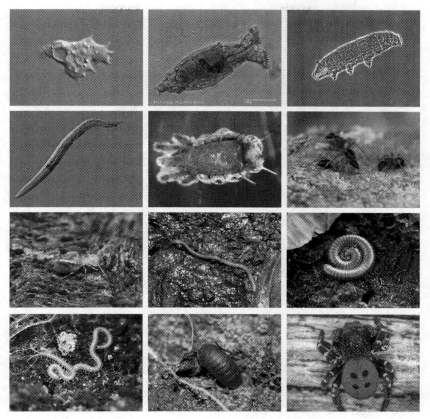

Figure 1.1 Examples of some common soil-associated fauna. Top panel (from left): Protozoa (*Acanthamoeba* sp.; courtesy of Stefan Geisen); the rotifer *Mniobia magna* (Rotifera; courtesy of Michael Plewka, Hattingen, Germany); the Antarctic tardigrade *Mesobiotus polaris* (Tardigrada). Second panel from top (from left): the nematode *Caenorhabditis elegans* (Nematoda; courtesy of Michael Plewka, Hattingen, Germany); oribatid mite (Acari: Oribatida); ant (Hymenoptera: Formicidae). Second panel from bottom (from left): termite (Isoptera); earthworm (Annelida: Megadrilacea); millipede (Myriapoda: Diplopoda). Bottom panel (from left): centipede (Myriapoda: Chilopoda); woodlouse (Isopoda); the spider *Eresus sandaliatus* commonly known as ladybird spider (Aranae; courtesy of Kenneth Tinnesen). Photos by the author unless noted otherwise.

of the astonishing diversity found belowground and its contribution to ecosystem services, there has to date been limited concern about the possible loss of soil biodiversity and the consequences for the future of soils (Veresoglou et al. 2015, Wolters 2001). Soil fauna has also been of more direct value to humans by providing a significant source of protein throughout history, and many indigenous peoples still consume a broad variety of soil-dwelling animals including earthworms, insect larvae, and termites (Decaëns et al. 2006). Indeed, Alfred R. Wallace described this phenomenon more than 150 years ago (Wallace 1853). Still, this is rarely taken into account when the value of soil fauna is considered today. I hope this book will pique interest in soil fauna assemblages and their role in ecosystems and encourage the development of stronger frameworks to promote the explicit consideration of soil fauna in conservation and land management more broadly.

With this in mind, the aim of this chapter is to provide an overview of the development of soil fauna ecology as a field of research, describe soils as a habitat for soil fauna, and introduce the main groups of soil fauna. Chapter 2 covers the contributions of this fauna to ecosystem processes. I define soil fauna broadly to include the heterotrophic, unicellular, eukaryotic Protozoa as part of the soil microfauna. The Protozoa are ubiquitous in soils and play a key role in carbon (C) and nutrient cycling but are rarely discussed in conjunction with bacterial, fungal, or Archaeal assemblages. I also include examples of 'part-time' soil fauna, i.e. fauna that spends only part of its life cycle in soil, where it is deemed to be particularly relevant to the functioning of the soil and plant communities, or when it influences the distribution of other soil fauna.

1.1 A Brief History of Soil Fauna Ecology As a Field of Research

Naturalists have long had a keen interest in the organisms that inhabit soils, both because of the interesting nature of the organisms found in soils and because it has been known for centuries that the functioning of soils itself is underlain by the intricate interactions between the myriad of organisms that live within. For example, although the ability of the earthworm *Lumbricus terrestris* to modify its environment was described in detail by Darwin (1881), even Aristotle understood the contributions of earthworms to organic matter decomposition (Edwards and Lofty 1977). Understandably, the investigations of soil fauna and its role in ecosystems were initially focused on the larger soil fauna because of the difficulties of observing the smaller soil fauna. Indeed, the vast majority of the soil fauna diversity was recognised only after the Dutch businessman and scientist Antoni van Leeuwenhoek modified the microscope to view biological samples in the late 1600s. He went on to describe a range of 'animalcules' using this design, including several types of soil microfauna

1.1 A Brief History of Soil Fauna Ecology As a Field of Research · 5

that we now know are common in soil, such as protists, rotifers, and tardigrades. Soil fauna ecology as a field of research has progressed rapidly since then, particularly since the beginning of the twentieth century.

Early work by the Danish biologist C. F. Bornebusch on the fauna of forest soil, particularly oak and beech, outlining the differences in relative abundance of key soil fauna groups (Bornebusch 1930) has since been validated by more recent work (Wallwork 1976). Similarly, feeding activity of collembolans was explored in the early twentieth century by Macnamara (1924), providing the first insights into soil food web interactions. While Protozoa were discovered by the users of the early microscopes, the field of soil 'protistology' did not begin in earnest until the early twentieth century when a few seminal studies began to unravel the importance of protozoans in soils through work undertaken in Rothamsted, England (Wilkinson et al. 2012). Later work by Weis-Fogh (1948) and Petersen and Luxton (1982) in consolidating contemporary knowledge of soil biota across biomes was hugely important to our understanding of belowground assemblages. The diversity and distribution of soil fauna, and its contributions to ecosystem functioning, have since these publications been the topic of several books, including *The Diversity and Distribution of Soil Fauna* by Wallwork (1976), *The Biology of Soils: A Community and Ecosystem Approach* by Bardgett (2005), and the third edition of *Fundamental of Soil Ecology* by Coleman et al. (2018). These books and others synthesise the literature and have provided great insight into the world belowground and the role of soil fauna in our ecosystems. They therefore helped to frame soil fauna ecology as a field of research and have substantially shaped the approaches we use today. While this book will cover some of the topics presented in these works where they intersect with soil fauna assemblages, I would implore anyone interested in soil ecology to revisit these books for a broader perspective. They also provide an interesting perspective into how our understanding of soil ecology has changed over time beyond the following overview.

This brings us to the conundrum of distribution patterns of soil fauna. As our knowledge of the diversity belowground increases, so does our understanding of the possible 'true' distribution of these organisms. At a global scale we recognise and describe broad patterns of species distributions in the field of biogeography, which originated as a field of research in the mid-eighteenth century, building on the early discovery by the French naturalist Georges-Louis Leclerc, Comte de Buffon (1707–88), that groups of organisms differ between geographical regions. Earthworms were similarly noted very early on to have achieved greater distribution than what was expected (Beddard 1912, Eisen 1900), indicating that human activities have long been modifying soil fauna assemblages. The origin of the biogeography of microfauna as a field dates back to the mid-nineteenth-century work by Christian Gottfried Ehrenberg, who noted that the ciliate fauna differed between mountain ranges (described in Heger et al. 2011). Biogeography has had a significant impact on ecology through the study of similarities, and dissimilarities, of fauna and flora of different patterns of the Earth. Early on it was recognised that the contemporary distribution of organisms did not reflect the current position of Earth's landmasses, giving rise to the hypothesis that these must have been placed differently in the past. However, this was against the paradigm that Earth's landmasses were fixed in position. A German meteorologist, Alfred Wegener, who recognised the discrepancies between the distribution of flora and fauna and global geography, challenged this idea in 1912. He posed that continents changed position over time through the process of 'continental drift' (see Chapter 4). Hence, biological evidence provided early indications of a heretofore unrecognised process. The acceptance of continental drift as a phenomenon was, however, not fully accepted until much later in the 1960s after geological data provided further supporting evidence given the initial reluctance to consider the idea more carefully. In terms of contemporary distribution patterns of flora and fauna the focus is generally on 'ecological biogeography'. That is, in very broad terms, why are species where they are, what restricts them from colonising other areas, why are there more species in some areas than others, what are the relationship with climate, topography, soil, latitude, etc.? By contrast, 'historical geography' addresses questions related to constraints on species ranges at geological timescales touching on evolutionary and phylogenetic relationships, influence of past geography and climate, and dispersal. For a more in-depth description of the evolution of biogeography as a field I encourage the reader to consult Cox et al. (2016). However, it is essential to recognise ecological and historical biogeography as important drivers of the patterns we observed today.

It is now evident that soil fauna assemblages are highly variable through both time and space. The next logical question is then, how does belowground variability in assemblage structure and composition influence ecosystem functioning? The progress in understanding the contribution of soil fauna to ecosystem functioning has largely been spurred by critical developments in the field, causing leaps in knowledge at particular times. As described in Huhta (2007) limited effort was

1.1 A Brief History of Soil Fauna Ecology As a Field of Research

made to quantify the role of soil fauna to ecosystem functioning until the era of litter bag studies began in the late 1950s. The litter bags were used to manipulate the soil fauna assemblages by limiting the access of organisms above certain sizes, for example, excluding macrofauna using mesh sizes of 2 mm diameter, or macrofauna and mesofauna by using smaller mesh sizes sometimes in combination with various biocides to exclude specific taxa, or conversely by containing soil fauna within the bags themselves (e.g. enchytraeids, Standen 1978). The contribution of the excluded (or contained) fauna particularly to litter decomposition could then be quantified by comparing the treatments with and without the fauna. The method has been criticised due to certain shortcomings, such as not accounting for litter mass loss due to fragmentation, changes in the microclimate, and unrealistic removal of soil fauna (see the discussion in Kampichler and Bruckner 2009; Chapter 2), but has provided significant insights into the contribution of soil fauna to ecosystem processes particularly in the early applications and is still a popular and useful approach to address certain questions. Early reviews of the method thus concluded that soil meso- and macrofauna contribute significantly to litter decomposition processes but had mixed effects on mineralisation processes (Edwards et al. 1970, Seastedt 1984).

Another period of significant progress in soil fauna ecology occurred during the International Biological Program from the late 1960s to the mid-1970s that had the main aim of quantifying patterns of metabolism, energy flow, and productivity among biomes (Huhta 2007). It provided new insight into soil food webs, with one of the main findings that the soil fauna decomposer assemblages generally had somewhat lower than expected impacts, usually less than 10% of all material assimilated (Petersen and Luxton 1982), on energy flows. However, these estimates largely exclude the contribution of protozoans due to technical constraints, and several studies provided evidence that the contribution of this group could be substantial, possibly exceeding that of all other soil fauna combined (Macfadyen 1963, Persson et al. 1980). Soil microcosm approaches have similarly provided substantial insights into ecosystem functioning but were not adopted to address questions related to soil fauna contributions until the early 1960s (Patten and Witkamp 1967). Since then, however, many key findings have been based on micro- or mesocosm approaches, with a particularly large interest in such studies in the 1980s and 1990s (Huhta 2007). These systems have allowed researchers to manipulate the soil food web to investigate effects on C and nutrient cycling, plant growth, and ecosystem function more broadly, and have provided substantial insight into the diversity–functioning relationship belowground. Most of the early studies found limited effects of species richness *per se*, with the main effects being driven by functional traits or by keystone species (Filser 2003, Huhta et al. 1998, Laakso and Setälä 1999b). Later reviews have supported these initial findings but suggest that there is a bit more to it and that the loss of soil biodiversity including fauna can substantially impact ecosystem functioning, particularly when the impacts on multiple functions are considered over temporal and spatial scales (de Graaff et al. 2015, Nielsen et al. 2011a).

Similarly, in the 1960s soil sterilisation using γ-irradiation was applied as a novel tool to address soil ecological questions, both in the field and in the laboratory, with David C. Coleman and colleagues largely pioneering this work. For example, they sterilised soil cores collected in the field, subsequently inoculating these with individual fungal strains, and then placed them at field sites and followed the colonisation of soil fauna, rationalising that mite and springtail species that colonised soil cores with individual fungi showed a preference for these (Coleman and Macfadyen 1966). They also used γ-emitting ^{65}Zinc radioisotopes to label soil fungi in the field and subsequently tracked the radioactive compounds as they moved through the soil food web to delineate soil fungal food webs (Coleman and McGinnis 1970). Since these early experiments, the use of stable isotope approaches, including stable isotope labelling, particularly using ^{13}C, ^{15}N, and, more recently, ^{18}O, have become more common and have provided substantial insight into the structure of soil food webs and potential food sources of soil fauna (see Chapters 2 and 3).

The latest substantial leap forward relating to the ecology and biogeography of soil fauna relied on the development of molecular sequencing approaches. These approaches were initially used in soils to investigate microbial assemblage composition but were soon adapted to the larger eukaryotic soil fauna as well (see Chapter 3 for a broader discussion of the application of molecular approaches to investigate soil fauna assemblages). The main advantages of sequencing approaches lie in their ability to provide higher resolution than morphological characteristics, thus allowing us to gain further insight into phylogenetic relationships, better distinguish closely related taxa, or provide insight into cryptic species complexes; with some limitations more recent high-throughput sequencing approaches can even provide whole assemblage fingerprints. However, getting relative abundance data from sequencing approaches remains a significant obstacle for multicellular taxa, which generally restricts us to using presence/absence data only or matching more focused sequencing approaches with abundance data gathered through quantitative polymerase chain reaction (PCR) assays, or by more 'old school' morphological counting. Moreover, we are yet to define robust species delineation protocols for soil fauna based on molecular tools. This is not a problem where reference sequences are known, but the existing databases are far behind.

1.2 Soil As a Habitat

To understand the complexity and diversity of soil fauna assemblages and how they are distributed through space and time it is necessary to consider the constraints imposed on soil fauna by soil as a habitat. Soil is a highly complex, three-dimensionally heterogeneous habitat consisting of mineral particles, air- and water-filled pores, as well as decomposing and living organic matter, including the soil biota itself. The mineral component can be characterised based on the relative size distribution of particles (Figure 1.2), with the particle size increasing from clay (0.000–0.002 mm) to silt (0.002–0.02 mm) to fine sand (0.02–0.2 mm) and coarse sand (0.2–2 mm), and the chemical characteristics of the mineral components. Soil texture exerts a significant control on soil structure and associated traits, such as water infiltration and water holding capacity. The chemical characteristics of the mineral component depend strongly on parent material, but also on geophysical and biological processes, and soil type and origin therefore moderate the availability of nutrients essential to plants and soil organisms. Soil structure is also greatly influenced by organic input of plant and animal origin. Indeed, the distribution of decomposing organic material and plant roots strongly influences the distribution and activity of soil biota, including the fauna, within the soil horizon but also contributes to distribution of soil fauna at larger scales (Beare et al. 1995). The authors recognised five 'arenas' of particular high biological activity in soils: the porosphere, the drilosphere, the rhizosphere, the detritusphere, and the aggregatusphere, while Lavelle and Spain (2001) identify another area of activity – the termitosphere.

The porosphere (*sensu* Vannier 1987) represents the system of pores of varying sizes, constructed through both physical and biological activity that is occupied by the soil biota. Larger types of soil fauna such as earthworms and some species of enchytraeids (Didden 1993, Hamilton and Dindal 1983) can physically engineer the soil structure, but most soil biota are dependent on pre-existing pores as their habitat. The drilosphere (*sensu* Hamilton and Dindal 1983) refers to the activity of

10 · Soil and Its Fauna

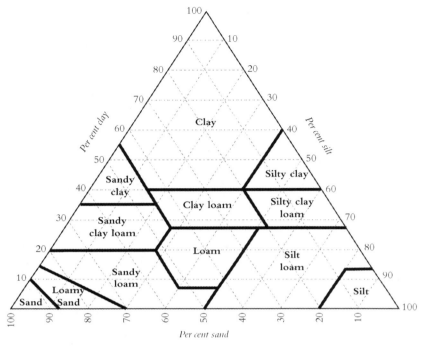

Figure 1.2 Soil texture is classified based on particle size distribution, specifically clay (0.000–0.002 mm), silt (0.002–0.02 mm) and fine sand (0.02–0.2 mm), and coarse sand (0.2–2 mm).
Modified from USDA (1951).

earthworms, both the formation of mounds and vertical distribution of fragmented litter, which leads to the formation of hotspots of organic materials (Maraun et al. 1999). During growth, several forms of organic compounds, such as sugars and amino acids, are 'leaked' from plant roots, which stimulate microbial activity (Feldman 1988). The rhizosphere, a term coined by Hiltner (1904), refers to the zone around the root where microbial and faunal activity is stimulated by plant influences, including exudates that comprise a significant proportion of plant photosynthetically derived C (Lavelle and Spain 2001). The zone of recognisable litter from plants composes the detritusphere, which is also sometimes referred to as the litter system. Both the quantity and quality of the litter can influence the biological assemblages that occur in the litter layer (Beare et al. 1995). Finally, the term aggregatusphere refers to the aggregations of particles in soils formed through physical, chemical, and biological processes (Lee and Foster 1991). Lavelle and Spain (2001)

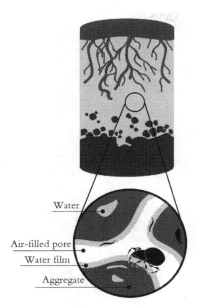

Figure 1.3 Most soil micro- and mesofauna are restricted to existing pores within the soil matrix. The microfauna, such as protists, nematodes, rotifers, and tardigrades, are essentially (semi-) aquatic organisms and require a water-filled pore or a water film on soil aggregates for feeding and movement. The soil mesofauna, such as mites and springtails, are generally confined to air-filled soil pores.

further identify the termitosphere as the area impacted by termite nests and browsing activities given the substantial impact of termites on landscape topography, distribution of organic material, and decomposition processes. Because the processes occurring within, and the structural differences between, these biological hotspots differ, the organisms found in these hotspots also differ predictably. Hence, the distribution of these hotspots has a profound influence on species distribution and assemblage composition of soil biota.

As mentioned earlier, many smaller types of soil fauna and the microbes are dependent on existing soil pores as a habitat. The 'aquatic' organisms, specifically protists, nematodes, rotifers, and tardigrades, are restricted to water-filled pores and water films around plant roots and soil particles or aggregates, while other taxa such as mites and springtails rely on air-filled soil pores (Figure 1.3). Hence, the pore size distribution of a given soil and its availability influence the abundance and distribution of individual soil fauna taxa (Ducarme et al. 2004, Nielsen et al. 2008). The distribution of soil pores is in turn influenced by larger soil fauna, such as earthworms, that can act as ecosystem engineers (*sensu* Jones et al. 1997; Chapter 2). Soil pores can be roughly divided into micro-, meso-, and macropores. Micropores are less than 0.15 µm wide and their volume/distribution depends on soil texture. The water in these pores is held tightly with water potentials exceeding −1.5 MPa, making it unavailable for plants. Mesopores are those between 0.15 and 30 µm in which the water potential is −1.5 to −0.05 MPa, with the water available to plants. These pores can be of biological origin or formed by physical processes. The macropores are those >30 µm from which water drains freely. These pores can be of various origins but are mostly due to soil bioturbation. The soil pore volume distribution thus interacts with soil water content to control soil fauna distribution and activity, at least those that cannot easily relocate to more favourable conditions. A good example is presented by the differences between the two dominant groups of soil microarthropods, the springtails and the mites. Isotomid springtails are sensitive to water potentials below −1.5 MPa, whereas most oribatid mites are not affected until water potentials approach −9.8 MPa (Vannier 1987). This difference in water affinity subsequently influences the distribution of mites and springtails, both within and among ecosystems. Furthermore, divergent physiological sensitivity to soil water availability is likely to contribute to taxa-specific responses to climate change, in this case specifically changes in soil water content driven by altered rainfall regime and/or increased temperatures (see Chapter 6 for discussion).

The majority of the soil biota is found in the organic (O) horizon. Accordingly, a substantial proportion of biological activities takes place in this horizon (Bardgett et al. 2005b). The O horizon is often subdivided into a litter layer (L), which consists mainly of fresh litter, a fermentation layer (F) comprised primarily of fragmented litter, and a humus layer (H) characterised by humified organic matter (Figure 1.4). The distribution and depth of these layers depend largely on biological activities, which have led to the classification of three main types of organic horizons with specific characteristics: mull, moder, and mor (Ponge 2003). Mull is generally characterised by rapid decomposition of litter and homogenisation of the layers by burrowing animals, such as earthworms (see Chapter 2). This also leads to an inconspicuous transition between the O horizon and the mineral horizon beneath (Ponge 2003). The biomass of soil fauna is often very high in this type of humus (Petersen and Luxton 1982, Schaefer and Schauermann 1990). In contrast, the lower biological activity associated with moder allows the development of distinct L, F, and H horizons (Schaefer and Schauermann 1990). Some groups of soil

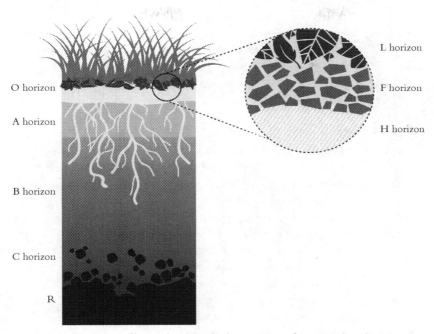

Figure 1.4 The soil profile can be described as a series of more or less distinct 'layers'. These layers commonly include the organic (O) horizon, which can be further divided into layers composed of fresh litter (L), fragmented litter (F), and decomposing organic material (H); a mineral (A) horizon incorporating degraded organic material; a mineral subsurface (B) horizon with limited rock structure or organic matter; and a mineral horizon (C) with unconsolidated rock structure overlaying bedrock.
Modified from Bridges (2007) with permission of Cambridge University Press.

fauna, such as the enchytraeids, are particularly abundant in this humus form (Didden 1993), but the biomass of soil fauna is generally small compared to that found in the mull-type humus. Moreover, due to low biological activity, decomposition and nutrient turnover rates are much slower, allowing humified litter and faecal pellets to accumulate (Ponge 2003). Also, the moder-type humus form is often more acidic than the mull-type humus form, and the microbial community is dominated by fungi. Finally, the mor humus form is characterised by an accumulation of undecomposed plant material due to very low animal and microbial activity (Ponge 2003). Most of the habitable pore space and resources are found in the upper parts of the soil horizon so most soil organisms are found in this space. The exception to this is the larger soil fauna including the earthworms that can construct their own living space and redistribute organic material at their will. For a more complete picture of soil development, with its chemical and physical properties, I refer the interested reader to consult the work by Coleman et al. (2004) and other books, e.g. Dindal (1980), Wallwork (1970), Lavelle and Spain (2001).

1.3 The Major Players

As highlighted earlier, soils are home to a myriad of fauna, ranging from the minute single-celled Protozoa to the small multicellular nematodes to the large earthworms, insects, and even vertebrates. In this section, I will provide a brief overview of the main groups of soil fauna that we are likely to encounter in most ecosystems. While the focus will be on the fauna that spends the entirety of its life cycle within or associated with the soil (i.e. the litter layer), I will also provide some information on fauna that is found in soils during specific life-cycle stages when it is pertinent to the topic at hand. It will quickly become evident that the diversity of soil fauna is significant, but it is worth highlighting early on that a large proportion of the small-sized soil fauna is yet to be described. The 'identification gap', i.e. the proportion of species yet to be described, is inversely related to body size so that we generally know less about the smaller species (Table 1.1). However, there is still substantial uncertainty about the true number of species that is found in soil.

The diversity of soil fauna and high proportion of species that have not been described present us with some difficulties when we try to describe or quantify soil fauna assemblages and soil food web structure. There are many ways that we might try to classify soil fauna to make this diversity more manageable. An early attempt at classifying soil fauna was made by Wallwork (1970), who used body length to categorise soil fauna. While this approach had some advantages, particularly that length is generally correlated with body mass, soil fauna is instead traditionally broadly categorised based on body width as microfauna, mesofauna, and macrofauna following Swift et al. (1979; Figure 1.5). I will follow this denomination because it fits broadly with differences in important life history and functional traits of the soil fauna. For example, most microfauna (i.e. <0.1 mm body width) are essentially aquatic, whereas the mesofauna (i.e. body width of 0.1–2 mm) generally lives in existing air-filled soil pores. As more species are described and information about their feeding habits is acquired, there is, however, great potential to further distinguish between organisms at different trophic levels or even functional guilds.

Table 1.1. *Overview of soil fauna diversity and approximate maximal abundances, estimated known and unknown species in soils, and the percentage of global species described to date*

Taxa	Local richness (per unit)	Approximate maximal abundance (per unit)	Described species (in soil)	Estimated species (in soil)	Per cent described (of global richness)
Protozoa	150–1,200 $(0.25\ g)^{-1}$	$10 \times 10^6\ g^{-1}$	40,000	200,000	0.7%
Nematoda	10–100 m^{-2}	$20 \times 10^6\ m^{-2}$	5,000	20,000	0.5%
Acari	100–150 m^{-2}	400,000 m^{-2}	30,000	80,000	2.8%
Collembola	20 m^{-2}	200,000 m^{-2}	8,000	24,000	27.1%
Enchytraeidae	1–25 m^{-2}	300,000 m^{-2}	600	1,200	50%
Annelida	10–15 m^{-2}	500 m^{-2}	3,600	7,000	47.6%
Formicoidea	–	–	8,800	15,000	58.7%
Isoptera	–	–	2,600	10,000	53.3%
Isopoda	10–100 m^{-2}	110 m^{-2}	3,600	No estimate	No estimate
Diplopoda	10–15 m^{-2}	300 m^{-2}	12,000	15,000	16.7%
Chilopoda	5–10 m^{-2}	600 m^{-2}	3,000	8,000	No estimate

Note: The richness and abundance of ants and termites are highly variable and therefore difficult to estimate.
Sources: Compiled using data from Decaëns et al. (2006), Bardgett and van der Putten (2014), Nielsen et al. (2015b), AntWiki (www.antwiki.org/wiki/), and the Global Soil Biodiversity Atlas (Orgiazzi et al. 2016).

Soil fauna in some taxa can also be characterised based on its occupancy of specific soil horizons. However, the terms differ somewhat between taxa. For example, epigeic soil fauna is mostly found on the surface or in the upper soil horizons, being particularly prominent in the litter layer and organic horizon. The endogeic fauna is for the most part found in the deeper soil horizons, while anecic species are commonly found throughout the soil. Many endogeic and anecic species, such as certain earthworms and ants, are ecosystem engineers that modify the soil structure and through this the belowground communities and ecosystem functioning more broadly. In comparison, when referring to microarthropods, the definitions used are generally epigeic, hemi-, and euedaphic for surface or litter dwellers, those that are found at the surface and in the soil matrix, and the true soil dwellers, respectively. Accordingly, there is

16 · Soil and Its Fauna

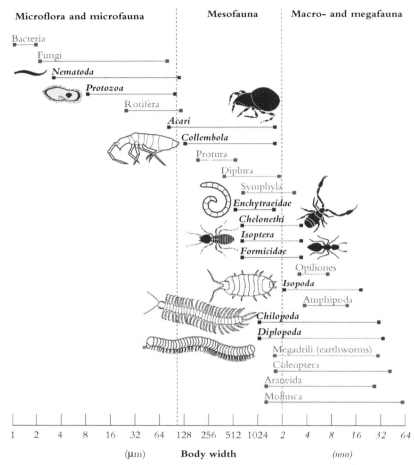

Figure 1.5 A schematic classification of soil biota based on body width. The grouping by body width fits reasonably well with key changes in life strategies, with microfauna being (semi-) aquatic organism that lives in water-filled pores or water films, whereas mesofauna is generally confined to air-filled pores or to the litter layer. The macrofauna, by contrast, can often modify the environment to create its own living space.
Modified from Swift et al. (1979) with permission from University of California Press.

generally vertical stratification of soil fauna assemblages that might moderate their contribution to ecosystem functioning (Chapter 6). In the following sections, I will provide examples of the role of specific taxa in the soil food web.

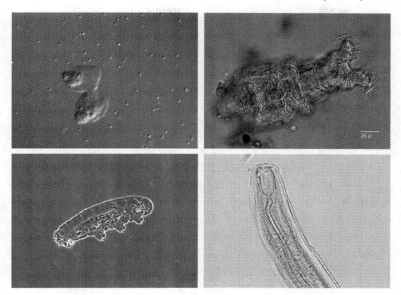

Figure 1.6 Examples of the main groups of microfauna. Top left: an amoeba from the genus *Stenamoeba* (courtesy of Stefan Geisen). Top right: the rotifer *Philodina rugosa* (courtesy of Michael Plewka, Hattingen, Germany). Bottom left: the Antarctic tardigrade, *Hypsibius antarcticus*. Photo by the author. Bottom right: the anterior of a predatory nematode (*Clarkus* sp.; courtesy of Patricia Gilarte).

1.3.1 Microfauna

Soil microfauna is loosely defined as soil fauna with a body width of less than 0.1 mm (Swift et al. 1979). The dominant groups of soil microfauna are the Protozoa and nematodes (Nematoda), but rotifers (Rotifera) and tardigrades (Tardigrada) are also common in some ecosystem types (Figure 1.6). Protozoa are often considered with the microorganisms more broadly (e.g. bacteria, fungi, Archaea) given their unicellular nature, but they are rarely given much attention. Our knowledge of the protozoans is therefore less than that of the 'true' microbes and the larger, multicellular soil fauna. This is problematic as they are recognised as essential components of the soil food web that contribute substantially to soil functioning. Fortunately, as we shall see later, the increasing use of molecular tools is helping us to fill that gap. Soil microfauna are essentially an aquatic organism, sometimes referred to as hydrobionts, that requires a water-filled soil pore or water film on soil particles or aggregates for movement and feeding. Because of their minute size and being limited to existing water-filled soil pores and water films, they have limited direct impact on the soil structure. Still, they can influence the soil structure indirectly through their interactions with other soil biota, particularly the soil microbes. Moreover, many microfauna are microbial grazers that have a substantial impact on ecosystem processes, particularly carbon (C) and nutrient cycling through turnover of microbial biomass and selective feeding (see Chapter 2).

The soil **Protozoa** are mostly small, heterotrophic, unicellular, eukaryotic organisms that represent various lineages of the tree of life essentially grouped together by not being animals, green plants, or true fungi. The group is thus paraphyletic, with critical discrepancies in taxonomic grouping, and the phylogeny of Protozoa is still being resolved. The soil Protozoa usually ranges in length from 10–50 μm, but larger specimens can be up to 1 mm (Geisen et al. 2017). The free-living soil Protozoa mostly belongs to Amoebozoa, Ciliophora, and Cercozoa, but there is increasing evidence that Apicomplexa can also be abundant in some ecosystems. Across these taxonomic units there is substantial variation in morphology, with four main types being recognised: ciliates, flagellates, naked, and testate amoeba (Bonkowski 2004). While the ciliates are monophyletic, the flagellate and naked and testate amoeba forms have evolved independently in several different lineages of Protozoa (Adl et al. 2005). The testate amoeba is enclosed within a shell more formally known as a 'test' that ranges in size from 5–300 μm. These tests can be made solely of secreted material (proteinaceous, calcite, or siliceous), or they can be agglutinated by incorporating material from the surrounding environment, including mineral particles (Wilkinson and Mitchell 2010). Most Protozoa predominantly feed on bacteria (Foissner 1999b) and are considered to be the main grazers of bacteria in soils thus forming the base of the bacterial food web channel. However, they represent a much broader range of feeding guilds than this, including both fungi, cyanobacteria, algae, organic matter, other Protozoa, and even multicellular soil fauna (Wilkinson and Mitchell 2010). There is recent evidence that mycophagous Protozoa are much more common in soils than previously assumed (Geisen et al. 2016).

The Protozoa are highly abundant in soils with numbers generally ranging from 10^4 to 10^5 per g dry soil (Clarholm 1981) or the equivalent of roughly 50 to 3,000 mg fresh weight biomass per m^2 (Petersen and Luxton 1982). They are particularly abundant in soils with greater organic matter content and are concentrated in the upper soil horizons where their prey or resources are found, but their abundances vary significantly (Stout 1963, 1968). Almost all soil-borne Protozoa can survive adverse environmental conditions as cysts. Despite their small size, soil protozoans make up a substantial component of the belowground invertebrate biomass. It has been estimated that in most soils the biomass of protozoans is equal to, or even exceeds, that of other invertebrate groups, except that of earthworms (Foissner 1987, Schaefer and Schauermann 1990, Sohlenius 1980). They occur in soil pore space, and it is thought that the pore-size distribution is a key factor in controlling their abundances (Stout and Heal 1967). Because they are aquatic, soil water content is another important variable that can limit the activity of protists. For example, it has been estimated that the theoretical limit for protist activity is −0.15 MPa, the water matric potential coinciding with all pores <2 μm being filled (Lavelle and Spain 2001).

Protozoa are often overlooked in soil ecological studies because they are difficult to quantify numerically, and consequently their role in soil processes is not well known. Although not much is known about protist life cycles it is very evident that population sizes fluctuate substantially both spatially and temporally (Bonkowski and Scheu 2004, Christensen et al. 1992, Clarholm 1989, Janssen and Heijmans 1998, Mulder et al. 2011). It has been estimated that some species have a minimum generation time along the order of two to four hours, and that their production rates can be in the order of 10 to 12 times their standing crop per year (Coleman 1994). Flagellates, ciliates, and naked amoeba have generation times measured in hours, and accordingly they exert a substantial grazing pressure on microbial biomass and through this C and nutrient cycling. Indeed, it has been estimated that 70% of the total respiration of soil fauna is accounted for by Protozoa (Foissner 1987, Sohlenius 1980). Testate amoebae are particularly abundant in organic-rich soils with low pH, where they can be the dominant type of microfauna. Because the tests in many cases are made of siliceous material it has been suggested that testate amoebae and also diatoms may be important in silicon (Si) cycling and creating soil biogenic Si pools (Creevy et al. 2016). Indeed, the pools of biogenic Si incorporated in Protozoa can be substantial, reaching up to 5 kg Si ha^{-1} in some forest ecosystems (Puppe et al. 2015). This pool of biogenic Si is made available when the Protozoa decompose. Given the fast life cycle and turnover of the protozoan biomass, the annual biosilicification rates can be substantial with that of testate amoeba alone being in the range of 17–277 kg Si ha^{-1} (Aoki et al. 2007, Puppe et al. 2015, Sommer et al. 2013).

The 'free-living' soil **nematodes** (Nematoda), also known as roundworms, are relatively small organisms, generally <1 mm long but with some species up to around 5 mm long. It is a highly diverse group and the most abundant multicellular animal on Earth, with an estimated possible one million species globally and numbers measured in millions of individuals per m^2 (Bongers 1999, Lambshead 1993). Nematodes are ubiquitous in practically all terrestrial soil ecosystems and can occupy functional roles at all trophic levels of the soil food web (Yeates et al. 1993). It is famously described that if all other matter were removed except nematodes, it would still be possible to make out the outline of Earth including the river valleys, deep seas, and mountain ranges (Cobb 1915). However, soil nematodes are particularly abundant in temperate ecosystems, with lower abundances in tropical regions and at high latitudes (Procter 1984, 1990, Sohlenius 1980). Interestingly, the biomass and density of nematodes can be significant in high-altitude ecosystems, and there is a tendency for larger body sizes at high elevation. Nematodes, namely *Caenorhabditis elegans*, have played a significant role in experimental biology as model organisms, due to their ease of culturing, fast life cycle, and tendency for eutely (cell constancy) of certain body parts (Cunha et al. 1999). For example, in 1998 *C. elegans* became the first organism to have its complete 97-megabase genome sequenced revealing over 19,000 genes (The *C. elegans* Sequencing Consortium 1998), which helped pave the way for the human genome project and the subsequent mapping of many other species' genomes. Nematodes have chemoreceptors, including specialised structures known as phasmids and amphids, and a variety of papillae, that likely aid in localisation of resources (Prot 1980). Nematodes have long been considered to be useful bioindicators because of their ubiquity in soils, a broad range of life history, and functional traits, high species diversity, and being numerically abundant. Their use for this purpose will be discussed in Chapter 3.

Nematodes show a great variability in life history traits. Some nematodes are free-living for their entire life cycle, while others are free-living during only some life stages and are functional parasites of plants or animals at other stages. Some of these can be of particular pestilence to animals and humans (parasites, pests of crops), while others can be utilised for biocontrol (i.e. entomopathogenic nematodes). Most nematodes have separate sexes and reproduce sexually. However, some species can reproduce by parthenogenesis, and others are hermaphroditic. Most nematode life cycles include an egg, four juvenile stages, and an adult stage. The juvenile stages look morphologically alike but differ in size. In some cases, the adult morphology is modified, such as in the case of the saccate females of the plant parasitic genus *Meloidogyne*. The life span of a nematode ranges from a few days to weeks to over a year. Plant parasites usually survive for about three to six weeks whereas common free-living species tend to have faster life cycles of one to two weeks (Norton 1978). However, it is worth mentioning that many nematodes have the ability to survive unfavourable environmental conditions for extended periods, which can substantially extend their potential life span. Some species of nematodes in the family Rhabditidae form dauer larvae, a resistant stage, in response to adverse environmental conditions. Other species, particularly those in hot and cold deserts, have the ability to survive desiccation, entering a state known as anhydrobiosis, where their metabolic activity is below our detection limits if any activity is present at all, and in this state they can survive for extended periods (Wharton 1986). In this state Antarctic nematodes are likely to stretch their life spans to many years and likely decades. Moreover, the first animal known to survive intracellular freezing (i.e. the formation of ice crystals inside the cells) was the Antarctic endemic nematode *Panagrolaimus davidi* (Wharton and Fern 1995). It is expected that other species found in similar environments might also have that ability. Recent evidence shows that infective juveniles of the entomopathogenic nematode *Steinernema feltiae* can similarly survive intracellular freezing down to a temperature of −3°C, but the ability is yet to be confirmed in other nematode species and soil fauna more broadly (Ali and Wharton 2014).

Nematodes occupy all trophic levels in the soil food web and have significant impacts on soil processes (see Chapter 2). Nematode-feeding types can be broadly categorised as plant parasitic, bacterial feeders, fungal feeders, predators, omnivores, and entomopathogenic (Figure 1.7), but various researchers have proposed more specific feeding guilds (e.g. Yeates et al. 1993). However, they all fundamentally feed on living protoplasm. These feeding types are briefly described here to provide context to their contribution to ecosystem functioning and their interactions with the environment including possible constraints on their diversity and distribution.

Plant parasitic nematodes feed on various plant parts throughout most of their life cycle. They can be classified broadly as sedentary parasites, migratory endoparasites, semi-endoparasites, and ectoparasites while others feed on epidermal tissue and root hairs or algae, lichen, or moss. They use hollow needle-like structures known as stylets to pierce plant cells and suck out the intracellular fluids. In some cases, feeding activities include the injection of enzymes such as chitinase and cellulase that can help break down the plant cell walls. They also possess a range of

22 · Soil and Its Fauna

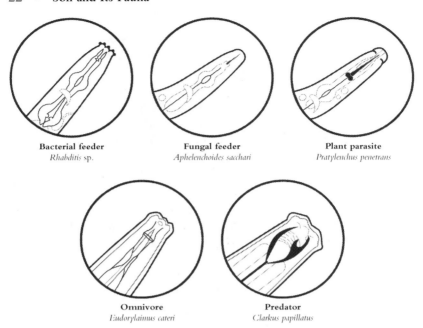

Figure 1.7 Schematic diagram of the main nematode-feeding types based on common nematode species.

'parasite genes' associated with adaptation to a parasitic lifestyle (Quist et al. 2015). These genes are, for example, involved with secretions that aid in penetration of the plant host cell wall and migration, formation of a feeding cell, production of peptides used for signalling, modification of the plant cell metabolism processes, and other functions (Davis et al. 2004). As such, plant parasitic nematodes are highly adapted to their lifestyle. Feeding by parasitic nematodes can have substantial impacts on plants directly and occasionally indirectly through the transfer of viruses. The migratory plant parasites can be ectoparasitic (e.g. *Longidorus, Xiphinema, Tylenchorhynchus*) where feeding occurs from outside the plant root or endoparasitic (e.g. *Pratylenchus*) where the nematode feeds inside roots. However, both types are free-living throughout their life cycle, and both sexes of migratory parasites are verniform to aid in migration between roots. By contrast, sedentary plant parasites are more specialised with some females forming cysts (e.g. *Heterodera*) and others galls (e.g. *Meloidogyne, Ditylenchus*) on plant roots and only migrate as juveniles. The males are, in comparison, free-living and migrate between hosts even as adults. Some plant parasitic nematodes, including species of

Meloidogyne and *Pratylenchus*, have a broad range of potential plant host species, while other species such as some *Heterodera* and *Globodera* have more limited host ranges. The ecology of some plant parasites is particularly well described given their detrimental impacts on agricultural and horticultural crops. They can be very abundant and substantially reduce the productivity and crop yield directly through feeding and, as mentioned earlier, through the transfer of important agricultural viruses (Holterman et al. 2017). By contrast, we know less about plant parasites in natural ecosystems, including their impacts on plant productivity, plant–plant interactions, and biochemical cycles.

Bacterial-feeding nematodes are, together with the plant parasites, the most abundant nematode feeding group in most soils (Boag and Yeates 1998, Nielsen et al. 2014). They are free-living and feed on bacteria by filtrating soil water or scraping bacteria off substrate surfaces. The bacterial-feeding nematodes generally have tubular mouths and, in some cases, elaborate external structures they use in feeding. Bacterial-feeding nematodes often have fast life cycles, ranging from days to weeks, and high rates of reproduction. Accordingly, their consumption rates can be very high. For example, it has been estimated that bacterial-feeding nematodes ingest up to six-and-a-half times their biomass daily, assimilating 40%–60% of the bacterial cells, resulting in a 4%–13% growth efficiency (Lavelle and Spain 2001). On a yearly basis, this can amount to the consumption of up to 800 kg bacteria per hectare, contributing to the turnover of some 20–130 kg N (Coleman et al. 1984).

Fungal-feeding nematodes can be abundant in some ecosystems and feed primarily on fungal hyphae using hollow stylets that are smaller and finer than those found in primarily plant-feeding nematodes. However, there is significant overlap between the plant parasite and fungal-feeding groups, with some species being able to utilise both resources at all life stages while other species switch feeding preference with life stage. Through their interaction with fungal hyphae, fungal-feeding nematodes can modify fungal assemblages and impact plant communities. The ratio of bacterial- to fungal-feeding nematodes provides insight into the dominant food web channels, with fungal-feeding nematodes more dominant in relatively stable environments with slower, fungal-based decomposition pathways whereas bacterial feeders are more dominant in disturbed or nutrient-rich environments (see the discussion of nematodes as bioindicators in Chapter 3).

Predatory nematodes are generally larger and less abundant than the other feeding types in most ecosystems. They can feed on a broad range of soil fauna types, including other nematodes. Predatory nematodes generally have one or more large teeth or a pointed spear that they use for feeding. Some species such as *Mononchoides* spp. also feed on bacteria during certain life stages or when other prey is not available, and can be cultured under laboratory conditions on bacterial cells. Similarly, *Pristionchus* spp. can be cultured on bacteria but switches to a predatory lifestyle during overcrowding (Susoy and Sommer 2016). Whether predatory nematodes have a significant impact on controlling the abundance of pest species including plant parasitic nematodes is yet to be determined, but it is well established that they can consume a very large number of nematodes in controlled settings.

A few groups of nematodes are *omnivores* that feed on a variety of resources ranging from plant roots to other soil fauna. Like the plant parasites and fungal-feeding nematodes, they have a hollow spear-like structure they use to penetrate animal or plant cells to access resources. Omnivorous nematodes are generally large, up to 5 mm, with slow life cycles and low rates of reproduction. They are therefore most commonly encountered in relatively stable environments. Most predatory and omnivorous nematodes are considered as K-strategists and hence used as indicators of soil food web structure and ecosystem maturity (Ferris et al. 2001).

The *entomopathogenic* nematodes (EPNs) represent a unique feeding type within the nematodes that is already used for biocontrol of important crop pests and have great potential for broader use in integrated pest management practices in the future (Chapter 9). There are currently some 60 described species of EPNs belonging to two families (Heterorhabditidae; Steinernematidae), each with one genus (*Heterorhabditis* and *Steinernema*, respectively) (San-Blas 2013). They are widely distributed throughout a broad range of ecosystems and are found on all continents except Antarctica. All species of EPNs are obligate parasites of arthropods, infecting their hosts during the infective third instar juvenile stage, through penetration of the host via natural openings such as the anus, mouth, or spiracles. Once inside a host organism they release an endosymbiotic bacterium (Enterobacteriaceae) that multiplies rapidly and kills the infected animal through septicemia (Stuart et al. 2006). The EPNs then feed on these bacteria and reproduce within the host. Eventually the animal bursts, thus releasing a new crop of infective juveniles. The infective juveniles employ different strategies to find new hosts to infect. Specifically, some species are predominantly ambushers that wait for a suitable host to come by while other species are predominantly stalkers that will actively seek out suitable hosts. However, it is clear that host recognition includes constitutive chemical clues as well as induced plant volatiles signalling root damage by herbivores (Ali et al. 2011). Host organisms are rarely infected by more than one species at a time, and there is evidence that *Heterorhabditis* and *Steinernema* cannot multiply on the bacteria from the other genus (Stuart et al. 2006). Still, co-infection does occur, and species of the same genus can co-exist and multiply within the same host. The horticultural and agricultural industry has been very interested in deploying EPNs for pest control and has had some success with this strategy. The use of EPNs as biocontrol agents relies on one of two approaches: (1) optimising soil conditions to maintain or improve naturally occurring populations of EPNs, or (2) applying EPN strains known to target specific pest species. There is a great need for improved knowledge of indigenous EPN species and their environmental requirements to facilitate greater pest suppression by naturally occurring EPNs. The main constraint with the latter approach is that it can be difficult to deliver the EPNs to a production system effectively and maintain effective populations in the field (Langford et al. 2014). The potential role of EPNs in agroecosystems is discussed in more detail in Chapter 9.

Two other microfauna taxa deserve a brief introduction, namely the rotifers (also called 'wheel bearers'; **Rotifera**) and tardigrades (also called 'water bears'; **Tardigrada**). Both of these groups can be abundant in some ecosystem types, but their phylogenies and ecologies are not well described. The rotifers are worm-like filterfeeders, whereas tardigrades are eight-legged semi-aquatic organisms that pierce plant, animal, or fungal cells for feeding. Both rotifers and tardigrades are important components of some soil communities. For example, tardigrades and rotifers are the only multicellular animals found in the simple soil food webs of particular interior Antarctic ecosystems found on nunataks in Ellsworth Land at ~75°–77°S and ~70°–73°W (Convey and McInnis 2005). A similar tardigrade- and rotifer-dominated ecosystem has been described from other continental Antarctic nunataks at 73°–75°S and 11°–14°W (Sohlenius and Boström 2005). In such ecosystems they are therefore likely to contribute greatly to soil processes, particularly biogeochemical cycling, as primary consumers.

Rotifers are minute organisms that generally vary in size from approximately 50–800 μm; however, the largest species can grow up to around 2 mm. Soil-dwelling rotifers belong to two orders, Bdelloidea and Monogononta, with the majority of species found in soil representing the former order. Rotifers can be observed in large numbers, particularly in mesic, organic-rich soils where they can reach abundances of 10^5 per m^2 (Wallwork 1970). They show significant, but weak, habitat specialisation and wide ecological niche breadths (Fontaneto et al. 2011). All rotifers have an anterior corona of cilia used for feeding and unique hard jaws (trophi). The bdelloid rotifers are vortex feeders that create water currents to filter food particles out of the water column. They use their sectorial rostral cilia and adhesive disk for locomotion. The reproductive life cycle of rotifers generally alternates between parthenogenetic and sexual reproduction in which a dormant embryo is formed. This embryo is also known as a 'resting egg' and is thought to function as a dispersal propagule. However, the bdelloid rotifers, and therefore most soil-dwelling species, are obligately parthenogenetic with no known males. Because rotifers are capable of reproduction through parthenogenesis, only a single female is required to establish a new population. All rotifers also produce certain resting stages that are tolerant to desiccation, high and low temperatures, including frost, that likely also facilitate dispersal (Wallace et al. 2006). These cysts allow them to survive during harsh environmental conditions or when resources are limited (Donner 1966).

The tardigrades are similarly small invertebrates, usually 100–500 μm long, but the largest species grow up to around 1.7 mm and are found in similar environments as the rotifers. They are more commonly known as water bears because of their bear-like appearance. Like the nematodes they belong to the monophyletic group Ecdysozoa that molts. There are two sub-phyla, Heterotardigrada and Eutardigrada, the latter of which is mostly terrestrial. Tardigrades have a long fossil record with a pre-Pangaean distribution pattern (Chapter 4). They have four pairs of legs, each with claws, and an eversible buccal tube with two stylets used to penetrate plant and animal cells during feeding. The cells' inner fluids are then sucked up using the pharynx. The shapes of the claws, buccal apparatus, and cuticle are all traits that are used for identification purposes. Many tardigrades reproduce both sexually and through parthenogenesis, which might promote successful dispersal. The eggs are 40–60 μm in size and are laid either singly or in multiples inside exuvia after molting and are smooth, or they are ornate and laid freely. In both cases they appear to be relatively resistant and may allow long-range dispersal. Tardigrades are among the better-known soil microfauna, largely because of their appealing appearance and amazing ability to survive extreme conditions. Tardigrades have, for example, been shown to survive being dipped into liquid nitrogen, high and low temperatures (up to 149°C, down to −272°C), high levels of radiation (5,000 rays of gamma radiation), and even exposure to the vacuum of space (see Weronika and Łukasz 2017 for references). The tardigrades' capacity to survive extended harsh to extreme environmental conditions is largely based on their ability to enter a state of reduced to completely halted metabolism, collectively referred to as 'cryptobiosis' (Keilin 1959). However, while the tardigrades' ability to survive such extreme conditions is truly impressive, it serves a much more fundamental survival strategy allowing them to exist in ephemeral environments (including moss on Antonie van Leeuwenhoek's roof) or prolonged periods with unfavourable environmental conditions only to resume biological activity when the conditions improve years or even decades later.

1.3.2 Mesofauna

The mesofauna is broadly defined as the soil fauna with body widths between 0.1 and 2.0 mm (Figure 1.8). In contrast to the microfauna,

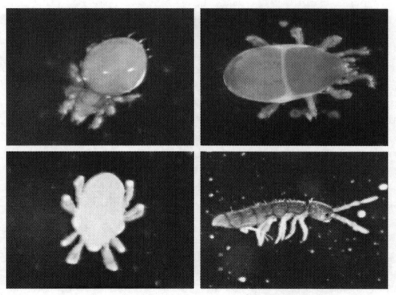

Figure 1.8 The most abundant type of mesofauna is the microarthropod, comprising mites and springtails. The oribatid mites (top left) are predominantly microbial grazers and decomposers. The mesostigmatid mites (top right) are mostly active predators, while the prostigmatid mites (bottom left) feed on more varied resources. The springtails (bottom right) are predominantly fungal grazers. Photos by the author.

the mesofauna occupies air-filled soil pores; however, like the microfauna the soil mesofauna has limited direct impact on soil structure, i.e. most of the taxa do not alter soil pore structure. The most numerically abundant and diverse types of soil mesofauna are the mites (Acari) and springtails (Collembola), but several other groups including the proturans (Protura), Diplura, Symphyla, potworms (Enchytraeidae), and pseudoscorpions (Chelonethi) are important members of the mesofauna. The mesofauna represents a very broad range of life history strategies and functional traits, and as a group contributes significantly to C and nutrient cycling, pest and disease suppression through selective feeding, dispersal of microbes, and in some cases ecosystem engineering (discussed in detail in Chapter 2). Only the most abundant or influential groups will be discussed in detail here.

The free-living soil mites (**Acari**) are highly diverse in soil systems, with roughly 40,000 species described across all taxa, and together with the springtails they are among the most abundant arthropods in most soils. The phylum is composed of the superorders Parasitiformes and Acariformes. The most ecologically important orders of Parasitiformes are the Ixodida (ticks) and the Mesostigmata, but only the latter are common types of soil fauna. Two orders make up the Acariformes, Trombidiformes, and Sarcoptiformes, with the suborders Prostigmata and Oribatida being the most species-rich and abundant representatives, respectively. The total abundance of mites varies among biomes from around 20,000 to 200,000 individuals per m^2, but abundances are often very low in cold and hot desert soils while a maximum of 1,783,000 individuals per m^2 were recorded in a beech forest in Germany (Petersen and Luxton 1982). Their abundances are positively related to mean annual temperature, and the biomass is in the 100 to 1,000 mg dry weight per m^2 but can reach 1,500 mg (Lavelle and Spain 2001). Mites are generally found in higher numbers in soils with considerable amounts of organic matter and prefer soils with higher soil moisture content and lower pH than the springtails (Wallwork 1976).

The mites are like other arthropods covered in a rigid exoskeleton that in many species is heavily sclerotized for protection. This is, however, not always the case, and juveniles are generally less well protected than adults, making them important prey for other soil fauna. Like their close relatives, the spiders, adult mites and nymphs have four pairs of legs, while the larval stage only have three pairs. Most Acari have six developmental stages, except the parasitic Ixodida (i.e. the ticks), which will not be discussed in detail here. It is worth noting that Ixodidae can be present in large numbers in soil and litter and may become prey of other soil fauna; however, they do not contribute directly to soil processes given their dependence on vertebrate hosts for resources. Mites have chelicerae that are used in feeding, and the shape of the chelicerae reflects feeding preferences. However, given that many species have not been described, there is uncertainty about general feeding preferences. The mites show substantial variation in life history traits and reproductive cycles. Most species have one generation per year, but some species of prostigmatid mites can complete their life cycles in less than three months whereas some species of oribatid mites can take up to five years (Krantz and Walter 2009). Morphological identification of mites is complicated by the fact that many mite species are polymorphic, and the juvenile stages do not closely resemble the adults. Many species of mites are heavily armoured and relatively insensitive to desiccation compared with the springtails discussed next. For example, it has been estimated that some oribatid mites can tolerate water potentials of −6.0 MPa. In comparison, most plants wilt at soil water potentials of −1.5 MPa (Lavelle and Spain 2001).

The mites can be broadly divided into three ecologically important groups that share some general morphological and functional traits. However, the phylogenetic relationship between groups is still not well resolved and many species of mites are yet to be described. The most diverse and abundant group in most ecosystems is **Oribatida**. The oribatid mites are generally more heavily sclerotized than other members of Acari with often-calcareous exoskeletons. They are highly abundant with up to several hundred of thousand individuals per m^2 in some ecosystems, with particularly high abundances in coniferous forests. Similarly, the diversity can be very high with more than 100 species not being unusual at a given site. The oribatid mites are broadly classified as saprophages, but some feed on decaying organic matter while others target microbes more specifically. However, more specific oribatid mite feeding guilds have been proposed, including fragment feeders (finely fragmented plant and fungal matter), panphytophage (plant and fungal matter), and micro- and macrophytophages (fungal hyphae and spores, and plant matter, respectively) that can be partly distinguished based on the size of the chelicerae (Kaneko 1988). The free-living soil mesostigmatid mites (**Mesostigmata**) are mostly predatory, while many non-soil species are animal parasites. They feed on a broad range of other soil fauna, but springtails and nematodes are common prey within the soil food web. The prostigmatid mites (**Prostigmata**) can be diverse and dominate the mite communities in some ecosystems. They present a broad array of feeding types ranging from herbivores to microbial grazers or decomposers to predators. Soil mites are therefore important to ecosystem functioning through several nodes of the soil food web.

The springtails (**Collembola**) are abundant hexapods closely related to the proturans, diplurans, and insects, with highest abundances observed in temperate mull-type soils. Most springtails are relatively small, usually less than 2 mm, but the largest species grow up to 17 mm long. The scientific name refers to the presence of ventral tube, the 'collophore' or alternatively 'glue piston' (Greek: kola = glue; embolon = piston), which is important in fluid and electrolyte control and has been proposed to also function as a way for the organism to adhere to the surface. They have three body regions like the insects but lack compound eyes and wings, and the abdomen has only six segments. They are known as springtails because of the ability of some species to jump significant distances (it is a common note that if springtails were the size of humans they would be able to jump over the Eiffel Tower). This ability comes from the furcula, which is found ventrally on the abdomen. The furcula is usually tucked away under the abdomen, held in place by a special catch mechanism that is released if the springtail is disturbed, thus making the animal jump. However, the furcula is absent in several groups. The springtails rival the mites in abundances, at least in some ecosystems, such as temperate grasslands and forest and even maritime Antarctic terrestrial ecosystems. Indeed, there appears to be a thermo-latitudinal relationship whereby particularly high abundances are observed in some cold environments. The highest mean abundances in a survey of 200 sites was thus reported from ornithogenic soils on Signy Island, Antarctica – a staggering 670,000 individual per m^2 – while lower abundances were observed in tropical savannas in Africa and the lowest in desert soils in California (Petersen and Luxton 1982). While abundant, the biomass of springtails is usually in the range of 80–200 mg m^{-2} (Lavelle and Spain 2001). It is a less diverse group than the Acari with approximately 8,500 species described to date, but there are still many undescribed species. They reproduce through parthogenesis or sexually whereby males deposit spermatophores that the females rub against for fertilisation. The juveniles develop through a series of 4–50 stadia, with development to reproductive instars taking 40–400 days (Lavelle and Spain 2001). The springtails are generally divided into three main groups based on morphological and phylogenetic similarities: Poduromorpha and Entomobryomorpha (both in the suborder Arthropleona) representing the 'linear' springtails to which most springtails belong and the spherical to globular Symphypleona. Springtails generally have life cycles that range from a few weeks to months, but can be up to several years, for example, in tundra (Addison 1977). Most species rely on existing soil pores for movement within the soil matrix, but a few species from the family Onychiuridae create microtunnels (Rusek 1985). They can also contribute to soil formation, particularly in weakly developed soils and early successional stages, where the soil profile can be made up almost entirely of springtail faecal pellets (Rusek et al. 1975).

Feeding activities of springtails have been explored by many scientists, beginning with the pioneering work of Macnamara (1924). Springtails feed on a very broad range of resources, but most species are saprophages or microbial grazers, particularly of fungi and algae (Petersen and Luxton 1982). A few species, such as some *Friesea* and *Isotoma,* are predators that feed on rotifers, tardigrades, and nematode eggs. Our understanding of springtail feeding preferences is largely based on direct observation, mouth-part specialisation and gut content analysis (Rusek 1998). Berg et al. (2004), for example, investigated enzyme activity of springtail gut contents in 20 different species from nutrient-poor peat meadows and defined four broad feeding guilds: fungivorous grazers, opportunistic herbofungivores, herbo-fungivorous grazers, and omnivores. Moreover, there is evidence that feeding preferences change among life stages (Jensen et al. 2006), contributing to difficulties attributing individual species to specific feeding guilds. While springtails are often considered generalist fungal grazers, there is some evidence that they show preferential feeding. For example, a study that compared fungal diversity of springtail gut contents with the surrounding soil using a sequencing approach found only one of 33 unique 18S ribosomal DNA operational taxonomic units (OTUs) in the soil in the springtail gut (Jørgensen et al. 2005). This strongly suggests that the springtail *Protaphorura armata* can be highly selective in its preference of fungi. The main constraints for gut content analyses using molecular approaches are the potential contamination by non-prey DNA and false negatives whereby prey DNA is not robustly amplified. DNA contamination is most problematic where whole individuals are isolated for DNA extraction because they are likely to be surface contaminated. This can in part be circumvented using prey-specific primer combinations, which at least avoids picking up other types of DNA. A better solution appears to be surface decontamination using bleach although the method is not perfect and may work only with certain types of fauna (Greenstone et al. 2012). The problem with prey DNA not being amplified should be resolved as analytical protocols are fine-tuned.

Springtails are broadly classified based on their habitat preference as epigeic, hemiedaphic, or euedaphic, with clear differences between the types in terms of morphology, ecophysiology, and population biology (see Verhoef and Brussaard 1990; Chapter 3). Their habitat preferences are also likely to influence how they contribute to ecosystem functioning, with surface-dwelling species (epigeic) more likely to be involved in the early stages of decomposition while the soil-dwelling species are more likely to contribute to the later stages of decomposition and mineralisation processes. Species found in the litter layer or upper soil horizons are generally larger, have a well-developed furcula, and are more colourful than springtails adapted to live within the soil horizon itself that also typically lack eyes. The family Sminthuridae has achieved much greater independence from soils than other springtail groups. They have trachea and do not need to breathe across the body surface so they can conserve water. This allows them to exist in microhabitats where other springtails are not generally present, and they are therefore more prominent on plants and tree trunks. Some Sminthuridae are phytophagous and can be significant pests of agricultural and horticultural crops. However, morphological adaptation is not always a proxy for microhabitat preferences displayed by springtails.

Finally, some springtails have adapted live in extreme environments, with some species being very cold tolerant. Many Arctic and Antarctic species produce antifreeze proteins that allows them to continue locomotion well below freezing, and they can survive much colder conditions; there is evidence that the Antarctic springtail *Anurophorus subpolaris* can survive temperatures down to $-50°C$ (Block 1983). There is some evidence of anhydrobiosis in springtails, but most species are limited in their desiccation tolerance, usually experiencing impacts below -5.0 MPa. One study showed that the activity of six Dutch springtails was generally affected once species have lost 16%–34% of the body water content (Vegter and Huyer-Brugman 1983). However, desiccation tolerance is generally lower for juveniles than for adults.

The potworms (**Enchytraeidae; Annelida**) are the smaller and lesser-known relatives of earthworms. Enchytraeids are relatively small (roughly 5–50 mm length) and are found in most ecosystems (Christensen and Glenner 2010). In acidic, organic-rich soils they can be found in very high numbers (hundreds of thousands per m^2). Most enchytraeids are found in the upper soil layers where most of the organic material occurs. Around 650 species are currently recognised (Erséus 2005), most of which are microbivore or saprotrophs (Briones and Ineson 2002, Didden 1990). Enchytraeids generally feed by ingesting plant fragments and mineral soil, but some species feed preferentially on fungi. It appears that most species rely on existing soil pores for movement although some can create their own microtunnels, and in this case they can act as ecosystem engineers. Like the earthworms, enchytraeids are hermaphroditic. Sexual reproduction usually includes the creation of a cocoon secreted by the clitellum containing one or more eggs, with some species covering the cocoon with a layer of organic and mineral debris (Christensen 1956). The time from cocoon formation to maturity is in the order of 65–120 days, with a maximal life span thought to be about one year (Dash 1990, Dósza-Farkas 1996). However, asexual reproduction through parthenogenesis, self-fertilisation, and even fragmentation is common in many species. Respiration in enchytraeids is cutaneous, and they require a wet integument for efficient gas exchange making them highly sensitive to drought. The threshold water potentials for survival has been estimated at -1.0 MPa (Lavelle and Spain 2001).

The **pseudoscorpions** (Chelonethi) are small charismatic arthropods (up to ~5 mm) closely related to other chelicerates including mites, spiders, and scorpions. They are often referred to as 'false scorpions' because they are nearly identical to their larger counterparts, except that they lack the extended post-abdomen and stinger characteristic of true scorpions. Pseudoscorpions do have pincer-like pedipalps that they use for catching prey and their two-segmented chelicerae are used for feeding. They have separate sexes, with the male producing spermatophores that are deposited and collected by the female when the male positions her over them. Interestingly, the female produces a silken brood sac in which she deposits 10–40 eggs and then carries it to the ventral surface of the opisthosoma. The pseudoscorpions have long life cycles, with adults living for up to three to four years. It is a diverse group with some 3,400 known species, but they are rarely abundant, with a maximal abundance of a couple of hundred individuals per m^2. They mostly occur in leaf litter, under bark, stones, and rocks, but also in the soil itself. They are sometimes considered beneficial to humans as predators of pests. They are widely distributed but tend to be of limited diversity at any given site. In temperate forests they can be found in excess of 500 per m^2 (Gabbutt 1967). Although they are likely important predators in some cases, it appears unlikely that they contribute substantially to suppress prey abundances in most soils.

The Protura and Diplura are commonly encountered in soils, but in lower numbers than most of the other mesofauna. **Proturans** are wingless, primitive hexapods, closely related to the springtails and insects, with some 700 known species. They are generally small, 0.5–2.5 mm long, and lack antennae and eyes. They favour organic-rich habitats, with abundances up to 85,000 individuals per m^2 observed, where they feed mostly on fungal hyphae and in turn are important prey of larger soil fauna. However, the biomass rarely exceeds a few mg per m^2. The **Diplura** are also wingless hexapods, ranging in size from around 0.3–1 cm, although some species can grow larger, with an elongated, often white or colourless, body. There are around 1,000 known species, but they generally occur in very low abundances (<50 individuals per m^2). Some Diplura superficially resemble earwigs (Dermaptera: Insecta) due to pincer-shaped abdominal appendages known as cerci, whereas in other species the appendages are filamentous. Most species are herbivores or detritivores, but some have well-developed mandibles and are predatory of other soil fauna.

Several other soil mesofauna, including **Pauropoda** and **Symphyla (Myriapoda)**, are found in soils in lower abundances and are encountered less frequently. Pauropoda are small (generally less than 1 mm long), eyeless, panphytophagous invertebrates mostly found in organic-rich environments in abundances up to a few thousand per m^2. Symphyla are similarly small, elongated invertebrates found to greater depth in the soil horizon. They are generally found in limited numbers, rarely more than a few hundred per m^2, but they can reach up to a few thousand in temperate and tropical soils (Lavelle and Spain 2001). The biomass of both groups can be up to a few g per m^2 but rarely amount to much more (Petersen and Luxton 1982). It remains unknown how much they contribute to ecosystem processes.

1.3.3 Macro- and Megafauna

The macro- and megafauna are defined as soil fauna with body widths above 2.0 and 20 mm, respectively. The macrofauna includes several well-known animals such as the earthworms (Annelida), termites (Isoptera), ants (Formicidae), beetles (Coleoptera), millipedes (Diplopoda), and centipedes (Chilopoda), as well as many lesser-known characters (Figure 1.9). Many macro- and megafauna, but in particular the ants, termites, and earthworms, are known as ecosystem engineers that modify their environment and contribute substantially to decomposition processes and nutrient cycling, water infiltration, pest and disease suppression, and community dynamics of other biota, which in turn can effect productivity, both positively and negatively (see Chapter 2). The focus here will be on the dominant and ecologically important groups.

The ants (**Formicidae: Hymenoptera**) are eusocial insects that live in complex colonies of varying sizes with a clear division of roles (i.e. castes: groups of individuals with similar roles). In most cases the location of the colony is fixed, but some ants, including certain species of fire ants, do not form fixed colonies. The colonies can be of substantial size and modify ecosystem topography. Ants have broad geographical distributions but are particularly common in tropical forests and arid grasslands, and are entirely lacking from cold environments such as the polar regions and alpine ecosystems. They likely evolved from a common ancestor living in the early Cretaceous period, although there is some discussion on the likely time this occurred (115–169 mya) (Brady et al. 2006, Moreau et al. 2006). It has been estimated that there are >20,000 ant species globally with some 12,600 described (Agosti and Johnson 2010). They represent a very broad range of feeding types though most are predatory or herbivores. Other ants feed on honeydew and some even cultivate fungi on harvested leaves. Ants are abundant in many ecosystems, and their biomass can exceed that of the vertebrates found aboveground in tropical forests. Because of their great abundance and affinity to modify the surrounding landscape, they can substantially impact soil fauna assemblages and ecosystem functioning.

The termites (**Isoptera**) are also eusocial insects with individuals representing castes that have different functional roles. However, termites are not closely related to the ants, instead being phylogenetically related to cockroaches. There are more than 2,700 recognised species of termites, most of which are associated with soils. Termites have a more restricted geographical distribution than ants. They are particularly abundant and diverse in the subtropical and tropical biomes and often dominate the soil arthropod assemblages of dry ecosystems (Kambhampati and Eggleton 2000, Thorne et al. 2000). However, they are virtually absent from temperate and colder regions. The highest termite diversities are found in lowland tropical forests where the species richness generally is in the range of 50–80 per hectare (Eggleton 2000). The termites owe their success to their social lifestyle and efficient digestive symbioses with a multitude of organisms including Protozoa, methanogenic Archaea, bacteria, and fungi that allow them to use a broad range of resources, including wood, that is not available to many other soil fauna (Bignell

Figure 1.9 Examples of common macrofauna. Top (left to right): earthworms (Megadrilacea), ants (Formicidae), and termites (Isoptera) are important ecosystem engineers that contribute significantly to ecosystem functioning and have substantial impacts on the structure of their environment. Middle (left to right): millipedes (Diplopoda) are decomposers, while their close relatives centipedes (Chilopoda) are predators. Isopods – the most successful terrestrial crustaceans, more commonly known as woodlice – are litter fragmenters. Bottom (left to right): white grubs, the larvae of scarab beetles (Scarabaeidae), feed on roots belowground before emerging to complete its life cycle aboveground. Cockroaches (Blattodea) are commonly found in the litter layer and decomposing organic matter. Many spiders build borrows and hunt actively or act as ambushers in the soil–litter interface. They are important predators of soil fauna.
Photos by the author.

2000). Because most of their food is high in C content, termites furthermore benefit from symbiotic N-fixing gut microbes to aid in N acquisition. Moreover, the association with gut microbes and protozoans contributes to the very high assimilation rates (54%–93%) of otherwise highly recalcitrant food sources, such as lignin, cellulose, and hemicellulose (Wood 1978). Termite-feeding types can be broadly defined as soil-feeders, soil-wood interface-feeders, wood-feeders, litter-foragers, and grass-feeders with other species feeding on algae, fungi, and lichens (Bignell and Eggleton 2000). Moreover, some species in the subfamily

Macrotermitinae cultivate fungi. The approximately 330 species in the subfamily of fungus-growing termites (Macrotermitinae) culture fungi (*Termitomyces* spp.) in subterranean chambers on masticated plant detritus. But establishing new colonies is difficult because the fungi generally have to disperse independently of the termites. However, there is substantial overlap between these groups, with some species feeding on multiple substrates under unfavourable conditions, and resource switches often occur between life stages. Their nests are constructed in a wide variety of microhabitats, ranging from subterranean, epigeal, intermediate on lower portions of trunks and in touch with the soil surface, arboreal, or within nests of other species (Lavelle and Spain 2001). Colonies vary in size from a few thousand individuals in 'dry wood' termites to hundreds of thousands in grass- and litter-feeding species. It is very difficult to estimate termite abundances reliably given the patchy distribution and complex nests, but maximal abundances approach 10^5 individuals per m^2 equal to more than 100 g fresh weight biomass (Eggleton et al. 1996). Given the size of the colonies it is not surprising that the territory of individual colonies can be large. Individual colonies can thus 'occupy' hundreds to thousands of m^2, sometimes leading to aggressive behaviour between colonies of the same species or with other species although this is not always the case. Termites are key prey to many more or less specialised vertebrate and invertebrate predators, including ants. Termites are ecosystem engineers that substantially impact their habitat and modify important ecosystem processes, particularly wood decomposition.

Earthworms (Annelida: **Lumbricidae**) are common in most ecosystems except hot deserts and the polar regions, and indeed dominate the soil animal biomass in most soils. There are approximately 7,000 known species, with an estimated global diversity of 30,000 species. Earthworms range in size from a few mm to around 2–3 m for *Amynthas mekongianus* and the 'Giant Gippsland Earthworm' *Megascolides australis*. However, most species are around 5–15 cm long. Earthworms are particularly common in grasslands and forests of temperate regions and because of their relatively large size can contribute substantially to the biomass of soil fauna in basic soils. Earthworm biomass is normally in the range from 30–100 g m^{-2}, but can be up to 400 g m^{-2}. By contrast, they are much less abundant in acidic soils and are generally absent from hot and cold deserts (Wallwork 1976). Ecologically, Lumbricidae and Megascolecidae are most important in Asia, Australia, Europe, and North America, whereas Eudrilidae and Glossoscolecidae are most important in sub-Saharan Africa and South America, respectively. They are semi-aquatic organisms that require enough soil water to maintain cuticular moisture to allow gas exchange. This poses some constraints on where earthworms flourish and they appear unable to survive extended periods with soil water potentials below −0.1 MPa (Lavelle and Spain 2001). However, some species have adaptive life history traits, such as quiescence or diapause, or constructs chambers where they might survive during stressful conditions. Other species actively avoid harsh conditions through migration to deeper soil horizons. Earthworms are hermaphroditic and generally reproduce sexually, although some species can reproduce through parthenogenesis.

Earthworms have contrasting life history strategies associated with their occupancy of the soil matrix. Epigeic earthworms predominantly inhabit the very shallow organic soil and litter horizon where they feed predominantly on organic material. Anecic earthworms gather leaf litter from the surface and pull it into their burrows, thereby mixing organic and mineral soil horizons. The action of both epigeic and anecic earthworms contributes to the formation of the characteristic mull-type soils, where the organic matter is well mixed within the upper mineral soil, through fragmentation and redistribution of organic matter. The anecic earthworms have substantial impacts on the soil structure through their burrowing, influencing water-holding capacity and infiltration rates, etc. (Chapter 2). By contrast, the endogeic earthworms feed on organic matter found within the soil matrix, with more limited impacts on the distribution of organic matter. Earthworms are efficient bioturbators of soils, ingesting and egesting up to 1,200 metric ton solid aggregates per ha per year while creating up to 900 m of galleries per m^2 (Lavelle and Spain 2001). However, a very small proportion of the ingested material is assimilated. For example, it has been estimated that the tropical earthworm *Reginaldia omodeoi* ingests up to 30 times its body weight every day, but only roughly 8% of this is assimilated, and even then over 90% of the C assimilated is respired through activities such as modification of the soil structure (Blouin et al. 2013). Similarly, earthworms in temperate ecosystems respire a very large proportion, up to ~90%, of the C assimilated during feeding and burrowing activities (Petersen and Luxton 1982). As such they are one of the key groups of soil ecosystem engineers, although not all types contribute equally to soil structure modification. The functional groups also differ in life span with epigeic earthworms usually living for about a year while endogeic and anecic earthworms can live up to 10 years (Sherlock 2012). However, there is substantial variation within the functional groups, with the epigeic earthworm *Eisenia andrei* known to live for more than eight years (Mulder et al. 2007).

Certain insects (**Insecta**) are commonly found in soils, particularly larval stages, and can reach significant densities. For example, many larval stages of Diptera are important root feeders, dung, or litter decomposers. Several members of Coleoptera (beetles) are important grazers of plant roots (i.e. scarab beetle larvae) (Frew et al. 2016), while many ground beetles (Carabidae) and rove beetles (Staphylinidae) are important predators in the litter layer and on the soil surface. Similarly, the larvae of Neuroptera are predatory soil dwellers bearing elongated mandibles. More broadly, saprophagous insect larvae include Tipulidae, Chironomidae, Lepidoptera, Muscidae, Mycetophilidae, and Dolichopodidae, while predatory insect larvae include dipteran Tabanidae. Of course, there are also the charismatic dung beetles that feed on the dung deposited on the soil surface and can play a key role in the decomposition process of dung in some ecosystems. It is noteworthy that insect root herbivores can reach astounding numbers and biomass. A classic example that illustrates the potential size of belowground herbivore populations is the case of cicada nymphs of the genus *Magicicada*. The nymphs spend most of their lives deep in the soil feeding on xylem fluid from the roots and rootlets only to emerge in 17-year cycles in northeast America (Karban 1980). They reach densities of more than 300 emerging cicadas per m^2 equalling the largest recorded biomass of any naturally occurring terrestrial animal. However, it appears that the higher temperatures in their southern ranges allow them to complete their life cycle faster, emerging every 13 years. Even some bees and wasps dig tunnels in the soil where they construct hives, store food, or hide, both solitary and colony forming. Other notable soil-associated insects include wasps that dig holes where they deposit paralysed prey inoculated with eggs to secure the future of their young and bees that nest in the soil.

The terrestrial crustaceans (**Isopoda**) known as wood lice or pill bugs and their relatives are probably best known because of the ability of some species to roll up into a tight ball when disturbed as a defence against predators. They are small arthropods, ranging from around 5–15 mm with a few smaller species. There are some 3,600 known species that are commonly found in, or at least associated with, moist organic deposits because of their incomplete waterproofed body surface. Isopods have three distinct body parts: cephalon (head), pereion (thorax), and pleon (abdomen). The head have eyes, two pairs of antennae although one pair is vestigial, and four pairs of appendages that are used in feeding. The thorax has seven pairs of walking legs, while the abdomen has five pairs of modified appendages used for respiration. The isopods have a well-developed olfactory sense, which might be related to their tendency for 'clumping'. The terrestrial isopods are important saprophages where they occur in larger numbers feeding on decaying organic material of plant or animal origin.

There are four classes of **Myriapoda** in soils. The millipedes (**Diplopoda**) and the centipedes (**Chilopoda**) are by far the most abundant and diverse Myriapoda, whereas the two lesser-known classes, Symphyla and Pauropoda, are less common and represent roughly 200 and 800 species, respectively. All myriapods have elongated bodies with many pairs of legs, a distinct head region, and a relatively uniformly segmented trunk. Symphyla can be distinguished from other myriapods by the presence of conical cerci on the posterior part of the body, while Pauropoda have small, branched antennae. Some species of Pauropoda and Symphyla can be significant pests of horticultural or agricultural crops. The 12,000 species of millipedes (**Diplopoda**) feed predominantly on decaying organic matter, but some can feed on living plant tissue. The millipedes' trunk is composed of fused segments (diplosegments) that make it appear like they have two pair of walking legs per segment. Contrary to popular belief and the suggestive common name, millipedes do not have a thousand legs, the record being 375 pairs in *Illacme plenipes*. Some of the larger millipedes, such as the African species *Archispirostreptus gigas*, can reach lengths of up to 30 cm. Most millipedes produce poisonous secretions or prussic acid (hydrogen cyanide) gas for defence. There are approximately 3,000 species of centipedes (**Chilopoda**). The first pair of walking legs are modified appendages, forcipules, that function as poison claws and contain venom used to catch and immobilise their prey. Hence, centipedes are thus predominantly predatory, although some species are able to live on, for example, leaf litter and decomposing organic matter for parts of the year.

Several other groups of fauna are commonly found in the soil or litter layer, where they forage. For example, while most spiders are not generally considered true soil fauna, many species including the wolf spiders (Lycosidae) hunt in the litter layer and could have a significant impact on soil fauna assemblages. Other spiders dig tunnels or other structures and through this modify soil conditions, including the ambush trapdoor spiders (Ctenizidae). Similarly, scorpions hunt in the soil litter interface and several species build tunnels that can contribute to alter the soil structure. Slugs and snails, the two primary terrestrial gastropods, are common pests in gardens. Most snails are herbivores while slugs feed on a broader range of organic matter including a few species that are predatory. Generally, only species that use soil as a habitat and for foraging are included in the soil megafauna. By this definition, soil megafauna includes a few vertebrates such as the worm-like amphibians, Caecilians, with reduced eyes and limbs that feed on insects and worms, and moles that dig tunnels and feed on lumbricid earthworms and other soil fauna. Other part-time soil fauna includes vertebrates such as voles, shrews (Soricidae), the naked mole rat, blind snakes, and legless lizards. Other large animals, including some reptiles, rabbits, hedgehogs, foxes, gophers, squirrels, tortoises, etc. may dig burrows but do not use the soil as a place for foraging. While these cannot be considered soil fauna in strict terms, their activities do influence soil fauna assemblages and ecosystem functioning.

1.4 Summary

The diversity of life in soil is astounding, and the organisms within display great variation in body size, life history strategies, and functional traits. We presently have a solid understanding of the types of fauna that call soil their home; however, there are still many species that remain to be described, particularly in the taxa dominated by smaller body sizes. Moreover, our knowledge of the soil fauna is biased towards countries with a historical interest in soil fauna; for example, it is unlikely that there are many more species of springtails to be discovered in the United Kingdom given the strong emphasis on this group over the past decades (Hopkin 2007). By contrast, there is a dearth of knowledge of the local soil fauna in countries with less historical interest, less densely populated areas, and more remote locations. There is a great need for more taxonomic expertise to resolve this knowledge gap. The rapid development of molecular techniques and their application to soil fauna assemblages (see Chapter 3 for further discussion on this topic) hold great promise to further our understanding of soil fauna species diversity and distribution. They may also provide more rapid approaches to quantify soil fauna assemblage responses to global change or experimental approaches. A discussion of the contribution of soil fauna to soil processes is in Chapter 2, and the methods available to assess this in more detail are discussed in Chapter 3.

2 · *Functional Roles of Soil Fauna*

Soil fauna is clearly important to ecosystem functioning, particularly through its contributions to biogeochemical cycling, interactions with other soil biota and the vegetation, and habitat modification. Indeed, fauna is even considered to be an essential facilitator of soil formation (Anderson 1995, Bardgett 2005). Quantifying the contribution of soil fauna to C and nutrient cycling has thus been a longstanding goal for soil ecologists, with research into their contributions gaining steam particularly in the 1960s, and which was later synthesised by other researchers. Seastedt (1984), for example, surveyed the contemporary literature for studies that measured the effects of soil animals on litter decomposition and concluded that the presence of soil fauna increased litter decomposition rates on average 23% across 15 studies. This has since been further corroborated by a growing literature, indicating that on average the presence of soil fauna ranging from Protozoa to microarthropods to earthworms substantially stimulates soil processes, including decomposition and mineralization, through their direct impacts on litter decomposition and indirectly through their interactions with the microbes (Mikola et al. 2002). One present key challenge is to consolidate existing knowledge to identify and address critical knowledge gaps to more robustly characterise the contributions of soil fauna to ecosystem processes. This is essential to better understand how our ecosystems function under contemporary conditions and predict their future state in the light of global changes. In the following sections, I will provide an overview of the contributions of soil fauna to ecosystem function, initially following the micro-, meso-, and macrofauna classification for simplicity. I will then try to tie this together by scaling functioning to the soil food web level to incorporate trophic interactions. I will wrap up with an introduction to a couple of developing topics in soil ecology: soil biodiversity–functioning relationships, aboveground–belowground linkages, and plant–soil feedbacks, with a focus on the soil fauna.

2.1 Ecosystem Functioning

Soil fauna is now broadly recognised to contribute to a wide range of ecosystem processes, and through this the provision of services (Table 2.1). The activities of soil fauna that influence biogeochemical cycling and litter decomposition in particular can be broadly defined as occurring through (1) selective feeding, (2) stimulation of microbe-derived hormones, (3) modification of organic matter, including fragmentation and mixing, and (4) ecosystem engineering. The first three categories follow that of Bardgett (2005). Ecosystem engineering effects are to some extent associated with modification of organic matter, but they are of great importance more broadly and specific to a few select taxa and therefore warrant a separate note. Selective feeding can occur at multiple levels, for example, through feeding preferences for certain types of microbes, leaf litter, prey or host-specificity of plant parasites, or belowground herbivores. Generalist feeding activities are likely to be important, with the effects likely to be resource-density dependent. Influences on the production of hormones that influence plant growth are associated with selective feeding. Fragmentation and mixing of the leaf litter or other organic matter, including that of animal origin, are mostly attributed to feeding activities of meso- and macrofauna. The effect of ecosystem engineers is often substantial, influencing the soil structure, distribution of resources, vegetation composition, and biogeochemical cycling. Where possible I will attribute soil fauna contributions to ecosystem functioning, but in most cases several mechanisms will be involved in moderating the effects.

Two further feeding types implicitly included in the aforementioned feeding categories warrant specific mention here because of their great impact on primary productivity and possible benefits in natural and production systems, respectively: belowground herbivores and soil fauna that provide biological control of pathogenic or pest species. For example, some beetle larvae, particularly members of the Elateridae (wireworms) and Scarabaeidae (white grubs), are detrimental root herbivores with substantial impacts on production systems unless managed appropriately (Frew et al. 2016). Other invertebrate root herbivores can also be problematic in production systems, including root-feeding dipteran larvae. By contrast, several types of soil fauna, such as predatory beetles and entomopathogenic nematodes, can provide biological control of said root herbivores (Sileshi et al. 2001, Susilo et al. 2004). More broadly, soil fauna can moderate successional patterns particularly through plant–soil

Table 2.1. *Key ecosystem functions that soil fauna activities contribute to, organised by broad functional groups, with examples of involved taxa. The activities of soil fauna contribute to the provisioning of ecosystem services such as soil formation, biochemical cycling, primary productivity, climate regulation, carbon sequestration, hydrological cycles, flood, and erosion control. Compiled based on Brussaard et al. (1997), Lavelle et al. (2006), and Barrios (2007).*

Functional groups	Example taxa	Actions	Ecosystem functioning
Decomposers	Oribatida Collembola Enchytraeidae Diplopoda	Litter fragmentation Production of faecal pellets/casts	Decomposition Nutrient cycling Soil respiration Soil aggregation
Microbial grazers	Protozoa Nematoda Collembola	Microbial grazing Production of faecal pellets/casts	Nutrient cycling Pathogen control Modification of the production of hormones that regulate plant growth Soil respiration Soil aggregation
Herbivores	Nematoda Collembola Coleoptera	Root feeding Production of faecal pellets/casts	Nutrient cycling Soil respiration Soil aggregation
Predators	Nematoda Mesostigmata Coleoptera Chilopoda	Predation Production of faecal pellets/casts	Biological control of pests Nutrient cycling Soil respiration Soil aggregation
Litter transformers	Oribatida Collembola Isopoda	Communition Production of faecal pellets/casts	Pedogenesis Decomposition Nutrient cycling Soil respiration Soil aggregation
Ecosystem engineers	Annelida Formicidae Isoptera	Bioturbation Redistribution of organic matter Dispersal of microbes Production of faecal pellets/casts	Nutrient cycling Soil formation Water infiltration and storage Nutrient cycling Soil respiration Soil aggregation

biotic feedbacks (e.g. van der Putten et al. 2013; Section 2.3). Accordingly, there is evidence that the addition of specific functional groups, particularly those that form close associations with plant roots including mycorrhizal-forming fungi, can promote the establishment of certain successional stage plant species and therefore would be useful to restoration practices (discussed in Harris 2009). Similarly, certain functional types of soil fauna may promote soil functioning or modify the soil food web to influence restoration practices (see Chapter 7).

2.1.1 Microfauna

The Protozoa and nematodes dominate the soil microfauna in most ecosystem types. Consequently, our understanding of the contribution of microfauna to soil processes is primarily based on these groups. The microfauna is often considered predominantly microbial-feeding organisms that modify microbial assemblages with cascading impacts on decomposition processes and biogeochemical cycling (Bardgett 2005, Hättenschwiler et al. 2005). However, as will become apparent, this may be too narrow a view of the extent of their contribution to ecosystem functioning. For example, it is well known that many nematodes are important plant parasites that can have substantial impacts on plant productivity, plant–plant interactions, and succession. There is also evidence that non-microbial-feeding protozoans may be of greater importance than previously thought. Moreover, the small size of microfauna limits their capacity to directly impact soil structure, but there is evidence that they can indirectly influence soil architecture through their interactions with other soil biota.

Protozoa

Our understanding of protozoan ecology is still rather limited, but there is increasing evidence that these minute organisms are of great importance to soil functioning, particularly as predators of bacteria. However, given recent evidence that Protozoa have a much broader range of feeding types that can also be common in soils, it has been suggested that their role in soil food web dynamics may need to be reconsidered somewhat. In particular, soil Protozoa feed on bacteria and fungi whilst they in turn fall prey to larger soil fauna. The Protozoa therefore present a key soil food web node whereby the fungal and bacterial food web channels come in close contact (Geisen 2016). However, protozoans broadly promote C and nutrient mineralization, which in turn often enhance plant nutrient uptake, and can under certain circumstances reduce microbial biomass or densities (Kuikman et al. 1990, Woods et al. 1982). Indeed, it has been estimated that Protozoa on average account for 70% of soil animal respiration (Foissner 1987) and that they are responsible for a high proportion of C and N mineralization, estimated at 10%–66% and 20%–40%, respectively (Ekelund and Rønn 1994, Griffiths 1994). For example, in an experimental arable field in the Netherlands, Bouwman and Zwart (1994) estimated that the average annual biomass of Protozoa (flagellates, amoeba) and nematodes (bacterivore, omnivore) under winter wheat amounted to 16 and 0.33 kg C ha^{-1}, with associated annual biomass production rates of 105 and 11.6 kg C ha^{-1}. They are particularly abundant in the rhizosphere soil (Rouatt et al. 1960) due to greater resource availability and play a critical role in this microhabitat. Indeed, the abundance of bacterial-feeding protozoans and nematodes can be up to 30-fold greater in the rhizosphere compared with the bulk soil due to the channelling of plant-derived C substrates (Griffiths 1990, Zwart et al. 1994). Protozoans are likely to play a particularly critical role in ecosystems where the abundance of other soil fauna is constrained by environmental conditions. For example, protozoans are common throughout the arid soils of the McMurdo Dry Valleys of Antarctica, including soils where no multicellular soil fauna is present (Bamforth et al. 2005). However, their contribution to C and nutrient turnover in these ecosystems are yet to be quantified reliably.

The composition of protozoan assemblages has been shown to influence bacterial assemblages. In a microcosm study, Rønn et al. (2002) inoculated soils with bacteria in the presence and absence of protozoans as a mixed culture or as individual species and investigated the effects on the bacterial community using denaturing gradient gel electrophoresis (DGGE) of PCR amplifications of 16S rRNA gene fragments. The results showed that the presence of the protozoan polyculture had a significant effect on the bacterial assemblage structure favouring G+C gram-positive bacteria related to *Arthrobacter* spp. whilst suppressing gram-negative bacteria. Moreover, the Protozoa monocultures had different impacts on the bacterial assemblage. Protozoa can similarly modify microbial assemblages through selective grazing of detrimental soil microbes. This in turn promotes plant health by facilitating beneficial rhizosphere microbes and modifying the production of plant hormones (Bonkowski et al. 2009, Scheu et al. 2005). Indeed, one study suggested that grazing by amoeba stimulated auxin-producing bacteria and increased the number and length of first-order lateral roots in five-day-old watercress seedlings (*Lepidium sativum*) (Bonkowski and Brandt 2002). These studies therefore provide strong evidence that protozoan assemblages influence microbial communities with cascading impacts on the plants.

The Protozoa may also interact with plant-associated fungi to influence plant growth. For example, it appears that mycorrhizal-forming fungi and Protozoa have contrasting effects on root development of plants. Mycorrhizae generally reduce root development as they take over the primary role of P acquisition, whereas Protozoa promote root development by facilitating N acquisition. In studies where both ectomycorrhizal (EM) fungi and Protozoa were added to pots with Norway spruce seedlings (*Picea abies*) the addition of Protozoa thus substantially increased root length relative to the Protozoa- and EM fungi-free controls. The addition of EM fungi reduced the positive impact of Protozoa albeit the root lengths were still greater than the control seedlings (Bonkowski et al. 2000, Jentschke et al. 1995). There is therefore a potential strong impact on plant growth and structure through indirect interaction between microfauna and plant symbionts likely due to competition for plant-derived C (Bonkowski and Scheu 2004). Similar interactions may occur between mycorrhizal-forming fungi and other bacterial-feeding microfauna.

Interestingly, there is recent evidence that some Protozoa may also serve as important predators of other soil fauna within the soil food web. In a laboratory experiment, Geisen et al. (2015a) found that the testate amoeba *Cryptodifflugia operculata* showed an elaborate pack-hunting technique to feed on bacterial-feeding nematodes. The impacts on nematode population sizes varied substantially between species, with juveniles being the preferred choice of prey. For example, *C. operculata* caused 89% and 25% reductions in *Rhabditis terricola* and *Rhabditis dolichura*, respectively. This laboratory study was supplemented with a survey of 12 soils from five locations throughout Europe, which showed that *C. operculata* was present in all soils and represented up to 4% of the active protist community in some soils. If these omnivore amoebas are similarly targeting nematodes under field conditions, they could have substantial impacts on both nematode abundances and assemblage composition. Protozoa themselves are prey for many multicellular soil-dwelling animals and create a link between the fungal and bacterial food web channels. However, their importance as prey is not yet well established given the inherent difficulties in manipulating these small organisms under realistic field conditions. A noteworthy study cultured protozoan assemblages from soils of two different ecosystems at Rothamsted, United Kingdom, and enriched these to ~83 atom% ^{13}C and 10 atom% ^{15}N before adding the cultures back to the soils in microcosms (Crotty et al. 2012a). The authors then tracked the fate of this ^{13}C and ^{15}N into the larger soil fauna for over 72 hours to determine who might feed predominantly on Protozoa. The results showed that most soil invertebrates were enriched in ^{13}C and ^{15}N, with evidence of C and N transfer from the Protozoa to the top predators of the soil food web, even within the limited time frame. However, there were clear differences between soil fauna, with nematodes, springtails, insect larvae, and earthworms acquiring the greatest proportion of Protozoa-derived C and N. One possible constraint of the experimental design is that many Protozoa are by nature not possible to culture under laboratory conditions. The study therefore favours the few species that flourish under these conditions, and the protozoan assemblages that were added to the soil are unlikely to be very similar to those observed under field conditions. This may have influenced the results somewhat. Still, the study provides strong evidence that the protists act as a link in the flow of C and N between the microbes and the larger multicellular soil-dwelling fauna. Further investigation of the contribution of soil protists to biogeochemical cycling is therefore warranted.

Nematoda
Soil nematodes are the most abundant and diverse multicellular soil fauna, and it is not surprising that they play a key role in ecosystem processes. A broad range of feeding types have been defined, but it is easier to summarise the impacts of nematodes based on trophic level, focussing on plant parasites, microbial feeders, and predators. Because there is substantial disparity in the resource use among these trophic levels, they will interact with other soil organisms and the plants differently and therefore contribute to ecosystem processes through different pathways, both directly and indirectly. In brief, plant parasitic nematodes have direct impacts on plant roots and indirect impacts on the soil microbial community by altering resource inputs (e.g. Bardgett et al. 1999a), microbial-feeding nematodes directly modify microbial communities which in turn may impact plant communities and indirectly influence microbes and plants through altered resource inputs, while predatory nematodes mostly have indirect impacts through changes in soil fauna assemblages at lower trophic levels and the release of nutrients. Omnivorous nematodes will bridge several of these trophic levels.

Plant parasitic nematodes are generally considered pests because of their substantial impacts on agricultural and horticultural productivity through grazing and transfer of detrimental viruses (Norton 1978), but there is substantial evidence that they play a critical role in biogeochemical cycling in natural and managed ecosystems (Yeates 1998). It has, for example, been estimated that plant parasitic nematodes consume 34.8–57 g m^{-2} belowground plant biomass at a range of prairie sites in Colorado and South Dakota, accounting for ~5.8%–12.6% of ANPP and surpassing the grazing by aboveground herbivores (Ingham and Detling 1984). However, although plant parasitic nematodes impact plant growth directly as plant feeders (De Deyn et al. 2003), causing C losses belowground through feeding and increased leaching, this does not always have negative consequences for plant productivity. Indeed, there is evidence that moderate levels of plant parasitic nematodes may actually promote plant biomass production similar to plant responses to herbivores observed aboveground. This effect may be caused by compensatory growth, altered plant C allocation, or enhanced activity of root symbionts such as N-fixers (Bardgett et al. 1999a). In a microcosm study of the impacts of the root-knot nematode, *Meloidogyne incognita*, on barley root architecture and rhizodeposition, Haase et al. (2007) accordingly found that intermediate densities of the root-knot nematode (~4,000 per kg dry soil) increased plant shoot biomass, plant N and P content after four weeks and initially (i.e. after one week) enhanced rhizodeposition of plant metabolites. However, the latter pattern was not sustained over the following weeks of the four-week-long study. Moreover, low levels of herbivory appeared to cause root elongation. Additionally, the sites of infection, i.e. the root knots, acted as independent microhabitats with reduced rhizodeposition and a greater fungal to bacterial ratio relative to the adjacent rhizosphere indicating altered biogeochemical dynamics at these microsites. The presence of plant parasitic nematodes has also been observed to have positive effects on the rhizosphere microbial community, likely by stimulating root exudation and through this, belowground activity (Poll et al. 2007, Yeates et al. 1998). However, this is not always the case, with some studies showing negative impacts of plant parasitic nematodes on microbial biomass production possibly due to the nematodes acting as a C and nutrient sink modifying the inputs to the microbial community (Maboreke et al. 2017). Through their feeding activities, plant parasitic nematodes may therefore modify plant C allocation, nutrient uptake, loss of C, and interactions with belowground microbial symbionts (Hofmann et al. 2010, van der Putten 2003). This in turn influences soil microbial communities with potential plant–soil feedbacks (Section 2.3). Conversely, there is evidence that indicates that mycorrhizal infection of plant roots inhibits plant parasitic nematode infections possibly because of competition for plant-derived C (Graham 2001, Ingham 1988). However, plant parasitic nematodes can also modify plant symbiotic relationships, reducing mycorrhizal root colonisation and sporulation (Francl 1993).

Several studies have used stable isotope labelling to investigate the role of plant parasitic nematodes in C and N dynamics belowground. For example, using ^{15}N labelling, a study showed that the presence of the plant parasitic nematode *Heterodera trifolii* increased the transfer of ^{15}N from the legume *Trifolium repens* to a neighbouring grass, *Lolium perenne* (Bardgett et al. 1999b). Similarly, another study found a positive relationship between the abundance of plant parasitic nematodes (*H. trifolii* and *Pratylenchus* sp.) and the transfer of ^{15}N from *T. repens* to *L. perenne* (Dromph et al. 2006). By contrast, a later study found a 13% reduction in ^{15}N transfer between the same two plant species (Ayres et al. 2007). The authors hypothesised that the different results were related to the time when the studies collected their samples. They collected their samples shortly (seven days) after the ^{15}N labelling, whereas the other studies allowed longer time for the ^{15}N to be distributed from the legume to the grass. Another recent experimental study using a ^{13}C pulse-labelling approach found that the presence of the root-feeding nematode *Pratylenchus penetrans* and the fungal-feeding springtail *Protaphorura armata* had no impact on plant growth when added to pots independently in microcosms, but when they were added together they synergistically reduced the biomass of oak (*Quercus robur*) inoculated with the ectomycorrhizal fungi *Piloderma croceum* (Maboreke et al. 2017). The authors hypothesise that the synergistic effect may be caused by changes in root morphology in response to collembolan grazing activity. It has previously been observed that plants produce longer, thinner roots when collembolans are present (Endlweber and Scheu 2006). This may promote nematode grazing because plant parasitic nematodes generally favour root tips for colonisation and feeding (Cohn et al. 2002). However, the experiment also showed that the presence of the nematode and springtail had contrasting impacts on the microbial community, with the nematode reducing and the springtail increasing microbial biomass, respectively (Maboreke et al. 2017). Interestingly, the presence of either feeding type still enhanced plant-derived ^{13}C incorporated into bacterial biomass indicating greater leaching, but there were limited collective effects. It was observed that the presence of microfauna, i.e. Protozoa and nematodes, in a microcosm experiment increased the N content of rye grass by 14% (Griffiths 1989), indicating their considerable impact on nutrient cycling through biotic interactions with the bacterial community. Other studies similarly showed increased plant nutrient uptake in the presence of microfauna (Bonkowski et al. 2000, Clarholm 1985), generally with positive effects on plant biomass production, although negative effects have also been observed (Bardgett and Chan 1999). Conversely, the increase in nutrients in mineral forms in the soil solution is often associated with increased loss of nutrients through leaching (Bardgett and Chan 1999, Bonkowski et al. 2000, Clarholm 1985).

A large proportion of the photosynthetically derived C produced by plants, estimated at up to ~40%, is released belowground through exudation by the plant roots (Lynch and Whipps, 1990), thereby fuelling the soil food web with particularly high activity observed in the rhizosphere, i.e. the zone immediately surrounding the root tips (Hiltner 1904). The free-living soil microbes are strongly C-limited (Wardle 1992) and would sequester this C, and associated essential nutrients, rapidly without the presence of microbivores (Wang and Bakken 1997). However, grazing by microbivore protozoans and nematodes helps re-mobilise important nutrients due to the predators' greater C:N ratios and low assimilation rates (10%–40% and 50%–70% for Protozoa and nematodes, respectively) (Ferris et al. 1997, Griffiths 1994) making the nutrients available for uptake by plants (Bonkowski et al. 2000). The surplus N is generally excreted as ammonium, making it readily available to other soil organisms as well as plants (Zwart et al. 1994). Bacterial-feeding nematodes have a higher C:N ratio (8:1 to 12:1) than their prey (3:1 to 4:1), leading to a surplus N intake during feeding (Wasilewska and Bienkowski 1985) that is usually excreted as NH_3 (Freckman 1988). Indeed, it has been estimated that approximately 90% of the N consumed by bacterial-feeding nematodes is not required for biomass production and is excreted to the soil, thus being made available for uptake by plants and microbes (Bardgett et al. 1999a). The effect of nematodes on N mineralization has, however, been shown to differ markedly between species with different biology or life history traits (Postma-Blaauw et al. 2005, Postma-Blaauw et al. 2006). Accordingly, a lab incubation study found that N turnover in sterilised soils inoculated with one of two species of bacterial-feeding nematodes (*Rhabditis intermedia*, *Protorhabditis oxyuroides*) differed substantially, and most processed involved in N cycling was only influenced by *P. oxyuroides* relative to a nematode-free control soil (Zhu et al. 2018). Feeding activities of nematodes have also been shown to influence P and S mineralization (Freckman 1988, Ingham et al. 1985), but the consequences of this have not been explored in detail. Given the potential competition for prey among bacterial-feeding Protozoa and nematodes, there are ample opportunities for biotic interactions. Indeed, it has been shown that co-occurrence of the bacterial-feeding nematode *Caenorhabditis elegans* and the amoeba *Acanthamoeba castellanii* in a laboratory experiment caused mutual toxicity (Neidig et al. 2010). However, the impacts of microfaunal biotic interactions on ecosystem functioning are not yet well characterised.

The effects of bacterivore soil microfauna, specifically protists and bacterial-feeding nematodes, on ecosystem functioning was assessed using meta-analyses tools in a recent paper. The authors data mined 41 experimental studies published between 1977 and 2014 that manipulated the presence of bacterivores and analysed the effects on 18 functions related to microbial and plant communities. Overall, their results showed that the presence of bacterivores had a negative effect on microbial biomass (−16%) and bacterial abundance (−15%), but increased soil respiration (29%) and the microbial metabolic quotient (35%), indicating greater microbial activity and turnover. Associated with this the authors observed greater phosphatase activity (7%) and increased rates of N (79%) and P (29%) mineralization. Moreover, the presence of bacterivores had a strong positive effect on plant shoot (27%) and root biomass (21%), and increased total plant shoot and root N and P content (in mg; N: 59% and 28%, respectively; P: 38% and 55%, respectively) (Trap et al. 2016). Similarly, an earlier meta-analysis concluded that increased soil fauna biomass (<2 mm body width) decreases microbial biomass and promotes plant productivity, with a larger effect observed for bacterial grazers than fungal grazers (Sackett et al. 2010). These results are consistent with the hypothesis that the main effect of microbivore microfauna on plant growth is due to increased N-mineralization (Clarholm 1985, Griffiths 1994, Zwart et al. 1994). The difference in plant productivity responses to bacterial and fungal grazing is likely associated with the preference of lower C:N substrates by bacteria, resulting in greater nutrient turnover and the concomitant lower C:N ratio of bacterial biomass, causing greater release of N when they are being grazed (Osler and Sommerkorn 2007). However, there appears to be more to the story as the presence of protozoans has been shown to have substantial effects on spruce seedling growth, even with a nutrient surplus (Jentschke et al. 1995).

Naturally occurring stable isotope ratios have also shown significant insight into the role of nematodes in soil food webs. The McMurdo

2.1 Ecosystem Functioning · 53

Figure 2.1 The McMurdo Dry Valleys, continental Antarctica, is dominated by polar desert. The soil mesofauna assemblages of the dry, salty soils are dominated by the nematode *Scottnema lindsayae*, with *Eudorylaimus antarcticus* and *Plectus murrayi* found more sporadically.
Photo by the author.

Dry Valleys in continental Antarctica are dominated by three genera of nematodes: *Scottnema*, *Eudorylaimus,* and *Plectus* (Nielsen et al. 2011b) (Figure 2.1). It is well established that *Scottnema lindsayae* and *Plectus murrayi* are bacterial feeders, but the feeding preferences of the indigenous *Eudorylaimus antarcticus* have been more contentious. The presence of an odonto-stylet that can be used for piercing plant and animal cells and other food sources, and the trophic classification of *Eudorylaimus* as omnivore-predators in temperate ecosystems (Yeates et al. 1993), indicated that the same may be true in Antarctic soil food webs (Virginia and Wall 1999). However, other studies speculated that the Antarctic dry valley *Eudorylaimus* may instead feed predominantly on algae (Powers et al. 1998), and they have indeed been observed using this resource (Wall 2007). A very recent study used $^{15}N/^{14}N$ and $^{13}C/^{12}C$ stable isotope ratios to provide more robust insight into the likely soil food web structure (Shaw et al. 2018). This study found strong evidence that dry valley soil food webs associated with cyanobacterial mats are composed of three trophic levels, with the cyanobacteria representing the primary trophic level, *P. murrayi*, rotifers, and the tardigrade *Acutuncus antarcticus* representing the primary consumers, and *E. antarcticus* the sole secondary consumer. This conclusion was based on an *E. antarcticus* $^{15}N/^{14}N$ ratio 2‰–4‰ higher than the primary consumers. Given that *E. antarcticus* is a common nematode throughout Antarctica, except in the driest and saline soils dominated by *S. lindsayae*, they may be one of the most important predators of continental Antarctic soils.

The free-living soil nematodes fall prey to many larger soil fauna, but how important they are as prey is not well defined. In a study using a targeted sequencing approach to determine whether a potential predator had consumed a given prey species, Heidemann et al. (2011) assessed the consumption of two pathogenic nematodes, *Phasmarhabditis hermaphrodita* and *Steinernema feltiae*, as a resource under laboratory (no-choice feeding experiment) and field conditions. In the no-choice feeding experiment using infective juveniles of the nematodes, both a known predatory mesostigmatid mite but also several 'detritivore' oribatid mite species consumed the nematodes, with prey DNA being picked up after as little as four hours of feeding. Following the no-choice feeding experiment, the authors added both dead and live infective juveniles of the two nematode species to plots in the field (live *P. hermaphrodita* with dead *S. feltiae*, and vice versa) to determine whether soil invertebrates feed on live nematodes directly or are more likely to scavenge on dead nematodes. They found that several oribatid mite species including *Liacarus subterraneus*, *Platynothrus peltifer*, and *Steganacarus magnus* feed extensively on nematodes. Moreover, live and dead *P. hermaphrodita* returned similar DNA signals indicating a high level of scavenging by the oribatid mites. These results thus highlight that nematodes are likely to be a substantial resource for larger soil fauna including species otherwise considered to be decomposers. The degree of scavenging is likely also much greater than currently assumed, and this warrants further investigation.

Finally, the discussion about the contribution of nematodes to soil processes and ecosystem functioning has so far focussed on 'free-living' soil nematodes. There is one more important group of nematodes that occurs in soil, that has important implications for plant productivity in particular – the entomopathogenic nematodes (EPNs). As described in Chapter 1, EPNs are parasites of many arthropods that spend part of their life cycle in the soil, including many important root herbivores that impact horticultural and agricultural crops. Several species of EPNs are currently being used for biological pest control (Chapter 7), and there is an ongoing effort to find EPN biocontrol agents for a broader variety of native and invasive pests. However, there is a significant gap in our knowledge about the impacts of EPNs on arthropods in natural and managed environments alike.

2.1.2 Mesofauna

Soil mesofauna plays an important role in ecosystems via direct and indirect effects on biogeochemical cycling, decomposition rates, primary productivity, and other processes. The two dominant groups of mesofauna, Acari and Collembola, are particularly important given their substantial abundances and diversity of functional traits. Mites and springtails contribute to ecosystem functioning through similar mechanisms, but the relative contributions differ between the two groups given contrasting predominant feeding preferences. As outlined in Chapter 1, both mites and springtails show a broad range of feeding types but are predominantly decomposers and fungal feeders, respectively. As such, mites would be expected to contribute more directly to decomposition processes than springtails, which would instead mostly influence ecosystem functioning ranging from plant growth to decomposition indirectly through their interactions with mycorrhizal-forming fungi.

It has, however, been shown that mite feeding groups impact soil processes differentially, making broad generalisation across high taxonomical groupings difficult. Mites have low C and nutrient assimilation rates, generally estimated to be in the range of 24%–52% (Luxton 1982), thus contributing to substantial C and nutrient turnover through their feeding activities. Siepel and Maaskamp (1994) investigated the effects of five different oribatid mite feeding groups (classified based on gut enzyme contents according to Siepel and de Ruiter-Dijkman (1993)) on microbial respiration during grass litter decomposition in microcosms. The authors found that only the feeding groups that interacted specifically with fungi influence microbial respiration, with fungivore browsers and opportunistic herbo-fungivores, and herbo-fungivore grazers and fungivore grazers, inhibiting and enhancing microbial respiration, respectively. By contrast, the herbivorous oribatid mite had no significant effect on microbial respiration. These results thus indicate that the impact of mites on decomposition processes depends on their feeding preferences and interactions with the leaf litter and microbial communities. The contributions of mites at higher trophic levels may also display feeding preference-specific influences on soil processes.

Springtails similarly represent multiple trophic levels. Some studies of springtail feeding activities suggest that springtails have limited resource specialisation with many species feeding unselectively on a broad range of plant litter and/or fungal biomass (Fiera 2014, Ngosong et al. 2011); however, there is evidence for trophic-level differentiation among springtails from stable isotope analyses. For example, Chahartaghi et al. (2005) measured $^{15}N/^{14}N$ ratios for 20 species of springtails and likely food sources in three deciduous forest stands in Germany and concluded that feeding preferences ranged from herbivory to primary and secondary decomposers. The authors defined trophic levels using a threshold of 3 δ ^{15}N units, with the results suggesting that the springtails represented three trophic levels. This indicates that springtails may have contrasting feeding preferences even within a group considered primarily food generalists. Indeed, they may even be relying more on plant material as a food source than previously considered (Endlweber et al. 2009). This in turn indicates that springtails can contribute to ecosystem functioning through multiple pathways. However, stable isotope measurements have various shortcomings, and the results should be considered with caution (Crotty et al. 2012b; Chapter 3).

Springtail feeding activities are known to moderate microbial assemblage composition with cascading impacts on soil processes. For example, fungivorous springtails have been shown to enhance microbial respiration and N and P mineralization rates during pine litter decomposition in microcosms through indirect effects on the microbial community (Teuben and Roelofsma 1990). The effects, however, appear to be density dependent. In a microcosm experiment, Hanlon and Anderson (1979) inoculated ground leaf litter with the fungus *Coriolus versicolor* and the springtail *Folsomia candida* at varying densities (0, 5, 10, 15, or 20 individuals). The presence of springtails enhanced microbial respiration at low density (five individuals) but suppressed respiration at greater densities indicating negative effects of high grazing pressures. Moreover, the presence of springtails caused a progressive bacterial dominance with increasing densities, indicating that the springtails feed preferentially on the fungi. Accordingly, it has been shown that springtails play a role in transferring litter-derived C into the soils through interactions with the fungal assemblages. One of the first studies to quantify the impacts of fungal grazing empirically — a pulse-labelling approach exposing the plant community to $^{13}CO_2$ for seven hours and then tracking this ^{13}C into root-free soil *in situ* — showed that the presence of springtails disrupts the flow of plant-derived C through the mycorrhizal mycelial network in a grassland (Johnson et al. 2003). Since then, multiple other studies have used similar and other approaches to quantify soil fauna impacts on biogeochemical cycling. Similarly, in an experimental laboratory approach to further quantify this link, Chamberlain et al. (2006) tracked the fate of C from ^{13}C-labelled alder litter into a soil with and without the springtail *Folsomia candida* present. While there were no significant differences in alder litter decomposition rates between treatments, the results showed that the presence of *F. candida* increased the translocation of C from the alder litter to the soil and also to the microbial community. They further estimated that the springtails consumed approximately 158 mg litter-derived C during the incubation, representing roughly 33% of the litter mass loss. Moreover, springtail grazing can modify mycorrhizal-forming fungal communities, and plant–fungal interactions in turn moderate plant performance (Ngosong et al. 2014) and fungal grazing by springtails have been found to modify hyphal morphology and enzyme production, with potential consequences for ecosystem processes (Hedlund et al. 1991). Hence, changes in springtail assemblage structure and composition can substantially modify ecosystem function.

The effects of springtail assemblages on ecosystem functioning are complex and context dependent. In a microcosm study carried out under glass house conditions, Eisenhauer et al. (2011b) found that springtail assemblage composition was a better predictor for their impact on ecosystem functioning than diversity (ranging from one to three species), with complex effects of species interactions. Springtails had a net positive but non-linear effect on plant shoot and root productivity, and influenced rooting depth distributions in a plant species-specific way. Interestingly, on average the presence of springtails had a negative effect on litter decomposition rates for forb and legume litter but not the grass litter they investigated. The authors highlight that this is in accordance with the conclusions drawn based on a meta-analyses undertaken by Kampichler and Bruckner (2009) after they corrected for the effect of mesh size. Being predominantly fungal feeders, it appears likely that high springtail densities may have suppressed fungal colonisation and utilisation of the litter enough to reduce litter decomposition. This effect may be particularly pronounced in a laboratory setting during initial leaf litter decomposition and where springtails are not influenced by interactions with other soil fauna, including potential predators. Indeed, there is evidence that the level of grazing by springtails has important consequences for mycorrhizal growth, with low to moderate grazing promoting growth and high grazing rates reducing growth, respectively (Kaneda and Kaneko 2004, Steinacker and Wilson 2008).

A recent review moreover discusses how mites and springtails may influence soil aggregation through direct and indirect pathways (Maaß et al. 2015). In brief, microarthropods are expected to contribute directly to aggregate formation through deposits of organic matter (faecal pellets, necromass, eggs, moulting, etc.) that may provide points of nucleation for aggregation, whilst possibly contributing to the destruction of soil aggregates through foraging and other activities. They are further likely to contribute indirectly to the formation or modification of aggregation through interactions with the soil microbial community, dispersal of microbial propagules, and reinforcement of existing structures made by larger soil fauna. The authors conclude that indirect effects likely will have a greater impact than direct effects; however, the size and direction of indirect effects are more difficult to predict given that they are mediated by mostly microbial contributions. For example, as outlined earlier, low to moderate grazing by springtails can promote fungal growth whereas high grazing pressures negatively impact fungal growth. Low to moderate grazing may therefore promote soil aggregate formation while higher grazing pressures could suppress aggregate formation. However, the mesofauna contributions to ecosystem functioning through these processes have not been quantified. Hence, there is substantial evidence that microarthropods influence ecosystem functioning and structure; however, the consequences of these activities are not well established.

Another group of mesofauna deserves mentioning here. The effects of enchytraeids on soil processes have received less attention than that of the larger earthworms, but it has been shown that they play important roles where they occur in abundance, particularly cold, organic-rich soils. For example, a microcosm experiment that incubated organic-rich upland soils from Cumbria, England, found increased amounts of dissolved organic C and greater microbial activity in the treatments when enchytraeids were present (Cole et al. 2000). The authors concluded that enchytraeids likely play a key role in decomposition processes and nutrient dynamics in such soils. Similarly, an earlier study found that the presence of enchytraeids enhanced nutrient mineralization during decomposition of Sitka spruce litter (Williams and Griffiths 1989). The authors hypothesised that the observed increase in leaching of nutrients in the presence of enchytraeids was due to reduced nutrient immobilization by microbes. Where earthworms are absent, the enchytraeids can contribute significantly to soil metabolism, with up to ~11% of total soil metabolism recorded comparable to that from *Lumbricus terrestris* in woodlands (O'Connor 1967, Satchell 1967). Their role as bioturbators have not been well characterised, but it is clear that enchytraeids can increase the soil pore volume (Topoliantz et al. 2000) and reduce soil compaction, and through this promote water infiltration and alter nutrient dynamics and oxygenation (van Vliet 1998). They are the dominant bioturbators of the subsurface horizons in soils where earthworms are not present and can be considered ecosystem engineers of the organic layer (Tyler et al. 2001). Hence, enchytraeids can promote the formation of aggregates in the 600–1,000 μm size range through the production of faecal pellets that can contribute substantially to the soil structure. Accordingly, it has been estimated that up to 30% of the Ah horizon in a Scottish grassland soil was enchytraeid faecal pellets (Davidson et al. 2002).

Given the significant contribution of soil mesofauna to soil processes such as litter decomposition and soil organic matter stability (Wolters 2000), there is a great need to further quantify how and to what extent they influence key processes. For example, in a perspectives paper, Soong and Nielsen (2016) highlighted the potential benefits of incorporating microarthropods into models of soil organic matter dynamics and how this might be achieved. The authors specified three main mechanisms through which they influence soil organic matter transformation: (1) releasing dissolved organic matter through microbial grazing, (2) increased inputs of free particulate organic matter allowing greater microbial access and an increased surface for leaching of dissolved organic matter, and (3) transfer of C and nutrients between mineral-associated organic matter and occluded particulate organic matter pools. These pathways may, at least in part, be quantified through stable isotope labelling techniques (see Chapter 3), and empirical evidence would substantially move forward our understanding of soil food webs and ecosystem functioning.

2.1.3 Macro- and Megafauna

Macro- and megafauna have considerable impacts on the ecosystem, in part driven by their larger sizes. They contribute to litter fragmentation and displacement, produce significant amounts of faecal pellets, and stimulate decomposition processes. Moreover, many are considered ecosystem engineers because they modify the environment through their feeding, burrowing, production of faecal pellets or cast deposits, and other activities (Figure 2.2). Macro- and megafauna thus produce lasting imprints on their environment including changes in soil structure and organic matter distribution, and through this influences soil edaphic

Figure 2.2 Soil macrofauna that can substantially impact their environment are known as ecosystem engineers. These ecosystem engineers include ants, termites, and earthworms. In this case, termite mounds in tropical Queensland, Australia, are pictured.
Photo by the author.

properties, soil biological assemblages, and biogeochemical cycling and ecosystem functioning more broadly. Three groups in particular, the earthworms, ants, and termites, have received significant attention because of their contributions to soil processes and ecosystem function as ecosystem engineers.

Earthworms

Earthworms are often thought of as litter transformers that promote litter fragmentation, and they deposit partly degraded organic matter that become hotspots of microbial activity. Moreover, there is evidence that earthworms, through their impacts as ecosystem engineers, increase the feeding activity of soil fauna, which across 92 managed grasslands in Germany was facilitated by an increase in collembolan abundances at sites with greater earthworm biomass (Birkhofer et al. 2011). As mentioned earlier, earthworms can be classified as epigeic, endogeic, or anecic based on their positioning in the soil horizon and associated morphological and behavioural traits. The epigeic earthworms are mostly small bodied, darkly pigmented, and agile species with high reproductive rates and rapid life cycles that live in organic substrates where they feed on

Figure 2.3 Anecic earthworms deposit large amounts of casts on the soil surface. The cast in the picture is approximately 5 cm high.
Photo by the author.

decaying organic matter. The anecic species are generally larger and produce relatively stable burrows, and feed on surface-deposited organic matter such as dead leaves. The endogeic species live in deeper soil horizons where they feed on soil organic matter. The anecic species have particularly large impacts on soil structure and the fragmentation and redistribution of organic matter within the soil matrix. The deposition of faecal casts by anecic earthworms (Figure 2.3) can be substantial, ranging from 40–70 to 500–1000 t ha^{-1} annually in temperate and tropical savannas, respectively, effectively contributing to turning over the soil (Bouché 1983, Feller et al. 2003, Lavelle et al. 1992). Earthworms also aid in mineral weathering, although it is still unclear whether it is the action of earthworms *per se*, their gut microbes, or an interaction between the two (Blouin et al. 2013). For example, Darwin (1881) noted the disappearance of the red colour of red-oxide sand after passage through the earthworms' digestive tract, possibly due to dissolution of the oxide by acidic enzymes. Much more recently, Pop (1998) found evidence that earthworms of the genus *Octodrilus* can dramatically promote the formation of illite in soil, and Carpenter et al. (2007) similarly found that the earthworm *Eisenia veneta* accelerates the weathering of anorthite, biotite, kaolinite, and smectite. The consequences for ecosystem functioning of these impacts are, however, not well known. Given the activities of earthworms it is not surprising that they have a substantial impact on soil structure; however, there are large variations in the effects of different earthworm species. Earthworms can therefore both increase and decrease bulk density, soil porosity, and aggregation. This in turn has idiosyncratic impacts on soil water infiltration, storage, and leaching, making it difficult to generalise on the contribution of earthworms to ecosystem functioning (Blouin et al. 2013). Earthworms can furthermore promote erosion through the deposition of unstable casts, particularly when these are deposited on hill slopes. It has, for example, been estimated that the production of casts by earthworms caused a loss of roughly 1,100 kg ha^{-1} year^{-1} at two different sites (Darwin 1881, Sharpley et al. 1979).

Many studies have shown that the presence of earthworms enhances C and nutrient mineralization (Binet and Trehen 1992, Haimi and Huhta 1990, Saetre 1998), which in turn can promote plant growth. A recent meta-analysis of studies that experimentally assessed the impact of earthworms on plant productivity showed that earthworms have substantial and consistent effects. In particular, the presence of earthworms increased crop yield by 25% and aboveground biomass by 23%, while also promoting total plant biomass (van Groeningen et al. 2014). In general, earthworms are likely to promote bacterial-dominated soil food webs with fast C and nutrient cycling or at least less fungal dominance (Wardle 2002). Hence, incorporating management practices that facilitate the persistence of earthworms may have net benefits to land managers (see Chapter 9). While the effects of earthworms are generally considered favourable, they can have undesirable effects in some ecosystems such as soil compaction, removal of organic matter from the soil, and deposition of fragile material promoting erosion, promoting leaching of nutrients through greater infiltration and loss of soil C through greater microbial respiration (Lavelle et al. 1998, Parmelee et al. 1998). Similarly, a mesocosm study found that an abundant and diverse earthworm assemblage increased plant biomass production and water drainage, but reduced soil water content (Schon et al. 2017). A mesocosm study found that the presence of endogeic earthworms resulted in lower total root biomass in a ruderal plant community and increased the establishment success of an introduced native forb, *Plantago lanceolata* (Wurst et al. 2011). Interestingly, it was also shown that the earthworms gained more weight in the presence of arbuscular mycorrhizal fungi and promoted fungal hyphal formation, but there were no interactive effects between fungi and earthworm impacts on the plant community responses. Earthworms also influence plant communities via the soil seed bank. Forey et al. (2011) summarised the main mechanisms through which earthworms influence the plant community via the seed bank by moderating seed survival on the soil surface' as well as in the soil, germination, and seedling establishment. However, the effects may be positive or negative on either of these stages. Earthworms may, for example, translocate seeds from the surface layer to more protected sites further into the soil horizon, thereby reducing seed predation, but if the seeds are buried too deep, they will not be able to germinate. The effects are further moderated by seed functional traits including size and dormancy strategies. Moreover, there is evidence that earthworms can act as predators of plant seeds.

Ants and Termites
Ants and termites are eusocial insects that have significant impacts on their environment through feeding activities, nest building, and construction of subterranean galleries. They have therefore been characterised as ecosystem engineers (Jouquet et al. 2006). Termites are particularly important as decomposers in tropical and subtropical regions including arid to semi-arid ecosystems, whereas ants are more widely distributed and use a broader range of resources. The resource preferences of termites can be somewhat reliably identified based on morphological adaptations of the mandibles and gut structure (Bignell and Eggleton 2000). Ants are key predators of herbivores in many ecosystems, but some species such as leaf-cutter ants in tropical ecosystems can impose strong impacts on the vegetation as herbivores. Ants have less impact on decomposition, soil formation, and turnover than termites but still modify their environment and contribute to soil structural changes, particularly through the construction of sub-surface nests and deposition of material on the surface (Lavelle and Spain 2001). Many species build epigeal nests similar to those of certain termites, engineering the topography of the landscape. Nests vary in size, with the larger compound nests reaching several meters in diameter, covering a significant proportion of the surface area and being composed of a substantially different soil composition (Cox et al. 1992). Even smaller nests can accumulate to significant coverage. For example, Wells et al. (1976) found up to 5,000 mounds per hectare for the epigeal ant *Lasius flavus* in a British grassland, estimated to cover over 15% of the soil surface.

Where termites are present they often consume more wood material than all other invertebrates combined (Ulyshen 2016). They have high C assimilation rates, generally above 50% and even approaching 100% for cellulose in some cases, and their wood utilisation can rival that of wood-rotting fungi (Breznak and Brune 1994, Wood 1976). While gut endosymbionts often contribute to wood utilisation and assimilation of recalcitrant compounds, there is increasing evidence that many wood-feeding invertebrates including termites produce their own cellulase and are therefore able to break down cellulose on their own (Watanabe and Tokuda 2010). Termites have been shown to account for 1%–2% of C mineralization in rainforests, up to 20% in dry Africa where they consume up to 1,500 kg ha^{-1} dry litter annually, including most woody litter, and a staggering 50% of grass litter and a considerable amount of mammalian dung (Wood and Sands 1978). Similarly, termites mineralise ~10% of the leaf litter in some Asian seasonally dry forests (Yamada et al. 2005). Hence, they have substantial impacts on decomposition, and consequently C and nutrient cycling, in most tropical to subtropical ecosystems (Schuurman 2012). On a global scale, termites are thus estimated to contribute 0.2%–2% of the global terrestrial CO_2 efflux (Sugimoto et al. 2000). Moreover, termites are well known to influence the soil structure and physical characteristics. Their feeding activities result in a significant turnover of soil, estimated at up to 4.7 t ha^{-1} soil annually (Lobry de Bruyn and Conacher 1990), thus influencing soil profile development. They also deposit a large number of faecal pellets and produce pellets of soil bound by saliva, that can make up considerable proportions of the soil profile, while their sub-surface galleries dramatically modify the soil structure (Holt and Lepage 2000). In general, the presence of termites will promote soil water infiltration rates because of the increased soil porosity, at least in the vicinity of the mound. In a study in Burkina Faso investigating the effects of various organic soil amendments it was observed that the presence of soil fauna, particularly termites, promoted water infiltration by breaking the soil crust, improved plant water use efficiency, and altered N use efficiency (generally increased except when adding low-quality amendments, *Andropogon* straw), with the increase in water use efficiency coinciding with greater plant species diversity (Mando et al. 1996, Mando et al. 1999, Ouédraogo et al. 2006). However, the mound itself may contribute to compaction of the surface and reduce water infiltration locally. The construction of mounds also modifies the distribution of nutrients within the local landscape.

Other Macro- and Megafauna
Other soil macro- and megafauna contribute less to ecosystem engineering but can have substantial impact on soil processes. Most soil macrofauna are expected to enhance soil processes such as litter decomposition

and nutrient mineralization (Teuben and Roelofsma 1990). Several studies have found that excluding soil fauna causes reductions in litter decomposition rates, with soil fauna being of greater importance in some ecosystems than in others. Rarely do individual taxa ingest more than 5%–10% of the standing litter biomass, but the collected effects can be substantial. For example, Handa et al. (2007) found that the exclusion of all soil fauna contributed to significant reductions in litter C and N mass loss across five different biomes, with a lesser reduction when only soil fauna with a body width above 1 mm was excluded. The effect size was particularly large in the temperate and tropical biomes coinciding with high abundances of millipedes and termites, respectively, indicating the importance of these decomposers. Accordingly, there is broad agreement that soil macrofauna contributes substantially to decomposition processes through feeding activities and interactions with the microbes and other soil fauna. Similarly, the suppression of microarthropod abundances during litter decomposition in a temperate and two tropical forests found that the effect was greater in the tropical forests where lower decomposition rates were already evident in the reduced microarthropod treatment after three months, whereas microarthropod effects were not evident in the temperate forest until close to a year after the litter bags were deployed (Heneghan et al. 1998). Researchers increasingly recognise that invertebrates, including many that fall within the soil fauna classification, also contribute significantly to wood decomposition, particularly Coleoptera and termites where they are present, with estimates of 10%–20% wood loss attributed to this fauna (Ulyshen 2016). Dung beetles have a unique life strategy that contributes substantially to ecosystem functioning through their role in the distribution and decomposition of the dung of large herbivores in some ecosystems (Lavelle and Spain, 2001). However, robust measures of soil fauna contributions to ecosystem functioning have proven difficult to attain given methodological and analytical constraints.

On average, it appears that low to moderate grazing by microbial-feeding soil fauna will promote microbial activity while high levels can suppress activity and through this biogeochemical cycling (Bengtsson and Rundgren 1983, Bretherton et al. 2006). The effects of macro- and megafauna such as isopods and millipedes are generally greater than those of mesofauna grazers (Crowther et al. 2011b, Crowther et al. 2011c). The effect of grazing by soil fauna is, however, species specific and density dependent, making it difficult to generalise impacts. For example, the effect of grazing by woodlice, millipedes, and springtails on two saprotrophic basidiomycetes increased with grazing densities, but the effect of the woodlice was greater than that of the other two grazers (Crowther and A'Bear 2012). Another study from the same lab showed that preferential grazing of the fungus *Resinicium bicolor* by *O. asellus* prevented competitive exclusion of two subordinate fungal species, while the nematode *Panagrellus redivivus* stimulates the growth of the same two subordinate fungi, shifting competitive hierarchies in microcosms (Crowther et al. 2011a). Similarly, another study showed that selective grazing of saprotrophic basidiomycetes, the dominant primary decomposers of temperate woodland soils, by the isopod *O. asellus* modify the competitive interactions among the fungi (A'Bear et al. 2013). The effects of *O. asellus* on fungal competition was moderated by the incubation temperature, indicating that climate change may modify fungal communities through changes in soil fauna assemblages. Moreover, faunal grazing on the hyphae produced by saprotrophic fungi can modify the growth and functional traits expressed by the fungi. In a microcosm study, Crowther et al. (2011b) inoculated soils in 24 cm × 24 cm bioassay trays with one of four saprotrophic basidiomycete fungi on wood blocks with or without the presence of one of four grazers (the isopod *Oniscus asellus*, the millipede *Blaniulus guttulatus*, the springtail *Folsomia candida*, and the nematode *Panagrellus redivivus*). The authors found that the presence of grazers influenced extracellular enzyme activities of the fungi. The effect on enzyme activity was moderated by the impact of the grazer with the greatest effects observed in the isopod and millipede treatments. Moreover, the impacts differed from positive to negative depending on the enzyme and fungal species. Grazing had significant impact on the activity of enzymes that are proxies for C, N, and P cycling, such as β-glucosidase, cellobiohydrolase, N-acetylglucosaminidase, acid phosphatase, and phosphodiesterase, indicating the importance of grazing by soil fauna to biogeochemical cycling.

Many macrofauna are important root herbivores that can have detrimental impacts on plant growth, whilst also influencing the soil biological assemblages more broadly, plant–plant interactions, aboveground food webs, and biogeochemical cycling (Johnson and Rasmann 2015). The most obvious, and often costly in production terms, effects are the direct impacts on plant growth. Root herbivory does not always culminate in substantial impacts on plant growth, however, with compensatory growth observed in many plant species (Wurst and van der Putten 2007). The damage caused to plant roots often results in changes in belowground carbon allocation and exudation (Schultz et al. 2013,

Wurst and Ohgushi 2015, Wurst et al. 2010), with knock-on effects on other belowground herbivores and the soil food web through changes in resource availability and quality. Moreover, root herbivores can influence plant–plant interactions. Certain species of weevils in the genus *Sitona* feed predominantly, or even exclusively, on root nodules of legumes with implication for N cycling. Accordingly, the presence of the clover weevil (*Sitona* sp.) has been found to increase the transfer of N from clover to a neighbouring ryegrass (Murray and Hatch 1994), thus shifting competitive interactions. The presence of root herbivores has also been shown to reduce plant water uptake, contributing to drought stress symptoms (Masters et al. 1993, Poveda et al. 2005) that could have substantial effects in future climates. Finally, the attachment to plant roots by belowground herbivores has been observed to induce systemic plant defence responses that can modify herbivore assemblages aboveground (Bezemer et al. 2003, Soler et al. 2005b, Wurst et al. 2008). Hence, the effects of belowground herbivores can be substantial and far reaching; however, the impacts have not yet been well quantified.

While most studies focus on the influence of soil fauna on biogeochemical cycling of the major elements such as C, N, and P, there is also evidence for their influence on other elemental cycles. For example, it has been posed that saprovore millipedes are important for calcium (Ca) cycling in forest ecosystems, processing 15%–20% of Ca inputs to forest floors in some cases (Coleman et al. 2004). The effects of macro- and megafauna feeding activities on soil processes and ecosystem function are complex and vary among species within and between taxa. Moreover, there is great spatio-temporal variability in their impacts making generalisations difficult. For example, an early study suggested that roughly 30% of all soil N mineralization was caused by soil animal activities, but there were substantial seasonal changes in the contribution (Verhoef and Brussaard 1990). Overall, it appears that soil fauna contributes less to decomposition processes and energy flow than nutrient mineralization, and that its indirect contributions outweigh direct impacts (Hättenschwiler et al. 2005).

2.1.4 The Soil Food Web

Soil fauna interacts in myriad ways within the framework of the soil food web to influence ecosystem structure and functioning (Figure 2.4). Broadly speaking, decomposers contribute to the turnover of C and nutrients, and through this influence the microbes and the plants aboveground,

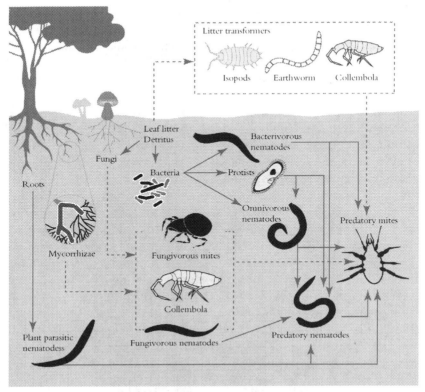

Figure 2.4 A simplified diagram illustrating the main linkages within the soil food web. It is important to note that many types of soil fauna are prey to predators aboveground, thus linking the soil food web with that above.
Modified from Nielsen et al. (2015b) with permission from *Annual Reviews*.

microbial grazers contribute to the turnover and mobilisation of C and nutrients tied up in microbial biomass, predators modify prey assemblages and through this biogeochemical cycling, while plant parasites exert direct impact on plant roots modifying vegetation productivity and composition. Many studies have investigated the effects of soil food web structure on ecosystem processes, generally focussing on C and nutrient dynamics or plant biomass production. These studies have provided novel and important insights into the contributions of soil fauna to ecosystem processes, although there are some methodological constraints. In one study, soil food webs were manipulated to incorporate omnivorous enchytraeids, a fungal-feeding springtail, and/or Oribatida to assess the effects on the growth of Scots pine with and without ectomycorrhizal fungi present (Setälä 2000). The author found that the presence of collembolans and enchytraeids enhanced pine biomass growth, in particular when ectomycorrhizal fungi did not colonise pine roots, whereas the presence of Acari had no impact. However, soil food web complexity did not have a substantial impact on pine growth as the effects of enchytraeids alone rivalled that of the most complex food webs. The study outlines that individual taxa contribute to different aspects of ecosystem processes and that interactions between different nodes of the soil food web moderate the outcomes.

The presence of decomposers generally promotes plant growth through enhanced nutrient mineralization, but there is also evidence that decomposer assemblage composition influences plant assemblage composition through changes in plant–plant competitive interactions. For example, by manipulating the structure of a model Mediterranean grassland decomposer assemblage comprising springtails, earthworms, and enchytraeids, Bonkowski and Roy (2012) showed that decomposer species richness, particularly of springtails, promoted grasses relative to forbs thereby effectively enhancing succession within the system. Interactions between large detritivores and microbes might influence functioning, but the effects of either on functioning are generally studied in isolation making it difficult to draw any strong, general conclusions. Hanlon and Anderson (1980) investigated the effects of microarthropod feeding activities on soil microbial respiration and biomass in a mesocosm experiment. Using additions of ground versus fragmented leaf litter with and without the decomposers *Oniscus asellus* and *Glomeris marginata* they found evidence that comminution of litter was the main decomposer effect on microbial activity, possibly by increasing the availability of resources. However, the addition of decomposers increased microbial respiration in the presence of fragmented litter in the short term. Interestingly, the presence of *O. asellus* reduced fungal standing biomass by roughly two-thirds, whereas there was a 10-fold increase in bacterial density, indicating a strong influence on microbial composition. Moreover, excessive decomposer density had a strong negative effect on microbial respiration. Another study similarly found that in the litter layer, fungal grazing by soil fauna stimulated the growth of fungi, thus immobilising nutrients whereas in the organic layer, soil fauna feeding tends to promote nutrient mineralization making it available to plant growth (Faber 1991). The influences of soil decomposer assemblages, however, change through litter decomposition stages (Van Wensem et al. 1993) and are moderated by assemblage or soil food web structure. In an experimental study, Wickings et al. (2012) found that grass and corn litter showed divergent patterns of litter chemistry during decomposition across three growing seasons. Moreover, by comparing patterns among three different agricultural management practices (conventional tillage, no-till, old field) they found evidence that the decomposer assemblages further moderated litter chemistry throughout decomposition, contributing to stark differences in litter chemistry at the final harvest when only ~10% of the litter mass remained.

The presence of predatory soil fauna reduces the density of microbial grazers by an average of 20%, but this does not generally incur a related change in microbial biomass or plant productivity (Sackett et al. 2010). The results of this meta-analysis and other studies suggest that trophic cascades are not common in soil food webs. Trophic cascades, however, have been observed in some ecosystems. Indeed, there is evidence that protozoan assemblages are modified by resource quantity and quality, top-down (predation), and competitive interactions (van der Putten et al. 2005). More evidence stems from Santos et al. (1981), who manipulated soil fauna assemblages during the early stages of creosote bush litter decomposition in the Chihuahuan desert using an insecticide (Chlordane, 1% by volume) that mostly suppressed the dominant predatory tydeid mites. They also included an insecticide-fungicide and an insecticide-fungicide-nematicide treatment. The highest litter decomposition rates were observed in the control treatments without any pesticides applied. The results showed that the absence of the predatory tydeid mites had a strong positive effect on bacterial-feeding nematode densities, which then in turn suppressed bacterial densities. These findings indicate that top-down control of bacterial-feeding nematodes by mites can be important to maintain ecosystem functioning. By contrast, it appears that fungi are generally not top-down regulated but rather limited by resource supply or bottom-up constraints. There are exceptions to the rule though, with experimental evidence of top-down control of fungal biomass in N-poor but not N-rich soils. More evidence for trophic cascades is presented by microcosm studies. Laakso et al. (2000) manipulated soil food web structure associated with birch seedlings in a microcosm experiment using leaf litter and humus from a boreal forest as the substrate. They manipulated both soil food web structure in terms of the number of trophic levels present and composition of assemblages representing these trophic levels. Following 37 weeks they destructively harvested the microcosms to assess effects of food web structure on plant performance and lower trophic levels. Their results showed that both predators and microbial grazers influenced their respective prey, and that the presence of predators increased microbial biomass, indicating the potential importance of trophic cascades in soil food webs. Similarly, in another microcosm experiment, Lenoir et al. (2007) established soil food webs with different trophic levels present in an N-poor and an N-rich humus substrate. One key relevant finding of that study was that the addition of a diverse fungal grazer community composed of springtails and oribatid mites suppressed the FDA-active fungal biomass in the N-poor substrate only. This indicates that the effects of grazers may be moderated by resource availability, or a trade-off between bottom-up and top-down constraints. Moreover, the study showed that the presence of predators could alleviate this effect, providing evidence for trophic cascades in nutrient-limited soil food webs.

Although trophic cascades may not be common in soil food webs, there are several other studies that have shown that top-down effects of bacterial grazers can be significant. In a microcosm study, Mikola and Setälä (1998) manipulated soil food webs to have one, two, or three trophic levels, with the microbial community made up of 20 species of bacteria and fungi, *Caenorhabditis elegans* and *Aphelenchoides* sp. representing bacterial and fungal grazers, respectively, and the predatory nematode, *Prionchulus punctatus*, the highest trophic level. These food webs were inoculated into a sterile humus and leaf litter substrate, regularly provided with a glucose media to support microbial growth, and followed for five months. While C and N mineralization rates and microbial productivity were greater in the presence of the higher trophic levels, the results did not provide evidence for strong trophic cascades given that bacterial densities were not influenced by food chain length, and fungal densities were higher in the presence of nematodes. Still, the experiment provides solid evidence that soil food web structure does influence ecosystem functioning. Similarly, Laakso and Setälä (1999a) established microcosms with different soil food web structures to assess the effect of top-down control of microbial-feeding nematodes by predatory mites. They grew birch seedlings in pots with a sterile leaf litter and humus substrate and inoculated this with bacterial and/or fungal-feeding nematodes with and without the presence of specialist or generalist predatory mesostigmatid mites. After 38 weeks, the presence of the specialist predator reduced nematode densities by more than 50%, while the generalist predator had limited effects on the nematodes with a weak increase in fungal feeders. Despite the substantial effect on nematode abundances, the authors found no differences in microbial biomass and only a moderate (<16%) increase in microbial respiration. Hence, high grazing pressures can cause top-down control of microbial grazers but appeared to have limited impacts on lower trophic levels. Slightly different results were observed in another mesocosm study with food webs constructed of one of three fungi (*Alternaria alternata, Fusarium oxysporum, Trichoderma viride*), a fungivorous springtail (*Folsomia fimetaria*), and a predatory mite (*Hypoaspis aculeifer*) (Hedlund and Öhrn 2000). The authors found the presence of all three trophic levels result in the highest respiration rates, while the lowest were observed in the mesocosms with fungi only. These results indicate that the low levels of grazing by springtails in the presence of a predator promote microbial respiration. Finally, another study showed that the presence of isopods suppressed the dominant cord-forming basidiomycete fungi in a fungal-dominated woodland soil (Crowther et al. 2013). This in turn contributed to substantial shifts in the soil fungal assemblage, including an increase in species richness indicating that the isopods prevented competitive exclusion, and modified the soil enzyme profile. Furthermore, the presence of isopods influenced the broader mycophagous soil fauna assemblage. Thus, top-down effects can be important, at least in some systems, with far-reaching effects on soil assemblages and ecosystem function. The study further provides evidence that there are keystone consumers among the soil fauna.

There is further evidence that predator–prey interactions can have impacts on soil fauna assemblages and through this ecosystem function. One hypothesis is that the presence of top predators that feed on other soil fauna can moderate their impacts either through suppression of their density or behaviour. If the predator targets a perceived beneficial organism, such as a decomposer, the effect could have negative effects on process rates. In the case of a decomposer this would result in reduced rates of decomposition and possible impacts on plant productivity because of reduced nutrient availability. However, there is limited evidence of the effects under field conditions and studies show idiosyncratic effects. For example, a study assessed the effects of predatory beetle presence on dung mass loss at a high-elevation alpine meadow on the Qinghai–Tibet Plateau under ambient and elevated temperature (~2.3°C) implemented by classical open-top chambers (Wu et al. 2011b). Prior to establishment, macroinvertebrates were culled inside mesh chambers using 40% chlorpyrifos to impose the treatments. They then added five large and/or 20 small predatory beetles (*Philonthus rubripennis* and *Quedius liangshanensis*, respectively), 40 coprophagous beetles (*Aphodius erraticus*), and a yak dung pat. The presence of the predatory beetles, either species in isolation or in combination, negatively influenced dung pat mass loss, with the greatest effect observed for the large predatory beetle. However, the effect on dung pat mass loss was only observed under ambient conditions.

The presence of predatory beetles in turn had a negative effect on plant growth, again largely driven by the presence of the large predatory beetle. A subsequent experiment confirmed that the large predatory beetle elicited a faster rate of consumption of the coprophagous beetles. The study therefore supports the hypothesis that the presence of predators can suppress decomposer assemblages, with cascading negative effects on soil processes and plant performance. By contrast, another study constructed mesocosms in which they manipulated the presence/absence of earthworms and predatory beetles at the same research site on the Qinghai–Tibet Plateau (Zhao et al. 2013). Following four months in the field, the plants in the mesocosms with both earthworms and predatory beetles showed greater growth, while earthworms alone had no effect. The effect appears to be due to a shift of earthworms to deeper soil horizons where their observed impacts on soil properties and nutrient availability may be of greater benefit to the plant. Unfortunately, the authors did not include a predator-only treatment, making it difficult to rule out possible alternative effects on plant performance, for example, through suppression of herbivores or other plant pests. Similarly, pathogenic or 'predatory' microbes may play a role in controlling the soil food web structure. For example, there is evidence that microbial enemies of plant parasitic nematodes moderate assemblage structure in sand dune systems (Costa et al. 2012). The authors collected samples from four different sand dune ecosystems over two years and quantified plant parasitic nematodes and their microbial enemies. Two microbial enemies, *Pasteuria penetrans* and *Catenaria* spp., were negatively correlated with plant parasitic nematode population sizes. In particular, *P. penetrans* appeared to exert a strong top-down control on *Meloidogyne* spp. populations, thereby indirectly facilitating *Pratylenchus* spp. population increases. Microbial pathogens of nematodes can therefore cause shifts in soil nematode assemblage structures that might in turn influence vegetation composition.

The soil fauna furthermore collectively produces a staggering number of faecal pellets that can contribute substantially to altering soil structure and modifying biogeochemical cycling. Unsurprisingly, this represents a unique resource that can be used by soil microbes as well as coprophagous soil fauna and several soil fauna taxa consume said faecal pellets. The ingestion of faecal pellets may serve multiple purposes but is centred on increased utilisation of nutrients or metals through direct uptake or by digesting the microbes growing within. The recycling of faecal pellets modifies microbial assemblages through the gut passage, generally with greater microbial biomass following ingestion compared to freshly fallen litter thereby promoting microbial decomposition activities (Hassall et al. 1987). While the N content and its availability may be greater initially (Hassall et al. 1987, Teuben and Verhoef 1992), subsequent ingestion tends to leave behind progressively more recalcitrant material (Gunnarson and Tunlid 1986). It is likely that this in turn produces faecal pellets that are more resistant in the long term, producing a highly recalcitrant pool of organic matter that can nucleate the formation or be incorporated in soil aggregates.

We are getting closer to providing empirical evidence to robustly structure food web models to evaluate the contributions of soil fauna to ecosystem functioning, but there are still important gaps. Several significant frameworks have been proposed that try to consolidate this knowledge and allow it to be incorporated into biogeochemical models. For example, Osler and Sommerkorn (2007) presented a framework based on prey preferences and C assimilation efficiencies of soil fauna to predict its contributions to dissolved organic matter pools and N mineralization. Soil fauna that are efficient C assimilators and preys on organisms with similar C:N ratios, such as bacterial-feeding protozoans and nematodes, is likely to contribute mostly to N mineralization. By contrast, varieties of soil fauna, such as fungal-feeding microarthropods and enchytraeids, that assimilate C less efficiently and use resources with higher C:N ratios are more likely to contribute to the dissolved organic matter pools. While the effectiveness of this framework is yet to be tested empirically, such efforts allow us to simplify the contributions of soil fauna to C and nutrient dynamics and possibly incorporate these activities more explicitly in biogeochemical models (see also Chapter 3).

2.2 Aboveground–Belowground Linkages

The literature on aboveground–belowground linkages is growing rapidly, sparked by the recognised importance of these linkages to ecosystem structure and functioning. I will not provide an in-depth discussion of aboveground–belowground linkages but rather will highlight a few key areas where there are particularly strong linkages between the soil fauna and the vegetation and animal assemblages aboveground. This is important to this book because these linkages are fundamental drivers of ecosystems and therefore shape assemblages both aboveground and belowground. Moreover, it has been highlighted that aboveground–belowground

2.2 Aboveground–Belowground Linkages · 75

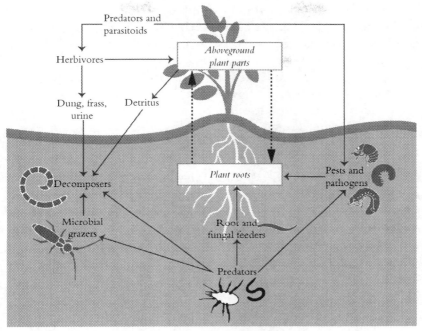

Figure 2.5 Simplified schematic illustrating the main aboveground–belowground linkages. The plants act as mediators linking the food webs, particularly as a resource for herbivores both aboveground and belowground that in turn are prey to predators and parasitoids. Moreover, plant litter and dung, frass and urine from aboveground fauna act as a resource for the decomposer assemblage, while much soil fauna is important prey for aboveground organisms.

linkages can provide insight into patterns of succession, agroecology, biological invasions, and global change impacts and may be critical for adaptive management (van der Putten et al. 2009). I refer the reader to the book *Aboveground-Belowground Linkages: Biotic Interactions, Ecosystem Processes, and Global Change* by Bardgett and Wardle (2010) for a more thorough overview of aboveground–belowground linkages. The main pathways through which soil fauna might be important are in aboveground–belowground linkages (Figure 2.5). In particular, soil fauna is likely to indirectly influence aboveground herbivores and their predators via changes in plant chemistry, growth, and vegetation composition. Root herbivores do this through direct interactions with the plant root as well as changes in the microbial assemblages; decomposers will do it by moderating nutrient availability and microbial assemblage composition, while predators exert their influence via changes in the decomposer and root herbivore assemblages and nutrient mobilization (i.e. excretion of nutrients following ingestion).

One of the most investigated aspects of aboveground–belowground linkages is the effect of belowground herbivores on aboveground herbivores, and vice versa, because of the expected strong interaction through feeding on the same host plant. Root-feeding nematodes have, for example, been shown to reduce aphid reproduction on plants aboveground (Bezemer et al. 2005, Sell and Kuo-Sell 1990). Despite an increasing number of studies on this topic, few general patterns have been identified to date. Indeed, one of the few publications that has tried to synthesise the literature through a meta-analytical approach found no strong evidence for directional effects of herbivores aboveground on those belowground or vice versa (Johnson et al. 2012). However, there was substantial variation in the outcomes of studies, with both positive and negative linkages observed. When this was investigated in more detail the data revealed that aboveground herbivores have a significant negative impact on belowground herbivores when the former arrive on a host plant before the latter. However, the effects were observed only on annual plant species. Moreover, the type of herbivore investigated moderated the outcomes. In particular, root herbivore Diptera had the strongest negative impact on aboveground herbivores, while the most widely studied belowground herbivores, Coleoptera, had positive effects on aphids and negative effects on sawflies aboveground, respectively. Conversely, a recent meta-analysis by Andriuzzi and Wall (2017) found that the presence of large herbivores aboveground had consistent negative effects on oribatid mites, total nematode abundances, and predatory nematodes, and that this effect was moderated by herbivore size, with no effect observed for small to medium-sized species.

There is also increasing evidence that other soil fauna groups influence aboveground–belowground linkages. For example, the presence of protozoans can impact plant interactions with organisms aboveground through changes in plant traits (Gange et al. 2002, Wurst et al. 2003). In a study investigating the effects of protozoans and earthworm presence on aphid performance on barley, Bonkowski et al. (2001) found that the presence of protozoans had greater effects than earthworms and increased biomass production by ~40%. Associated with this the authors saw a doubling in aphid biomass and abundance. However, the presence of protozoans also promoted barley reproductive rates (biomass of ears, number of seeds, seed weight) and indicated greater plant tolerance to aphid herbivory. Similarly, the presence of springtails and/or earthworms influenced the reproductive performance of the aphid *Myzus persica* on *Poa annua* and *Trifolium repens* (Scheu et al. 1999). Earthworms promoted plant biomass production of both species, and particularly *P. annua*, whereas springtails reduced biomass production. Similarly, the presence of earthworms enhanced aphid reproduction, whereas springtails increased aphid reproduction on *P. annua* but reduced reproduction on *T. repens*. The authors were unable to determine what caused the idiosyncratic responses but speculated that springtails decrease reproduction on palatable host plants and increase reproduction on less palatable host plants. Moreover, the presence of earthworms moderated springtail exploitation of deeper soil horizons and contributed to shifts in the relative abundance of the two species used in the experimental design. Decomposers generally increase aphid reproduction and pathogen infection on plants aboveground, possibly because they increase the palatability of the plant biomass (Bonkowski et al. 2001, Poveda et al. 2006, Wurst et al. 2003). By contrast, the presence of earthworms had no effect on leaf chewer (*Mamestra brassica*) biomass and increased leaf chewer mortality, despite an increase in foliar nitrogen content in another mesocosm study (Newington et al., 2004). These studies highlight the complex linkages between soil fauna and herbivores aboveground, but our understanding of such linkages is still limited.

It is furthermore important to recognise that these aboveground–belowground linkages work at a variety of spatial and temporal scales to affect ecosystem processes and properties. It is possible to identify impacts of aboveground–belowground that occur at relatively defined temporal scales (Bardgett et al., 2005a). In particular, the authors identify three main timescales: (1) interactions among plants, microbes, and consumers cause changes in C and nutrient dynamics at short timescales, i.e. hours to seasons, that in turn influence the plant community; (2) influences of changes in resource supply and plant–soil feedbacks are manifested at longer timescales, from decades to hundreds of years, causing changes in biogeochemical cycling and succession; and (3) at even longer timescales, i.e. hundreds of years to millennia, aboveground–belowground linkages respond to changes in resource supply and can be manifested in changes to nutrient availability and ecosystem productivity. Similarly, spatial scale can be expected to differently influence aboveground–belowground linkages. The soil fauna assemblages are key players in the aboveground–belowground that, as described in later chapters, contribute to biogeochemical dynamics, promote succession, and influence ecosystem productivity. However, the contributions are not well quantified, and there is a great need for a better understanding of aboveground–belowground linkages.

2.3 Plant–Soil Feedbacks

The contribution of plant–soil feedbacks in structuring ecosystems has similarly received increasing attention over the past couple of decades and is now recognised to play a key role in coexistence of plant species. Indeed, the plant–soil feedback is a specific component within the aboveground–belowground linkages framework, explicitly focussed on the feedback between the plant and the soil it grows in (Figure 2.6). Generally, plant–soil feedbacks are considered at the plant species level

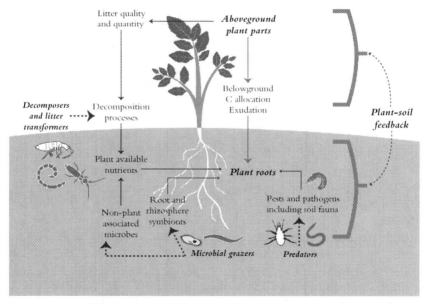

Figure 2.6 Simplified schematic illustration of the main pathways that contribute to plant–soil feedbacks. For example, changes in plant chemistry can impact (1) root-associated soil fauna via changes in the soil microbial assemblage or root resource quality and (2) the decomposer assemblage via changes in litter quality and quantity. This in turn can influence plant primary production via changes in herbivory (i.e. compensatory feeding) or impacts on nutrient cycling. The combined plant–soil feedback effects can be either positive, whereby plant primary productivity increases due to the impacts belowground, or negative, in which case primary productivity decreases.

and the idea is that a given plant species may foster soil biological assemblages or conditions that either benefit (i.e. positive feedbacks) or reduce (i.e. negative feedbacks) the performance of an individual of the same species subsequently growing in the same soil relative to their growth in a sterile soil or a soil modified by another species. However, one can similarly quantify plant–soil feedbacks where the effect of one species on another species is investigated or at the community level, although so far only a few studies have done this. A decade ago, the first meta-analysis of plant–soil feedbacks indicated that most plant species experience negative plant–soil feedbacks when they are grown in a soil that previously hosted an individual of the same species, although this was not universally true (Kulmatiski et al. 2008). By contrast, plant–soil feedbacks at the community level appear to be neutral to positive, indicating a potential role in stabilising the communities. The latter findings were, however, based on only two publications and need further examination. Plant–soil feedbacks are clearly important in ecosystem dynamics, may be important in moderating global change impacts, and should be considered in land management practices (Kardol and Wardle 2010, Mariotte et al. 2018, van der Putten et al. 2013). For example, rare species often experience more negative plant–soil feedbacks than common and exotic plant species (Klironomos 2002), and the escape from natural enemies including soil fauna that causes negative plant–soil feedbacks likely contributes to the success of invasive plant species in new environments in some cases (Reinhart and Callaway 2006, van der Putten et al. 2013). However, our understanding of the mechanisms that cause negative versus positive feedbacks is still limited, and in particular the contributions of soil fauna are largely unexplored. Soil fauna can contribute both directly and indirectly to plant–soil feedbacks, i.e. directly through herbivory and indirectly through their impacts on soil properties, C and nutrient cycling, and modification of the belowground community more broadly including populations of beneficial organisms, pest, and pathogens. Direct impacts are most likely to be negative whereas indirect effects could range from negative to positive depending on the pathway. Plant–soil feedbacks are now being incorporated into dynamic global vegetation models (DGVM) in an effort to better represent the global C cycle. However, as highlighted by Ostle et al. (2009), there are critical challenges and knowledge gaps that hinder our ability to construct realistic and robust models. In particular, they call for (1) an evaluation of the representation of plant–soil feedbacks in these models; (2) increased supply of robust data and knowledge to be integrated; and (3) thorough tests of the models against observational data collected along environmental gradients and realistic large-scale multifactor experiments.

It is still uncertain how plant–soil feedbacks influence ecosystem structure through space and time. Recent modelling work indicates that plant–soil feedbacks can enhance plant species diversity by delaying community convergence which eventually would cause changes in species composition (Fukima and Nakajima 2013). While negative plant–soil feedbacks may act to suppress the competitive dominance of plant species within a plant assemblage, there is evidence that negative plant–soil feedbacks can promote succession, generally by reducing the performance of early successional plant species (Brown and Gange 1992, De Deyn et al. 2003, Schädler et al. 2004, Verschoor et al. 2002) (see Chapter 7). Moreover, there is still uncertainty around the relative contribution of plant–soil feedbacks at given successional stages or environmental conditions. It has been proposed that positive plant–soil feedbacks are relatively more important in early successional stages and under stressful conditions where the plants rely on mutualists to access resources, with negative feedbacks contributing to species turnover and diversification in later successional stages (Reynolds et al. 2003). In particular, later successional plant species may be less influenced by negative feedbacks from soil pest and pathogens, and may possibly rely more on positive feedbacks (Kardol et al. 2006, van der Putten et al. 2009). However, this might be a too simplistic view as it appears likely that the influence of plant–soil feedbacks is not directly related to the level of negative versus positive plant–soil feedbacks experienced by a given individual *per se* but rather the relative contribution of these. For example, hypothetically, as succession proceeds, the level of both negative and positive plant–soil feedbacks may increase. Still, negative feedbacks are likely to influence some species more than others, and those tolerant of the pathogens and pest species that build up in the soil over time are likely to survive as succession proceeds (van der Putten et al. 2009). Much of this and the previous section have focussed broadly on aboveground–belowground linkages that may be influenced by soil fauna. However, there is still much to discover, particularly how soil fauna influences aboveground–belowground linkages and what their role is in plant–soil feedbacks under contemporary and future conditions.

2.4 Soil Biodiversity and Ecosystem Functioning

One of the more contentious topics in ecology over the past couple of decades is that of the biodiversity-ecosystem functioning (henceforth BEF) relationships (Figure 2.7). The BEF relationship discussion was

2.4 Soil Biodiversity and Ecosystem Functioning · 81

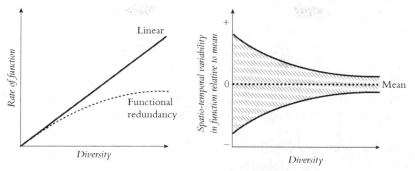

Figure 2.7 Schematic of hypothetical diversity-functioning relationships. Left: In theory, functioning may increase in a linear fashion with increasing species richness when the addition of new species promotes a given function (left). However, most evidence to date favours an asymptotic pattern whereby there is significant 'functional redundancy' and additional species have limited impact on functioning, even at low levels of diversity. Right: There is some evidence that increased species richness can stabilise process rates (here presented as reduced variability around a mean process rate) suggesting that species richness might be important to maintain functioning through time in a variable environment.

initially focussed mostly on the effects of plant species diversity (see, e.g., Hooper et al. 2005), but it has since then naturally become a topic of discussion in soil ecology. It is beyond the scope here to provide an in-depth review of the literature on this topic, but the nature of BEF relationships is of high relevance to the contributions of soil fauna to ecosystem functioning and therefore deserves a separate section in this chapter.

The main constraints for drawing robust conclusion on, or formalising general patterns about, BEF relationships in soil still lies in the dearth of studies that have addressed this question belowground, particularly involving soil fauna specifically, and methodological constraints (Mikola et al. 2002, Nielsen et al. 2011a). Early work suggested that species richness *per se* might not have substantial impacts on ecosystem functioning, but rather that the identity of the species present (i.e. assemblage composition, keystone species) and the number of trophic levels were more important (Hättenschwiler et al. 2005). It was further found that there was high functional redundancy and that the effect of species richness within functional groups was unclear (Heemsbergen et al. 2004, Laakso and Setälä 1999b, Liiri et al. 2002). This in turn suggested that strong biodiversity effects were most likely to be observed in ecosystems with inherently low soil biodiversity such as the polar deserts of the McMurdo

Dry Valleys or in highly impacted soils (Nielsen et al. 2011a). However, as indicated above, the early literature reviews and syntheses were based on relatively few studies, and many of the existing studies imposed unrealistic soil biodiversity manipulations. While methodological constraints are still a concern, recent approaches to quantify soil BEF relationships have provided further insights as the number of studies increases. In particular, a meta-analysis of the impact of soil biodiversity on C cycling processes and pools provides stronger evidence for positive soil BEF relationships at broader scales (de Graaff et al. 2015). The authors used data from 45 published studies to quantify the effects of soil biodiversity (albeit biodiversity was rarely quantified at the species level) on plant biomass production, soil respiration, litter decomposition, and soil C pools. Their analyses showed that the loss of soil biodiversity had a strong negative impact on soil respiration (−27.5%) and litter decomposition (−18%), including effects caused by species loss within and between body size groups. Their results further showed that the loss of soil fauna diversity negatively impacted litter decomposition processes, while the loss of microbes had no discernible effects. In fact, the average reduction in the 14 studies that quantified litter decomposition due to the loss of soil fauna species richness far exceeded that observed across all studies (i.e. a reduction of 37% versus 18%, respectively), likely due to the effects of soil fauna-feeding activities in the early stages of litter decomposition (Heemsbergen et al. 2004, Milcu and Manning 2011). By contrast, there was no effect of soil biodiversity on plant biomass production or soil C content, but there were only three studies reporting on the latter making statistical inferences difficult. These results point towards the potential importance of soil fauna in ecosystem processes but simultaneously illustrate that there are significant gaps in our knowledge that require a concerted effort to address. In particular, there is a great need for studies that use robust experimental approaches to assess the effects of soil biodiversity, and particularly soil fauna biodiversity, on ecosystem processes beyond litter decomposition. Moreover, the studies should cover a range of environmental and climatic conditions so that the impacts of global change may be predicted.

There are other ways in which biodiversity may be important to soil functioning that is not captured by the meta-analysis mentioned in the previous paragraph. For example, there is evidence that species richness within functional groups can be important to soil processes. It has accordingly been shown that the diversity of decomposer assemblages influences both the rate of litter decomposition and the 'stability' of decomposition rates. In a simple mesocosm-based litter decomposition study, Kitz et al. (2015) manipulated decomposer assemblages creating diversity gradients from one to three species, represented by a fungus gnat larvae, a millipede, and an earthworm. The authors found that an increase in the richness of decomposers accelerated litter decomposition rates but also that the variability in decomposition rates in the three species mixture was much smaller than any of the other treatments. This indicates that biodiversity may stabilise ecosystem functions, which could be of substantial consequence under natural conditions where assemblages are constantly exposed to variation in environmental conditions. While the diversity of macrofauna decomposers used in this experiment is low compared to that generally observed under field conditions, it does suggest that at least a threshold of species diversity will be required to maintain functioning over time. Other studies similarly indicate that functional diversity may be important. For example, Heemsbergen et al. (2004) found that mean functional dissimilarity within an assemblage was positively related to gross N processes. Moreover, the contribution of decomposers to litter decomposition is modified by environmental conditions. In a mesocosm study where the authors manipulated the decomposer assemblage (one millipede, two species of isopods) and investigated the effect on the decomposition of two contrasting litter types ('recalcitrant' versus 'easily degradable') under two soil moisture regimes, it was found that all macrofauna contributed equally to litter decomposition processes in well-watered, but not water-limited, conditions (Collison et al. 2013). Their results indicate that decomposer diversity may mediate potential impacts of environmental fluctuations under field conditions.

A more recent approach taken to investigate BEF relationships focus on the effects on multiple functions (i.e. multifunctionality; henceforth, BEMF relationships) rather than individual functions. The rationale behind the BEMF relationships is that organisms may only contribute to certain ecosystem functions and possibly only at certain times of the year or under particular conditions. Hence, longer-term maintenance of multiple functions is a result of the soil assemblage as a whole, with individual species playing key roles only under certain conditions. Research has again primarily focussed on plant biodiversity where species richness and functional diversity can be manipulated relatively easily compared to soil assemblages, either through planting or removal experiments. To give an example, Fanin et al. (2018) used a plant-removal approach to investigate BEMF relationships over 19 years on islands of three size classes (large, medium, small) in Swedish lakes. The removal of plant species or plant functional groups generally, but not always, had negative effects on individual ecosystem function and structure, including soil nematode density, and there was a net positive biodiversity effect on multifunctionality when two or more plant species were present. The effects, however, were dependent on the size of the island, so that the removal of certain plant species or functional groups had island size specific effects. In essence, some plant species contributed more to certain functions on given islands than other plant species. Through investigations of the relationship between plant biodiversity and fungal assemblages, it was evident that many of the biodiversity effects of plants on ecosystem functioning were mediated by impacts on the fungal assemblages, particularly fungal diversity. This finding highlights the strong linkages between aboveground and belowground communities and the substantial contribution of soil fungi to ecosystem functioning.

Similarly, there is experimental evidence that soil biodiversity influences multifunctionality. In one of the first studies to address the BEMF relationship through manipulation of the soil assemblage, Wagg et al. (2014) found that the loss of species diversity and simplification of the soil food web have strong negative effects on key ecosystem functions, including nutrient cycling and retention, decomposition and plant diversity. The authors manipulated the soil communities by sequentially sieving a soil inoculum through a series of decreasing mesh sizes and inoculating microcosms using these diversity dilutions. The dilutions represent non-random, and likely unrealistic, diversity losses based purely on the body size of the soil organisms but created otherwise robust diversity gradients. In each of the microcosms, the authors planted 40 individual plants representing 10 common temperate European grassland species. The authors then characterised the soil biodiversity of the microcosms and related this to eight ecosystem functions, finding a strong linear positive BEMF relationship across all functions. Although some methodological concerns with this study make it difficult to evaluate the likelihood of similar patterns under field conditions, it does strongly support the hypothesis that soil biodiversity is critical to maintaining 'whole' ecosystem functioning (i.e. multifunctionality). It thus seems highly likely that soil fauna diversity plays a key role in maintaining ecosystem functioning under current and future conditions, with species losses presenting a risk to ecosystem functioning. The high diversity of soil fauna, including generalist feeders, observed in natural ecosystems suggests that there is likely to be relatively high functional redundancy in soil food webs in general. However, there is still a great need for further studies that assess soil BEF/BEMF relationships using robust approaches that mimic realistic biodiversity losses under field conditions to guide the management of soil fauna assemblages to maintain ecosystem function. One option is to use a hierarchical framework approach as suggested by Kardol et al. (2016), whereby diversity at different 'levels', i.e. genetic, functional, feeding type and trophic level, can be explicitly assigned contributions to ecosystem processes or services at a given spatial or temporal scale. This requires a very targeted approach but is likely to result in more applicable outcomes.

2.5 Summary

As highlighted throughout this chapter, soil fauna plays a critical role in soil processes and ecosystem function, thus underpinning soil formation and critical ecosystem services supporting human health and wellbeing (Wall et al., 2015). Our understanding of the contributions of soil fauna to these processes has increased dramatically over the past few decades. Most of this knowledge is, however, based on *qualitative* insights, and there is still a great need for further *quantitative* studies that provide empirical evidence. The rapid development of novel statistical techniques, more advanced and increasingly sensitive analytical equipment, and molecular approaches hold great promise for further insights over the coming years (as discussed in Chapter 3). Future investigations of soil fauna contributions to ecosystem functions should be guided by current information and target known knowledge gaps, and, where possible, should emphasise hypothesis-driven research. It may be of significant value to group soil fauna by feeding guild or functional characteristics as a way to reduce the complexity of the soil food web. However, there is strong evidence that greater taxonomic resolution can provide insights not attained by such grouping. Indeed, resolving the functional characteristics and feeding preferences of individual species is required to more robustly group soil fauna in soil food webs. Finally, focussing on improving our conceptual understanding of the influences soil fauna have on ecosystem functioning through aboveground–belowground linkages is likely to move the field forward substantially.

3 · Approaches to Studying Soil Fauna and Its Functional Roles

The previous two chapters provided a brief overview of the most common and functionally important groups of soil fauna, and how each of these qualitatively, and where possible quantitatively, contribute to ecosystem functioning through their feeding, burrowing, and other activities. Most soil fauna are too small to be seen and counted by the naked eye, and given the inherent difficulties working with fauna within the soil matrix, scientists have had to come up with various techniques to extract and then quantify the fauna. Abundance estimates using extraction and morphological identification is, however, often time consuming and requires expert knowledge for robust implementation of data. The larger soil fauna are easier to work with as they can be counted without the use of a microscope, but it generally involves sorting through large quantities of soil or the application of stimulants that encourage the fauna to emerge from the soil. There has furthermore long been an interest in quantifying the influence of soil organisms on ecosystem functioning, but it is inherently difficult to manipulate soil food webs *in situ* because of the intricate nature of soils and the small size of the organisms without altering other important parameters or imposing unexpected non-target effects. Hence, most of the knowledge we have today stems from laboratory incubations with manipulated and often simplistic soil food webs, which may not reflect soil organisms' role in ecosystem functioning under field conditions realistically. In this chapter, I will present an overview of some of the methods that have been employed to quantify soil organisms and their contributions to ecosystem functioning. I will highlight new methodological and analytical tools that promise to move forward our understanding of soil fauna's role in ecosystems through an improved capacity to quantify key parameters more accurately, particularly through more sophisticated molecular, analytical, and statistical tools.

3.1 Quantifying Soil Fauna

Protozoan assemblages have historically been assessed using the 'most probable number', which is essentially a culturing-based technique. This involves incubating small quantities of soil from a dilution series in wells with bacteria as a food source and then using the presence or absence of protozoans in each well to estimate the population density. This, however, is a rather rough estimate and is likely to miss certain feeding types. Other researchers use direct counting of Protozoa, usually dissolving 5–30 mg of soil in water and then counting the number of protozoans under a microscope. Due to the very limited amount of soil being screened, rare species are again likely to be missed. Moreover, this technique is very time consuming, which usually limits the number of samples a person or a lab can physically handle. Given these constraints, our knowledge of protozoan assemblages is very limited, even compared with that of other soil fauna. More recent approaches to estimate protozoan biomass include molecular and biomarker approaches. Phospholipid fatty acids (PLFAs) have long been used as a way to estimate soil food web structure (Frostegård et al. 1997), and the fatty acid 20ω4 is related to the abundance of protozoans in soil, but it can also occur in other eukaryotes. It is useful in that it is a reliable tool to get a fingerprint of the microbial assemblage, including the Protozoa, that provide biomass estimates, but it is unlikely to be a robust tool for assessing soil food web structure more broadly.

Most other types of soil microfauna, i.e. nematodes, rotifers, and tardigrades, are usually extracted and enumerated using variations of the fundamentally similar water-based extraction techniques given their aquatic nature. These techniques are generally divided into active, predominantly modified Baermann funnel approaches, and passive or floatation techniques (sugar centrifugation, elutriation, decanting, and sieving). The traditional way of extracting nematodes is based on variations of the Baermann funnel technique (Baermann 1917) (Figure 3.1). The method was developed specifically for the extraction and quantification of nematodes and relies on the active movement of the soil fauna. In very simple terms, the approach is to suspend soil placed on top of coarse tissue paper supported by a metal mesh screen in a water solution and collect the organisms after they have migrated out of the suspended soil. Glass funnels fitted with a rubber hose sealed with a hose clamp are usually used so that the organisms can be collected by removing a set quantity

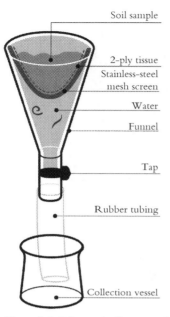

Figure 3.1 Schematic diagram of a common Baermann funnel setup, based on descriptions by Baermann (1917). Briefly, the method relies on suspending a known quantity of soil in water and letting the microfauna migrate through this medium. Usually, soil is homogenised gently and placed on two-ply tissue paper held by a stainless-steel mesh in a glass funnel. A rubber hose with a hose clamp is placed on the funnel stem so that water can be collected every 24 hours over a set time (usually 72 hours). The enchytraeid mesofauna can be collected in a similar way but generally requires larger quantities of soil to be processed and an external heat source used to encourage migration.

of water after a specified time (usually 48–72 hours). The main bias of this method is that it represents only individuals that are active when the soil is suspended in water. This may include specimens that were dormant in the soil but miss less active nematodes, including many plant parasitic nematodes. Therefore, the methods may overestimate the number of nematodes that are active at a given time but miss many other nematode species. The passive or floatation-based methods, such as sugar centrifugation and elutriators, are generally less biased and will collect all free-living soil nematodes, including dormant and dead individuals, but generally require a more elaborate setup. Plant parasitic nematodes, however, require other approaches that generally rely on direct counts of gall-inducing females or stained individuals within the root itself.

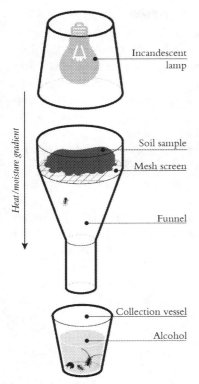

Figure 3.2 Schematic diagram of a Tullgren funnel setup based on descriptions by Tullgren (1918). This method is used primarily for extraction of microarthropods and other small soil fauna. A known quantity of soil, usually an intact soil core or litter, is placed in a container with a mesh screen bottom. Incandescent bulbs are used to create a heat and moisture gradient that encourages downward migration of the soil fauna into a collection vessel. Usually the fauna is preserved in alcohol, but the technique can also be used to collect live specimens for culturing.

A slightly modified version of the Baermann funnel approach can be used to extract enchytraeids, but this requires larger quantities of soil and usually encourages migration using a heat source.

Most mesofauna are not aquatic, except Enchytraeids, and therefore requires other extraction techniques. Mesofauna are still too small and numerous to be sampled individually, so we again rely on extracting individuals from known volumes or quantities of material (soil, leaf litter) generally using Tullgren (or Berlese) funnels (Tullgren 1918) of various designs (Figure 3.2). In principle, these funnels function by encouraging the soil mesofauna to abandon the soil or litter using heat to create a heat and/or moisture gradient. The extracted soil fauna can then be collected either live for culturing or in preservative for later identification. The volume or quantity of material that is processed can be modified based on the abundance of mesofauna expected at a given site to ensure robust quantification of soil fauna abundances or assemblage structure. A main limitation of the method is that it is somewhat biased in extraction efficiency, with some species being more likely to remain in the soil or litter material. Other approaches to quantifying mesofauna generally rely on specific gravity or hydrocarbon floatation techniques and produce better results for substrates with a low organic matter content such as sandy soils (Krantz and Walter 2009). Specific gravity floatation using salt or sugar is used to separate dense soil particles from lighter-bodied mites but may underestimate larger-bodied, denser mite species. Hydrocarbon floatation, in comparison, relies on the adhesion of certain hydrocarbon compounds to mite cuticle. One drawback of the hydrocarbon floatation approach is that it often relies on noxious chemicals, such as kerosene, and is more laborious than funnel-based approaches. These methods moreover work best when the samples are low in organic particles that would float in the dense salt or sugar solutions or bind to hydrocarbons. Indeed, the Tullgren funnel approach is much better suited for highly organic substrates including litter. Each of the techniques has its own shortcomings, varying in extraction efficiencies across soil types, and displaying biases towards the extraction of certain taxa. Finally, a relatively large number of soil samples is generally required for an accurate representation of the mesofauna assemblage structure and estimates of site diversity. Indeed, using the data in Nielsen et al. (2012a) it was estimated that more than 20 soil samples (3.5 cm diameter, 5 cm depth) were required to accurately predict mite species richness of a given site.

The larger soil fauna generally requires approaches such as Malaise or pitfall traps (Figure 3.3) whereby larger numbers can be collected passively, utilize irritants (e.g. mustard, soap, electricity) that induce species to leave the soil matrix, or can be hand sorted to allow larger volumes of soils to be processed. Indeed, robust characterisation of soil fauna assemblages is greatly dependent on our ability to capture and classify enough individuals of a given taxa for statistical procedures to be completed. The methods listed so far all provide count data that can be transformed into densities that are often presented in number of individuals m^{-2} or kg^{-1} dry soil. Biomass is more difficult to quantify and requires either direct measurements of dried individuals, which is often prohibitive due to the small size, or estimates of biomass based on

Figure 3.3 Schematic diagram of a pitfall trap used to collect more mobile, predominantly surface- and litter-dwelling soil fauna. A trap, usually a plastic container, is placed in the ground aligned with the soil surface, and a preserving agent is added to immobilise the unfortunate soil fauna.

existing information. This is a time-consuming exercise, but it can be an immensely useful one to quantify soil fauna biomass.

Once information on the species present in a given assemblage has been obtained, the next step is generally to characterise the assemblage in ways that allow us to compare patterns through time and space. It is beyond the scope of this chapter to provide a detailed account of the methods employed, but a few concepts are worth highlighting. The simplest way to compare assemblages is using species richness, either expressed per sample or per unit area or volume, that can be calculated based on direct counts or estimated based on species-richness estimators and rarefaction curves. These are powerful tools because the number of samples required to sample all species of a given taxa is usually prohibitive. Rarefaction curves further allow direct visual comparisons of the accumulation of species as the number of individuals or samples increases, providing insight into differences among different sites or ecosystems. Species richness can be defined as alpha(α)-diversity, beta(β)-diversity, and gamma(γ)-diversity, where α-diversity refers to point- or plot-level measures and γ-diversity to the total richness observed across plots or sites, respectively. β-diversity generally refers to the turnover in species among plots or sites, but it can also be used to quantify the total amount of variation in assemblages across all samples. More complex measures that target assemblage structure include various diversity and evenness indices that compare the relative abundance of species within assemblages generally using count data. Such measures are very useful for monitoring purposes. By contrast, multivariate statistics and modelling approaches are required to quantify relationships between soil fauna and environmental variables or to assess the mechanisms that govern assemblage composition in more detail (see Section 3.6). I would encourage the interested reader to consult books such as *Measuring Biological Diversity* by Magurran (2004) and *Spatial Analysis: A Guide for Ecologists* by Fortin and Dale (2005) for a more in-depth introduction.

It should be no surprise that the molecular sequencing approaches have fundamentally altered our ability to assess microbial and soil fauna assemblages. These techniques can be very useful for some organisms, particularly where the abundances or biomass is difficult to estimate using other techniques but have their own potential biases due to extraction efficiencies, PCR amplification bias, and general limitations in the amount of soil that can be processed. In terms of soil processed, DNA is usually extracted from less than 1.5 g of soil and only the smaller organisms are likely to be well enough represented in such a small volume to be robustly quantified, even if the sample is well homogenised before the DNA is extracted. There are methods that allow larger quantities of soil to be processed, but these methods are often cumbersome and not easily implemented across large sample numbers. Hence, there are still clear constraints and considerations that should be applied in the use of molecular approaches to investigate soil fauna assemblages (Bik et al. 2012, Porazinska et al. 2009). This is exemplified in a study by Geisen et al. (2015b), where the authors created artificial protist communities and used 454 high-throughput DNA metabarcoding to evaluate the assemblage structure of these in the presence of micro- and mesofauna. The authors found that ciliate sequences were highly overrepresented in the data, whereas sequences of amoebas and flagellates were underrepresented or even absent. In addition to this, the authors discovered protist sequences representing a range of species, including 20 potential parasites of micro- and mesofauna that had not been added to the artificial communities. These results highlight that sequencing data should be interpreted with care due to sequencing biases between taxa but also that the presence of other organisms can contribute non-target DNA that can fundamentally alter perceived assemblage structures. Indeed, while sequencing-based approaches appear to be robust in some circumstances or for very specific purposes, it is necessary to treat broad sequencing efforts with some restraint. Orgiazzi et al. (2015) categorised the upcoming challenges focussing on metabarcoding soil biodiversity as (1) clarification and standardising of terminology across taxa; (2) developing standardised protocols and optimising protocols for a broader range of taxa; (3) development of common databases for sequencing data; and, (4) enhanced usage of existing and new data generated, but these points apply to molecular approaches more broadly. Hence, these techniques are still in the early stages and will require a significant amount of finessing before it can truly be applied and contribute to soil ecology as a field in broad terms, but there is already evidence that it is possible to reliably pick up changes in soil fauna assemblages using sequencing.

Another option is to extract soil fauna from a larger sample first and then use quantitative-PCR (qPCR) or sequencing approaches with taxa-specific primers to quantify biomass (or relative abundance) and assemblage composition, respectively. The main constrain of qPCR is that it is limited to species or other phylogenetic groups for which there are specific primers, with each reaction providing data for only one target taxa. Hence, if one were to quantify all nematode species in a sample or at one site using qPCR, it would possibly require hundreds of reactions. However, the approach is very powerful for screening soil samples for specific organisms or comparing relative abundances of individual species or higher phylogenetic groups across samples. For example, Quist et al. (2017) recently used qPCR to assess the spatial distribution of nematode-feeding types in arable fields and semi-natural grasslands on three different soil types. Their results showed that many bacterial- and fungal-feeding nematodes were widely distributed and had high detection probabilities across samples, whereas predatory nematodes and some omnivores showed greater degrees of spatial clustering. Similar approaches have been applied for several other groups.

RNA approaches have also been used to assess active Protozoa and the approach looks reasonably promising. For example, Urich et al. (2008) used an RNA-centred meta-transcriptomics approach to assess soil assemblages of a sandy soil with the basis that RNA mostly represents the active organisms. They generated cDNA from the transcriptome and subjected this directly to pyrosequencing without any prior PCR or cloning steps. Each unique rRNA-derived sequence was identified as a ribo-tag whereas each mRNA was identified as an mRNA tag and was used to probe assemblage structure and functional attributes, respectively. The results were dominated by prokaryotic ribo-tag sequences but also included a variety of eukaryotic organisms dominated by plants (~50%), fungi (20%), and metazoan (~10%). These data confirmed the presence of a broad range of Protozoa dominated by slime moulds (Mycotozoa) followed by Cercozoa, Plasmodiophorida, and Alveolata with other groups being rarer, representing fewer than 40 ribo-tags each. The authors recognised potential problems due to the ribosome content varying substantially based on the organisms' physiological states and between taxa. However, they still considered each ribo-tag a proxy for a taxon's assemblage-level cellular biomass. Such techniques may prove particularly useful for minute and highly abundant organisms including the Protozoa that are otherwise inherently difficult to quantify reliably. By contrast, our ability to generate robust assemblage-level assessments of larger soil fauna using molecular techniques is still somewhat limited.

3.2 Diversity, Distribution, and Phylogeny

The investigation of soil fauna diversity, distribution, and phylogeny traditionally based on morphological identification is time consuming and requires expert knowledge. The DNA barcoding and qPCR techniques mentioned earlier appear to be ideally suited to investigate the distribution of specific soil fauna species or groups from local patterns to global scales. For example, barcoding techniques can target various regions of the genome depending on the scale of the investigation and are therefore also powerful tools to investigate phylogenetic patterns within taxa and even dispersal patterns within species. These techniques are very promising in that they allow us to rapidly process large numbers of samples and diverse taxonomical groups without *a priori* expert knowledge. The main constraint is generally that the techniques are still best applied by targeting individual specimens. Indeed, the investigation of biogeographical and macroecological patterns in soil fauna ecology should give further consideration to phylogenetic history (Webb et al. 2010), because phylogeny can substantially influence observed patterns, whereby distribution may be an artefact of evolutionary history rather than ecological constraints.

High throughput sequencing (HTS) approaches are getting increasingly powerful as more sophisticated bioinformatic procedures are developed, allowing more robust analyses of soil fauna assemblages. These tools are likely to be particularly relevant for the smaller microfauna that occurs in high densities; the microfauna are very species diverse and can be nearly impossible to reliably identify morphologically even with expert knowledge. Quite a few studies have now employed HTS approaches to assess soil fauna assemblages. An early study that was focussed on soil fauna used HTS to assess nematode diversity in tropical rainforests in Costa Rica (Porazinska et al. 2010). The results showed that the diversity of nematodes of the rainforests is high, exceeding that of temperate ecosystems. The authors further highlighted that many of the operational taxonomical units (OTUs) were unknown, possibly indicating a high level of endemicity and undiscovered biodiversity. One caveat of this conclusion is that the number of nematode species-specific sequences in relevant databases still remains limited so that the likelihood of finding a match is limited. In another recent study, an HTS approach was used to investigate microfauna of East Antarctic soils at three sites across an elevation gradient in the Prince Charles Mountains (173–3,330 m, 70°–73°S) (Czechowski et al. 2016). The results showed that the most widespread phylotypes were fungi but also that non-algal protists were widely distributed. Similarly, Emerson et al. (2011) highlighted how high-throughput sequencing combined with mtDNA barcoding provide a robust tool to investigate phylogeographical patterns of springtails and other soil fauna. In particular, they outline how these approaches can provide insights into the distribution of cryptic species that are poorly defined morphologically.

Several DNA barcoding techniques, where DNA is extracted from individual specimens and sequenced, have been powerful tools used to investigate soil fauna assemblage structure, biogeography, and phylogeny. For example, a survey of mite assemblages in a tundra–taiga transition in subarctic Canada provided novel insights into the diversity of the Acarine fauna (Young et al. 2012). The authors collected samples from a variety of ecosystems and microhabitats near Churchill, Manitoba, and successfully sequenced DNA (COI) from 6,365 individuals. The sequences were assigned to nearly 900 species, but the total richness was estimated at around 1,200 based on species accumulation curves. This is much greater than what would generally have been expected based on previous studies using morphological identification techniques. The data further revealed that the Trombidiformes was the most diverse group, with an estimated species richness of 633, whereas the estimated richness of Sarcoptiformes and Mesostigmata was 423 and 173, respectively. However, it is constrained by the requirement for high sample processing and taxa-specific DNA extraction and amplification success rates. In the aforementioned study, the sequencing success averaged 77% but ranged from 68% to 80% in the Trombidiformes and Sarcoptiformes, respectively (Young et al. 2012). This is problematic given that it may cause potential biases in assemblage structure.

Similarly, there are substantial technological developments that will likely aid in our understanding of soil fauna assemblages from very fine to global scales. For example, there are now satellite-based high-resolution measurements of biologically relevant variables such as soil temperature and moisture contents that could substantially improve our ability to map the distribution of soil fauna based on its environmental envelopes at landscape scale to global scales. For example, NASA's Soil Moisture Active Passive (SMAP) mission recently provided a global map of soil water content using a satellite fitted with a sophisticated radar sensor based on data gathered between 31 March and 3 April, 2015. Similarly, higher-resolution characterisation of microclimatic conditions at biologically relevant scales, including daily to seasonal variability, would provide much greater insights into the constraints on key soil organisms. At smaller scales, technologies that allow us to look inside the soil matrix itself to investigate biotic interactions in natural settings would provide new insights. Nano sensors and X-ray computed tomography provide techniques for visualising the distribution of soil fauna and interactions between different organisms within soils without disturbing the soil structure (Coleman 2008, Young and Crawford 2004). As more data become available it has also become possible to map soil fauna diversity and abundances in much more detail. Noteworthy examples include first the European Atlas of Soil Biodiversity (Jeffery et al. 2010) and the more recent Global Soil Biodiversity Atlas (Orgiazzi et al. 2016), but other independent efforts are also worth highlighting. For example, a compilation of data on local abundances and diversity of earthworms was used to produce abundance and diversity maps for most of Europe (Rutgers et al. 2014). The study showed that it was possible to produce robust predictive maps based on existing data despite obvious knowledge gaps and that such efforts allow us to establish broad generalisations about the possible constraints on assemblages. In this case, the main drivers of earthworm assemblage structure were land use and geological history, with greater earthworm abundances and diversity predicted in grasslands. By contrast, fewer earthworms and lower diversity was predicted in cropland, heathland, vineyards, and forests. Such collation of information allows us to more accurately predict on current and future distribution and abundances of soil fauna.

3.3 Soil Fauna Functional Traits

Investigations of functional traits can be an immensely powerful tool to characterise soil fauna assemblages and quantify soil food web structure and contributions to ecosystem function. In most cases, functional traits of soil fauna are based on life history traits such as feeding mode, dispersal, and reproduction (Siepel 1994, Yeates et al. 1993). Functional traits can be measured at the individual level and used comparatively across species; they can include physiological, morphological, behavioural, and life history traits (McGill et al. 2006). These traits are often classified as either response or effect traits. Response traits govern the response of an individual to the environment whereas effect traits influence, for example, ecosystem functioning (Pey et al. 2014). Response traits are therefore particularly useful to investigate the mechanisms that govern soil fauna assemblages, whereas effect traits can provide insight into the contribution of soil fauna to ecosystem functioning under current and future scenarios. The main constraints for using functional traits for soil fauna is that the ecology of many species is not well known and that many species are yet to be described. However, traits can provide substantial insight into the distribution of soil fauna and the mechanisms that structure assemblages. Because functional traits are not well quantified for all soil fauna I will focus on a couple of key examples, in particular springtails. I will provide more detail on functional traits in Section 3.5, including a discussion of the use of nematodes as bioindicators.

A substantial amount of effort has gone into determining functional traits for springtails and their functional importance in relation to interaction with other biota and habitat preferences. For example, the presence of well-developed legs, furcula, and visual aids (eyes) has long been thought to be related to dispersal and living in exposed habitats (i.e. in or on the litter, open vegetation types) (Ponge et al. 2006). Similarly, sensory organs and their level of development including antennae length, number of ocelli, the presence of trichobothria, and the complexity of post-antennal organs are all expected to vary between habitat types (Hopkin 1997, Salmon et al. 2014). Pseudo-ocelli appear to play a role in protection against predation through the exudation of repellent fluids

(Hopkin 1997, Rusek and Weyda 1981). Pigmentation and scales appear to be involved in signalling and environmental buffering, particularly temperature and UV protection (Hopkin 1997). Body size and shape is also likely to be influenced by habitat, with larger bodies providing protection against frost and desiccation in epigeic habitats and open vegetation types (Bokhorst et al. 2012). Finally, reproductive mode appears to be associated with dispersal and survival strategies (Chernova et al. 2009).

Springtail functional traits can therefore provide substantial insight into the distribution of species and their habitat preferences. In a synthesis of the distribution of springtails in Europe, consolidating information from more than 900 samples, Salmon et al. (2014) found that vertical stratification (i.e. epigeic to edaphic) and air temperature strongly moderated the variation in 12 functional traits. Moreover, there was some convergence between vertical distribution and habitat structure, with epigeic and 'open habitat' springtails showing similar functional trait compositions. In particular, the species in open habitats have better-developed legs and furcula, have sensorial organs sensitive to air movement, are larger with spherical body sizes and pigmentation, and generally reproduce sexually. By contrast, edaphic species and those in closed habitats have shorter locomotion organs, smaller body sizes, more defence organs (pseudo-ocelli), post-antennal organs, and they often reproduce through parthenogenesis. However, trait distributions are also influenced by climate, particularly temperature, and especially traits that are found in epigeic or open habitat species. Vertical stratification and temperature thus play a significant role in determining the functional traits of springtails. Similarly, functional traits can be useful in quantifying climate change impacts. For example, simulated extreme winter warming in the Arctic caused a shift in community-weighted springtail functional types, with more hemiedaphic and less euedaphic species found in the warming treatments, respectively (Bokhorst et al. 2012). Moreover, it has been shown that many surface-dwelling springtail species show substantial physiological plasticity adjusting the relative abundance of fatty acids during temperature acclimation that increases their heat tolerance, whereas no response was observed in soil-dwelling species (van Dooremalen et al. 2013). This has potential implications for the state of springtail assemblages in the future. The forecasted increase in heat waves may be detrimental to euedaphic springtails in particular unless they can escape to deeper soils where temperature fluctuations are more buffered.

Similarly, gut content enzymatic activity has been used extensively for assessing potential feeding guilds for soil fauna including springtails

(Berg et al. 2004), mites (Siepel and De Ruiter-Dijkman 1993), and enchytraeids (Urbášek and Chalupský 1992). For example, the presence of cellulase would indicate the ability to break down cellulose, a key component of plant cell walls, and trehalase would indicate the ability to break down carbohydrates stored as trehalose, particularly in fungi, but also in lichens and bacteria. Similarly, chitinase would indicate the ability to break down chitin, a key component of arthropod exoskeletons and fungal cell walls (Urbášek and Rusek 1994). Using gut content enzymatic activity, Siepel and de Ruiter-Dijkman (1993) accordingly defined seven feeding groups (herbivore grazers, fungivore grazers, herbo-fungivore grazers, fungivore browsers, opportunistic herbo-fungivores, herbivore browsers, and omnivores) among 49 oribatid mites and an acaridid mite species collected from a range of ecosystem and microhabitat types. It is still uncertain whether these enzymes are produced by the soil fauna itself or its gut microbiota, but the presence of specific enzymes can provide insight into the diet of soil fauna.

The functional trait distribution within assemblages can provide useful insight into the likely drivers of assemblage structure. In particular, assemblages where species share key functional traits are likely to be under high environmental selection, i.e. there is convergence in traits. By contrast, assemblages where species have more diverse functional traits with limited overlap among species, i.e. an overdispersion of traits, are likely to be under selection pressure through competition (Figure 3.4). For example, it has been shown that functional traits can be strongly correlated with environmental variables, particularly in ecosystems with strong known environmental gradients (Widenfalk et al. 2015). Differences in trait versus species turnover can also be an indicator of possible species overlap in resource requirements and competitive interactions. Essentially, species with similar traits are less likely to co-occur because of limited resource availability and increased competition for these, so that species show greater turnover between samples than traits (Widenfalk et al. 2015). However, strong environmental filtering can force species with similar traits to co-exist more often than would be expected by chance.

Another possible functional approach is to focus on stoichiometry and allometric scaling as tools to better describe soil food webs and predict consequences of changes in these. As an example, Mulder et al. (2013) provides an excellent synthesis that outlines how allometry and stoichiometry might be used to predict changes in food webs based on environmental conditions and construct models that better link the

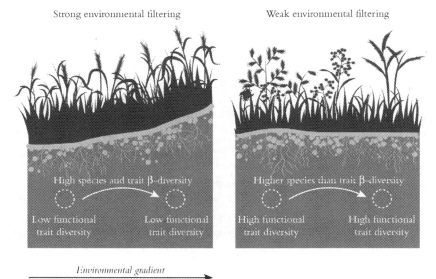

Figure 3.4 Simplified diagram illustrating how environmental filtering can contribute to over- or underdispersion of functional traits. In ecosystems where there is strong environmental filtering (left panel), species at a given location are likely to be functionally similar through adaptation to the environment (i.e. an underdispersion of traits). If there is an environmental gradient within the site, there will be turnover in functional traits and species as the environmental conditions change. By contrast, in a homogeneous ecosystem where environmental filtering is weak (right panel), species are likely to show overdispersion in traits with species being functionally dissimilar to avoid competitive interactions. In this case, most traits are likely to be found throughout the ecosystem, and there will be limited turnover in traits between sampling points. However, there might be turnover in species identity due to biotic interactions.

aboveground and belowground components of our ecosystems. Indeed, ecosystem stoichiometry (i.e. C:N:P) is closely linked to microbial, invertebrate, and plant assemblages, thus influencing ecosystem functioning and constraining possible management actions, with cascading effects on allometry. However, the authors highlight that stoichiometrical and allometric plasticity is greater than previously recognised and needs to be taken into account when considering potential future scenarios. Moreover, it can be difficult to disentangle the influences of changes in stoichiometry imposed by external forces (i.e. nitrogen deposition) and underlying geology from the inherent effects of the vegetation and soil organisms imposed on stoichiometry.

3.4 Contributions to Ecosystem Processes

Significant efforts have been made to manipulate soil fauna assemblages *in situ*. Classic work often used pesticides to suppress certain types of microbes or soil fauna or used litter bags sometimes in combination with naphthalene to exclude soil fauna during decomposition. Other classic work studied the effect of the addition of non-native species, either incidentally or intentionally. The latter scenario can provide useful insights into the effect of species additions, but it is much more difficult to study the effect of species removal, particularly belowground. Both pesticides and litter bag experiments have been heavily criticised for potential non-target effects or for altering the microclimate and, through this, impacting the study outcomes (Kampichler and Bruckner 2009). However, these approaches have collectively provided critical insights into soil functioning that have furthered our understanding of soil food webs and soil fauna assemblages more broadly. This in turn has promoted our capacity to formulate hypotheses that can now be tested empirically using more robust approaches. Modelling approaches have been used to estimate the contribution of soil food web structure and specific taxa over the past few decades based on substantial field data and theoretical knowledge. In the early days, the soil food webs were compartmentalised to group organisms with broadly similar feeding guilds, such as in the work by Hunt et al. (1987) in which the authors explored N cycling in a shortgrass prairie. Through this work it was estimated that bacteria account for the largest contribution to N mineralization (4.5 g N m^{-2} $year^{-1}$), with the soil fauna accounting for another 2.9 g N m^{-2} $year^{-1}$. They further estimated that bacterial-feeding protozoans and nematodes accounted for 83% of the N mineralization by soil fauna, a testament to the substantial contribution to biogeochemical cycling accounted for by these organisms. Similarly, De Ruiter et al. (1993) used soil food web modelling to estimate that the amoeba and bacterivore nematodes directly accounted for 18% and 5% of the total N mineralization occurring in a winter wheat field, respectively. However, deleting these two groups from the soil food web resulted in a 28% and 12% decrease in N mineralization, indicating that these groups have further indirect effects. A similar pattern was observed for other groups. For example, the direct contribution of predatory nematodes to N cycling accounted for 1.4% of the total mineralization, but deletion of the group from the food web resulted in a 12% decrease in mineralization. Since then, soil food web modelling has been improved substantially but is still strongly dependent on compartmentalisation of the food web. The inherent intricacies of the myriad interactions taking place within the soil matrix make it difficult to assess the contribution of individual taxa. However, the broader approach taken in food web modelling is valuable to generalise patterns and frame hypotheses.

Testing the outcomes of model predictions in turn requires *in situ* manipulation of soil fauna assemblages or other methods to track the flow of C and nutrients. Several methods have been used to assess the role of soil fauna in litter decomposition, including litter bags where fauna of certain body size widths is excluded using mesh of different sizes (e.g. Kampichler and Bruckner 2009, Figure 3.5) and naphthalene addition to which some taxa show strong response (e.g. Cotrufo et al. 2014). Both methods have their own potential drawbacks but can be useful tools for *in situ* manipulations with limited impacts on other aspects of the ecosystem. The main criticisms of the litter bag method are (1) that it excludes only fauna of a certain body width, making it virtually impossible to target individual taxa or feeding types, and (2) that it is likely to influence the microclimate differentially within bags with mesh of different sizes during litter decomposition with potential unquantifiable cross-treatment effects. Similarly, naphthalene addition can be used to suppress certain soil fauna, but it rarely fully excludes individual taxa and may have undesirable non-target effects. Still, these methods have contributed substantially to our understanding of the contribution of soil fauna to ecosystem processes. For example, Wall et al. (2008) used naphthalene in combination with litter bag exclusion of soil macrofauna to assess the contributions of mesofauna to leaf litter decomposition at a global scale. To do this, the authors deployed a common grass litter substrate (*Agropyron cristatum*) in 20 cm × 20 cm glass fibre litter bags with a 2 mm mesh size at 30 sites on six continents, representing a broad range of biomes and latitudes from 43° S to 68° N. They then applied naphthalene to half of the litter bags at each of the sites to quantify the effect of reduced soil mesofauna abundances on leaf litter decomposition. This ambitious project showed that soil mesofauna contributes substantially to litter decomposition processes albeit only in some biomes. In particular, they promote litter decomposition in temperate and wet tropical climates but not in cold or dry biomes. The authors therefore conclude that soil mesofauna contributions to litter decomposition processes are relevant only where temperature or water availability does not constrain biological activity. The project highlights how important it is to assess the contribution of biological processes at a global scale to be able to

3.4 Contributions to Ecosystem Processes · 103

Figure 3.5 An example of a litter bag used to investigate the effects of elevated CO_2 concentrations on litter decomposition in the Eucalyptus Free Air Carbon Enrichment (EucFACE) facility in Richmond, New South Wales, Australia. Photo by the author.

draw generalisable conclusions. However, one potential shortcoming of this study is that it quantified changes in litter decomposition based on *reductions* in soil mesofauna densities only and further excluded the macrofaunal effects by using a relatively small mesh size. Macrofauna, such as earthworms and termites, can have a particularly large impact on litter decomposition, and the study therefore likely underestimates the true impacts of soil fauna on litter decomposition via fragmentation and degradation substantially including in cool and dry climates. A recent meta-analysis of litter bag or chemical soil fauna suppression studies support this. Garćia-Palacios et al. (2013) conducted a literature search to recover 75 articles in which soil fauna densities were manipulated using either litter bags (comparing a large and a fine mesh size) or chemical suppression (no dose versus dose) representing a total of 440 individual cases distributed across 129 sites on all continents except Antarctica. They found that the suppression or exclusion of soil fauna reduced litter decomposition rates by 35% at a global scale across all sites and plant species. As in the study by Wall et al. (2008), there was substantial variation in the effect on litter decomposition rates between biomes, with a reduction of 47% in humid grassland versus 13% in coniferous forests and 18% in cold or dry biomes (Garćia-Palacios et al. 2013). The authors further note that the differences in soil fauna contributions to litter decomposition rates depend on both direct effects of climate and indirect effects of climate through changes in leaf litter chemistry, particularly the litter C:N ratio. Climate change may therefore affect litter decomposition differentially across biomes and through different mechanisms in part by altering the soil fauna assemblages. However, the potential consequences of climate change effects on decomposition processes via impacts on soil fauna assemblages are still unknown in part because we have limited understanding of belowground responses to climate change (see Chapter 7).

Moreover, there is strong evidence that litter quality (i.e. litter stoichiometry and composition relative to the grazer stoichiometry and capacity to degrade specific plant chemical compounds) to a large degree controls the rate of litter decomposition but that soil fauna moderates the effect of litter quality on decomposition processes. For example, Carrillo et al. (2011) followed N dynamics during the decomposition of six different types of leaf litter over time with and without the presence of meso- and macrofauna (exclusions established using mesh sizes of 40 μm and 5 mm). They found that litter decomposition rates varied widely between the different litter types, but that the presence of larger-bodied soil fauna promoted N mineralization across all litter types, with particularly large effects observed for faster decomposing litter types. Along the same lines, Wickings and Grandy (2011) showed in a microcosm experiment that the presence of the oribatid mite, *Scheloribates moestus*, enhances extracellular enzyme activities, microbial respiration, and water-extractable organic C and N during the decomposition of both corn (*Zea mays*) and oak (*Quercus rubra*) litter, whilst also decreasing the relative abundance of polysaccharides in the decomposing corn litter. This provides evidence for multiple ways by which the presence of soil fauna species as well as soil food web structure may moderate litter decomposition processes including the cycling of C and nutrients therein.

The development of our understanding of the soil food web has relied heavily on the use of stable isotopes, and it is a method that is still very promising as a tool to investigate soil fauna's contribution to ecosystem functioning, particularly through the application of labelled substrates or by pulse-labelling atmospheric CO_2 or N_2 to investigate the flow of photosynthetically derived C and nitrogen fixed from the air through the soil food web, respectively. Stable isotopes have been used to investigate resource use in several soil fauna groups, with the results indicating relatively broad feeding preferences even within closely related organisms. For example, the use of stable nitrogen isotope ratios in one study suggested that oribatid mites in a temperate forest represented at least four different trophic groups, coarsely identified as lichen and algae feeders, detritivores, fungal feeders, and bacterial feeders (Schneider et al. 2004). Similarly, Pollierer et al. (2009) used stable isotope ratios for $^{13}C/^{12}C$ and $^{15}N/^{14}N$ to assess the structure of the soil food web of a temperate deciduous forest in Switzerland. The results suggested that the soil food web is strongly compartmentalised, composed of decomposers, earthworms, fungal feeders/predators and predators, with a large proportion of the soil fauna feeding on fungi. This corroborated earlier results from the same site, with root-derived C likely comprising the primary source of C. However, it should be noted that preferential microbial use of ^{14}N (and ^{12}C) complicates the interpretation of studies utilising naturally occurring stable isotope ratios (Dijkstra et al. 2006). Stable isotope probing measures the incorporation of a stable isotope labelled (or depleted) substrate to quantify activity organisms (Neufeld et al. 2009). This method has been used extensively over the last few decades but has been somewhat constrained by analytical practicalities. Ideally, the stable isotope ratios of species would be assessed for individual specimens, but this has not been possible for most fauna given the equipment material requirements. It is therefore necessary that either multiple specimens of a given species be processed at once or that one works with trophic groups or feeding guilds instead. However, the sensitivity of the analytical equipment is increasing, making it possible to work with much smaller quantities and in some cases even with individual specimens. The continued fine-tuning of such equipment is therefore likely to facilitate greater detail of feeding preferences of soil fauna.

In a very informative experiment, Strickland et al. (2012) used ^{13}C-labeled glucose to investigate the potential fate of low molecular weight compounds released by plant roots via exudation in three pasture and forest soils in South Carolina, USA. The authors quantified the proportion of ^{13}C-glucose-derived C in CO_2, dissolved and soil organic C pools, the microbial biomass and soil fauna (springtails, oribatid, and mesostigmatid mites) after 72 hours and found that the glucose-derived C had already propagated throughout the soil food web. The largest proportion was found in the soil microbial biomass and soil organic C followed by CO_2, dissolved organic C, and the microarthropods, including the predatory mites. Interestingly, the only variable that significantly explained the differences in distribution of glucose-derived C across sites was the abundance of predatory mites. Greater abundance of predatory mites was associated with reduced glucose-derived C in the CO_2 indicating greater retention of C belowground, with potential implication for ecosystem level C cycling. A slightly different approach needs to be taken to quantify photosynthetically derived C that enters the belowground food web via root exudation or allocation to microbial symbionts, particularly mycorrhizal-forming fungi. For example, Ostle et al. (2007) pulse-labelled 12 unimproved upland grassland plots with a 50 atmosphere % $^{13}CO_2$ tracer and tracked the ^{13}C pulse into soil food web, specifically earthworms, enchytraeids, mites, and collembolans, over 20 days. Earthworms made up 93% of the extracted soil fauna biomass with the remaining groups accounting for only 7%. All taxa showed incorporation of plant-derived ^{13}C within a week from the pulse, and a time × animal group interaction suggested that the incorporation differed between groups. Interestingly, by far the largest proportion of the ^{13}C tracer was found in the springtails, estimated at nearly 45%, with mites and earthworms showing roughly similar incorporation, and the enchytraeids showing the least incorporation over the 20-day time span. The study thus provides insight into the short-term fate of plant-derived C and that the soil mesofauna rapidly incorporates this C. Several studies have since used similar approaches to investigate soil food web structure and functioning.

In another study, a free air carbon dioxide enrichment facility (Swiss Canopy Crane) was used to assess whether soil fauna acquires its C from leaf litter or belowground sources (i.e. directly from roots or through root exudates including C allocated to mycorrhizal fungi). The authors used reciprocal leaf litter transplants from ambient and elevated [CO_2] treatments to create an experimental design where the leaf litter and/or root-derived C was depleted in ^{13}C. This was possible because the CO_2 that was used to increase the atmospheric [CO_2] was depleted in ^{13}C and incorporated into the plant biomass. By comparing the ^{13}C values across treatments it was then possible to determine whether soil fauna predominantly acquired its C from the litter or belowground sources (including feeding on fungal hyphae and microbes more broadly). A large proportion of the soil fauna, including mites, springtails, isopods, centipedes, and earthworms, that were extracted from the plots with only labelled root-derived C were depleted in ^{13}C indicating that they predominantly acquired their C from belowground sources. This was true across primary and secondary decomposers and higher trophic levels including predators. By contrast, only three taxa including juveniles of a dominant millipede were depleted in ^{13}C in the plots with only labelled leaf litter. This indicates that root-derived C may contribute a larger part of soil fauna diets than previously assumed (Pollierer et al. 2007). However, a very large proportion of the plant-derived C that enters the soil food web does so via the roots through exudation, losses to root herbivores and leaching following damage caused by root herbivory, and C allocation to mycorrhizal symbionts. It appears possible that a higher proportion of ^{13}C allocation belowground could mask the contribution of leaf litter derived C. In any case, this warrants further investigation into the origins and fate of plant-derived C in the soil food web.

Radioisotopes such as ^{14}C and ^{32}P can also be employed in studies investigating the role of soil fauna in food webs. For example, ^{14}C has been used to calculate the age of substrate used by different species of soil fauna. One study found that epigeic earthworms use photosynthetically derived C about zero to four years old, whereas endogeic earthworms use C when about five to nine years old (Briones et al. 2005). Similarly, differences in substrate use have been found between grass-feeding termites and soil- and wood-feeding termites, which use 7–12 and 8–21-year-old C, respectively, using ^{14}C (Hyodo et al. 2008). It therefore seems that life history strategies can be useful indicators of food web contributions. The use of ^{14}C generally takes advantage of naturally occurring abundances (i.e. the 'bomb peak'). In comparison, few studies have used ^{32}P *in situ* given the constraints of releasing radioactive material into our ecosystems. However, ^{32}P and ^{14}C labelling have been used in a laboratory experiment to assess the ingestion and retention of P and C from a bacterial prey (*Escherichia coli*) in the bacterial-feeding nematode, *Caenorhabditis briggsae* (Nicholas and Viswanathan 1975). The study found that some 20%–50% of the C and 19%–35% of the P from *E. coli* was assimilated by the nematode. Similarly, ^{18}O labelled H_2O can be used to label active microbes and follow this marker through the food web. Moreover, our analytical equipment is increasingly more sensitive making it possible to get robust data from even minute samples, such as a few nematodes or mites, where the quantities required earlier restricted our options for separating taxa to higher taxonomical levels or even functional or trophic group levels due to the minute size of many types of soil fauna.

Fatty acids similarly have a long history as indicators of soil food web structure as a proxy for biomass of key organisms, although there is some overlap in fatty acids between organisms (e.g. Frostegård et al. 1997). Indeed, many fatty acids are common across multiple taxa and are therefore not suitable as biomarkers. Still, a recent paper investigated the potential for neutral lipid fatty acids (NLFAs) and amino acids to establish feeding in the oribatid mite, *Archegozetes longisetosus* (Brückner et al. 2017). The authors reared the mite on ten different substrates and analysed NLFAs and amino acid composition. They found that NLFA composition reliably reflected changes in diets, but that diet had no influence on amino acid concentrations. Hence, NFLA composition may be a useful biomarker to determine food preferences in mites and other soil fauna although this will require further investigation. Another approach combines biomarker fatty acids with stable isotope probing (i.e. NFLA-SIP, PLFA-SIP) to more specifically assess trophic links and carbon fluxes (Ruess and Chamberlain 2010). The origin of fatty acids in a target animal can be traced to its food source because biomarker fatty acids are predominantly found in certain organisms and it is more economically efficient to incorporate unmodified fatty acids directly into body tissue so that the fatty acid will have the $^{13}C/^{12}C$ signatures of the resource rather than the consumer. The use of other biomarkers to provide quantitative or qualitative insight into soil fauna is still under evaluation. Several biomarkers including gut content barcoding, fatty acids, and amino acid composition have been suggested. A simple approach to determining feeding preferences is to explore the gut contents of target organisms. Historically this would have been done visually by extracting the gut contents via dissection and then classifying this under a microscope. This approach is, however, limited to larger types of soil fauna given the constraints in physically accessing the gut of animals. More recent approaches can overcome this constraint using molecular techniques. For example, Juen and Traugott (2006) presented an optimised targeted sequencing approach to detect *Amphimallon solstitiale* (Coleoptera: Scarabaeidae) mitochondrial DNA in the invertebrate predator, *Poecilus versicolor*, larvae. Using this method, they were able to reliably detect the consumption of a single *A. solstitiale* egg eight hours after it occurred and, in some cases, up to 32 hours, with larger consumption rates detectable for even longer. While this example is limited to one prey, the method can be applied more broadly provided that resource-specific primers are identified.

Importantly, we can use a combination of techniques to address specific questions about the contribution of soil fauna to ecosystem functioning. For example, Soong et al. (2016) used stable isotope labelling techniques in combination with modelling approaches to quantify empirically the effect of reduced microarthropod density on short-term C and N cycling in a tallgrass prairie in Kansas, and then used a modelling approach to predict longer-term impacts. Specifically, the authors used naphthalene to suppress microarthropod abundances by roughly 38% over a three-year period. At the start of the study, they deposited ^{13}C- and ^{15}N-labelled big bluestem (*Andropogon gerardii*) leaf litter on the soil surface and tracked the fate of the litter-derived C and N into the soil organic matter fractions and the microbial community over the next three years. Suppression of soil microarthropods reduced litter mass loss and incorporation of litter-derived C and N into the soil organic matter and microbial biomass over the first 18 months of the study. Moreover, while all leaf litter C and N was eventually incorporated in all treatments, there was a lower early-stage supply of leaf litter C to the microbial community and a reduced C:N ratio of leaf litter-derived organic matter inputs to the mineral soil fractions. Using the DayCent model, the authors predicted that suppression of soil microarthropods would reduce total soil C and N mineralization rates and plant net primary productivity in the long term (Soong et al. 2016). This study illustrates how short-term studies may underestimate the true long-term impact because the system has not yet acclimated to the novel conditions, whether that is caused by altered soil food web structure, nutrient input, or climate change.

Modelling is a powerful tool to provide insight into ecosystem functioning responses to the changes in soil food web structure, but these responses should be interpreted with care. A better use would be to use models to formulate new testable hypotheses. Early modelling work suggested that although deleting specific soil fauna groups influences the abundance of other soil fauna groups or microbial communities, only the removal of plant parasitic nematodes from the model results in as much as a 10% change in ecosystem functioning, including nitrogen mineralization and primary production (Hunt and Wall 2002). This promoted the view that there was great functional redundancy in the soil food web and that the loss of species and even feeding groups might not have a great impact on ecosystem functioning. However, there is now much evidence that indirect effects of soil fauna might contribute further to functioning. Accordingly, there is a push to incorporate soil fauna more explicitly in models of biogeochemical cycling (Soong and

Nielsen 2016). A proposed approach to do this for microbes is to focus more explicitly on population and community ecology, which would allow density-dependent effects of biotic interactions to be incorporated in more detail (Buchowski et al. 2017). Similar approaches could be used to quantify and incorporate key plant–soil fauna, microbe–soil fauna, and soil fauna–soil fauna interactions emphasising both the abundance of individual taxa and shifts in assemblage composition. While this may not be useful for large-scale modelling of biogeochemical cycling in the short term (Grandy et al. 2016), it would allow us to test theoretically how changes in soil fauna assemblages might impact biogeochemical cycling under specific circumstances. This in turn would also provide a tool for establishing hypotheses related to key constraints on biogeochemical cycling and potential impacts of changes in soil fauna assemblages that can be tested empirically. In the longer term, such knowledge could drastically improve our ability to predict the impacts of global changes such as climate change or land use management.

3.5 Soil Fauna As Bioindicators

It has long been evident that soil fauna assemblages are influenced by environmental conditions, leading researchers to the eventual proposition that the fauna may itself be a good indicator of ecosystem state. Such organisms are known as biological indicators or, more briefly, as bioindicators. Ritz et al. (2009) presented one of the most robust evaluations of the use of soil biological indicators in ecological monitoring programs, addressing the applicability of individual methodologies (i.e. morphological versus molecular, abundance versus assemblage composition) using the 'logical sieve' approach. The paper grouped the most promising methodologies based on their 'readiness' and the type of information they provide, including several soil fauna-based options. Indeed, the soil nematode, mite, and protozoan assemblages were identified as valuable indicators of soil food web energy transfer, microbial activity, pest and disease suppression or transfer, habitat suitability for plants, and soil biodiversity reservoirs (genetic, taxonomic, functional). These are generally broad variables that still provide useful insight into ecosystem characteristics relevant to management. The paper further identified morphological approaches as being more easily applicable than molecular approaches, which at that point was limited to T-RFLP-based assemblage fingerprints for nematodes and Protozoa. Since the paper was published nearly a decade ago, the molecular techniques have improved substantially and several new approaches, such as high-throughput sequencing, whole genome sequencing, and qPCR, hold great promise for the future of soil monitoring based on soil fauna bioindicators.

As outlined above, the potential use of various soil-dwelling invertebrates as bioindicators have been suggested; however, the most advanced soil fauna-based bioindicator schema is undoubtedly that established for nematodes. Few soil organisms have received as much attention as the soil nematodes given their ubiquitous presence in soils, high diversity and abundance, and various life history and functional traits. It is evident that this combination of characteristics makes them ideal prospects as bioindicators. Several nematode indices have been developed that reflect changes in nematode assemblage structure and, more importantly here, that act as proxies for shifts in ecosystem functioning. The use of nematodes as bioindicators was initially made possible through the recognition that nematode species could be arranged along a coloniser–persister (cp) scale ranging from 1 to 5 based on life history traits and sensitivity to disturbances including pollution and land use management. The coloniser–persister scale is broadly equivalent to an r to K life strategy classification with colonisers (i.e. low cp values) having short life cycles and generally tolerant of disturbance, whereas persisters (i.e. high cp values) have longer life cycles and are more sensitive to disturbance. This eventually culminated in the development of the maturity index (MI) posed by Bongers (1990), which the author showcased as being indicative of pollution and eutrophication impacts. In both cases, the MI decreases with increasing pollution or eutrophication, albeit for slightly different reasons, with greater impacts of pollution than eutrophication. Pollution causes a substantial decrease or even a complete loss of persisters depending on the level of impact but has limited impact on the density of colonisers, therefore causing large decreases in MI. By contrast, eutrophication, which is generally associated with disturbance and increased nutrient availability such as that caused by fertilisation or other inputs, have limited impacts on persisters but promotes the density of colonisers. This impacts MI negatively but less so than pollution. Plant parasitic nematode assemblages, however, behave differently from other free-living nematode species. Accordingly, MI is usually computed for the free-living nematodes less plant parasites, and another index – the plant parasite index (PPI) – can be calculated to assess impacts on the plant parasite assemblage. Since the inception of MI and PPI these indices have been applied to various cases with great success, but the results can be difficult to interpret in a useful manner.

Multiple other nematode-based indices have since been established for various purposes. One of the next major steps forward was the application of the cp continuum to feeding guilds, expressed as Ba_{1-5}, Fu_{1-5}, Ca_{1-5}, and Om_{1-5} for bacterial feeders, fungal feeders, carnivores, and omnivores, respectively. This forms the foundation for calculating the structure (SI), enrichment (EI), and channel (CI) indices (Ferris et al. 2001). A 'structured' nematode assemblage indicates greater occurrence of high cp value nematode taxa that are likely to be negatively impacted by environmental stress or disturbance. The enrichment index increases when nutrients are readily available and is characterised by large densities of bacterial feeders, but not necessarily low abundance of high cp value taxa. The channel index indicates whether the food web is predominantly fungal or bacterial dominated. Many other indices have been derived since the publications mentioned here, but it is beyond the scope of this book to describe the workings of these in detail. However, the brief description of the use of nematodes as bioindicators provided here hopefully convinces the reader that there is much to gain from investigating nematode assemblage structure. Conveniently, a group of researchers have provided an online platform making it possible to calculate most of the validated nematode-based indices using the online tool NINJA (Sieriebriennikov et al. 2014). While the use of nematodes as bioindicators has been broadly accepted it is clear that more work is needed to further evaluate the use of the above indices and that some care should be taken in how they are applied. In particular, the indices appear to provide useful insight into changes in ecosystem functioning and soil food web structure over time for a given plot or site associated with, for example, altered management practices or seasonal changes, and it allows the user to compare the impacts of similar land use management practices within a given area. However, it is uncertain how broadly such principles can be applied, and comparing different ecosystem types should be avoided as differences in bioindicator indices could be caused by other underlying mechanisms. A recent paper provides a good attempt at assessing the use of nematodes as bioindicators in a landscape framework. Tsiafouli et al. (2017) collected samples from five contrasting microhabitats at ten locations that differed in altitude, aspect, and vegetation type on Mt Holomontas, Greece. Through modelling they showed that microhabitat could be predicted reliably based on all nematode indices calculated, except the maturity index and the fungivore/bacterivore ratio. Similarly, a robust knowledge of desirable nematode assemblage bioindicator characteristics would be necessary for monitoring ecosystem state.

The use of nematodes as bioindicators is still limited by the expert knowledge required for reliable identification at appropriate taxonomical resolution and a lack of time. There is promise, however, in the adaptation of molecular tools to solve this. For example, Vervoort et al. (2012) showed how quantitative PCR (qPCR) techniques could be applied to monitor seasonal chances in nematode assemblages under field conditions. The authors used a library of ~2,400 SSU rDNA sequences to design nematode taxa-specific qPCR primers and testing a subset of these primers for taxon-specificity and the relationship between qPCR outputs and the number of nematodes before application to samples collected from the field. They surveyed nematode assemblages of two contrasting field sites in the Netherlands, an abandoned arable field and a forest, over 40 weeks (March–December). Nematodes were extracted from 100 ml subsamples using elutriators before being concentrated using centrifugation, and then DNA was extracted from the remaining 140 μl following removal of the supernatant. To reduce the number of qPCR reactions required they first surveyed the nematode assemblages in weeks 1 and 39, recovering 38 and 25 genera in the field and forest, respectively. Within these they then selected 15 candidate genera covering 59% and 72% of the genera found in the field and forest, respectively. Their results showed significant seasonality in nematode assemblages within both ecosystems, which supports the idea that qPCR-based approaches can be targeted to investigate nematode assemblages.

A few other noteworthy candidate bioindicator taxa include protozoans, ants, mites, springtails, and earthworms. Soil Protozoa have, for example, been highlighted as a potential bioindicator phyla given their ubiquity in terrestrial ecosystems, their high abundance, and fast life cycles, and the apparent near-cosmopolitan distribution of many taxa allowing comparison at species resolution across sites (Smith 1996). Indeed, protozoans are likely to be useful bioindicators for monitoring global change impacts. However, we currently know less about the ecology and distribution of soil Protozoa than we do about nematodes, and they are inherently difficult to identify and quantify, making this a less suitable candidate phylum at this stage. The rapid development and implementation of molecular techniques may, however, make this feasible in the near future. Similarly, ant assemblages have been used to evaluate restored Australian abandoned mining sites (see Chapter 7), while oribatid mites (Behan-Pelletier 1999) and earthworms (Paoletti 1999) appear to be good bioindicator taxa for land use.

3.6 Statistical Tools

Several new statistical techniques have been applied recently in soil ecology with great success, and they are likely to promote our understanding of soils and its inhabitants more broadly if they are implemented correctly. A few techniques in particular are worth highlighting here, notably variance partitioning, structural equation modelling, and network analyses.

A method that has been used in several studies to investigate the spatial patterns of distribution of soil fauna within ecosystems is variance partitioning (Figure 3.6). Briefly, the method partitions the amount of variation in the spatial distribution that can be attributed to environmental variables and spatial positioning of the samples, respectively, and the variation that is attributed to spatially autocorrelated environmental variability where the effect of space and environmental variability cannot be separated. Often, the environmental variables are 'lumped' based on their relevance, generally vegetation and edaphic variables when soil fauna is considered. Several different approaches are used to represent spatial variables, but they all fundamentally aim to capture patterns in assemblages through space. One of the first studies that applied variance partitioning to soil fauna assemblages was performed by Borcard et al. (1992). The authors applied variance partitioning to identify the variability in assemblage composition that can be explained by pure spatial, spatially structured environmental variation, and pure environmental influences leaving a further component of undetermined variability that was unrelated to the geographical location of the samples collected or the environmental variables. One of the study systems was oribatid mite assemblages in a Canadian sphagnum moss and peat blanket. The authors collected 70 samples (5 cm diameter, 7 cm depth) across a 10 m × 2.5 m sampling area and identified the oribatid mites and key environmental characteristics. Using these data, they were able to explain 57% of the variation in oribatid mite assemblage structure, including 12.2% explained by pure spatial patterns, 13.7% pure environmental influences, and 31% explained by spatially structured environmental variation. Similarly, Mitchell et al. (2000) studied testate amoeba assemblages in a small *Sphagnum magellanicum*-dominated patch (40 cm × 60 cm) of upland peatland in the Swiss Jura Mountains at high spatial resolution. The sphagnum patch showed

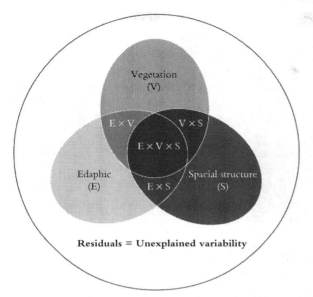

Figure 3.6 Variance partitioning is often used to illustrate influences of spatial and environmental parameters. In this schematic, the 'circle' represents the total amount of variation in assemblage composition within a given area. Part of this variation can be explained by a spatial structure (S), variation in vegetation (V), and edaphic (E) variables, and their interactions. Vegetation and edaphic variables are often spatially structured (i.e. V × S, E × S, E × V × S), making it difficult to separate spatial and environmental influences. Moreover, vegetation and edaphic variables are often correlated (E × V), making it troublesome to separate their influences. The pure spatial structure (S) is thought to be governed by biological processes, such as dispersal and behaviour. The residuals equal unexplained variation in assemblage composition that is unrelated to spatial patterns and environmental influences of the variables measured. There is often a large component of unexplained variation in assemblage composition in variance partitioning of soil fauna assemblages.

no measurable ecological gradients but did vary in topography (up to 6.6 cm difference in 'altitude'). They found a strong spatial structure that explained 36% of the variation in assemblage structure across the patch, which was in part related to fine-scale variation in microtopography within the plot. A large number of studies using similar and modified approaches have been published since then providing further insight into the likely contributions of environment and spatial structure. Moreover, the statistical methods have become progressively more sophisticated. While the spatial structure was initially modelled using relatively simple terms, for example, using a cubic trend surface (i.e. x, y, x^2, y^2, xy^2, x^2y,

x^2y^2, x^3, and y^3), the common method for 'capturing' the spatial structure has more recently been using principal coordinates of neighbour matrices (PCNM) analysis (Borcard and Legendre 2002, Dray et al. 2006). However, common for all studies is that they generally explain only a relatively small proportion of the variation in assemblage structure. It is uncertain what causes this 'gap' in our ability to accurately account for the variation in assemblage structure through space, but it is likely to be caused by multiple underlying factors including an inherent inability to measure all relevant environmental variables at scales relevant to target organisms and that different drivers control individual species within an assemblage. More recently, variance partitioning has been combined with null- and neutral-model approaches to provide further insight into the drivers of soil fauna assemblage structure with great success. This is discussed in more detail in Chapter 5.

Structural equation models (SEMs) have been used extensively in certain disciplines including psychology in the latter part of the twentieth century and have more recently been adapted by ecologists to better understand possible causal relationships. While the SEM approach has been somewhat underutilised in regard to belowground assemblages (Eisenhauer et al. 2015), there has been much greater emphasis on their use over the past couple of years. Structural equation models are powerful where they allow the investigator to formulate *a priori* relationships between explanatory and response variables based on existing knowledge, using either experimental (i.e. manipulation) or survey-based methods, that can then be tested using the SEM analyses. The SEM can therefore be used to test hypotheses using manipulative experiments where the possible effects (direct and indirect) can be assessed statistically against alternate hypotheses or to formulate hypotheses based on best model fits utilising survey data. A couple of recent examples using SEM are worth highlighting here to showcase the potential use of this quantitative modelling approach. In a combined field and laboratory study, de Vries et al. (2012b) investigated the resistance and resilience of extensively managed grasslands and intensively managed wheat fields to drought. The drought treatments were implemented in the field (April–July) after which soils were collected, rewetted, and incubated at 60% water holding under laboratory conditions to assess impacts on resistance and resilience. Soil samples were collected over time (up to 77 days) to quantify resilience. Interestingly, their results showed that on average the fungal channel was more resistant but less resilient to drought than the bacterial channel, indicating that there is a trade-off between resistance and resilience of soil food webs. More relevant to the discussion here, the authors followed this analysis up with an SEM approach to investigate the role of soil food web structure on C and N dynamics characterised by respiration and N_2O production and N leaching, respectively. The SEMs, one for each sampling date, were constructed using the residuals of the complete data set after the main treatment effects (i.e. ecosystem type and drought treatment) had been accounted for. The final models showed that the fungal:bacterial channel ratio played a key role in moderating soil C and N dynamics, including through modification of, or interactions, with the microarthropod assemblage. In particular, microarthropods increased N leaching 77 days after the soils had been rewetted indicating increased N mineralization. Because there were no plants present in the microcosms in the laboratory settings, this N was, however, lost rather than incorporated into plant biomass.

In another study, Eisenhauer et al. (2013) investigated the long-term (13 years) effects of plant species richness, elevated CO_2 and N deposition on the soil food web in a grassland experiment (BioCON), focussing on soil microbes, nematodes, and microarthropods. Overall, their results showed that plant species richness has a much greater effect on belowground communities than elevated CO_2 and N deposition. The strong effects of plant species richness observed here contrasts with other mostly shorter-term experiments as summarised by Bardgett and Wardle (2010). The authors speculate that this is because soil legacy effects or pretreatment of experimental soils may mask the plant diversity effects in the short term. Indeed, another paper by the lead author found that plant diversity treatment effects increase with treatment duration and generally do not become apparent until after four to six years (Eisenhauer et al. 2012). Moreover, the authors then used SEM to assess the effect of plant species richness on the soil food web in more detail. One of the SEMs indicated that plant species richness increased root biomass, soil pH, N concentration and water content, and through this positively affected the abundances or biomass of both micro- and mesofauna detritivores. Another SEM indicated that the nematode trophic structure was influenced by changes in soil microbial biomass and root biomass. This study provides significant insight into the belowground responses to multiple global change drivers under realistic field conditions. However, increasing the plant species richness from four to nine species had more limited effects than did increases from one to four species. Monocultures are unlikely to be common in grasslands of this kind suggesting that plant species richness effects may not be relevant in all cases, i.e. an increase from very low to moderate or high richness is likely to incur responses, but further improvements are unlikely to be observed at higher diversity. Similarly, in a small field experiment we recently used SEM to assess the direct and indirect effects of P-fertilisation on belowground assemblages in a Eucalyptus forest (Nielsen et al. 2015a). The study was limited in scope with only ten plots each with one *Eucalyptus tereticornis* being sampled, i.e. five with and five without added P (superphosphate equivalent to 50 kg P ha^{-1} over six months), therefore effectively violating the basic assumptions of sample size requirements. Still, the study indicated that P-fertilisation had a positive effect on springtail abundances and a negative effect on predatory nematode abundances. The resulting SEM model indicated that P-fertilisation had direct effects on springtail abundance as well as indirect effects caused by increases in root biomass, whereas the negative effect on predatory nematodes was related to changes in pH mediated by the addition of superphosphate. The results therefore warrant some consideration when interpreting the effects of imposed experimental treatments. Without assessing the potential indirect effects, we would have concluded that P availability has a negative direct impact on predatory nematodes, while in reality the effects appear to be caused by treatment side effects. This should take into account the interpretation of other studies as well. The study, however, also allowed us to establish new hypotheses about belowground responses to fertilisation and the possible direct and indirect effects implied by these hypotheses that can be tested under more controlled conditions. Indeed, the ability of SEMs to form a framework for establishing or testing novel hypotheses is one of the main strengths of the method. Obviously, some restraints should be taken in the application of SEMs in soil ecology. The underlying assumptions of model requirements and fitting the data need to be valid, and enough information should be included to allow robust conclusions to be drawn. One common shortcoming of many studies that use SEM is low sample size relative to the number of parameters, with the recommended sample size being a minimum of 50–200 samples depending on the objectives and at least five to ten samples per parameter in the model (Grace 2006).

Another statistical method that is being used increasingly more in soil ecology is network analyses based on correlation matrices. For example, Morriën et al. (2017) used network analyses to assess possible changes in soil food web structure through interactions between different organisms during restoration of former arable land. The authors found that soil organisms interacted more strongly in mid to late successional stages compared to recently abandoned arable land. Moreover, stable isotope labelling indicated that this was linked to greater C uptake efficiency and nutrient cycling apparently associated with changes in fungal community composition or activity. Similarly, Creamer et al. (2016) used network analysis to assess the interconnections among soil biodiversity and ecosystem functioning. The authors collected soil samples from three land use types (forestry, grass, arable) in 11 European countries representing five biogeographical regions associated with the project EcoFINDERS and completed a detailed analyses of soil properties, soil biodiversity, and proxies for ecosystem functioning. The network analysis showed much greater network densities in the forest soils with lowest densities in the arable soils. These analyses allowed the authors to identify the biota that dominated specific land use types or had the most 'neighbours' and therefore were more connected within the food web. This could then be linked to C and nutrient cycling to provide insight into the key taxa involved in biogeochemical cycling. The analyses also highlighted that the networks differed between land use types based on soil characteristics, particularly soil organic matter content and pH, both factors that are well known to influence belowground organisms. Such tools can therefore provide great insight into ecosystem function and which management practices can be used to modify the soil to better suit a given purpose.

3.7 Summary

Soil ecologists still rely heavily on methods that have been around for a long time to quantify or estimate soil fauna abundances, biomass, and assemblage structure and composition, particularly by culturing or directly counting soil fauna. The techniques used depend mostly on the size of the organisms under investigation with direct counts mostly employed for the larger soil fauna. However, several new technologies, including molecular, analytical, and statistical approaches, hold great promise in advancing our understanding of soil fauna assemblages, the positioning of phylogenetic groups within the soil food web, and their contributions to ecosystem functioning. In particular, the molecular techniques ranging from qPCR that target individual organisms to sequencing of whole soil samples (DNA or RNA) are likely to become more widely accessible and provide new insights. These techniques will be particularly important for organisms that we currently have limited capacity to quantify robustly, such as Protozoa, or where taxonomical expertise is a main limiting factor. Sequencing techniques have already provided new insights into species delineation, phylogeny, and distribution patterns beyond what traditional morphological approaches can provide. However, there is a clear need not to treat soil fauna as operational taxonomical units (OTUs) only but also acquire knowledge of their functional properties or traits. This will require that molecular identification of soil fauna be coupled to morphological identification and assessments of probable feeding preferences. Combined with the improved sensitivity and development of new analytical tools and more sophisticated statistical and mathematical approaches, this is likely to provide substantial new insights at a much higher level of resolution than what has previously been possible. Collaring and interpreting this data will present a new challenge.

4 · *Soil Fauna Biogeography and Macroecology*

Our knowledge of biogeographical and macroecological patterns of soil fauna is still limited relative to taxa found aboveground, particularly for smaller organisms (Decaëns 2010). The soil fauna assemblages are well described in some areas, for example, in Europe, but species-level knowledge is often lacking from more remote areas in less densely populated countries and where there has been less focus on exploratory research historically. Moreover, comparisons across studies are complicated by the use of non-comparable methodological approaches. However, in a notable review of the literature, Fierer et al. (2009) compiled data from more than 400 soils representing seven different biomes in an effort to describe and generalise global patterns of biomass and composition of belowground assemblages. While not being focussed on soil fauna *per se*, the work did highlight some key patterns relevant here. In particular, microbial biomass carbon was found to represent 0.6%–1.1% of the total soil organic carbon and is in the range of 1%–20% of plant biomass across biomes, while soil fauna biomass is approximately equal to 2% of the soil microbial biomass with some notable exceptions. However, the approach taken is likely to underrepresent the influence of larger soil fauna due to the sampling techniques applied and many studies not reporting soil fauna abundances. Moreover, the authors found that bacterial community composition was relatively predictable from soil pH, while C:N ratio was a good predictor of the fungal:bacterial gene ratio (Fierer et al. 2009). Given that microbes are the main resource for many soil fauna and the foundation of the soil food web, changes in pH and C:N ratios are therefore likely to be reflected at higher trophic levels, although other mechanisms could overrule the influence of these variables. Importantly, this work provides strong evidence for the existence of macroecological patterns belowground that allows us to make predictions about the biological assemblages of a given site. Similar studies with a more explicit focus on soil fauna could provide substantial new insights and address some of the knowledge gaps outlined later in this chapter and elsewhere in the book.

This chapter will focus on the biogeography and macroecology of soil fauna, i.e. global-scale patterns of soil fauna distribution, diversity, and assemblage composition. I will develop the discussion around the three broad soil fauna classifications based on body width introduced in Chapter 1 (micro-, meso-, and macrofauna) because size is likely to play a key role in the large-scale distribution of soil fauna. In particular, it has been proposed that smaller organisms, particularly those with a length below ~1–2 mm, are less likely to have restricted distributions due to greater dispersal abilities and large population sizes. Essentially, a given species present in the global species pool can be considered to have to pass through a series of nested filters before it can join a local assemblage (Hillebrand and Blenckner 2002, Poff 1997, Soininen 2012). Importantly, the filters differ somewhat among taxa due to their inherent life history traits, rates of evolution and dispersal abilities, contributing to observed differences in biogeography between the small unicellular microorganisms and the larger fauna and flora, in particular. This suggests that species of microfauna are more likely to be cosmopolitan whereas meso- and macrofauna are likely to show more restricted distribution. The view of biogeography of soil fauna, and specifically the smaller microfauna, is strongly influenced by how species are classified. Taxonomists can be described as 'lumpers' or 'splitters' depending on their affinity to define a species. The 'splitters' are more likely to find geographically restricted distributions simply by recognising more distinct species than the 'lumpers'. This should, therefore, be taken into account when conclusions on the biogeography of soil fauna are formulated. Reviews of the literature by Decaëns (2010), Brussaard et al. (2012), and Soininen (2012) provide an excellent framework for understanding soil fauna biogeography and macroecology. It will become apparent that there is still limited evidence for strong biogeographical patterns of microfauna, with notable exceptions, while the larger soil fauna often shows distinct distributional patterns at continental to global scales.

4.1 Biogeographical Patterns

Current biogeographical patterns are driven by both ecological and geological influences. Briefly, the evolutionary history of a given taxa combines with the pattern of continental drift to control the distribution of species in geological timescales (Figure 4.1). In ecological terms, biogeographical patterns are influenced by environmental conditions and biological interactions. Older lineages can therefore be expected to

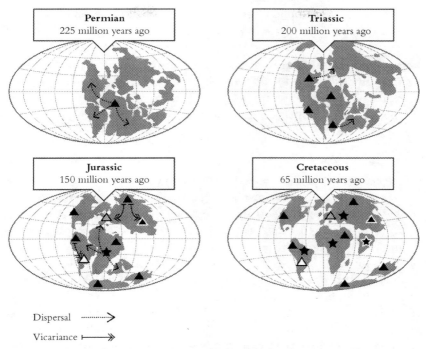

Figure 4.1 A simplified diagram illustrating the influence of post-Permian continental drift on the present distribution of organisms. Hypothetically, a lineage that evolved more distantly (i.e. the triangle) would have had greater dispersal opportunities due to greater connectivity between continents in the distant past and more time for vicariance (i.e. evolution of new species) to take place. A lineage that evolved more recently (i.e. the star) will have had less opportunity to disperse and evolve, and is likely to show a more restricted distribution at present day. However, species with greater dispersal abilities might overcome this perceived limitation to show (near-)cosmopolitan distributions, particularly if gene flow restricts vicariance.

be more broadly distributed than more recent lineages simply because they have been around for longer. Similarly, higher taxonomic levels will show broader geographical distributions with more restricted distributions observed at the family, genus, or species level. The pattern, however, also reflects differences among taxa associated with body size, life span, and dispersal ability. Specifically, it is expected that smaller organisms with fast life cycles and great dispersal abilities are more widely distributed than larger-bodied organisms with longer life spans and more limited dispersal ability. In extension, areas that are geographically isolated are likely to have unique faunas due to dispersal limitations. Dispersal limitation is, for example, a significant contributor to the very high proportion of endemic species in Antarctica. Antarctica is isolated from the other continents and nearby islands by the Southern Ocean and the polar jet stream, making it very difficult for organisms to colonise from even nearby habitats. Most of the indigenous taxa that managed to colonise the continent early on and survived during the glaciations have had the opportunity to evolve into new species.

4.1.1 Microfauna

There has been a rather heated debate about the possible distribution of microorganisms, including the **Protozoa**. One camp favours the 'Everything is everywhere, [...] the environment selects' hypothesis (EiE) dating back to Baas Becking (1934), which is also known as the cosmopolitan hypothesis (e.g. Finlay 2002). The EiE hypothesis is difficult to disprove because the absence of viable individuals of a species is attributed to ecological filtering. Many protists appear to be widely distributed with near-cosmopolitan status as proposed by Finlay (2002). Indeed, several studies have concluded that many protozoan morphospecies (Smith and Wilkinson 2007, Wilkinson 2001) as well as many cercomonad genotypes (Bass et al. 2007) are cosmopolitan in nature. Most of the data is from marine or freshwater ecosystems that might be less isolated spatially or at least present less vigorous dispersal barriers than soil habitats. Soils are extremely heterogeneous at fine to large scales, making it less likely for an organism to find a suitable spot through passive dispersal. Indeed, passive dispersal poses challenges for the protozoan fauna that some taxa might be better able to tackle than others. However, it appears that many protists show broad environmental niches so they can exist in more habitats making them appear more cosmopolitan than larger organisms. The other camp favours the 'Moderate Endemicity Model' (e.g. Foissner 2006), in which it is predicted that many species may be cosmopolitan but that at least some species show restricted distributions. Accordingly, there are robust examples of restricted distribution in groups as diverse as the protozoans, nematodes, springtails, and earthworms, and the Moderate Endemicity Model is now favoured by most in the field. However, the biogeographical pattern is not uniform across taxa. Specifically, there are reasons why smaller organisms with greater dispersal abilities, such as the protozoans, may be more widely distributed than larger organisms. For example, most small organisms produce small and resistant resting stages that can be passively dispersed over great distances and are likely to persist in most environments (Finlay 2002). Provided this is true for a given organism, they are therefore likely to be distributed globally, but may not be able to survive in a given ecosystem.

The debate about biogeographic patterns is further influenced by how species are delineated. For example, Finlay and Fenchel (1999) estimated that the global diversity of Protozoa, including soil-dwelling species, is in the order of 12–19,000 species, with approximately 3,000 species of free-living ciliates. However, Foissner (1999a) proposed that this probably substantially underestimated the true global diversity of protists, particularly rare species with more limited ranges. Moreover, the author gave examples of ciliates that are likely to have very restricted distributions. He listed several 'flagship' species that are morphologically recognisable and would be unlikely to be missed if present in a given sample. Several of these flagship species have been found only in certain regions of the world, suggesting that there are indeed dispersal-limited protists with non-cosmopolitan distributions. For example, the protozoan *Apodera vas* is considered a 'flagship species' that is thought to have a restricted biogeographical distribution (Mitchell and Meisterfeld 2005). More recent molecular evidence suggest that this genus evolved on the former Gondwana and has not yet been able to colonise several biogeographical regions (Lara et al. 2008). Smith and Wilkinson (2007) proposed that the continental distribution of *A. vas* occurred via continent drift following its origin no later than the Mesozoic, and its presence on Southern Hemisphere islands happened by wind dispersal from South America. Similarly, several species of testate amoeba appear to show regional, and even local, endemism (Smith et al. 2008a). Hence, there is substantial evidence that at least some protists show restricted biogeographic distribution.

One ongoing concern about making strong conclusions on the distribution of protists is that the ability of traditional morphological techniques to distinguish between species is severely limited. In accordance with this, studies that apply molecular techniques (i.e. sequencing) to assess protist assemblages and distribution generally find strong evidence for much greater species richness, both locally and globally, and also often the presence of many rare species. For example, Howe et al. (2009) used 18S rRNA gene sequencing to explore the diversity of protozoan assemblages among four sites on different continents (United Kingdom, Chile, Panama, Australia) and cross-referenced the results from environmental samples with those from culturing-based techniques. The results from the environmental samples (i.e. DNA extracted directly from the soil) and cultures showed substantially different patterns in assemblage composition supporting the notion that many soil microorganisms are not culturable (although this might be overcome by using a broader range of media and more replicates). Therefore, results based on culturing techniques need to be interpreted with care. Moreover, the authors found that individuals defined as the same species using morphological techniques were often highly divergent on a molecular level, indicating that they should be considered different species. Through the sequencing approach they defined 29 new species of cercozoans (gliding flagellates), which they placed in new genera and morphologically distinctive families. The cercozoan species richness was estimated to be in the hundreds at a temperate site with a likely global estimate in the thousands, and there was substantial turnover in species among sites. The limited number of sites used in the study and a high likelihood of missing rare species, however, make it difficult to use these data to interpret biogeographical patterns. More recent work based on the development of molecular techniques has contributed to resolve this issue. In a study assessing the protist assemblages in soils from 40 sites covering a wide range of ecosystem types using high-throughput pyrosequencing of the 18S ribosomal RNA (rRNA) gene, Bates et al. (2013) found that only a few protists show a broad geographical distribution across North America, South America, and Antarctica. The authors discovered a total of 1,014 unique OTUs across the 40 sampling sites with 84% of the phylotypes restricted to five or fewer samples and only one that was found in more than 75% of the samples. This suggests that there is some potential endemism in protists, which has also been found in terrestrial ciliates (Chao et al. 2006). An earlier investigation of the heterotrophic flagellates, cercomonads, using molecular techniques (18S rDNA genotypes) similarly noted that certain genotypes within some morphospecies showed restricted environmental or geographical distribution (Bass et al. 2007).

Finally, the Protozoa are even widespread in the Antarctic, often being the only soil fauna present, indicating very simple soil food webs. For example, in a study where the authors collected 50 soil samples across 12 different geographical regions in the McMurdo Dry Valleys, protozoans were present in all samples. The protozoan assemblages were dominated by small flagellates and amoeba, with few ciliates and no testacean protists recorded (Bamforth et al. 2005). None of the protozoans recorded were endemic to Antarctica, with the common species shared with dryland ecosystems elsewhere. However, a subsequent incubation study showed distinct physiological phenotypes of two dominant species,

Acanthamoeba and *Hartmannella*, indicating that the Antarctic species may be genetically distinct from those found in temperate dryland ecosystems. It is not yet clear what governs the distribution of Protozoa in these ecosystems, although soil pore size distribution and soil water content are likely critical factors. Again, molecular approaches would help resolve such issues.

The **nematodes** are larger, multicellular, and therefore likely to show different distributional patterns. However, many nematode genera show near cosmopolitan distributions (Hodda 2007), while Antarctica as discussed below is an outlier with a high level of endemism. The broad distribution of nematodes is likely associated with their long evolutionary history and perceived ability to disperse over long distances. It is considered an ancient phylum, and many genera diverged early on. For example, it has been estimated using molecular clocks based on globin and cytochrome c sequencing that the genera *Ascaris*, *Caenorhabditis*, *Nippostrongylus*, *Pseudoterranova*, and *Trichostrongylus* from the order Rhabditida diverged some 550 million years ago (mya) providing plenty of time for these genera to attain a global distribution (Vanfleteren et al. 1994). Still, there is evidence that biogeographical restricted species and genera do occur. For example, early work by Andrássy (1964) indicated that 84% of the Actinolaimidae has an entirely Gondwanian distribution. Two later syntheses similarly found that almost all species of the genus *Tyleptus* are entirely Gondwanian in distribution (Ferris et al. 1976, Ferris et al. 1981). Moreover, the isolation of Australia and New Zealand, combined with human-assisted immigration of plant parasitic nematodes, has helped shape the local nematode assemblages. Several species and genera mostly representing Criconematoidea, Dolichodoroidea, Radopholinae, and Tylodorinae, and the genus *Fergusobia*, are endemic to the region, whereas there appears to be few native species of Heteroderidae, Meloidogynidae, and Pratylenchinae (Hodda and Nobbs 2008). Hence, there is significant evidence that not all nematodes are cosmopolitan.

One continent in particular, Antarctica, presents a special case where substantial dispersal barriers and a harsh climate have reduced the opportunity for species to colonise and establish a viable population, respectively (Convey et al. 2014, Nielsen and Wall 2013). Therefore, a large proportion of the terrestrial fauna is endemic, including the 22 nematode species recorded in continental Antarctica. For example, the dominant species in the polar deserts of the McMurdo Dry Valleys, *Scottnema lindsayae*, is endemic and the only representative of the genus. It is also the nematode with the southernmost distribution (Adams et al. 2007). A recent review of the biogeography of nematodes of Victoria Land,

Antarctica, highlighted that all nematode species found in this area are endemic to Antarctica, but that most of the known species are common and well distributed within this geographical area (Adams et al. 2014). The high proportion of endemic species is a testament to the long isolation of Antarctic from source populations but also limited interaction between more isolated or remote geographic areas. The broad distribution within biogeographical regions suggests high dispersal rates at local to regional scales, likely while specimens are in anhydrobiosis (Nkem et al. 2006). The indigenous species have seemingly occupied Antarctica for an extended period of time, surviving in refugia during the previous glacial maxima, and evolving and diversifying locally. Recent work provides strong evidence that geothermal activity may have played a key role in supporting local populations, with greater biodiversity of plants and fungi observed near sites with known geothermal activity along the Antarctic Peninsula and on continental Antarctica (Fraser et al. 2014). The pattern was less pronounced for soil invertebrates and only significant on continental Antarctica, but the authors highlight that there were few records for soil fauna and also that 'glacial islands' (nunataks) may have been more important during the Last Glacial Maximum. However, given the strong association with vegetation it seems likely that at least some soil fauna may also have survived in refugia created by geothermal activity.

Molecular techniques promise to provide further insight into nematode biogeography. For example, many species of nematodes show very limited morphological differentiation, but differ significantly in their genomic profiles. A greater reliance on DNA sequencing could reveal more biogeographically distinct patterns of distribution, whereas greater geographical coverage could expand the current ranges of species with observed limited geographical distribution simply because they have not yet been looked for. For example, Wu et al. (2011a) provide a great example of how the greater taxonomic resolution achieved through molecular approaches can inform the biogeography of soil fauna. The authors collected soil samples at 11 sites on a global scale, with samples collected on most continents, and assessed the soil fauna assemblages (20 phyla) through sequencing of environmental 18S rRNA. Of more than 2,200 OTUs recovered, not a single OTU was found at all sites, and only 14 were common to four or more sites (at 99% similarity). If the classification of OTUs was relaxed to approximate family level, the number increased to 34 OTUs with a distribution of four or more sites. These results suggest that most types of soil fauna are limited in their biogeographical range. One limitation of the study is that the sites were classified as a broad range of biomes, making it difficult to counter the old statement that 'everything is everywhere, [...] the environment selects'. Ideally, a similar study covering more sites but targeting similar ecosystem types across a large geographic scale should be established to test this idea within soil fauna assemblages.

Much less is known about the biogeography of **rotifers,** but there is evidence for restricted distribution in this phylum as well. A decade-old synthesis of the literature focussed mostly on aquatic rotifers (some of which also occupy soil habitats) and concluded that 44% and 23% of all monogonont rotifers are endemic to restricted biogeographical regions and cosmopolitan, respectively. The pattern is even more pronounced in bdelloid rotifers with 51% apparently having limited distribution and only 13% currently considered cosmopolitan (Segers 2008, Segers and De Smet 2008). Whether soil-dwelling rotifers show the same pattern is yet to be confirmed, but it seems likely, particularly given the potential isolation of species across, and even within, continents. A criticism of this approach is that its interpretation is constrained by sampling effort, with many regions having received very limited attention. It is therefore not unlikely that many so-called rare species that are classified in this review are more broadly distributed but have simply been missed. A counterargument to this is the evidence from 'flagship' species of rotifers, similar to the definition presented for Protozoa above. Some rotifers are relatively abundant and have unique features that make it highly unlikely they would be overlooked in samples. An example of one such flagship bdelloid rotifer species with apparent restricted biogeography is described in Kaya et al. (2010). The authors surveyed bdelloid rotifers of 41 moss and lichen samples collected on Svalbard and found an impressive 52 taxa including 18 species new to the region. This represents roughly one-fifth and one-eighth of the European and globally known bdelloid rotifer species richness, indicating the broad distribution of many species. However, one of the species recovered, *Pleuretra hystrix*, has been found only in the European Alps, the Lake District in the United Kingdom, and the Canadian Arctic, making it a likely candidate for an arctic-alpine species. Moreover, it has not been found in the southern hemisphere. Given that it has characteristic morphology, and therefore is unlikely to be missed during sample processing for bdelloid rotifers by any expert, it is likely endemic to the northern hemisphere.

A more recent analysis of terrestrial bdelloid rotifer assemblages at a global scale using molecular techniques targeting the COI gene found that there was very limited overlap in species between distant sites and a high level of unique operational taxonomic units despite rarefaction curves indicating that local assemblages were well assessed (Robeson et al. 2011). Moreover, molecular approaches show surprisingly high levels of endemism and diversity in Antarctic rotifers (Velasco-Castrillón et al. 2014a). The authors sequenced the COI gene of 514 individual bdelloid rotifers extracted from sites covering the main biogeographical regions of continental Antarctica, the Antarctic Peninsula, and a reference site in Tierra del Fuego, South America. They identified 37 distinct lineages, representing 40 putative species, from the Antarctic samples. All of the Antarctic rotifers were considered endemic, and only one lineage (*Adineta cf. gracilis*) occurred in both continental Antarctica and on sites in the Antarctic Peninsula. However, several lineages showed pan-continental Antarctic distributions, indicating that dispersal is not a strong limitation within continental Antarctica. They highlight that it is problematic that most studies assign rotifer morphotypes found in Antarctica to species described elsewhere, likely causing substantial misrepresentation of the local fauna and underestimating the global richness of rotifers.

Our understanding of the biogeography of **tardigrades** is also limited and likely to be modified as molecular analyses of more assemblages are undertaken through the discovery of new species and more robust distributional data. However, McInnis and Pugh (2007) provided a substantial synthesis of tardigrade biogeography based on an earlier paper on the same topic. They created a database incorporating tardigrade distributions among 11 biogeographical regions based on 856 publications. To distinguish between endemic and cosmopolitan species, genera, or families they defined endemism as a taxon being present in only one biogeographical region while cosmopolitan species are present in all 11 biogeographical regions. Their synthesis provided strong evidence of endemism within the tardigrades at a species level, with the pattern being much less pronounced at the genus or family level. The data support the view that many Antarctic species are endemic, with 58% of the 64 tardigrade species recorded in Antarctica endemic to the biogeographical region. Fewer tardigrades were endemic to the other biogeographical regions, but the proportion of endemic species still ranged from 8.4% on the Pacific Islands to 45.4% in Europe among biogeographical regions where tardigrades were present. The results moreover indicate that some families have a Laurasian origin while others have a Gondwanan origin. One significant caveat of the study is that it is somewhat biased by a high number of publications that describe new species that may well be found in other biogeographical regions as the number of records increase. This, in turn, may be buffered by the splitting of cryptic species complexes into more robust species designations based on molecular techniques. These conclusions are broadly supported by an earlier literature review by Pilato and Binda (2001).

4.1.2 Mesofauna

Given the larger size of the soil mesofauna, one would predict that there is a greater level of biogeographically restricted species. A synthesis of the distribution of oribatid mites in Antarctica, sub-Antarctica, and nearby islands including New Zealand and neotropical South America provides insight into the possible limited distribution of soil fauna (Stary and Block 1998). The authors provide evidence for a high level of endemism in continental Antarctic (60%) and sub-Antarctic islands (63%), but not maritime Antarctica (18%) or the Falkland Islands (18%). They also show that the endemism of oribatid mites in New Zealand and neotropical South America is very high (83% and 89%, respectively). These results strongly suggest that many oribatid mite species have very restricted distributions. They further speculate that the oribatid mites likely arose after the breakup of Gondwanaland based on the similarity, or lack thereof, of the oribatid mite fauna found in the regions they investigated and that the most likely mode of dispersal was via what is now continental Antarctica. Another study applying a meta-analytical approach investigated oribatid mite assemblages at a global scale using 25 published datasets representing Africa, Australia, Europe, Japan, Malaysia, New Zealand, and the United States (Osler and Beattie 1999). A total of 253 genera representing 97 families and 43 superfamilies were identified across the datasets. The data suggested that few oribatid mites are cosmopolitan with only two families and four superfamilies found in more than 90% of the studies. Similarly, Marshall and Pugh (1996) found that 42.5% and 85.7% of mite species in maritime and continental Antarctica, respectively, are endemic. Moreover, there was little overlap in assemblages among habitats at a family level, with common families differing between habitats. There is less information about the possible biogeography of mesostigmatid mites, and it is difficult to make strong predictions of their distribution because of limited observations at the species level. However, there is some evidence for the existence of both geographically restricted and cosmopolitan species. In particular, the relatively well-studied

Phytoseiidae include a large proportion of species that appears to be endemic to Australia (Beaulieu and Weeks 2007). Moreover, a synthesis of the Phytoseiidae more broadly based on seven biogeographical regions (Australasian, East Palaearctic, Ethiopian, Nearctic, Neotropical, West Palearctic, Oriental) showed that species richness was particularly high in the Neotropical, Oriental, and Palaearctic, where there were also many endemic species (Tixier et al. 2008). The number of species was lower in the other biogeographical regions. The authors speculated that the family Phytoseiidae, which likely diverged from its sister group Ascidae some 80 mya, has a Gondwanian origin with contemporary patterns of distribution being driven by dispersal and vicariance.

Other studies have shown that there is considerable similarity in the composition of soil microarthropod assemblages among similar biome types at the global scale. For example, Noble et al. (1996) studied microarthropod assemblages of semi-arid soils in New South Wales, Australia, and found that they were very similar to assemblages observed in semi-arid ecosystems in Chile and North America at the genus level. However, it is unknown if the same pattern holds at the species level. The authors speculate that the seemingly large-scale distribution of species could be due to long-distance dispersal of fauna after the breakup of Pangaea and Gondwana or to convergent evolution of fauna present within Pangaea or Gondwana prior to their breakup. These hypotheses can be tested using contemporary molecular methods described in Chapter 3 that were not available when the work was published, but the cause of the pattern has still not been resolved. Presenting clear biogeographic patterns of soil fauna is complicated by unresolved phylogeny in many taxa. A good example of this is presented by the Antarctic springtail genus *Cryptopygus*. A phylogenetic survey of individuals of *Cryptopygus* from a broad range of locations using mitochondrial (COI) and ribosomal (18S, 28S) DNA revealed that the genus is likely paraphyletic, with multiple cryptic species and a diverse evolutionary history with seemingly frequent colonisation events and episodes of vicariance taking place *in situ* over a long timescale (McGaughran et al. 2010). The deepest evolutionary split within the genus was estimated at >20 MA, and the species would have had to survive through multiple subsequent cycles of glaciation.

The biogeographical patterns of other soil mesofauna are not well characterised but is likely to reflect that of the Acari and Collembola. Some evidence points to restricted biogeography of some enchytraeids. For example, the species-rich Arctic enchytraeid assemblages have a high proportion of endemic species indicating a long evolutionary local history and survival in glacial refugia from which recolonisation could occur (Christensen and Dózka-Farkas 2006). Similarly, a review of the enchytraeids of Latin America found a substantial species diversity, including several species that do not appear to occur, or are rare, in other biogeographical regions (Schmelz et al. 2013). The authors further noted that 17 of the 62 known Latin American enchytraeids were possible peregrine species. However, these patterns are yet to be explored in detail.

4.1.3 Macro- and Megafauna

There is substantial evidence for restricted distribution of macro- and megafauna. Clear biogeographical patterns have been observed within the termites with certain families being widely distributed in tropical and subtropical biomes, while other families have very narrow ranges. For example, the termite families Termitidae and Rhinotermitidae are widely distributed whereas Termopsidae and Mastotermitidae show more restricted distribution (Brussaard et al. 2012). Ants display similar large-scale biogeographical patterns with a clear distinction between the species occupying New and Old World biogeographical regions. For example, the predatory army ants (Aenictinae, Dorylinae, Ecitioninae) evolved in the mid-Cretaceous (94–116 mya) and have a pan-tropical distribution (Brady 2003), whereas the fungus-cultivating leaf cutter ants (tribe Attini in the Myrmicinae) that evolved some 8–12 mya are only present in the Neotropics (Schultz and Brady 2008). Similar patterns are found in earthworms with Glossoscolecidae in South America being a sister taxon to the African Eudrilidae consistent with the breakup of Gondwana, while the Ocnerodrilidae and Benhamiinae are present in both areas. However, endemic genera have evolved within both regions following the original colonisation/shared ancestry (Brussaard et al. 2012). The termites show asymmetric distributions across latitudinal and longitudinal gradients and biomes largely driven by idiosyncratic differences in the distribution of clades leading Eggleton (2000) to conclude that termites likely evolved before the breakup of Pangaea, with diversification within clades following breakup and no significant migration of species between the new large land masses. Indeed, there is limited evidence supporting termites as strong dispersers across geographical barriers, and there are no known peregrine termite species. The termites thus show a substantial level of endemism (~60%–80%), particularly in the tropical and oriental regions. Other soil-associated insects also show

134 · Soil Fauna Biogeography and Macroecology

restricted distributions. For example, there are only two recognised insects in Antarctica, both wingless chironomids of the genus *Belgica* (Figure 4.2). One, *B. antarctica*, is common through most of the northern Antarctic Peninsula, while the other, *B. albipes*, is endemic to the sub-Antarctic archipelago Îles Crozet. Molecular investigations of their likely origin show that several *B. antarctica* haplotypes exist in relatively close geographical proximity. This indicates that multiple colonisation events took place in the Pleistocene and that the populations survived in local refugia during successive glacial maxima (Allegrucci et al. 2012).

Given their large size and long appreciation of their contribution to ecosystems our understanding of the biogeography of earthworms is reasonably well developed compared with many other soil fauna taxa. Earthworms are interesting in that they generally show rather restricted distributions, possibly linked to a more recent post-Pangaean evolutionary origin and dispersal limitation. Even at the family level, there is strong evidence for restricted distributions, many families occurring in only certain biogeographical regions (e.g. Hendrix et al. 2008). However, many earthworm species have proven to be highly invasive often assisted by human activities, with more than 120 species classified as peregrine with broad distributions. While a relatively large proportion

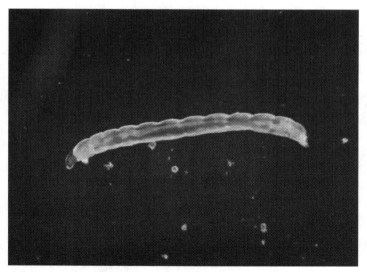

Figure 4.2 A chironomid larvae of the genus *Belgica* from maritime Antarctica. The two wingless midges are the only insects considered native to Antarctica. Photo by the author.

of earthworm species have likely been described, there are still new species to be discovered, and many of these are likely to also show limited distribution. For example, there are more than 200 endemic species of earthworms (Megascolescidae) in New Zealand, with many species yet to be described (Boyer et al. 2011). There is also evidence for restricted biogeographical distributions of centipedes, which often show very narrow geographical distributions (Edgecombe and Giribet 2007). For example, the Scutigerinidae is endemic to Madagascar and southern Africa, whereas Pselliodudae is endemic to the Neotropics and tropical Africa. However, species within all the major clades have near cosmopolitan distributions, including *Lamyctes emarginatus* that can reproduce by parthogenesis. It is clear that many macro- and megafauna taxa show broad restricted distributions albeit with noteworthy examples of peregrine species, but the resolution is generally substantially low with a high level of underexplored areas. Indeed, the high level of endemism might be caused by an emphasis on recording new species.

4.2 Species–Area Relationship

The species–area relationship was one of the first macroecological patterns described, with species richness increasing as larger areas were sampled following a power law (e.g. Arrhenius 1921), and it is considered one of the few laws of ecology (Figure 4.3). The species–area relationship in and by itself does not have significant meaning but rather expresses the influence of sampling effects, habitat diversity, and other ecological mechanisms. Differences in the slope of the species–area relationship among taxa thus informs us about the contribution of these variables to the distribution of these although it is generally difficult to interpret the relative influence of individual underlying factors. The species–area relationship is driven by different mechanisms depending on the scale of study. In short, an increase in species with area sampled is likely to reflect an increase in the inclusion of more rare species as more individuals are identified at small scales, whereas at larger scales an increase in habitat diversity as the area sampled increases is a likely driving factor (Decaëns 2010). The theory of island biogeography (MacArthur and Wilson 1967) further predicts that islands far from continental influences will have fewer species due to less dispersal events and higher extinction rates. However, environmental stability is also likely to increase at larger scales promoting immigration of species to reduce the risk of and compensate for extinction. A recent paper described the possible application of

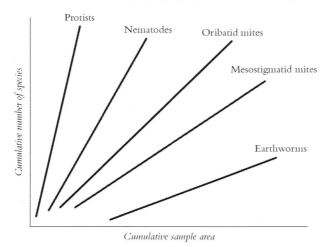

Figure 4.3 A hypothetical schematic of species-area relationships. The species richness of smaller organisms is expected to increase more rapidly with the size of the area sampled than the species richness of larger organisms.
Modified from Bardgett et al. (2005b) with permission from Cambridge University Press.

a species co-existence–area relationship built on similar principles. The authors highlight that species co-existence will increase with the size of the area sampled because of three main factors: (1) a weakened influence of demographic stochasticity reduces the potential for species to go extinct as their population sizes increase, (2) increased environmental variability allow for 'space' for more species, and (3) increasing probability that the environmental variability exceed dispersal abilities of species so that ecologically similar species can occupy remote patches of similar habitats (Hart et al. 2017). Given that the number of species increases with the area sampled, this indicates that landscape patterns of biodiversity can be caused by differences in area. This may have particularly large implication for altitudinal gradients where the area of a given elevation will decrease towards the peak of a mountain (Rahbek 1995).

There are few publications focussed on assessing species-area relationships for soil fauna to date (Decaëns 2010). However, a positive species-area relationship has been shown across a range of soil fauna including ants of the Melanesian archipelago (Wilson 1974) and the British Isles and northern Europe (Cushman et al. 1993), oribatid mites on islands and mainland countries (Maraun et al. 2007), springtails across 35 European countries and large islands (Ulrich and Fiera 2009), centipedes on

Mediterranean island groups (Simaiakis et al. 2012), and earthworms in Europe (Judas 1988). Some of these studies as well as Stanton and Tepedino (1977) also indicate that islands support fewer species per unit area. For example, ant species richness decreased with latitude in Ireland, Britain, and northern Europe, but predictive models were more accurate when they included area as a variable for both Ireland and Britain (Cushman et al. 1993). This pattern was not observed in the northern European sites, but that could be due to the area sampled being continuous. By contrast, Ulrich and Fiera (2009) found no difference in the species-area relationship for springtails between islands and mainland Europe after correcting for climate and longitude. The sparse information we have to date supports the notion that soil fauna species richness on an island is governed by the equilibrium between immigration and extinction rates and that species richness is negatively impacted by isolation (Bardgett et al. 2005b). However, work on boreal lake islands observed a neutral or even negative relationship between island size and soil invertebrate richness (spiders, beetles, springtails, mites, and nematodes) and also a neutral or positive relationship between richness and island isolation (Jonsson et al. 2009). A noteworthy paper provided more insight into this by modelling species-area relationships for 17 different taxa using data from the volcanic Aeolian Islands near Sicily to assess the general dynamic model of island biogeography proposed by Robert J. Whittaker and co-workers (Fattorini 2009). The author showed that species accumulation and richness at equilibrium differed substantially among the taxa. Furthermore, the species accumulation curves were much greater for oribatid mites and springtails than other soil fauna such as isopods and millipedes, but the richness at equilibrium was estimated to be roughly 100 and 55 for oribatid mites and springtails, respectively. However, it was estimated that it took hundreds of thousands of years to reach equilibrium richness in most taxa, which may explain the contrasting results of other studies. Overall, it appears that the slope of the species-area relationship is generally steeper for smaller-bodied organisms and could be an artefact of the smaller size of the organisms inhabiting soil and great spatial patchiness (Decaëns 2010).

4.3 Distance-Decay Relationships

The similarity of species assemblages generally decreases with increasing distance between samples. The slope of this distance-decay curve is indicative of the turnover in assemblages and can be caused by biological

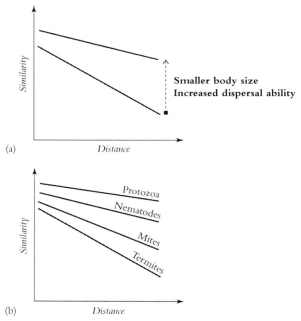

Figure 4.4 A hypothetical schematic of distance-decay relationships. (a) Smaller body size and increased dispersal ability is expected to 'shift' the distance-decay relationship. (b) It has therefore been hypothesised that smaller organisms with great dispersal abilities will show less variation in assemblage composition with increasing distance than larger-bodied organisms with more limited dispersal ability.

interactions, dispersal processes, and environmental variability. The steeper the slope is, the more the assemblages differ between spatially separated locations. The steepness of the slope can be used to compare the relative importance of both neutral (i.e. dispersal) and niche-based (i.e. habitat requirements, competition) processes in structuring assemblages of different taxa. Indeed, any decay in assemblage similarity with increasing distance that cannot be attributed to changes in the environment or biological interactions would indicate that neutral processes structure the assemblages. Because of the smaller size and the substantial capability of prokaryotes to disperse, they generally show less steep distance-decay relationships than the larger and more dispersal-limited eukaryotes (Soininen et al. 2011). Similarly, one can hypothesise that larger and/or more dispersal-limited soil fauna are likely to show steeper distance-decay relationships (Figure 4.4), but there is limited evidence that provides robust insight into this pattern for soil fauna assemblages. However, evidence for such a pattern exists when comparing distance-decay relationships for unicellular and multicellular organisms more broadly. For example, Hillebrand et al. (2001) found that unicellular microalgae and Protozoa had higher local species richness to global species richness ratios and shallower slopes of distance-decay relationships than polychaetes and corals. Both patterns indicate that the smaller unicellular organisms are more widely distributed than the larger metazoans. The fact that the unicellular microalgae and protozoan assemblages became more dissimilar with increasing distance provides evidence for dispersal limitation even within these groups. Rotifer assemblages similarly show decreasing assemblage similarity with increasing distance at least at small scales. This pattern was not reflected at scales larger than 50–100 m where assemblages were generally highly dissimilar (Robeson et al. 2011). The authors conclude that their results supported the conclusion that not all rotifers are cosmopolitan, but this pattern could also be interpreted as a sign of assemblages under high influence of stochasticity. By contrast, no distance-decay was observed in rotifer assemblages in moss and lichen in low-elevation (850–1,810 m) and high-elevation sites (2,984–4,527 m) in the French, Swiss, and Italian Alps across distances of up to 420 km, but the authors note that this could be due to low sampling efficiency and high environmental stochasticity (Fontaneto and Ricci 2006). Distance-decay relationships have also been observed in nematode assemblages. In a study of 30 semi-natural grasslands on three neighbouring chalk hill ridges in the United Kingdom, the authors observed strong distance decay patterns across a range of 1–198 km of both nematode and bacterial assemblages that were unrelated to vegetation composition or soil properties (Monroy et al. 2012). The authors noted that the pattern observed for the nematodes were in part related to a difference in assemblage structure, with assemblages on one ridge being fundamentally different from those on the other two ridges, possibly due to past land use management. There is a clear gap in large-scale studies that investigate distance-decay relationships in soil fauna assemblages.

4.4 Latitudinal Gradients

The study of latitudinal and altitudinal patterns of diversity has been instrumental to the development of theories of the mechanisms that structure species assemblages and biodiversity (Hillebrand 2004, Rahbek 2005). One of the first biogeographical patterns observed related to latitude was that species found at higher latitudes generally have broader geographical ranges than species at lower latitudes. The observation was first made by E. H. Rapaport in the 1970s, prompting Stevens (1989) to coin the term 'Rapaport's rule' to describe the phenomenon. Since then the majority of studies that have investigated latitudinal patterns agree that high-latitude species generally have broader geographical, altitudinal, and ecological ranges. However, Rapaport's rule does not appear to explain latitudinal changes in biodiversity.

Several groups of taxa aboveground show a pronounced increase in species richness per unit area as you go from the Polar Regions towards the tropics. This latitudinal pattern has been associated with multiple different factors, including a larger geographical area, greater productivity or habitat diversity, and environmental stability, but the underlying drivers are still unresolved (Gaston 2000). It has been proposed that latitudinal gradients may not be as prominent belowground given that many types of soil fauna taxa appear to be cosmopolitan and limited latitudinal variation in edaphic properties (De Deyn and van der Putten 2005, Maraun et al. 2007, Wardle 2002). Indeed, several studies have investigated latitudinal gradients in soil fauna and found that protozoans (Foissner 1999a), oribatid mites (Maraun et al. 2007), and earthworms (Lavelle et al. 1995) show limited evidence for a strong latitudinal gradient in richness with rather similar species richness observed from low to intermediate latitudes, albeit with a significant decrease in species richness in the Polar Regions (Figure 4.5). Accordingly, the diversity of protozoans is, for example, negatively correlated to latitude moving south from the sub-Antarctic islands, with a seeming 81° S limit to their presence (Smith 1996) and the diversity of microarthropods decrease along the maritime Antarctic Peninsula, likely associated with lower temperatures (Bokhorst et al. 2008). Similarly, one of the few studies that has used molecular approaches to assess soil fauna assemblages at a global scale found no significant latitudinal patterns in soil fauna species richness, diversity, or evenness (Wu et al. 2011a). The study was, however, limited to below 68° latitude, making it impossible to compare with higher latitudes. The study therefore provides support for the lack of strong latitudinal trends across tropical to arctic regions observed using morphological approaches but was unable to corroborate the decrease in richness observed for several taxa at high latitudes. Indeed, many studies are constrained by limited latitudinal coverage and methodological inconsistencies making it difficult to draw strong conclusions.

One of the first efforts to assess latitudinal patterns in soil nematode diversity was by Procter (1984), who concluded that nematode diversity

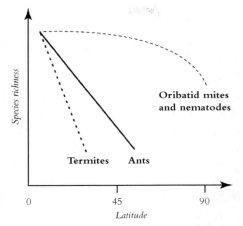

Figure 4.5 Schematic of possible latitudinal richness patterns in soil fauna. There is evidence that the species richness of termites and ants decreases in a near linear fashion from the tropics to temperate regions, with the richness of termites showing a steeper decrease than the ants. By contrast, several soil fauna groups, such as oribatid mites and nematodes, show limited evidence for a significant decrease in richness with increasing latitude except in the Polar Regions and, in some cases, the richness even appears to peak in temperate regions.

increases towards higher latitudes. However, this finding was founded on an observed increase in diversity from the tropical to temperate regions and included very few high-latitude observations. Several more recent papers have since reviewed the latitudinal patterns of nematode diversity. For example, Boag and Yeates (1998) surveyed the existing literature and concluded that nematode diversity is greatest in temperate broadleaf forests (~62 species per sample) followed by, somewhat surprisingly, agricultural soils, grasslands, tropical rainforests, temperate coniferous forests, and polar vegetation. Moreover, they concluded that on average nematode diversity peaks at 30°–40° latitude with lower diversity in the tropics consistent with the observation made by Procter (1984). However, the authors included several studies with very low diversity in the Polar Regions, at least at the sample level. Hence, the available data now indicate that nematode diversity is relatively similar across most latitudes, peak at intermediate latitudes, and is substantially lower in the Polar Regions (Nielsen et al. 2014). However, the spatial coverage is still very poor, and robust assessments of nematode assemblages are sparse, making it very difficult to draw strong conclusions on latitudinal gradients of this group. Indeed, the low Polar Regions species richness observed to date might well be an artefact of limited sampling effort and logistical constraints. At least, several studies indicate that the nematode species richness at regional scales can be high in these environments, except perhaps the most stressed environments such as the McMurdo Dry Valleys, continental Antarctica. For example, Loof (1971) reported 89 nematode species across a range of sites at 79° N in Spitzbergen in the Arctic, while Nielsen et al. (2011b) reported 37 taxa from samples collected on Byers Peninsula (62° N), maritime Antarctica. Moreover, a recent study using molecular methods confirmed that the species richness of high Arctic tundra can be surprisingly high, with α-diversities comparable to those observed in Malaysian tropical rainforest and a significant overlap in species (defined as 99% OTU similarity) among the tropical and tundra sites indicating potential broad distributions (Kerfahi et al. 2016). However, nematode β- and γ-diversity was observed to be greater in the rainforest likely driven by greater plant diversity and environmental variability. Finally, the authors found that there were relatively more omnivore and insect parasites in the tundra site. Hence, it is clear that there are substantial gaps in the coverage of existing datasets, and greater taxonomic resolution is required for more robust conclusions to be drawn.

Ant species richness has long been known to decrease with latitude (Kusnezov 1957). Using a survey of published records of ants from 65 sites in the British Isles and northern Europe, Cushman et al. (1993) found that ant species richness decreased with increasing latitude. The authors interestingly also found evidence that ant body size increased with increasing latitude. Similarly, a survey of more than 5,000 ant species records from 49 locations in the Americas showed strong decreases in species richness with increasing latitude, with the pattern being robust across different plot sizes (Kaspari et al. 2003). The distribution of ant species diversity is, however, asymmetric with more species in the southern hemisphere than in the northern hemisphere at comparable latitudes (Dunn et al. 2009). This pattern is in part explained by differences in contemporary climate and phylogeny (see Section 4.1). Furthermore, another study suggested that ant species diversity and predatory function decrease as you move from the tropical regions to temperate and cold regions (Jeanne 1979), indicating a shift in the functional attributes of ant assemblages. Termites are also more diverse in subtropical and tropical biomes (Eggleton 1994, Lavelle and Spain 2001), but as for the ants the pattern is asymmetric (Eggleton 1994), with the southern hemisphere supporting more species than similar latitudes in the northern hemisphere possibly driven by differences in climate (Dunn et al. 2009,

Eggleton 2000). In the case of termites, there are also substantially more endemic species in southern temperate regions. In particular, it has been proposed that the protection from repeated glaciation episodes dating as far back as the Permian may have benefitted the assemblages in the southern hemisphere. Moreover, there is a correlation between termite richness, at the genus level, and net primary productivity (NPP), but at similar levels of NPP there are substantial differences in genus richness among biographical regions with more species in Afrotropical than Neotropical and Oriental biomes possibly driven by differences in rates of speciation (Eggleton 2000).

Other soil fauna taxa similarly show latitudinal species richness gradients. For example, the species richness of springtails increases with latitude through central Europe (Ulrich and Fiera 2009) and in a synthesis of the distribution of earthworms in France, Mathieu and Davies (2014) found evidence of latitudinal gradients in earthworm diversity. However, contrasting patterns were observed for α- and γ-diversity defined as earthworm site-level diversity and regional (150 km radius around a sampling site) diversity, respectively. The authors found that earthworm γ-diversity decreased at higher latitudes but that α-diversity increased. This pattern appeared to be associated with past glaciation patterns, with higher diversity at the site level outside the refugia. The authors propose that this could be due to competitive exclusion at sites where earthworms have been present for longer. The study also showed that γ-diversity increased with the (estimated) temperature during the last glacial maxima and present-day mean annual precipitation. By contrast, α-diversity decreased with the temperature during the last glacial maxima. Moreover, the authors determined that species found in the more northern latitudes have greater latitudinal ranges. The fact that the complexity of earthworm assemblages is greater at lower latitudes (Lavelle 1983) and that there is an exceptionally high level of earthworm endemism in tropical rainforests (Lavelle and Lapied 2003) further indicate the existence of a latitudinal species richness gradient in earthworm assemblages.

Hence, it appears that we are yet to fully understand the mechanisms that contribute to the observed latitudinal gradients in biodiversity. A recent paper provides a new take on the possible mechanisms underlying observed differences in the diversity–latitude relationship slope among taxa. The authors used field data and literature records to investigate differences in diversity gradients among a broad range of taxa from prokaryotes to soil micro- and mesofauna to larger organisms such as trees (Weiser et al. 2018). The results indicated that the steepness of the diversity–latitude relationship slope was influenced by both the body size of the organisms and the likely population size prompting the authors to support the abundance-adaptation hypothesis. Briefly, the abundance-adaptation hypothesis states that both geologically older taxa and taxa that have faster generation times (such as smaller organisms) have had more opportunity to disperse to, and diversify within, novel habitats. This requires the assumption that taxa have their roots in tropical environments, that taxa from older clades have produced more individuals than those from more recent clades, and that clades with faster generation times have higher rates of evolution and therefore potential for adaptation to the new environmental conditions. Their results fit this pattern very well, with smaller and widespread taxa showing more shallow or even insignificant diversity–latitude slopes, while larger taxa with longer generation times such as trees, bats, and birds, showed steeper slopes. This is an intriguing approach that provides possible mechanisms to explain the observed differences in diversity–latitude gradient slopes among taxa that deserve further exploration with more robust data.

4.5 Altitudinal Gradients

Similar to latitudinal patterns one could expect that the diversity of soil fauna would decrease with increasing latitude due to a decrease in the quantity and diversity of resources, harsh environmental conditions, and smaller geographical areas with habitable ecosystems (Gaston 2000). However, the pattern can vary substantially between taxa with some showing linear decreases in species richness as altitude increases and others a humpbacked relationship with highest species richness at intermediate elevation (Figure 4.6). Indeed monotonic decreases in species richness with increasing elevation may not be the norm, with many taxa showing either insignificant decreases in species richness until mid-elevation or a peak at lower to mid elevations and then decreases with increasing elevation (Rahbek 1995). The author highlights one notable explanation for this pattern: Particularly prominent in the tropical regions is the presence of a condensation zone somewhere along the elevation gradient where clouds are more common. This alters the microclimate, in many cases favourably, and can therefore increase species richness causing these hump-shaped species richness–elevation relationships.

Altitudinal patterns in soil fauna diversity have received a fair bit of attention. The current literature indicates that species richness per unit area generally decreases with increasing altitudes, but as mentioned it is

4.5 Altitudinal Gradients · 145

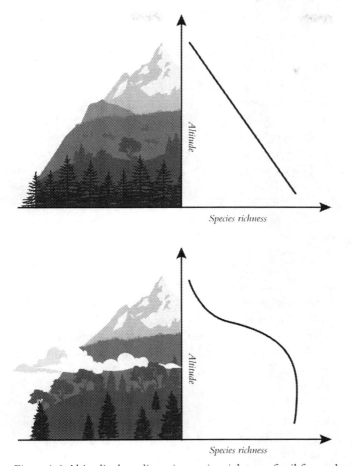

Figure 4.6 Altitudinal gradients in species richness of soil fauna show contrasting patterns. While there are examples of near-linear decreases in species richness with increasing elevation (upper panel), there are also many examples where soil fauna species richness peaks at intermediate elevation (lower panel). In many cases, this appears to be related to climatic conditions, particularly zones of cloud formation, or the existence of ecosystem transition zones that provide greater habitat variability. However, the existence of less favourable ecosystems at low elevations, such as deserts or degraded sites, can also contribute to such a pattern. Moreover, there can be divergent patterns within groups of soil fauna.
For example, cold adapted species might show a humpbacked relationship with elevation at mid- to high-elevation but be competitively excluded by warm adapted species at lower elevation. Where the two groups overlap, there might be a peak in species richness.

not always a linear relationship. For example, nematode and rotifer abundance and species richness was observed to show a humpbacked relationship with elevation at two contrasting altitudinal gradients in Indian Himalayan cold deserts (3,800–4,700 m and 4,500–6,200 m, respectively) (Devetter et al. 2017). However, the relatively low species richness and abundances observed at the lower elevation sites is likely caused by these being cold deserts. Indeed, the highest abundances and species richness were observed in more fertile samples found at mid-elevation sites in this study. Moreover, there were changes in feeding strategies with increasing elevation, coinciding with ecosystem changes. The abundance of nematodes but not species richness was observed to decrease with elevation in New Zealand tussock grasslands (Yeates 1974). However, some studies have observed changes in assemblage structure along elevational gradients. For example, it was observed that bacterial-feeding nematodes dominated at 1,000, 2,000, and 3,000 m in a tropical montane rainforest in the Andes, but that plant parasitic nematodes were replaced by hyphal-feeding nematodes with increasing elevation (Traunspurger et al. 2017). The change in nematode assemblage structure was strongly correlated with shifts in litter C:N ratio and fungal biomass.

The decrease in species richness with increasing elevation seems like a robust pattern in ant and termite assemblages. This has been observed in ants in the Smoky Mountains (Cole 1940, Sanders et al. 2007) and along an altitudinal gradient in Malaysia (Brühl et al. 1999) and in termites in Sarawak (Collins 1980). Similarly, Brühl et al. (1999) investigated leaf litter ant assemblages along an altitudinal gradient ranging from 560 to 2,600 m in primary forests in Malaysia. They found a very strong, exponential decrease in ant species richness with increasing elevation, with no ants at all found at the site at 2,600 m. Moreover, there was high species turnover between sampling locations, with 73% of all 283 species present at only one elevation, indicating that ant species at this site have very narrow altitudinal range. Another study examined ant assemblages along altitudinal transects of 12 South Korean mountains up to approximately 2,000 m elevation and found that ant species richness was negatively related to elevation across all sites (Kwon et al. 2014). However, the authors also noted that this was not uniformly true across all taxa, with the richness of known cold-adapted species showing a humpbacked relationship with elevation. A likely explanation of this pattern is that cold-adapted species may dominate high-elevation sites because they are better able to survive these conditions, but too severe of a temperature will inevitably limit the richness of even cold-adapted species. At the same time, cold-tolerant

ant species are likely to be outcompeted by more competitive species at lower elevation. Together these constraints would predict a unimodal distribution of cold-adapted ant species across an altitudinal gradient. Several other studies support the general decrease in ant species richness at high-elevation relation to lowland ecosystems even though they do not provide specific insight into the pattern across elevational gradients. For example, Brown (1973) reported markedly lower ant species richness in high-elevation tropical forests compared to lowland forests, and no ants were found at Mount Mulu, Sarawak, at 2,376 m (Collins 1980) or Volcan Barva, Costa Rica, at 2,600 m (Atkin and Proctor 1988). A study of ant assemblages in six subregions of the Australian wet tropics covering elevations ranging from 100–1,300 m altitude found no significant relationship between ant species diversity and elevation, except for a slight peak at mid-elevation (Nowrouzi et al. 2016). However, there was a strong shift in ant assemblage structure across the altitudinal gradients in all subregions, with a particularly noticeable turnover in composition from 600–800 m elevation. The authors note that this shift is aligned with the persistent orographic cloud formation and an associated change in vegetation type. Other studies have also shown species richness of ants peaking at mid-range elevations. For example, ant species richness along four elevational transects on mountains in Madagascar peak at around 800 m elevation and one study hypothesised that this was due to the mixing of a low-elevation and high-elevation assemblage (Fisher 1999a, Fisher 1999b). As a final example, a study that assessed ant assemblages at 22 sites in the Great Smoky Mountains National Park found that there was a monotonic decrease in ant species richness with increasing altitude across an elevational gradient from 379–1,742 m (Sanders et al. 2007). The authors concluded that the best predictor of ant species richness was temperature.

Several other studies have produced evidence for a humpbacked relationship with elevation so that species richness is greatest at mid-range elevation, i.e. dipteral richness was greatest at 1,300–1,700 m elevation and beetle richness at 500–1,200 m in Sarawak (Collins 1980). Similarly, Loranger et al. (2001) found that springtail species richness showed a humpbacked relationship with elevation peaking at 950–2,150 m elevation in the French Alps. González et al. (2007) found that the species richness of earthworms increases from 0–1,000 m elevation in Puerto Rico. It seems likely that the species richness would decrease at even higher elevation, with these findings supporting a humpbacked species richness-altitudinal gradient for earthworms as well. There is also evidence that dung beetle species richness show a humpbacked relationship with elevation. A survey of dung beetle assemblages along elevation gradients of ~1,000–2,250 m elevation in five regions of the Columbian Andes found that the species richness of dung beetles overall did decrease significantly with elevation, but that there was a peak in richness at mid-level elevations, i.e. 1,250–1,500 m (Escobar et al. 2005). Hence, these are clear but contrasting changes in soil fauna diversity and abundance across altitudinal gradients. Specifically, one can expect a gradual decrease in species richness at least above low- to mid-range elevations. The existence of a richness peak at mid-range elevation is generally associated with vegetation transition zones or the cloud formation zone whereby more species can co-exist in a narrow elevation range. However, different functional groups will show contrasting patterns depending on their life history traits and feeding preferences.

4.6 Regional versus Local Species Richness

A recurring theme within macroecology is that local species richness is (intuitively) limited by regional species richness, and that local species richness is positively correlated with the regional species pool size. This pattern can be measured at multiple scales comparing, for example, the species richness of a given site to that of a region or a region to a continent, but it can also be approached at smaller scales. In essence, the species present within a given area is a subset of the larger species pool at the next level (i.e. plot versus site, site versus landscape, landscape versus region, etc.). A strong linear, non-asymptotic relationship between regional and local species richness indicates that local assemblages are not saturated in species, instead being limited by the regional species pool. At very fine scales local species richness that display saturation relative to the regional species pool would indicate that the richness of local assemblages might be limited by biotic interactions. Many studies that have investigated soil fauna species richness across spatial scales would provide insight into this pattern, but few studies explicitly report on the pattern. However, the few studies available indicate that small-scale species richness is strongly related to and limited by species richness at a larger scale. For example, Nielsen et al. (2014) found that nematode family richness at the plot level was positively related to site-level family richness across 12 sites at a global scale. Similarly, Sanders et al. (2007) found that ant species richness in 1 m^2 plots within a site was strongly related to species richness of a larger 50 m × 50 m plot. Another study found that the species richness and co-existence of earthworms in agricultural fields in France were always lower than expected based on regional species richness, leading the authors to conclude that competitive exclusion played a role in structuring local earthworm assemblages (Decaëns et al. 2008). This finding supports the value of comparing local and regional species richness to investigate patterns in soil fauna assemblage structure. Data mining of existing datasets could likely provide substantial insight into these relationships.

4.7 Distribution of Rare versus Abundant Species

The abundance-range relationship appears to be a universal macroecological pattern, whereby species that are locally more abundant have greater ranges at regional to global scales. The relationship was observed as early as through the work by Darwin (1859), and has since been validated for a broad range of multicellular organisms (Brown 1984, Gaston et al. 1997, Soininen and Heino 2005). There are still uncertainties as to what causes this pattern, but Gaston et al. (1997) discuss eight different mechanisms that might contribute. Two mechanisms are non-biological, sampling effects and phylogenetic interdependence, whereby undersampling contributes to the underestimation of rare species' ranges and phylogenetic relationships can result in sampling independence, respectively. These non-biological effects should be taken into account during data analysis and interpretation, but the authors note that they are unlikely to be the main cause of observed abundance-range relationships. The biological drivers include range position, resource breadth and abundance, habitat selection, meta-population dynamics, and vital rates. Specifically, species that are found close to the edge of their geographical range may only be present in a small part of the study area, while species that use a broader range of resources or a resource that is available in larger quantities are likely to be more common. The habitat selection mechanism proposes that species occupy more habitats and larger ranges when they are abundant through density-dependent habitat selection driven by intraspecific competition. The existence of meta-population dynamics would allow an abundant species to be more widespread through continuous dispersal into less favourable habitats, and, lastly, species with lower density-dependent mortality rates may attain higher population sizes. There was some support for individual mechanisms, but there was not unequivocal support for any of them either. These mechanisms have yet to be tested belowground. As outlined above, there is robust evidence for positive abundance-range relationships in aboveground assemblages. There is less evidence of abundance-range relationships belowground, but there is no reason to expect that soil fauna should not conform to this pattern. There are few reported abundance-range relationships published for soil fauna, despite the increasing number of large-scale surveys. The existing data, however, suggest that abundance-range relationships are the norm. For example, in a global scale investigation of nematode assemblages, Nielsen et al. (2014) found that families that were more abundant within sites were also distributed more broadly across both plots and sites. However, the relative influence of the mechanisms outlined by Gaston et al. (1997) may differ among soil fauna taxa and compared to organisms aboveground.

4.8 Summary

There is clear evidence from a broad range of taxa that soil fauna shows distinct biogeographical patterns with noticeable differences among phyla. There is currently substantial evidence that at least a few species of most common soil fauna phyla have restricted biogeographical distributions. Differences in biogeography among phyla appear to be related to aspects of their evolutionary history, in particular when phyla diverged and the rate of evolution, their body size, and dispersal ability. Hence, smaller-bodied soil fauna with efficient dispersal strategies are likely to be predominantly of cosmopolitan distribution, whereas larger-bodied soil fauna with lesser dispersal abilities are likely to show more restricted geographical distribution. However, there are a few exceptions to this pattern, with the notable ones being that species that evolved more recently are increasingly likely to show geographically restricted distribution patterns simply because they have not yet had time to disperse to new habitats. Along the same line, species are unlikely to successfully disperse to highly isolated areas such as mountain tops and Antarctica that are in turn highly likely to support a greater proportion of endemic species. Moreover, soil fauna shows macroecological patterns that are at least in part similar to those found aboveground. For example, it appears that the species richness of soil fauna is related to latitude, with three divergent patterns recognised: (1) the species richness of some taxa, such as ants and termites, decreases in a near linear fashion with increasing latitude; (2) the richness of other taxa, including nematodes and mites, is relatively stable across latitudinal gradients, but decreases rapidly with increasing latitudes in the Polar Regions; and, (3) the species richness of some taxa may be highest in the temperate zones. Moreover, the species richness–latitudinal gradient is asymmetric in the ants and termites, seemingly due to environmental conditions and their evolutionary history. Similarly, the species richness of soil fauna decreases with increasing altitude, although mid-elevation peaks in richness are commonly observed. This is often associated with zones of cloud formation or transitions in vegetation types or can be related to the conditions at lower elevation. There is also robust evidence for significant species-area and distance decay relationships that are moderated by the dispersal ability and body size of the organism. Local species richness is correlated with regional species richness indicating that local assemblages are rarely saturated in species. However, this is based on very few observations and requires further evaluation. Finally, there is some evidence that rare types of soil fauna have more restricted distributions than common and abundant species, but this pattern similarly needs further quantification. A concerted effort to address biogeographical patterns in soil fauna assemblages could provide substantial insight into the mechanisms that structure assemblage structure and composition.

5 · *Soil Fauna Assemblages at Fine Scales to Landscapes*

Chapter 4 provided an overview of the mechanisms that influence the distribution of soil fauna at large scales (i.e. continental to global scales). Ultimately, the controls exerted on soil fauna distribution at these scales strongly modify the assemblage structure and composition at smaller scales from landscapes to ecosystem level to microhabitat scales. However, other mechanisms come into play at smaller scales. Ettema and Wardle (2002) and HilleRisLambers et al. (2012) provide robust frameworks that outline the likely controls on soil fauna distribution across scales (Figure 5.1). In brief, large-scale gradients in climate, soil, and vegetation type provide an environmental filter that controls which species occupy a given region. The species found at the regional scale essentially make up a 'regional species pool' from which the assemblages at smaller scales are derived. The main mode of dispersal within the region is passive and the ability of species to disperse moderates the assemblages at smaller scales. Vegetation composition and structure, the spatial distribution of individual plant species, and variation in edaphic variables become more important at the ecosystem level. The effects of ecosystem engineers including the soil fauna itself, however, influence the variability in the vegetation and edaphic properties. Moreover, biological processes such as reproduction, mortality, and active dispersal, and biotic interactions are likely to also become more important. At the finest scales, the spatial soil structure and distribution of resources (roots, organic particles) and biotic interactions including trophic interactions and competition likely dominate assemblage structure. In this chapter, I will provide an overview of the patterns of soil fauna assemblage structure observed at landscape scales, within ecosystems, and at fine scales, and the likely mechanisms underlying the observed patterns.

5.1 Landscape to Continental Scales

The identity of soil fauna found within a given defined and coherent terrestrial area is fundamentally governed by geological processes and evolutionary patterns, and the ability of an organism to disperse passively as discussed in Chapter 4. Within these boundaries, the structure and composition of soil fauna assemblages across large spatial scales, here defined as a smaller area encompassing a matrix of ecosystem types (henceforth, landscapes) to continental scales, is moderated by gradients in climate, and the spatial distribution vegetation and soil types (Ettema and Wardle 2002). Climate can often act as a robust proxy for broader environmental influences due to the role of rainfall and temperature in moderating the distribution of vegetation types and edaphic properties. However, the distribution of soil types is moderated by the geological history of the area, which, in turn, influences vegetation type and soil chemistry, with cascading impacts on soil fauna assemblages. Moreover, the distribution of vegetation and soil types is influenced by biological influences on the vegetation and edaphic variables, global changes, and disturbances and recovery through the process of succession with the dispersal ability of individual soil fauna taxa playing a significant role in the presence and absence of species. All these factors hence combine to influence soil fauna assemblages. The relative influences of these drivers of assemblage structure and composition differentially affect individual soil fauna taxa, but it is possible to make some broad generalisations as outlined below. These relationships are best explored through landscape scale to national or continental scale studies that sample a broad range of biomes, and such studies will be the focus of this section.

Climate plays a significant role in the spatial distribution of soil fauna assemblages but, as mentioned, the influences of climate are in part manifested through associated impacts on vegetation type and edaphic properties. Indeed, climate will often act as a 'proxy' that incorporates the influences acting via vegetation type and edaphic properties. Climate has accordingly been shown to be a good predictor of soil fauna assemblages as varied as protist (Bates et al. 2013), nematodes (Nielsen et al. 2014), mites (Nielsen et al. 2010a), springtails (Salmon et al. 2014), and enchytraeids (Briones et al. 2007a). Similarly, ant species diversity is moderated by climate, and, in particular, temperature with only a weak negative relationship between ant species diversity and rainfall (Dunn et al. 2009, Jenkins et al. 2011). Temperature therefore plays a key role in ant species distribution, with high species densities found in the wet tropics and in some dry tropical ecosystems (e.g. Bishop et al. 2014, Jenkins et al. 2011, Kaspari et al. 2004). While ant species diversity is not strongly related to rainfall, there is evidence that ant species richness

154 · Soil Fauna Assemblages at Fine Scales to Landscapes

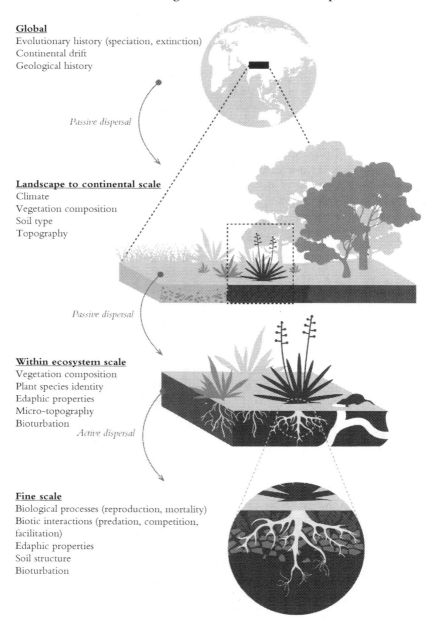

Figure 5.1 Schematic diagram illustrating patterns of environmental and biological filtering of soil fauna assemblages from global to local scales. In essence, the distribution of soil fauna at the global scale is largely governed by the geological history of Earth and the evolutionary history of the lineage investigated. However, the ability of a given organism to disperse passively will modify its distribution at

often increases with rainfall within biomes unless this is countered by increases in temperature (Chaladze 2012, Fisher 1999a, Pfeiffer et al. 2003). Hence, aridity may be a better predictor of ant distribution at smaller scales. However, the relationship between ant species diversity and rainfall shows contrasting patterns between continents. For example, Parr et al. (2004) found a strong relationship between ant species diversity and rainfall in tropical savannas in southern Africa. Similarly, a recent study of ant assemblages across a ~20° latitudinal gradient in the Brazilian Cerrado savanna found a positive relationship between rainfall and ant species diversity (Vasconcelos et al. 2018). By contrast, ant species richness is not strongly related to rainfall in north Australia. Sampling ant assemblages on silt, loam, and sandy soils in a single biome (tropical savanna) across a rainfall (650–1,400 mm rainfall per year) and latitudinal (12°50′ S–17°21′ S) gradient, Andersen et al. (2015) found no significant change in total ant species richness. On average the species richness of ants was considerably lower on clay (40) compared to sand (85.4) and loam (82.2), and the assemblages differed between clay on the one hand and sand and loam on the other. While total ant species richness was not related to latitude, rainfall, or temperature, the richness of individual genera showed contrasting relationships with rainfall ranging from positive to negative. Hence, there was a significant shift in ant assemblage structure across the rainfall gradient. The authors hypothesised that Australian ant assemblage diversity may be less sensitive to changes in rainfall than ant fauna elsewhere because of an evolutionary history associated with aridity.

Similar patterns are likely to be found for other soil fauna taxa. A recent study showed that oribatid and mesostigmatid mite assemblage structure in alpine moss-dominated ecosystems across 36 sites in the United Kingdom is related to climate, and that oribatid mite species richness was negatively related to daily maximum temperature, but positively

---

← the global scale. At a landscape to continental scale, the influence of climatic gradients, vegetation composition, soil type, and topography become more important. Whereas within ecosystems, the vegetation composition and plant species identity, variation in edaphic variables, micro-topography, and bioturbation is of greater importance. At this scale, active dispersal also becomes more important. At the finest scales, it is expected that biological processes and interactions combined with the microscale variation in edaphic, soil structure, and distribution of roots have a greater influence. The diagram is largely based on Ettema and Wardle (2002) (with permission from Elsevier Science Ltd), with additional information from HilleRisLambers et al. (2012) and Soininen (2012).

to minimum daily temperature, respectively (Mitchell et al. 2016). The authors indicated that projected climate changes for the UK alpine ecosystems might therefore negatively impact oribatid mite species richness in these ecosystems. Similar responses of alpine mite communities to variation in climate were observed by Hågvar and Klanderud (2009). There is, similarly, evidence that climate influences earthworm assemblages, but again the responses are context dependent. For example, the density and diversity of earthworms were not strongly related to climate in the Inland Pacific Northwest cereal production region, USA, across four land use management practices, instead showing a threshold of 330–370 mm MAP under which there were no earthworms present (Walsh and Johnson-Maynard 2016). Finally, wood- and grass-feeding termites are negatively related to rainfall, whereas this is not the case for soil-dwelling species (Bignell 2006), while climate moderates wire-worm (click beetle larvae; Coleoptera: Elateridae) assemblages in Russian oak forests across a 1,100 km latitudinal gradient (Penev 1992). Hence, climate can substantially influence soil fauna assemblages, but the patterns are not always straightforward. Indeed, mean annual precipitation and temperature may be important in describing large-scale patterns, but conditions at daily to seasonal and annual scales may be of greater importance. However, these relationships are rarely investigated in detail.

There is substantial evidence that vegetation type and edaphic properties influence soil fauna assemblages. For example, a regional-scale study of plant and nematode assemblages in 220 plots across 44 grassland sites on the Mongolian Plateau provided significant insight into the distribution of nematodes (Chen et al. 2016). Nematode biomass was strongly correlated to plant biomass across all sites, and nematode and plant α- and γ-diversity was similarly strongly related. Structural equation modelling indicated that these relationships were driven by climate and edaphic properties, but even when this was accounted for there was a weak positive relationship between nematode and plant biomass, and a stronger positive relationship between plant and nematode diversity. Similarly, a substantial landscape-scale study by Reay and Wallace (1981) of plant parasitic nematodes in South Australia, representing more than 600 samples collected at 108 sites distributed within a 75,000 km^2 area, showed that the distribution of nematodes was associated with vegetation composition (i.e. host plant preferences), which, in turn, is moderated by rainfall. The relationship with rainfall is not unexpected given that nematodes are essentially aquatic organisms. Indeed, nematode species often show distinct distributions related to soil water availability of habitats. For example, Yeates (1974) found that the plant parasitic nematode genus *Paratylenchus*, known to have a drought-resistant preadult stage, is common in dry tussock grasslands in New Zealand. By contrast, the Mononchoidea were restricted to wetter grasslands. The other microfauna is likely to show similar patterns given their fundamentally aquatic nature.

The soil meso- and macrofauna are also moderated by vegetation composition and edaphic properties and likely by associated changes in the microbial assemblage. For example, an early study observed significant changes in soil fauna across a sandy plain moisture and vegetation gradient in Denmark, with springtails and prostigmatid mites being predominant in drier soils and oribatid mites more abundant in wetter soils (Weis-Fogh 1948). In a recent large-scale project, EcoFINDERS, the investigators assessed mite assemblages at 36 sites in ten countries representing three different land-use types (arable, grassland, forestry), a latitudinal gradient and four bio-climatic zones (Creamer et al. 2016). Mite assemblage structure showed consistent patterns across land-use types and bio-climatic zones, but not latitude. Moreover, mite assemblage structure showed limited correlation with microbes, nematodes, or enchytraeids, but there was a significant correlation with springtail assemblage structure ($r = 0.43$, $p < 0.001$). Similarly, vegetation is one of the most important drivers of ant assemblage structure (Gotelli and Ellison 2002), with indirect impacts through alterations in the microclimate, and soil biological and physical properties, but there are also direct impacts associated with vegetation composition. One observed pattern is that ant species richness often increases with plant species richness. This has, for example, been observed in coastal dune vegetation (Chen et al. 2015). There is also evidence that ground-beetle assemblages are governed by geomorphology and elevation at large geographical scales (Schuldt and Assmann 2009) and vegetation type (e.g. meadow, marsh, heather, woodland) at the landscape scale (Scott and Anderson 2003). Moreover, significant influence of soil moisture on ground-beetle abundance and diversity was observed in German grasslands, with greatest diversity and abundance observed at intermediate soil moistures (Tietze 1968). Moreover, there is some evidence for a relationship between species richness of soil fauna and landscape-scale heterogeneity (Chust et al. 2003, Eggleton et al. 2005, Vanbergen et al. 2007), although this relationship has not yet been fully explored.

In a large-scale study in Scotland, Nielsen et al. (2010a) collected soil samples in two contrasting ecosystems (birch woodland, heather moorland) at 12 sites representing a broad range of environmental and climatic conditions to provide insight into the drivers of belowground assemblages focussing on mites and microbes. The authors found that among the mites, only the oribatid mites showed consistent differences between the two ecosystems across all sites, whereas mesostigmatid mite assemblages were only weakly related to vegetation type. However, both oribatid and mesostigmatid mite species richness was greater in the birch woodland than in heather moorland. Across all sites, oribatid and mesostigmatid mite assemblages were influenced both by vegetation composition, edaphic properties, particularly pH, and mean annual precipitation. The relationship with climate is likely stronger than their analyses suggest given the indirect effects on vegetation composition and soil properties. Moreover, the significant relationship with precipitation was not unexpected given that the sites represented a substantial rainfall gradient with MAP from roughly 700 to 2,250 mm. The temperature across the sites was less variable, likely contributing to rainfall being the main climate driver. In another large-scale study, the authors collected 684 samples across Wales associated with a national soil-monitoring program, providing insight into the environmental constraints on mite and springtail assemblages in particular (George et al. 2017). Across all sites and land-use types, all mesofauna except Mesostigmata were most abundant in lowland forests and least abundant in agricultural sites. Oribatid mites were least abundant in mineral soils and were related to all edaphic variables measured, except soil moisture. Mesostigmatid mites and springtails showed reduced abundance in peatlands, likely because of the high soil moistures observed in these ecosystems. The main taxonomic groups defined by the authors showed contrasting relationships with edaphic variables in general, with oribatid mites in most cases responding opposite to mesostigmatid mites and the springtail superfamilies Entomobryoidea and Poduroidea. For example, Oribatida was positively correlated with total C, total N, C:N ratio and 'soil water repellancy' (used as a proxy for water infiltration resistance), whereas the reverse was true for the mesostigmatid mites and the springtails. Similarly, oribatid mite abundance was negatively related to total P and pH, while the other groups were positively correlated to these variables or showed no correlation. Finally, while mesostigmatid mite and springtail abundances were negatively related to soil water content, oribatid mite abundances were not related to soil water content. Because of the inverse relationships with edaphic variables among taxa, the total mesofauna abundances show more limited effects, with a negative correlation with soil water content and pH, and positive correlation with soil water repellancy. These results highlight that soil fauna abundances show group-specific relationships with environmental variables that may be useful for characterising ecosystems. However, greater taxonomic resolution will be essential for using such investigations for bioindication purposes.

Very few studies have investigated soil fauna assemblages at large scale in Australia. However, in a notable exception, Wood (1971) studied microarthropod, crustacean, and nematode fauna of arid, semi-arid, and sub-humid soils of Australia, focussing on the distribution of the springtail *Folsomides deserticola*. From samples collected at 184 sites, he found that *F. deserticola* is more or less confined to arid to semi-arid ecosystems and was most frequently found in desert sclerophyllous grassland and desert steppe. More broadly, the densities of microarthropods other than *F. deserticola* decreased with increasing aridity, both in terms of annual and seasonal aridity. Despite springtails often being considered more sensitive to water stress, the abundances of springtails often exceeded that of mites across the dryland habitats. This pattern was strongly influenced by the high population sizes of *F. deserticola* though. Prostigmatid mites dominated the mite assemblages, although oribatid mites were important at many sites as well. The prostigmatid to oribatid mite ratio generally increased with aridity, a pattern that reflects results from other studies. Mesostigmatid mites were found in low densities, particularly in the arid sites. Interestingly, the crustaceans, dominated by calanoid Copepoda and bosminid Cladocera generally considered aquatic to semi-aquatic, were relatively common in the arid to semi-arid ecosystems and less prevalent at wetter sites. The author further investigated nematode assemblages at nine sites in Southern Australia and found that their densities were low and correlated positively to the sand fraction and negatively to soil water content. He noted that soil water content was related to clay content and that soils with greater water content do not necessarily contain more available water. While the abundances (17,600–313,500 ind. m^{-2}) are lower than in many other ecosystems, they are comparable to those found in other dryland ecosystems.

A survey of the spatial distribution of three Antarctic springtail species across a latitudinal gradient in Victoria Land, continental Antarctica provided high-resolution insight into large-scale patterns of distribution (Caruso et al. 2009). More than 130 sites were surveyed over a ten-year period for the presence of *Friesea grisea*, *Gomphiocephalus hodgsoni*, and *Gressittacantha terranova*. It was noteworthy that none of the three species showed similar distributional patterns, with various longitudinal and latitudinal patterns being the norm. The spatial patterns were to some degree related to spatially structured climatic gradients, but the results suggested that past geological events have greatly influenced present-day distribution. The study illustrates how difficult it can be to accurately describe species distributional patterns let alone whole assemblages. Similarly, a large-scale survey of soil fauna assemblages of East Antarctica covering more than 2,000 km from Framnes Mountains to Bailey Peninsula provide insight into the distribution of soil fauna (Velasco-Castrillón et al. 2014b). The most common and widespread organisms were rotifers occurring in 87% of the 109 samples processed. Nematodes and tardigrades were relatively common (71% and 57% of samples, respectively), while ciliates and mites were relatively rare and occurred in smaller numbers. In all cases, the abundance and composition of assemblages were related to soil properties, particularly P, NO_3^-, and salinity, and the highest total soil micro- and mesofauna abundances were observed where visible vegetation was present. However, the correlation with edaphic variables varied both within and between the groups of soil fauna surveyed. The authors conclude that continental Antarctic soil fauna assemblages are likely to be the result of present environmental conditions and legacies of landscape formation, with limited influence of geographical region. It is clear that soil fauna assemblages are moderated by climate, vegetation, and soil type but that the relative influence of these variables differ among soil fauna taxa.

5.2 Ecosystem Scales

As highlighted in the previous sections, soil fauna assemblages are at the ecosystem level modified by mechanisms that govern the distribution of soil fauna at the landscape scale. In particular, climate, vegetation, and soil type play a key role in structuring soil fauna assemblages at landscape scales. Within ecosystems the role of vegetation structure, plant species identity, the distribution of resources and gradients in edaphic properties become more important. Furthermore, biological processes, such as aggregation behaviour, active dispersal, and biotic interactions, more strongly influence soil fauna assemblage structure and composition. The influences of biological processes on the distribution of individual populations will, however, differ substantially between soil fauna taxa with divergent life history strategies and functional traits. This likely contributes to the seemingly rather random nature of shifts in soil fauna assemblage structure and composition through space and time observed within ecosystems.

5.2.1 Vegetation

There is substantial evidence that the plant community modifies belowground assemblages and soil food web structure (Bezemer et al. 2010, De Deyn et al. 2004, Keith et al. 2009, Viketoft et al. 2009). Hence, it follows that the spatial distribution of plant species and their litter will influence the distribution of soil fauna and soil food web structure both within and among ecosystems. In extension, the presence of herbivores aboveground is likely to modify belowground assemblages, particularly through their interactions with the plant assemblage. The spatial structure of the vegetation even influences the distribution of macrofauna (Mathieu et al. 2009), which in turn would influence the distribution of micro- and mesofauna. Conversely, the distribution of soil fauna within ecosystems modifies the vegetation composition aboveground. For example, it has been shown that the plant community growing in mounds built by ants in the Netherlands (Blomqvist et al. 2000), termites in eastern Australia (Spain and McIvor 1988), and gophers in Californian grasslands (Hobbs and Mooney 1985) differ from that of the surrounding vegetation. This in turn will impact soil fauna assemblages more broadly.

The distribution of plants within an ecosystem is an important driver of soil fauna assemblages. For example, nematode assemblages have been shown to be plant species specific with distinct assemblages found in the rhizosphere of eight different plant species in an experimental grassland, while soil food web structure and mite, enchytraeid, and soil macrofauna assemblages differed between the legume *Lotus corniculatus* and the non-leguminous forb *Plantago lanceolata* (Bezemer et al. 2010). There is similarly evidence that plant species identity influences mesostigmatid mite assemblages. For example, a study compared mesostigmatid mite assemblages of three plant species (the grass: *Bromus sterilis*, legume: *Medicago sativa*, and herb: *Taraxacum officinale*) in Austrian grassy arable fallows of different ages (2–3, 6–8, or 12–15 years) by collecting soil samples associated with each of the plant species (Wissuwa et al. 2012). The results showed that the age of the grassy fallows had a substantial impact on mesostigmatid mite assemblages. Moreover, mesostigmatid mite densities differed between three plant species, and there was a weak albeit significant shift in assemblage structures. The authors hypothesised that the high mesostigmatid mite abundances associated with the grass *B. sterilis* was likely due to higher springtail abundances and therefore greater prey availability. Similarly, in a relatively homogenous Arctic *Saxifraga*-lichen heath, the dominant plant species supported distinct microarthropod assemblages within a 20 m^2 patch (Coulson et al. 2003).

Another study found limited evidence for a strong host-specificity of oribatid and mesostigmatid mites in Australia (Osler and Beattie 2001). The authors surveyed mite assemblages underneath three potential host trees (*Eucalyptus pilularis*, *E. propinqua*, *Allocasuarina torulosa*) known to have differential effects on soil properties. Of the 79 oribatid and 34 mesostigmatid mite species discovered, only three oribatid mite species, and no mesostigmatid mite species, showed signs of host-specificity. However, tree-host identity had consistent effects on mite assemblage structure. Hence, the distribution of canopy species can modify the spatial distribution of soil fauna assemblages, even if they have limited impacts on individual species. Some plants, however, have particularly great impacts on belowground assemblages. For example, in a ten-year-long plant removal study conducted during primary succession, St John et al. (2012) found that the absence of the dominant nitrogen-fixing shrub, *Carmichaelia odorata* (Figure 5.2), had substantial negative effects both above- and belowground. The removal of the shrub contributed

Figure 5.2 The N-fixing shrub *Carmichaelia odorata* has been shown to play an important role during primary succession in a New Zealand South Island montane river valley.
Courtesy of Chris Morse.

to lower biomass of all soil fauna groups observed including plant parasitic, bacterial-feeding and predatory nematodes, fungal-feeding and predatory mites, enchytraeids and rotifers, with bacterial-feeding fauna being more negatively affected than fungal-feeding fauna. The impacts on the soil fauna thus span at least three trophic levels. Moreover, the shrub removal reduced the overall α- but not β-diversity of soil fauna assemblages. These effects were likely related to the significant reductions in the biomass of other woody plants that form relationships with AM fungi, soil C and N levels, and microbial biomass, suggesting significant bottom-up constraints on soil fauna abundances. This point to a potential great effect of the loss of key functional types of plant through their effect on litter inputs and changes in biogeochemical cycles.

Patchiness in leaf litter is another driver of soil fauna assemblage structure by moderating the quantity and quality of detrital resources to the decomposer assemblage (Wallwork 1976). In particular, leaf litter C:N ratio is important to palatability, with lower C:N ratios generally associated with greater decomposition rates. However, cellulose, lignin, and secondary metabolite contents are also important in litter decomposition processes. Accordingly, it was found that litter from eight New Zealand rainforest canopy and understory plant species differently influence soil fauna assemblages, each favouring particular subsets of the local soil fauna assemblage (Wardle et al. 2006). However, soil micro- and mesofauna abundance showed limited responses to litter mixing (two, four, or eight species compared to monocultures), contrasting somewhat with effects observed in other studies. There were at times impacts of litter mixing on nematode and macrofauna diversity, but the responses were idiosyncratic and weaker than litter identity. Another mesocosm study found that plant shoot litter identity had a greater impact on soil decomposer assemblages than the live plant itself, with *Trifolium repens* litter supporting greater abundances of oribatid mites and higher body mass ratios of earthworms than *P. lanceolata* likely due to a great plant shoot N content (Eisenhauer and Reich 2012). Hence, the spatial distribution of plant species can modify the distribution of soil fauna within ecosystems, while differences in plant species contribute to differences among ecosystem types. Accordingly, there is evidence that soil fauna, including nematodes and microarthropods, show spatial patterns that are correlated with individual trees (Görres et al. 1998, Klironomos et al. 1999). By contrast, increased canopy heterogeneity can weaken spatial patterns (Aubert et al. 2003).

It has been hypothesised based on literature reviews of experimental data (e.g. Bardgett and Wardle 2010) that plant species richness should have limited effects on belowground assemblages. However, a recent long-term study concluded that plant species richness has a much greater effect on belowground assemblages and food web structure than either CO_2 or N deposition and with no interactive effects on soil fauna assemblages (Eisenhauer et al. 2013). In this study, the authors found strong effects of plant species richness on several groups of soil nematodes and microarthropods. Increased plant species richness generally had a positive effect on both nematode and microarthropod abundances, and on soil fauna species richness overall, although in some cases the effects peaked at intermediate plant species richness (i.e. four plant species treatments had greater abundance of some groups than one or nine plant species treatments). As outlined in Chapter 3, it appears likely that the limited effects of plant species richness in other studies were due to short treatment durations (Eisenhauer et al. 2012). It therefore appears that plant species richness may be a more important variable than previously acknowledged, and it may be important to maintain aboveground species diversity to support belowground biodiversity (Eisenhauer et al. 2013). Another large grassland plant diversity manipulation provided further insight into the effect of plant species diversity on above- and belowground food web structure (Scherber et al. 2010). In this case, plant assemblages in 82 plots each measuring 20 m × 20 m were manipulated to provide a plant species gradient ranging from 1 to 60 species native to the area. To do this, plots were seeded with 1, 2, 4, 8, 16, or 60 plant species and the effects on above- and belowground food webs were followed from 2002 to 2009. In this study, the realised plant species richness had significant effects on the abundance and species richness of both above- and belowground fauna, but the effects decreased at higher trophic levels and for omnivores, although the effects were lesser belowground than aboveground. Belowground, particularly the protozoans and herbivores including plant parasitic nematodes and macrofaunal grazers showed strong responses. The authors hypothesised that the positive effects were mediated by increased root biomass production or exudation by plants. There was therefore strong evidence for substantial bottom-up effects on the soil food web. Most groups responded positively to increased plant species richness, but this was not the case across all taxa, with less invasive species in the diverse plant assemblages aboveground. While this was not evaluated belowground, it appears likely that increased plant diversity may also suppress invasive species belowground. Similarly, Zaller and Arnone III (1999) found that earthworm biomass and density increased with plant species in an experimental grassland with treatments ranging from 5 to 12 to 31 species in a calcareous grassland, mainly due to the increase in the abundance of the endogeic species *Allolobophora rosea* and to a lesser degree *Nicodrilus caliginosus*. Observational studies further support the hypothesis that vegetation diversity is important to soil fauna assemblages. For example, in a study of 92 temperate grassland soils in Germany, Birkhofer et al. (2011) found that legume and grass species richness was positively related to soil fauna feeding activities facilitated by changes in resource availability and microclimate. This indicates that plant diversity is strongly related to soil fauna activity with knock-on effects on soil processes that could have positive feedbacks on plant productivity through increased nutrient turnover.

Given the established link between the vegetation aboveground and the biota belowground, including the soil fauna, there has long been an interest in the effects of herbivores. The main pathways through which herbivores influence belowground communities include changes in vegetation composition and biomass through consumption and damage, impacts on C and nutrient availability, and spatial distribution through the deposition of dung and urine, and impacts on soil physical characteristics caused by trampling and burrowing (Ayres et al. 2004, Bardgett and Wardle 2003, Eldridge and Koen 2008). The effects of herbivores on belowground assemblages were assessed using a meta-analysis by Andriuzzi and Wall (2017). The authors canvassed the literature to recover 278 cases from 61 publications where belowground responses to herbivores were assessed through herbivore exclusions. Herbivores were broadly classified as small (lagomorphs), medium (sheep, deer, reindeer), and large (cattle, moose) to allow comparison across body sizes. Most of the soil animal responses were for mesofauna, with microfauna and macrofauna represented by nematodes and earthworms only, respectively. Across all studies, the microfauna (i.e. nematodes) showed a significant response, with lower abundances when herbivores are present. When considering trophic levels, belowground herbivores and decomposers tended to be negatively impacted by aboveground herbivore presence, but the response was not significant. Similarly, only some taxa showed consistent responses to herbivory, with more Oribatida and predatory nematodes in the absence of large herbivores. The soil fauna responses to herbivores were, however, moderated by herbivore body size and climate. In particular, the presence of small to medium herbivores had no effect on soil fauna abundances, whereas the presence of large herbivores had significant negative effects. The authors speculated that large herbivores have greater impacts than small to medium-sized herbivores because their presence causes more disturbance and compaction and have greater impacts on the vegetation. Moreover, the response of decomposers switched from negative to positive at around 850 mm mean annual precipitation. Finally, they proposed a framework for predicting the effect of herbivores in which the impact of herbivores increases with body size and switches from positive in productive ecosystems with limited abiotic disturbance to negative in less productive and more disturbed ecosystems. They highlight that more data are needed across biomes, particularly tropical regions, with better representation across soil animal groups including protists and macrofauna, and more detail on soil physical and chemical characteristics. There is also more recent evidence that the effect of herbivores is moderated by vegetation composition itself. In an herbivore exclusion and plant removal study in an alpine meadow on the Tibetan Plateau, Wang et al. (2018) found that the presence of yak as the main grazer moderated the effect of a dominant shrub *Dasiphora fruticosa* on nematode abundances. Specifically, the shrub had limited effects on nematode assemblages in the absence of the yak. By contrast, a strong negative direct effect of shrub presence on nematode abundance was observed in the presence of yak, although the negative direct effect of the shrub was somewhat compensated for by an indirect positive effect on nematode abundances via an increase in grass biomass. The presence of the shrub also had a minor impact on the nematode assemblage composition in the presence of the herbivore. This study highlights how intricate the aboveground–belowground linkages are, making it difficult to predict the consequences of herbivores across ecosystem types. One potential criticism of such studies is that they often have unnaturally high densities of livestock causing unrealistic impacts through disturbance and soil compaction.

5.2.2 Edaphic Variables

There is substantial evidence that soil properties and chemistry influence soil fauna assemblages, with the key variables being soil organic matter content, elemental stoichiometry, pH, and soil water content. For example, the biomass of soil fauna is likely to increase with soil organic matter content at least until a certain threshold, with shifts in assemblage structure and composition moderated by the C:N ratio. Specifically, soils with 'low' C:N ratios are likely to be dominated by the bacterial food web, with the relative abundance of fungi increasing in 'high' C:N soil food webs, which in turn moderates the soil fauna assemblages (Bardgett 2005).

Similarly, very low or very high soil pH will constrain soil fauna diversity and biomass, with greater richness and biomass observed at near neutral pH. Associated with this is a shift in soil fauna assemblage structure and composition acting over more moderate soil pH gradients. Finally, soil water content is a critical resource, with biological activity impaired at very low soil water content. By contrast, water saturation will have detrimental effects, particularly when soils become anoxic and soil fauna is unable to escape to more favourable conditions. Noteworthy, however, is that soil water content is highly variable through both space and time, generally making it difficult to correlate soil fauna assemblages with soil water content measurements. Moreover, several other edaphic variables can influence soil fauna assemblages through various mechanisms, and edaphic variables often interact to influence soil fauna assemblages, making it difficult to tease apart the critical drivers of assemblage structure and composition.

Organic matter is a key component of the soil and an essential resource fuelling the detrital food web and modifying soil fauna assemblages. Moreover, soil organic matter exerts a substantial impact on soil structure and water-holding capacity, which in turn modifies biological activity. It is well known that soil biotic communities differ between soils with varying levels of soil organic matter, although the patterns may not always be clear. For example, a study of microarthropod assemblages in two contrasting semi-arid ecosystems in eastern Australia found a positive relationship between soil organic carbon, a robust proxy for soil organic matter content, in the soil surface and the richness and abundance of mites at only one of the sites. One of the key differences between the sites was related to their soil organic C contents, with 0.4%–1.75% and 4%–9.5% at the two sites, respectively (Noble et al. 1996). It appears that soil organic C was a limiting factor at the site with medium-textured soil but not at the site with heavy-textured clay soil, so that other variables may instead be limiting mite abundances here. Similarly, sites with high organic matter concentrations can be biological hotspots. Much soil fauna is accordingly attracted by dung patches, and it has been shown that, for example, lumbricid earthworm assemblages in soils associated with dung pats differ from soils without dung pats (Boyd 1958). Hence, the distribution, composition, and quantity of organic matter is a strong driver of soil fauna assemblage composition.

Soil water content is highly important to soil biological assemblages, both directly by moderating the habitability of the soil itself with many organisms highly sensitive to very low soil water content or saturation of the soil but also indirectly via impacts on microbial and plant assemblages. Accordingly, many groups show a strong correlation with soil water content characteristics both within and among ecosystems. For example, it appears that protist assemblages are best understood in terms of soil water availability at an annual scale (Bates et al. 2013), with limited contribution of other edaphic variables known to influence these minute soil fauna. In particular, Dinophyceae were dominant in arid soils, while Ciliophora and Apicomplexa were more abundant in more humid soils, and Cercozoa was widespread with some tendency for higher dominance in drier soils. Soil moisture is, however, by nature a highly spatiotemporally variable factor, and it can be difficult to quantify the impacts of changes in soil moisture regimes. Hence, the conditions under which samples are collected may dictate how strong a relationship is observed between soil fauna assemblages and soil moisture. A better way to represent these relationships would be through spatial or temporal variation in soil moisture, for example, by quantifying mean soil moisture levels or extreme events that may have particularly large impacts on soil fauna assemblage structure. For example, research in the McMurdo Dry Valleys, Antarctica, has shown that flood events can have long-term impacts on assemblage structure that can be quantified in the following dry years (Barrett et al. 2008, Nielsen et al. 2012b). Importantly, extreme events, both drought and water logging, that expose indigenous species to conditions they cannot tolerate or avoid could impact on species distribution.

There is also strong evidence that soil pH influence soil fauna assemblages ranging from protozoans to nematodes to enchytraeids and earthworms (Wallwork 1976). It is well established that nematode assemblages are strongly governed by edaphic properties, including soil pH. In a survey of soil nematode assemblages on Byers Peninsula, Livingstone Island in maritime Antarctica, it was found that nematode densities, generic richness, and assemblage composition were best explained by variation in soil pH across the sampling sites (Nielsen et al. 2011c). Similarly, in a grazing exclusion and plant removal study undertaken in an alpine meadow, nematode assemblage structure was much more strongly related to soil organic matter content, soil water content, and pH than to the presence of a dominant shrub or yak, the regionally dominant large herbivore (Wang et al. 2018). Enchytraeids often dominate acidic soils where other ecosystem engineers are limited (Coulson and Whittaker 1978, Cragg 1961) and soil type, pH, and organic matter quality appear to be the main drivers of enchytraeid distribution (Briones 2009).

However, enchytraeid species richness is generally not reflected by high abundances, with species richness being positively related to pH (Nowak 2001, Standen 1984) and negatively with soil organic matter content (Kapusta et al. 2003). Other soil fauna assemblages are also related to soil pH. For example, the abundance of terrestrial litter-dwelling molluscs increases with pH from 4 to 6, while species richness peaks at around pH 5.5, across a range of ecosystems in the Pukeamaru Ecological District, northeast New Zealand (Barker and Mayhill 1999).

While soil organic matter, pH, and soil water content appear to be significant edaphic drivers of most soil fauna assemblages through direct and indirect effects, there are many other factors that can moderate soil fauna assemblage structure and composition. For example, the availability of calcium carbonate is important to arthropods such as snails, millipedes, and mites as they use this compound for strengthening their exoskeleton. Indeed, it has been estimated that up to 50% of the dry weight of the box mite *Steganacarus magnus* is calcium carbonate (Wallwork 1976). Soil pore air composition may also impact soil fauna, at least under extreme conditions, particularly oxygen concentrations. For example, in early work Van Gundy and Stolzy (1961) found that the development of galls on tomato roots decreased dramatically under reduced atmospheric oxygen concentrations, with a significant reduction in gall formation when oxygen concentrations were reduced from 21% to 5.5%. Nematodes were not able to develop successfully at concentrations below 3.5%. Hence, oxygen depletion of soils could have substantial effects on soil fauna assemblages, particularly over longer time spans. Finally, distinct zonal patterns were observed in mite community structure in salt marsh in South Wales associated with changes in inundation frequency and salt influences (Luxton 1967). Similar patterns observed for springtails in the Netherlands where topography, and accordingly, the likelihood of inundation, was a strong predictor of springtail assemblage structure and community-weighted functional trait composition (Widenfalk et al. 2015).

5.2.3 Spatial Patchiness

It is clear from the previous section that vegetation composition and edaphic properties modify soil fauna assemblages in ways that can impose spatial patchiness. Accordingly, soil fauna, including protists (Robeson et al. 2011), nematodes (Ettema et al. 1998, Ettema et al. 2000, Görres et al. 1998, Robertson and Freckman 1995), microarthropods (Fromm et al. 1993, Klironomos et al. 1999, Nielsen et al. 2010a), enchytraeids

(Lavelle and Spain 2001), ants (Blomqvist et al. 2000), termites (Crist 1998), earthworms (Decaëns and Rossi 2001), and even gophers (Ayarbe and Kieft 2000) are generally aggregated at various spatial scales related to the size and lifestyle of the taxa in question. For example, protozoan assemblages show spatial autocorrelation at ranges of 54–133 m, with very limited similarity between assemblages at larger scales (Robeson et al. 2011). However, another study found spatial patchiness of testate amoebae at a much smaller scale (tens of centimetres) across 96 samples collected in a 40 cm × 60 cm patch of *Sphagnum* in the Swiss Jura Mountains (Mitchell et al. 2000), while ciliates in subtropical forests aggregate at scales of 3–8 m (Acosta-Mercado and Lynn 2002). Soil nematodes show spatial patchiness, even in agricultural systems that have been tilled and are under monocropping for extended periods (Robertson and Freckman 1995). It has even been shown that plant parasitic nematodes show spatial patterns reflecting that of crop inter-row distances in sugarcane (Delaville et al. 1996).

The spatial patterns of populations and assemblages can be influenced by biological processes such as active dispersal and aggregation behaviour (Decaëns and Rossi 2001, Ettema and Wardle 2002). Many arthropods, including species of Acari, Collembola, and Coleoptera, are known to produce and use aggregation pheromones (Wertheim et al. 2005), which can contribute to observed spatial patterns. For example, spatial aggregation driven in part by the use of pheromones has been observed in springtails during moulting, egg laying, mating, and migration (Benoit et al. 2009, Leinaas 1983, Verhoef et al. 1977). Similarly, it has been shown that sex pheromones are used in the search for mates in plant parasitic nematodes, but this has not been well characterised (Perry 1996). It seems very likely that similar chemical cues are used more broadly in soil fauna. Importantly, the use of such aggregation pheromones will contribute to the existence of spatial population structures that might be picked up in assemblage patterns. Species that produce and utilise such behaviour are therefore likely to show greater spatial aggregation unrelated to environmental heterogeneity, although overlap will often occur when pheromone-driven aggregation behaviour is driven by resource availability or habitat suitability, including sites for egg laying. It seems likely that other soil fauna similarly uses chemical cues that may contribute to observed spatial distribution patterns. For example, ground-beetle assemblages are influenced by microhabitat-type distribution within forests (Niemelä et al. 1992) but also inter-specific differences in behaviour such as egg laying, larval survival, and foraging patterns cause horizontal and vertical stratification at fine scales (Loreau 1987). The patterns of biodiversity at local scales are moreover likely to depend on the dispersal ability of the organism studied. Types of soil fauna that have different dispersal rates are likely to show contrasting patterns of distribution. For example, whereas earthworms are known to migrate up to 1 m per day (Caro et al. 2013), another study found that migration rates varied from 0.3 to 2.1 cm per day among 17 species of oribatid mites (Lehmitz et al. 2012). It is therefore obvious that life history traits and dispersal ability contribute to contrasting spatial distribution among populations of individual species. Dispersal and behavioural-related influences on the spatial distribution of individual species thus contribute to the spatial patterns of soil fauna assemblage composition and will be reflected in the 'pure spatial' component, i.e. the spatial structure that is unrelated to quantified environmental variables, in many studies.

Teasing apart the influences of environmental and 'pure spatial' patterns are commonly done with variance partitioning (Chapter 3, Section 3.6), with the environmental variables often further divided into edaphic versus vegetation components. Using this approach, we can then identify shifts in soil fauna assemblages related to the vegetation, edaphic variables, and space, alone and together, which hints at the likely key drivers of assemblage composition. However, there is often great overlap in the spatial structure of vegetation and edaphic variation that cannot easily be teased apart. The 'pure spatial' component not including spatially structured environmental gradients is as previously outlined related to biological processes or unmeasured variables that vary in space. For example, a study used a spatially structured sampling design to investigate the contributions of vegetation composition, edaphic variables, and pure spatial configuration to the variability in oribatid and mesostigmatid mites in two contrasting ecosystems, namely birch woodland and heather moorland (Nielsen et al. 2012a). The two main findings were that there were differences in the amount of variation in assemblage composition that could be attributed to variables associated with the vegetation, soil, and space between the oribatid mite and mesostigmatid mite assemblages, and the pattern differed between the ecosystems (Figure 5.3). In particular, we could explain more of the variation in oribatid mite than mesostigmatid mite assemblages in both ecosystems, and the amount of variation explained was substantially greater in the birch woodland, with a large 'pure spatial' component in the heather moorland. We hypothesised that this was related to greater environmental

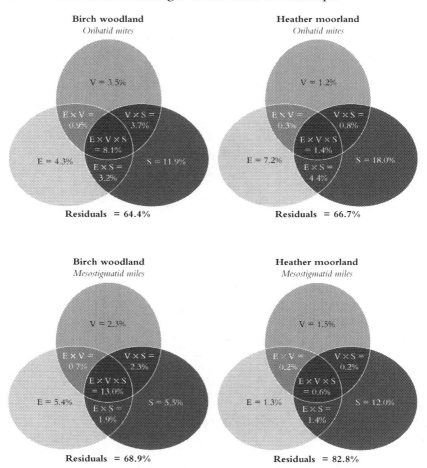

Figure 5.3 An example of variance partitioning for Scottish mite assemblages. In this case, the influences of space (S), edaphic variables (E), and vegetation composition (V) on oribatid and mesostigmatid mites were investigated in two contrasting ecosystems: birch woodland and heather moorland. Note that more variation in oribatid mite assemblages could be explained in both ecosystems and that the pure spatial influence was much greater in the more uniform heather moorland.
Modified from Nielsen et al. (2012a) with permission from Elsevier Science Ltd.

variability in the more environmentally structured birch woodland. The influences of vegetation and edaphic properties could be mediated by a change in resources including the microbial assemblage that would likely have stronger direct effects on the predominantly detritivorous oribatid mites than the predatory mesostigmatid mites. Similarly, a few studies have assessed the spatial, vegetation, and edaphic influences on soil fauna assemblages. For example, Lindo and Winchester (2009) collected soil samples around, and canopy samples from, Sitka spruce trees across five neighbouring watersheds in temperate rainforests in British Columbia to investigate differences in spatial assemblage structure and likely drivers underlying different patterns. The authors indeed found different spatial structures for soil and arboreal assemblages, with the arboreal assemblages being more strongly related to environmental variables, whereas soil assemblages showed a large pure spatial structure that was unrelated to environmental variables. However, the variation in soil assemblage structure among the watersheds was related to predator abundance (i.e. mesostigmatid mites), moisture, and soil type. The authors concluded that the large spatial structure in the soil assemblages (22%) that was unrelated to environmental variability is likely caused by limited long-distance dispersal opportunities in the oribatid mites. Another study found that spider assemblages in an upland moor site in northeast England showed a significant spatially structured distribution that was unrelated to variation in vegetation or soil properties. In contrast, carabid beetle assemblages at the same site showed a significant correlation with soil properties (Sanderson et al. 1995). This indicates that spider and carabid beetle assemblages are structured by contrasting drivers. Hence, both life strategy and habitat structure appear to play critical roles in structuring soil fauna assemblages.

Spatial patterns are greatly influenced by ecosystem characteristics. For example, the distribution of springtails and their functional traits in a salt marsh in the Netherlands was strongly correlated with spatially structured environmental gradients, with very limited pure spatial patterns observed (Widenfalk et al. 2015). The authors assessed springtail assemblages across 172 sampling points within a 35 m × 25 m plot using a spatially structured sampling design. The main predicted driver of springtail assemblage structure was expected to be elevation (i.e. topography) as this is strongly related to the likelihood of a given sample to be inundated and its soil moisture content. The results indeed showed that topography alone could explain 22% and 19.5% of the variation in assemblage and trait composition, respectively. This study provided strong evidence for environmental filtering, i.e. only species with certain traits can survive in a given area, and competitive exclusion whereby species with similar traits are less likely to co-occur. Another paper by the same lead author investigated springtail assemblage composition in a Scots pine forest in Sweden and found rather different patterns (Widenfalk et al. 2016). In this paper, the investigators collected 100 soil samples within a 5 m × 20 m homogeneous plot with limited evidence of significant environmental variability using a slightly different spatially structured sampling design. Here the springtail assemblage composition showed significant spatial structuring for both species and functional trait composition that was not related to environmental variables. There was therefore limited evidence for any significant environmental filtering for springtail species or traits within the Scots pine forest, which contrasts with the strong environmental filtering observed in the salt marsh. Moreover, all functional traits except life form were overdispersed in the Scots pine forest, indicating there is greater diversity of functional traits within a given local assemblage than expected by chance (for over- and underdispersion, see Chapter 3). The authors explain that this is likely to be a consequence of mechanisms that limit species trait similarities such as competition for resources.

A further complication with this approach is that species show variability in their preferences for environmental driver and tendencies for biological self-organisation driven by behaviour and other biological factors. For example, when the spatial distribution of two dominant springtail species was assessed in a high Arctic meadow, it was observed that one of the species, *Hypogastrura tullbergi* (Figure 5.4), was predominantly displaying spatial structures unrelated to environmental variability. By contrast, *Folsomia quadrioculata* showed a stronger correlation with environmental variables, including the spatially structured variability (Widenfalk et al. 2018). The authors predicted this pattern based on known social behaviour in the genus *Hypogastrura*, whereby species aggregate independently of environmental conditions or resource hotspots due to intraspecific interactions (Lyford 1975), which has not been observed in *Folsomia*. Hence, both species are known to show spatial aggregation, but the underlying reasons appear to be different. Moreover, the results showed that the drivers of springtail distributional patterns differ among life stages, with generally stronger spatial patterns observed in the early life stages. This is not surprising given that many springtails deposit eggs in batches and that dispersal limitation is likely to be more common in younger and smaller individuals (Hopkin 1997, Leinaas and Fjellberg 1985), but such patterns could well contribute to the large amount of unexplained variation in soil fauna assemblages observed in most studies.

Figure 5.4 Aggregation behaviour in the springtail *Hypogastrura viatica* feeding on cyanobacteria, Svalbard.
Courtesy of Hans Petter Leinaas.

5.3 Fine-Scale Patterns of Biodiversity

The astounding species diversity of soil fauna at fine spatial small scales was already recognised more than four decades ago in an article entitled 'The Enigma of Soil Animal Species Diversity' (Anderson 1975), and it is still not entirely clear what mechanisms maintain this diversity (Bardgett 2002, Berg 2012, Wardle 2006). In part, this is because the mechanisms driving species diversity in soils have received little attention relative to the effort put into explaining the patterns of species richness observed aboveground. The mechanisms influencing species richness and assemblage composition aboveground have been quite well explored, and it has been proposed that some of these mechanisms might be relevant for belowground communities as well (Wardle and Giller 1996). While organisms belowground are receiving more attention due to the increasing recognition of their contributions to ecosystem functioning, there is still a need for a more thorough exploration of the factors that influence both the species richness and composition of belowground assemblages (Bardgett 2005, Coleman and Whitman 2005). One of the main hypotheses is that high soil fauna diversity can be maintained at fine scales due to the substantial temporal variability and highly heterogeneous, three-dimensional nature of the soil matrix itself under the assumption that biotic interactions and niche differentiation is important. The scale of interaction varies from cm to m depending on the body size, mobility, and life history traits of the taxa being studied, but the high spatial and temporal heterogeneity at various scales make it difficult to interpret the drivers of soil biodiversity at fine scales. For example, the species richness of nematodes ranges from around 10 to more than 100 species in a given sample of soil, often as little as 100 g, with a significant co-occurrence of species with similar feeding types. This is well above what one might expect if there is strong competition for resources, which would eventuate in competitive exclusion in equilibrium assemblages. It has accordingly been hypothesised that fluctuations in environmental and climatic variables, disturbance, and predation prevent nematode communities from reaching equilibrium states and through this avoid local competitive exclusion (Ettema 1998). Moreover, spatiotemporal variability in population dynamics (Berg and Bengtsson 2007) and bioturbation (Young and Ritz 2000) may contribute to allow co-existence.

5.3.1 Spatial and Temporal Habitat Heterogeneity

Soil fauna assemblages are characterised by highly patchy patterns of fine-scale diversity hotspots surrounded by more or less infertile soils. For example, the abundance of protozoans and nematodes is greater within 0–1.8 mm from plant roots, i.e. the rhizosphere (Rønn et al. 1996), with up to 70% of all bacterial- and fungal-feeding nematodes also found in the rhizosphere (Ingham et al. 1985). Similarly, patches of decomposing organic matter can be areas of high biological activity, with nematodes actively seeking out these 'hotspots' (Griffiths and Caul 1993). The distribution of various biological hotspots that vary in key characteristics such as resources and microclimate can thus influence the distribution of soil fauna and allow more species to co-exist. Accordingly, Anderson (1978a) found that oribatid mite species richness is related to microhabitat diversity, and Nielsen et al. (2010b) experimentally showed that small-scale heterogeneity in soil properties (e.g. soil moisture) promote species richness of oribatid mites, springtails, and nematodes without any differences in abundances. In the same study, no effect was found on mesostigmatid mite species richness, but this was hypothesised to be due to the larger size and greater mobility of most mesostigmatid mites compared to the other taxa investigated. This corresponds with earlier work that shows that many oribatid mite species as well as many springtails show relatively strong microhabitat preferences (Wauthy 1982, Wauthy et al. 1989, Weis-Fogh 1948), whereas the predatory mites show limited signs of microhabitat preferences (Čoja and Bruckner 2003). This is further supported by a stronger relationship observed between oribatid mites and environmental characteristics in two contrasting ecosystems relative to that observed for mesostigmatid mites (Nielsen et al. 2012a), and that oribatid mite assemblage composition – but not mesostigmatid mites – show strong ecosystem influences (Nielsen et al. 2010a).

Microarthropod species richness in litter similarly appears to be related to the complexity and heterogeneity of the litter layer (Gill 1969, Hansen 2000, Stanton 1979). The diversity of soil mites is related to the diversity of microhabitats within a site (Anderson 1978a, Anderson 1978b), and several other studies have correlated soil fauna diversity with microhabitat diversity, comparing single-leaf litter with mixed litter (Hansen and Coleman 1998, Kaneko and Salamanca 1999). There are two main ways in which the leaf litter layer can influence soil fauna assemblages: (1) it structures the microhabitat in terms of patchiness and microhabitat complexity, and (2) it provides the resources available to the consumers (Hättenschwiler et al. 2005). The litter layer is a highly important habitat for feeding fauna but can be considered ephemeral in that it is habitable only at certain times due to fluctuations in microclimate. It is therefore expected that the assemblages found in the litter layer are more variable through time and space than the subterranean habitats underneath. Conversely, litter-dwelling soil fauna is generally quicker to colonise disturbed areas or new habitable patches than fauna more adapted to live within the soil itself, and litter-associated assemblages may therefore recover faster following disturbance. This has potential implications for the persistence of soil assemblages, which have been hypothesised to show limited resilience to disturbance based on observed long recovery and reorganisation times following disturbances (Bengtsson 2002).

Soil fauna assemblages, particularly those limited to existing soil pores, can be modified by the soil structure itself, with evidence that the availability of soil pore volumes of certain sizes can limit the abundance of both nematodes and microarthropods (Ducarme et al. 2004, Hassink et al. 1993, Nielsen et al. 2008, Strong et al. 2004). For example, across 12 soil samples varying in soil pore volume distribution collected in a pasture in Belgium, Strong et al. (2004) found that nematode biomass was positively related to the volume of pores between approximately 15 and 60 μm. These results compare well with earlier results that showed a strong positive relationship between nematode biomass and soil pores between 30 and 90 μm (Hassink et al. 1993). Similarly, Nielsen et al. (2008) found that the abundance of oribatid mites was positively related to the volume of pores in the 60–300 μm range in both birch woodland and heather moorland, whereas the abundance of mesostigmatid mites was related to pore volume in the birch woodland only. Moreover, there is also experimental evidence that changes in soil structure moderate mite assemblage composition. In this study, the soil structure, and through this soil pore volume distribution, was manipulated by creating artificial soil with different grain sizes (i.e. 'fine', 'medium', 'large'). PVC pipes with the different grain sizes were placed in the field in autumn with a litter layer on top and collected the following spring in a spruce forest in the Colorado Rocky Mountains (Figure 5.5). Any differences in mite

Figure 5.5 Photo of a spruce forest used to investigate impacts of soil structure on soil fauna assemblages located in Pingree Park, the Rocky Mountains, Colorado, USA.
Photo by the author.

abundance and mite assemblages would therefore be due purely to variation in the soil structure. There were no differences in mite abundances between the soils with different grain sizes, but the oribatid mite assemblage was related to grain size, with smaller species predominantly found in the treatment with fine grains and larger species in the treatment with large grains, respectively (Figure 5.6). Hence, soil structure can moderate mesofauna communities directly by limiting the abundance and size of its

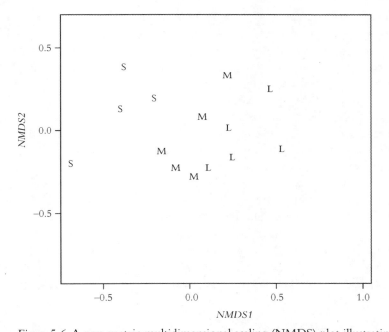

Figure 5.6 A non-metric multidimensional scaling (NMDS) plot illustrating the effects of soil structure on oribatid mite assemblage composition in an experimental study in the Rocky Mountains, Colorado. The authors manipulated the soil structure in PVC pipes with a mesh bottom by adding small (S), medium (M), or large (L) grains. The PVC pipes were then placed in the organic horizon of a spruce forest over winter with a litter layer added on top, effectively functioning as a place to take refuge only, i.e. no food source was added to the mixture. After the samples were collected in spring, microarthropods were extracted using Tullgren funnels, and the oribatid mites were identified to species level. There was no difference in mite abundances between the treatments, but there was a substantial shift in oribatid mite assemblage composition, with fewer large individuals in the treatment with smaller grain sizes, indicating that the soil structure alone imposes a significant influence on assemblage structure. Note that in NMDS plots, sample points that are more distant to each other have more dissimilar assemblages. Nielsen et al., unpublished data.

occupants. Interestingly, another study found that the abundance of mites was positively related to the volume of soil pores in the 1.2–6 μm range (Vreeken-Bruijs et al. 1998). The authors hypothesised that this was due to increased access to suitable protected sites for egg-laying. Hence, soil structure may impose other controls on mesofauna abundances.

Finally, the richness and diversity of soil fauna at very fine scales are further likely to be influenced by stress (e.g. resource or abiotic limitations) and perturbation (e.g. grazing, fire, tilling). It has been hypothesised that species richness should show a humpbacked relationship with stress and perturbation gradients (Grime 1973, Huston 1994, Wardle 2002). It proposes that too high stress or perturbation filter out all but the most tolerant species, whereas very stable environments may favour competitively superior species or provide limited habitat diversity (Tilman 1982). However, observed stress-species richness relationships often diverge from this pattern, and it may not be a general pattern (Mittelbach et al. 2001). It appears likely that the continuous disturbance of soil contributes to the maintenance of soil fauna biodiversity. Indeed, ecosystem engineers that cause bioturbation may promote the diversity of other soil fauna. For example, the presence of earthworms has been found to promote species richness of soil macrofauna (Decaëns et al. 1999, Loranger et al. 1998), likely through an increase in resource availability and habitat complexity and availability (Decaëns 2010). In short, there is very little evidence for a decline in diversity belowground with increasing productivity (Bardgett 2002), and it has been suggested that competitive exclusion is unlikely to occur belowground (Wardle 2002). However, biotic interactions are more likely to influence soil fauna assemblages at these fine spatial scales (Ettema and Wardle 2002, Wardle 2006).

5.3.2 Vertical Stratification

Most soil fauna assemblages are concentrated in the litter layer and the upper few cm of the soil proper. Due to a reduced influence of the litter layer and constraints of the soil matrix there is a general change in soil fauna assemblage structure and composition with increasing depth. This phenomenon is referred to as vertical stratification and is commonly observed in soil fauna assemblages, including nematodes (Liang et al. 2005), microarthropods (Berg et al. 1998), carabid beetles (Loreau 1987) and beetles more broadly (Andújar et al. 2015), and macroarthropods (Mathieu et al. 2009). Moreover, there is a general decrease in the abundance of most soil fauna with increasing depth, most likely related to reduced resource availability. However, much soil fauna can be found at even greater depths. For example, most protozoans are thought to be found in the upper few cm of the soil horizon but can be observed much deeper in the soil, with many soil protozoan commonly found associated with groundwater reservoirs. Similarly, nematodes are commonly found in the presence of plant roots at depths up to 12 m in the playa of the Chihuahuan desert, New Mexico (Freckman and Virginia 1989), and the species *Halicephalobus mephisto* was described from samples collected at deep mining sites in South Africa at an astounding 1.3 km depth, with DNA suggesting the presence of other nematode species at 3.6 km depth (Borgonie et al. 2011).

The shift in assemblage composition and decreasing abundance of microarthropods with soil depth is likely due to the broad reliance on resources provided by, or associated with, the litter layer. However, there are also differences in the morphology of springtails with larger, more pigmented species in the litter layer versus deeper in the soil and similar trends have been observed in mite assemblages. Many species of collembolans are known to feed on fungal hyphae, which are likely to be most dominant in the litter layer (Ekelund et al. 2001) or decaying organic matter (Hopkin 2007). Similarly, many species of oribatid mites are fungal grazers (Kaneko 1988, Luxton 1972) and are therefore likely to favour the soil horizon immediately associated with the litter layer. By contrast, many mesostigmatid mites are predatory (Ruf and Beck 2005) and are as such not directly related to the litter layer. However, the higher occurrence of prey items in the litter layer may explain a large part of the decrease in abundance with increasing depth observed for this group. Furthermore, many species of microarthropods are relatively large, which may make it difficult for them to move into the deeper parts of the soil. In contrast, the abundance of enchytraeids and the nematodes is less influenced by soil depth, at least in the upper soil horizons. However, the enchytraeids are capable of manipulating the soil and, hence, are not dependent on pre-existing soil pores for movement (Didden 1993). The nematodes do not have this ability, but many species are so small that their movement through the O horizon is unlikely to be restricted by the soil structure. Hence, soil structure is most likely to be a constraint for organisms that cannot create their own habitable pore space.

A key characteristic of the soil vertical profile is the depth of the organic layer. Since much soil fauna is predominantly found in this layer, a reduction in soil organic matter is likely to negatively influence soil fauna abundances, and possibly even assemblage composition due to changes in soil physico-chemical properties. As part of another study, we manipulated the organic matter depth distribution of small plots *in situ* to investigate potential vertical stratification of soil fauna within an otherwise homogeneous soil horizon (Nielsen et al., unpublished results). Specifically, the depth of the organic layer was manipulated to create three treatments with either a deep (12 cm), a medium (7.5 cm), or a shallow (3 cm) organic horizon. Two different sampling regimes were then used to test whether the abundance of soil fauna and assemblage composition are related to O-horizon thickness and depth. The authors found that the community composition of soil biota in the uppermost 3 cm of organic matter below the litter layer was generally not influenced by O-horizon thickness. Interestingly, the study showed that the abundance of oribatid mites at 0–3 cm depth was greater in a shallow O horizon compared with the deeper O horizons, with the relationship apparently caused by a negative relationship between oribatid mite abundance and soil moisture content across the treatment plots. However, the abundance of all microarthropods decreased significantly with depth, whereas the abundance of nematodes and enchytraeids remained constant. Furthermore, all microarthropods showed vertical niche differentiation, possibly indicating their association with the litter layer and higher abundances in the upper organic horizon (Figure 5.7). These findings are consistent with another study that showed a significant decrease in the biomass of soil mesofauna after organic matter removal (Battigelli et al. 2004), but they contradict the suggested inverse relationship between biomass of soil biota and the amount of accumulated organic matter on the soil surface (Petersen and Luxton 1982, Schaefer and Schauermann 1990, Scheu et al. 2003). However, the results presented here compare the relationship between abundance and organic matter depth within a uniform O horizon, whereas the previously suggested inverse relationships were based on comparisons of different humus forms. These contrasting conclusions can be explained by the differences in perceived impacts. The removal of organic matter from a given ecosystem is likely to have negative effects due to the associated decrease in resources, habitat, and possibly also the disturbance that underlay this removal. By contrast, differences among soil types with different O horizons are more likely associated with differences in resource quality and food web structure.

5.3.3 Biotic Interactions

The effect of biotic interactions such as competition, predation, and even facilitation on soil assemblage structure is expected to be more important

5.3 Fine-Scale Patterns of Biodiversity · 183

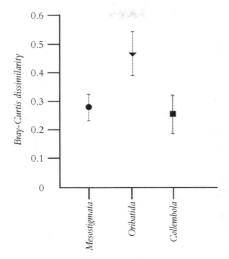

Figure 5.7 A graph illustrating the turnover in mesostigmatid mite, oribatid mite, and springtail assemblage composition between the top 0–3 cm and 3–6 cm of an organic soil horizon in an experimental study in a birch woodland in Scotland. Note that a greater dissimilarity indicates greater turnover between the top 0–3 cm and the underlying 3–6 cm. The dissimilarity is different from 0 for all taxa indicating significant vertical stratification. It is expected that this is due to a combination of more limited influences of the leaf litter layer and the restricted movement of larger individuals at greater depth.
Nielsen et al., unpublished data.

at smaller scales (Wardle 2006). The importance of predator–prey interactions was already mentioned in Chapter 2 because of the resulting influences on ecosystem functioning, and there is substantial evidence that predation moderates soil fauna assemblage structure. There is less evidence that facilitation plays a large role, except in that microhabitat modifications – including effects on soil structure, increased availability of C and nutrients of organic matter during decomposition, and creation of resource hotspots by certain soil fauna – could benefit other organisms. For example, several studies have reported greater diversity of soil fauna in patches with high densities of earthworms (Loranger et al. 1998) or associated with earthworm casts (Decaëns et al. 1999). A review by Decaëns (2010) indicates that soil fauna is not governed by the same factors as aboveground taxa, with very limited evidence for competition playing a significant role and that the diversity is mostly controlled by the habitat heterogeneity and constraints imposed by soils as a habitat. Having said that, more recent evidence indicates that competition may play a significant role or at least help shape assemblages under certain circumstances.

Self-organisation of soil fauna assemblages based on mutualism or non-trophic interactions appears to prevail in soils; however, there is increasing evidence of 'negative' biotic interactions between soil fauna (i.e. predation, competition). Non-trophic biotic interactions are receiving more attention and can have significant effects on soil fauna assemblages. In a literature review combined with a meta-analytical approach, Eisenhauer (2010) synthesised the effect of the three different ecological groups of earthworms – epigeic, anecic, and endogeic – on microarthropods. The effect of epigeic earthworms appeared to be density dependent, with positive effects on microarthropod abundances at moderate densities, whereas negative effects were observed at high earthworm densities. Endogeic earthworms generally had negative effects on microarthropods, likely due to competition for resources, whereas anecic earthworms had positive effects on the microhabitat scale and neutral effects on the habitat scale. However, given the idiosyncratic and species-specific results observed to date it appears too early to draw even broad generalisations about the impacts of non-trophic interactions.

There is more evidence that predator–prey interactions are involved in structuring soil fauna assemblages. The density of nematodes is generally suppressed in the presence of predators, both microbial and other soil fauna. The effect is often density dependent, with predators relying mostly on chance encounters with prey and display limited resource specificity (Yeates and Wardle 1996). For example, the density of two dominant nematodes species was strongly affected by the presence of arthropod predators whereas no effect was observed on two subordinate nematode species (Hyvönen and Persson 1996). Similarly, there is evidence from spatially explicit data that predator abundance can influence oribatid mite assemblage structure (Lindo and Winchester 2009). In this study of oribatid mite assemblages in British Columbia temperature rainforests, the authors found that predator abundance, specifically mesostigmatid mites, together with moisture and soil type explained part of the variation in assemblage structure across three watersheds with no other environmental variables being included in the final model. Moreover, some studies have found that the use of pesticides with preferential impacts on soil fauna can influence predator–prey interactions, with impacts on soil fauna assemblages. For example, in early studies on the impact of pesticide use, it was found that reductions in mesostigmatid mite abundances were associated with an increase in springtail abundance, one of their prey items, suggesting predator release effects (Wallwork 1976). Hence, top-down forces may limit soil fauna abundances or contribute to shifts

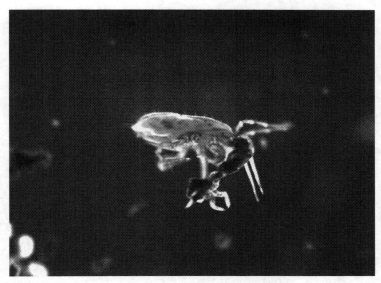

Figure 5.8 A mesostigmatid mite, *Gamasellus racovitzai*, found feeding on a springtail, *Cryptopygus antarcticus*, in a sample collected in maritime Antarctica. Such predator–prey interactions can influence soil fauna assemblage composition. Photo by the author.

in soil fauna assemblage composition (Figure 5.8). While trophic interactions are well recognised, there is less emphasis on competition and other intra-trophic level interactions as drivers of soil assemblage structure.

Whether competition is a significant driver of belowground assemblage structure is, in comparison, under significant debate. There is increasing circumstantial evidence that suggests competition may indeed contribute to observed species distribution pattern, with multiple studies finding patterns of community assembly that cannot be attributed solely to environmental variables or stochastic events. For example, the fact that the beta-diversity or turnover of functional traits between samples within ecosystems is often substantially lower than that observed at a species level hints at possible competitive exclusion of species with similar functional traits (Widenfalk et al. 2015). Specifically, interspecific competition for resources predicts that species that compete for the same resource would be expected to show lower-than-expected co-occurrence (Diamond 1975, Gotelli and Graves 1996), and if species co-occur they likely show limited niche overlap or greater morphological differentiation than expected by chance alone (Schoener 1974). Several studies have reported lower-than-expected species co-occurrence, suggesting that competition might be a structuring force, but this in itself does not provide unequivocal evidence for competition (Decaëns 2010). It is moreover complicated by phylogenetic influences that can nonetheless be accounted for using statistical procedures (Helmus et al. 2007). Still, clear evidence for competition between some plant parasitic nematodes utilising the same host plant has been documented (Alphey 1985, Johnson and Nusbaum 1968, Sikora et al. 1979), and competitive exclusion has been implicated in the spatial distribution of earthworm assemblages (Decaëns et al. 2009, Jiménez et al. 2006) and the distribution of ants' nests (Traniello and Levings 1986). For example, in a survey of 44 sites across a range of land-use types from forest to extensively managed grasslands and intensively managed arable land, Decaëns et al. (2008) found that the local species richness of earthworms, which never exceeded nine species, was well below that expected by chance and concluded that species richness at a patch scale is governed by competitive exclusion. A comparison of the body size distribution of predatory *Pterosticus* spp. (Carabidae) in central Europe similarly indicated that competition moderated assemblages in habitats that were not exposed to significant disturbance (Brandl and Topp 1985). By contrast, this pattern was not observed for meadows or pastures under management.

Several other studies provide some evidence that biotic interactions play a role in structuring soil fauna assemblages. For example, microarthropod assemblages from 80 moss samples collected on four islands in the Argentine Islands, maritime Antarctica showed very limited spatial autocorrelation (1% of the variance explained) or correlation with environmental parameters (<1% of the variance explained). In comparison, island of origin accounted for 7% of the observed variation in assemblage structure. However, it was evident from comparing assemblage structure with predictions from neutral models that species were co-occurring less frequently than predicted by chance (Caruso et al. 2013). This provides at least circumstantial evidence that negative biotic interactions may play a role in structuring Antarctic soil fauna assemblages. Moreover, there is evidence for competitive exclusion in earthworm communities (Chauvel et al. 1999, Decaëns et al. 2004), likely driven by the high adaptability and functional plasticity (Decaëns et al. 2008), and it has been suggested that the spatial distribution of both ants and earthworms is driven by intra- and inter-specific competitive exclusion (Decaëns et al. 2009, Jiménez et al. 2006, Jiménez and Rossi 2006, Traniello and Levings 1986). Similarly, neotropical grassland earthworm species were aggregated at a scale of 20–40 m, but two species with similar patch sizes were spatially segregated indicating possible niche overlap and competitive exclusion (Jiménez et al. 2006). Biotic interactions, specifically competition, could be avoided by the population size of co-occurring species peaking at different times of the year. For example, it has been found that the dominant carabid beetles in sand dune systems in Wales differ in their temporal population dynamics (Gilbert 1956). Hence, competition can be avoided through spatial and temporal separation.

Finally, there is also evidence that chemical warfare between organisms that use the same resources may play a key role in moderating assemblage structure. For example, the amoeba *Acanthamoeba castellanii* can produce compounds that suppress population growth of the bacterial-feeding nematode *Caenorhabditis elegans*, with the nematode also being repelled by the compounds produced by the amoeba. However, the amoeba in turn responded to compounds produced by the nematode with increased encystment. The antagonistic compounds produced by the nematode did not inhibit the growth of the amoeba, but the increased encystment would contribute to a reduced fitness in the longer term given that these individuals are not feeding or reproducing (Neidig et al. 2010). Chemical interactions between organisms that utilise similar resources may therefore be important to maintaining diversity in soil systems.

5.3.4 Deterministic versus Stochastic Influences

All the information in the previous section contributes to the discussion of whether soil fauna assemblages are structured by deterministic or stochastic processes unrelated to niche differentiation or biological interactions. If deterministic processes dominate, soil fauna assemblages should be predictable through space and time, whereas assemblages structured by stochastic processes cannot be predicted based on environmental parameters. However, assemblages will generally be influenced by both deterministic and stochastic processes at any given time. Disturbance can cause substantial disruptions of soil fauna assemblages that hinder strong biotic interactions and competitive exclusion. Indeed, there is considerable evidence to support that disturbance influences soil fauna assemblages negatively. For example, traditional intensive soil management practices associated with agricultural systems have been found to cause a reduction in the species richness of nematodes (Bloemers et al. 1997), springtails (Chauvat et al. 2007), earthworms (Decaëns et al. 2003), termites (Gillison et al. 2003), and macrofauna more broadly (Decaëns et al. 1994, Mathieu et al. 2005). Soil fauna assemblages are therefore likely to be governed mostly by stochastic processes in highly disturbed ecosystems, such as production systems. Moreover, if dispersal rates are high enough it is predicted that species can be found in suitable and unsuitable habitats alike simply because the high number of immigrants counteract lower competitive abilities (i.e. source-sink or meta-community dynamics) (Shmida and Wilson 1985). This in turn may override the effects of environmental variation, causing spatial patterns more similar to those predicted by neutral theories. Relatively few studies have addressed this question explicitly for soil assemblage structure, but some noteworthy exceptions provide significant insights.

A recent paper provided evidence for deterministic processes being involved in the organisation of oribatid mite assemblages (Caruso et al. 2012). In this study, the authors collected soil samples in two contrasting habitats, a beech forest and natural grassland, in Italy using a hierarchical sampling scheme. Specifically, they identified a large 500 m × 500 m representative area within each habitat and outlined four 10 m × 10 m plots within this area. Within the four plots, they established three 1 m × 1 m subplots, and within each of these three soil samples were collected for extraction of oribatid mites and a characterisation of key soil properties (i.e. $n = 36$ for each habitat type). The data analysis specifically assessed the influence of spatial positioning of the samples and soil properties as well as estimated neutral diversity and immigration parameters. Key to our discussion here is that the patterns of assemblage structure were different from those predicted by the neutral models, indicating that both deterministic and stochastic influences are at play. The authors concluded that oribatid mite assemblages are structured at least in part by environmental filtering, competition-driven niche differentiation, or both. Such patterns can also be compared across taxa within the same studies. For example, a study that assessed oribatid mite and springtail assemblages at nunataks of varying soil ages and nearby non-isolated deglaciated areas found that there is environmental species sorting in both taxa, with oribatid mite and springtail assemblage structure being most strongly correlated with soil age and plant species richness, respectively (Ingimarsdóttir et al. 2012). The authors found no sign of strong dispersal limitation for either group, although the oribatid mites were slower to colonise, and there was clear evidence of species sorting further indicating that the environment explains part of the variation in assemblage structure. The variation in assemblage structure explained by spatial and environmental variables was much greater for the oribatid mites than the springtails, suggesting that the two taxa are influenced by different drivers. Similarly, it has been shown that spatial patterns and environmental variation explain more of the variation in oribatid mite assemblage structure than that of mesostigmatid mites in heather moorland and birch woodland in Scotland (Nielsen et al. 2012a). Furthermore, an assessment of mite assemblages of three 5 m × 5 m plots using a spatially structured sampling design ($n = 100$ per plot) in temperate deciduous forests in China indicated that the assemblages displayed significant spatial structures that were not related to environmental variables in either of the three plots (Gao et al. 2014). However, the authors compared species' co-occurrence with null and neutral models and found evidence for some environmental filtering. Signs of overdispersion in traits have also been found in earthworm assemblages in Columbian grasslands, specifically body weight, length, and diameter, indicating that competitive interactions moderate assemblage structure (Decaëns et al. 2009). Moreover, strong environmental filtering was observed at larger spatial and temporal scales, highlighting the influence of multiple drivers of earthworm assemblage structure that act at different spatial and temporal scales.

A more recent approach to investigate whether soil fauna assemblage structure is deterministic or governed by stochasticity and neutral processes is based on patterns of beta diversity (Maaß et al. 2014). The basic idea is that spatially structured assemblages should show lower turnover or beta-diversity within an ecosystem than predicted by patterns observed under neutrality. This was recently used to provide insight into springtail assemblages in forests of different ages (young: 30–40 years; intermediate: 50–70 years; old: 150–200 years) across 11 years (Dirilgen et al. 2018). In each year, the authors collected 100 soil samples from each forest along five 40-meter-long transects. They then calculated total beta-diversity as the total variance of the assemblage matrix and local contributions to beta-diversity as an estimate of the uniqueness of individual sample points following the methods developed by Legendre and De Cáceres (2013). They further compared individual- and sample-based rarefaction curves as a measure of assemblage heterogeneity, with the notion that heterogeneity is present if the individual-based rarefaction curve increases more rapidly than the sample-based rarefaction curve following Colwell and Coddington (1994). The results suggested that the springtail assemblages at these sites were not predominantly different from what could be expected if neutral processes structure the assemblages, with 26 of the 33 year by forest combinations fitting the neutral model and displayed limited difference between sample- and individual-based rarefaction curves. However, there was a tendency towards spatial structuring in the older forest where the beta-diversity was less than that predicted by the neutral model in five of the 11 years. These results indicate that springtail assemblages are not in equilibrium, particularly in the young to intermediate aged forests, reducing the influence of deterministic processes.

Finally, it has been proposed that strong environmental filtering would result in phylogenetically clustered assemblages by favouring species with similar traits that are more likely to be closely related. By contrast, strong biotic interactions and, particularly, competition for resources would result in phylogenetically overdispersed assemblages where species are less closely related than could be expected by chance (Webb 2000). Similarly, we can hypothesise that strong competitive interactions are likely to result in assemblages where the members are more divergent in life history and functional traits than could be expected by chance alone, whereas strong environmental filtering would promote assemblages dominated by species with similar traits. There is some evidence that soil fauna assemblages follow this pattern. For example, Moroenyane et al. (2016) used a molecular approach, sequencing the 18S rRNA gene to investigate nematode assemblages of 23 soil samples across five Fynbos ecosystems. They found that nematode assemblages showed a significant phylogenetic clustering, indicating habitat filtering with local assemblages composed of species more closely related than would be expected by chance alone. The authors claim that this is an indication that deterministic processes are more important than stochastic events, but that is not well quantified particularly given that nematode assemblages showed no significant correlation with environmental variables. It does appear likely that habitat filtering contributes to assemblage structuring, but it is likely to be a continuum from nearly only influences of deterministic processes to mostly stochastic and neutral process influences, rather than one or the other *per se*. Still, only a few studies have taken this approach to assess the mechanisms that structure soil fauna assemblages, but it appears to be a powerful tool to gain further insight.

5.4 Summary

We have a robust understanding of the mechanisms that influence soil fauna assemblage structure and composition at various spatial scales. Climate and soil type can be considered landscape scale drivers of soil fauna assemblages that integrate effects of variation in the vegetation and edaphic properties. They are therefore likely to be good proxies that can

5.4 Summary

be used to predict soil fauna assemblage structure and composition with relatively high precision although the effects are moderated by other factors, such as disturbances and global change (see Chapters 6 and 7). Large-scale studies of soil fauna assemblages are difficult to undertake given the logistical constraints and taxonomic expertise required to reliably identify the specimens, but ideally, more studies will be designed to investigate soil fauna assemblages at these scales to provide further insight. Variation in edaphic properties and vegetation structure and composition becomes more important, particularly to soil fauna that uses specific host plants, within ecosystems, while the distribution of plant roots, patches of resources, and soil structure become increasingly more important at the finest spatial scales where biotic interactions are also most likely to be observed. There is some evidence that competition can be a driver of soil fauna assemblage structure and composition, but this may be the exception rather than the norm. Indeed, competition is rarely considered a main driver of soil fauna assemblages, even where it is observed. Other biotic interactions, specifically predator–prey relationships, are more likely to be of significant influence. Moreover, soil fauna assemblages and populations of individual species show spatial patchiness that can be driven by biological processes (dispersal, aggregation) and environmental variation. The eusocial termites and ants, for example, show strong behavioural influences on their distribution, but many other soil fauna taxa display spatial patterns that are in part related to the distribution of resources and behavioural aggregation patterns that can be established using chemical cues such as pheromones. There is clear evidence that soil fauna assemblages are modified by environmental filtering, but the outcome can range from underdispersion to overdispersion of species and functional traits depending on how strong the environmental filtering is. Specifically, very strong environmental filtering (i.e. harsh environmental conditions) promote assemblages consisting of functionally similar species, whereas more favourable conditions are likely to promote assemblages consisting of functionally dissimilar species due to competitive exclusion, at least in ecosystems with limited disturbance. As such, niche differentiation is more likely in relatively stable ecosystems with limited environmental stress. However, soil fauna assemblages are on average highly variable in nature, and this variability is rarely well explained by environmental characteristics or spatial structure indicating a large degree of stochasticity and assemblages moderated predominantly by neutral processes.

6 · *Anthropogenic Impacts on Soil Fauna Assemblages*

Human activities impact natural ecosystems directly through conversion to production systems and development of infrastructure and housing, and indirectly through changes in climate and other external pressures such as nutrient deposition. Approximately 40% of Earth's terrestrial surface area is presently managed for agricultural purposes (Foley et al. 2011), a substantial proportion, at least 15%, is degraded (Bridges and Oldeman 1999), and desertification is increasing due to human activities (Reynolds et al. 2007). The construction of infrastructure has detrimental impacts through habitat loss, and urban ecosystems often support altered assemblages (Francini et al. 2018, Pavao-Zuckerman and Sookhdeo 2017). The loss of habitat is one of the key threats to soil fauna, and there is substantial evidence that it can cause local extinctions. In contrast, the effect of habitat loss and modification on global diversity of soil organisms is more difficult to assess (Veresoglou et al. 2015). Moreover, since 1860 the external contribution of nitrogen and phosphorus to Earth's ecosystems has increased from 15.3 and <0.3 Tg nitrogen and phosphorus per year to 175–259 and 14–16 Tg nitrogen and phosphorus per year, respectively, in the early twenty-first century due to fertiliser application and atmospheric deposition (Peñuelas et al. 2012). Much of this nitrogen and phosphorus are applied as inorganic fertilisers, but organic fertilisers, including manure and planting of leguminous crops, are another considerable source of nitrogen that contributed a substantial 40 Tg nitrogen in 2005 (Galloway et al. 2008). Similarly, the widespread use of agrochemicals can have unexpected and sometimes detrimental impacts on soil fauna assemblages, with knock-on effects on ecosystem functioning and service provision, including pest and pathogen suppression.

These human-driven global changes have already contributed to changes in Earth's ecosystems, including soil fauna assemblages, with associated impacts on ecosystem functioning. For example, a meta-analysis provided evidence that species losses are likely to have profound impacts on ecosystem functioning. By collating results from a broad range of studies, Hooper et al. (2012) found evidence that the loss of decomposer species has negative impacts on decomposition rates (~8% reduction) that at intermediate levels of species loss rivals or exceeds the effects of elevated atmospheric CO_2 concentrations and fertilisation. While the study is not exclusive to litter decomposition in terrestrial ecosystems, it provides robust evidence for the impacts of species loss on this important ecosystem process. Indeed, a key rationale for understanding possible impacts of global change on soils is that it is currently the largest terrestrial reservoir of carbon, exceeding that found in the vegetation and atmosphere combined (Lal 2004). Global change often results in increased soil respiration, with possible feedbacks on climate change due to the contribution to greenhouse gas emission. Great benefits could be gained from developing evidence-based land use management practices that limit greenhouse gas emission or contribute to soil carbon sequestration. It is, however, of concern that there is a long-lasting legacy of land use that may impede successful modifications of soil processes that promote sustainable use. For example, it was shown in a microcosm experiment that soil processes were strongly influenced by past management (intensively managed wheat field; extensively managed grassland) even after the soils had been homogenised in terms of soil structure and soil fauna assemblages (Liiri et al. 2012). Another possible concern with land use practices that has received less attention is the fact that it generally contributes to homogenisation of biological assemblages. For example, Gossner et al. (2016) showed that even moderately intensive land use practices caused multitrophic homogenisation of organisms ranging from microbes to arthropods to plant assemblages. Increased land use intensity thus reduced β-diversity of the organisms studied in a non-linear way, with the greatest reduction occurring associated with the change from extensively to intermediate intensity managed grasslands. In this chapter, I will first provide an overview of the observed impacts of common management practices on soil fauna assemblages. A key problem as outlined above is the increasing use of fertilisers and, similarly, nitrogen deposition, which will be discussed in a separate section before we have a look at the impacts of agrochemicals and pollution more broadly. I will wrap the section up with an introduction to invasion ecology in soil, specifically focussing on impacts of invasive species aboveground, both plants and animals, and belowground invasive species.

6.1 Management Practices

The conversion of natural ecosystems ranging from grasslands to forests into production systems is known to impact belowground assemblages (Figure 6.1). For example, several studies have found that conversion of

194 · Anthropogenic Impacts on Soil Fauna Assemblages

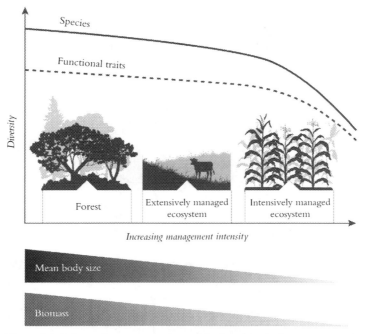

Figure 6.1 Schematic representation of the hypothetical management impacts on soil fauna assemblages. It is expected that soil fauna species richness, mean body size, and biomass decrease with increasing management intensity. Similarly, the diversity of functional traits is likely to decrease with management intensity, but the effect may be less pronounced.

natural ecosystems has negative effects on the diversity of termites, favouring r-strategists and pioneer species (Collins 1980, Eggleton and Bignell 1995, Johns 1992), reduces the species richness of ants (Dunn 2004a), and modifies assemblage structure (Fayle et al. 2010), while habitat degradation often results in more negative interspecific interactions (Floren et al. 2001). In a meta-analysis, Alroy (2017) showed that habitat disturbance has substantial negative impacts on species richness of plants (~30% for trees) and animals (8% to 65%) in tropical forests. The impacts were disproportionally large for certain taxa, including ant and scarab beetle species richness, and the impact on species richness increased with the level of disturbance. Moreover, fragmentation results in reduced species diversity and altered assemblage structure of termites at least in the mid- to long term (>5 years) (Brussaard et al. 2012), indicating disturbance beyond the impacted area. Biodiversity loss associated with global change and, in particular, land use changes, are thus significant threats to ecosystems worldwide. While the effects belowground have been difficult to estimate beyond local shifts in assemblage diversity and structure and possible local extinctions, there is substantial evidence that anthropogenic activities negatively impact plant diversity aboveground (Loreau et al. 2001, Sala et al. 2000, Vitousek et al. 1997b). Because the plants largely govern carbon and nutrient inputs to the soil, and thus fuel the soil food web, it should not be surprising that this will impact belowground assemblages and through this ecosystem processes. However, there is ongoing debate about the importance of plant species versus plant functional diversity and productivity as key drivers of belowground impacts, with many studies giving limited notion of species richness (Hooper et al. 2005). This may in part be driven by a lack of robust, long-term studies. For instance, Eisenhauer and co-workers (2011a) investigated the effects of plant species (1–60) and functional (1–4) diversity on soil biota in a grassland field experiment established at Jena, Germany, after two, four, and six years. The authors found that the importance of plant functional group diversity on soil macrofauna decomposers diminished through time, while the effect of plant species diversity was more constant through time and remained after the effects of functional group diversity and productivity had been accounted for. This suggests that diversity may be a more significant driver of belowground diversity and density than previously assumed. However, the effects on decomposers only appeared after four to six year's treatment duration, indicating that short-term studies may underestimate impacts of plant species losses belowground. The effects on the soil mesofauna, springtails and oribatid mites, were more variable across the three sampling dates, with density and diversity of both groups being influenced by multiple plant community properties. Maintaining plant biodiversity in production systems may therefore be key to promoting belowground biodiversity. Indeed, because of the reduced soil biodiversity observed under intensive management practices, soil fauna generally plays a lesser role in ecosystem processes. For example, Beare et al. (1992) used biocides to manipulate soil food webs in conventional and non-tillage agroecosystems and investigated the contributions of key taxa to litter decomposition processes. The work confirmed that fungi and bacteria were the main decomposers of litter on the surface and within the soil matrix, respectively, and also showed that the suppression of soil microarthropods had very limited effects on litter mass loss (<5% reduction in mass loss when absent). Still, the interactions between fungal-feeding microarthropods and their resource moderated litter N dynamics, indicating that they play an important role.

It is widely accepted that intensive management practices have detrimental impacts on soil fauna, albeit with taxa-specific responses to management regimes (Wallwork 1976). For example, heavy machinery and high levels of traffic associated with intensive management practices tend to cause considerable compaction of the soil. This is problematic as much soil fauna relies on existing soil porosity for habitat (Chapter 5), and accordingly lower abundances of soil fauna are often observed in soils that are compacted or show reduced structural complexity (Battigelli et al. 2004, Borcard and Matthey 1995, Heisler and Kaiser 1995). Hence, any agricultural practice that causes soil compaction or modifies the spatial configuration will likely impact soil fauna assemblages. Moreover, there is substantial evidence that the intensification of land use management associated with production systems generally promote bacterial-dominated soil food webs (e.g. de Vries et al. 2012b, Eisenhauer and Schädler 2011, Giller et al. 1997), which in turn will have cascading impacts on soil fauna assemblages. Specifically, intensive land use management practices such as tillage and fertilisation tend to favour bacterial-feeding organisms whereas extensive management promotes fungal-feeding organisms through a switch in soil food web structure (deVries et al., 2012a). Indeed, there is evidence that no-tillage practices support greater bacterial and fungal biomass, but they do support higher fungal:bacterial ratios, as opposed to conventional tillage, which increases soil aggregate formation (Beare et al. 1997) and likely carbon sequestration (Six et al. 2006).

The impacts of management practices on soil fauna assemblages have been studied extensively. For example, a study found that earthworm abundance and biomass differed predictably across management regimes ranging from conventional practices, in this case wheat–soy rotations with conventional tillage and fertiliser and herbicide applications to no tillage and tilled with organic input practices, old fields, a conifer plantation, and old-growth deciduous forest (Smith et al. 2008b). Earthworm abundances responded positively to the switch from conventional to no tillage and organic management practices. There was no additional increase in earthworm density in the old fields or the conifer plantation, but the old growth forests supported much greater densities of earthworms. Similarly, Kuntz et al. (2013) found higher earthworm densities, particularly juvenile earthworms, and cocoons in reduced tillage production systems compared to conventional tillage after nine years. The authors also found greater PLFA indicators of protozoans in the topsoil. Moreover, experimental slurry additions had a positive effect on juvenile anecic earthworm density but reduced microbial biomass. In comparison, oribatid and mesostigmatid mite assemblages showed contrasting shifts across a land use intensity gradient ranging from cornfields to hardwood forests in New York (Minor and Cianciolo 2007). In particular, the species richness of oribatid mites of a given sample (α-diversity) and that of the ecosystem (γ-diversity) increased with decreasing management intensity, whereas no such pattern was observed for the mesostigmatid mites. However, there were clear shifts in assemblage composition of both mite groups along the management intensity gradient.

Management practices appear to have fewer direct effects on carabid beetle assemblages, which are instead related to landscape complexity. In a survey of conventional and organic farming practices in Germany, it was found that carabid beetle diversity and abundance was positively related to the percentage of grassland cover of the surrounding landscape (1.5 km radius), with no differences observed between organic and conventional farms (Purtauf et al. 2005). A related study using the same sites found an increase in ground-dwelling spiders in the organic farming plots, and the density of spiders in the conventional farmed plots increased with the proportion of non-crop habitat in the surrounding area (Schmidt et al. 2005). Moreover, spider species richness increased in both management types in complex landscapes with higher non-crop habitats. Spiders and carabid beetles are important predators of potential plant pests and the incorporation of more diversity in the landscape could thus benefit farm productivity. Similarly, a survey of macrofauna densities and ecosystem services at 270 sites in southern Columbia and northern Brazil representing several different land use types (annual and perennial crops, pasture, fallow, forest) showed significant correlation between macrofauna assemblages and landscape characteristics (Marichal et al. 2014). Moreover, there was a significant correlation between several ecosystem services and macrofauna assemblages indicating that the presence of this fauna is important to maintaining functioning. Finally, pastures located less than 100 m from a forest supported greater densities and diversity of macrofauna than comparable pastures that were not near a forest. Given the correlation between ecosystem services and macrofauna assemblages the proximity to a forest may hence contribute to greater service provisioning.

Tillage is a common agricultural practice used to suppress weeds, prepare the seedbed, and manage soil-associated pests and pathogens. The practice further contributes to the dispersion of soil macroaggregates and modifies the soil physical structure influencing the soil water-holding capacity, infiltration, and leaching, and temperature and gas dynamics. This generally accelerates decomposition and causes reductions in soil organic carbon content. There is also evidence that tillage directly (i.e. by causing death of resident soil fauna through disturbance) and indirectly influences soil fauna (Ayuke et al. 2011, Birkhofer et al. 2011, Roger-Estrade et al. 2010); however, the impact is moderated by tillage intensity and soil type. Due to the significant disturbance caused by tillage the practice favours early successional species (Swift et al. 2004). The negative impact of agricultural practices on soil fauna abundance and diversity has been known for a long time. For example, a study by Raw (1967) comparing a permanent grassland with arable fields found a reduction in arthropod abundance of an order of magnitude due to cereal crops, particularly due to a reduction in mite and springtail abundances, and that several arthropod groups were not present in the tilled fields (i.e. Araneida, Thysanura, Protura, Pauropoda). Tillage is therefore generally perceived as a disturbance that negatively impacts soil fauna diversity and density, but this is not always the case. Indeed, strategic tillage can be employed to aerate densely compacted soil, which will benefit both soil organisms and the crop. Moreover, tillage combined with fallows can be used to manage soils that are heavily infested by soil fauna pests, including plant parasitic nematodes. Finally, it should be noted that tillage does not influence all soil fauna equally so that functioning is not necessarily lost entirely.

Switching from conventional tillage to no-till or conservation tillage can therefore positively influence soil fauna abundances. For example, springtail abundances were greater in winter wheat maintained using conservation tillage compared to conventional methods, although there was no difference in species richness between the two regimes (Brennan et al. 2006). Moreover, the effects were species specific with most species showing a positive response, while *Folsomia candida* that is known to reproduce rapidly was more abundant in the conventional tilled plots. It seems likely that the release from competition for resources due to lower abundances of other springtails contributed to this pattern. Similarly, several other studies have found that microarthropod abundances are higher in conservation or reduced tillage systems (Alvarez et al. 2001, Fox et al. 1999). There is also evidence that switching from conventional tillage to reduced tillage can improve earthworm abundances and modify earthworm assemblage structure. For example, nine years after the implementation of reduced tillage in a six-year organic spelt crop rotation, earthworm abundances were greater in the reduced tillage system than treatments with conventional tillage, mainly due to more juveniles, and there was a difference in the species composition between the two tillage regimes (Kuntz et al. 2013). Hence, tillage regimes can be used as a tool to manage earthworm assemblages in agro-ecosystems. Similarly, conversion of extensively managed grassland to arable land, and vice versa, had substantial impacts on soil fauna assemblages in an experimental field facility in the Netherlands (Postma-Blaauw et al. 2010, 2012). The investigators converted part of a long-term arable field (crop rotation: oat, maize, barley, potato) to grassland, while existing grassland was converted to arable fields, and assessed impacts on bacteria, nematodes, enchytraeids, earthworms, and predatory mites. The conversion of grassland to arable land had detrimental impacts on the soil fauna, with a dramatic decrease in taxonomic diversity and richness observed shortly after conversion, particularly pronounced in the larger bodies' soil fauna. In contrast, the establishment of extensively managed grasslands contributed to the recovery of earthworm assemblages and a species-rich nematode assemblage but had limited effects on predatory mites and enchytraeids. Several other studies support these findings, with general negative impacts of intensive management practices on soil fauna density and diversity that are particularly pronounced for larger-bodied organisms (Culman et al. 2010, Ponge et al. 2013, Tsiafouli et al. 2015). However, negative effects of reduced tillage have been observed in some systems (De Ruiter et al. 1993), indicating that this is not a universal outcome. In particular, tillage can help aerate the soils, increase the number of habitable pores, and distribute organic matter which can be beneficial to soil fauna if the soils are suffering from compaction. Still, the disturbance imposed by tillage generally negatively impacts soil fauna. Moreover, tillage can increase the abundance of root herbivores, including beetle and dipteran larvae with negative impacts on crop productivity.

There is still discussion about the possible effect of organic farming practices on belowground organisms. However, some studies point towards the benefits of organic farming on soil fauna assemblages and the soil processes to which they contribute. For example, when comparing organic farmed arable fields with conventional and no-till systems, it was found that the organic fields supported much greater densities of mesofauna and macrofauna than the conventional and no-till systems (Domínguez et al. 2014). Moreover, decomposition rates were substantially greater in organic farming systems. Two early reviews of organic farming showed similar patterns (Bengtsson et al. 2005, Hole et al. 2005). There is general evidence that soil fauna biomass and species richness is greater in organic farming systems than conventional systems, but with taxa-specific responses. It appears that the number of carabid beetles increases due to an increase in plant cover, whereas the number of earthworms and other soil fauna increases due to greater organic inputs (residue, manure). Hole et al. (2005) found an increase in bacterial-feeding nematodes in organic systems associated with greater bacterial biomass. A more recent meta-analysis showed that organic farming supports 34% higher species richness than conventional farming systems, with positive effects on pollinators, predators, and herbivores, but no significant effect on decomposer diversity (Tuck et al. 2014).

There is further evidence that some management practices have unexpected, sometime beneficial, non-target effects on soil fauna. For example, there is great interest in management practices that promote pest and disease suppression, including ameliorating or reducing the effects of plant parasitic nematodes. There are multiple potential mechanisms through which soils can become suppressive to certain pests and pathogens, and it is a topic of great interest given its potential to substantially improve yield while reducing costs in agroecosystems. One practice that has received some attention in this regard is mulching. Mulches can influence soil fauna in multiple ways including providing a more suitable habitat. In particular, mulches generally reduce evaporation thereby promoting soil water retention, which is essential to most soil fauna. However, mulches or residue addition does not always result in positive outcomes for soil fauna, and often the effects are species specific (Brennan et al. 2006). For example, a recent study found that organic soil amendments, and poultry litter in particular, reduced the density of plant parasitic nematodes and increased the density of other free-living soil nematodes likely through improved soil structure in an Australian vineyard (Rahman et al. 2014). This study is consistent with the findings of other studies. Suppression of soil pests and pathogens may be achieved through antagonistic bacteria and fungi (Kerry 2000) or the release of nematocidal compounds during decomposition (Thoden et al. 2011). Another option is that soil food web complexity aids in disease and pest suppression. A microcosm study, for example, showed that more complex or longer soil food webs effectively suppressed the plant parasitic nematode *Meloidogyne incognita* (Sánchez-Moreno 2010). The authors incubated soils collected in an oak forest and a vineyard imposing different management regimes including two with pesticide applications, two types of nitrogen fertilisation, and a tillage application. They then used nematode assemblage structure as a proxy for food web complexity and found that soil suppresiveness of *M. incognita* increased with greater predator–prey ratios and in soils with higher prevalence of predators and omnivores. Their results thus indicate that soil food web structure as impacted by management regimes influences the ability of soils to suppress pests and pathogens. Accordingly, Stirling (2011) showed that control soils suppressed the multiplication of the root lesion nematode *Pratylenchus thornei*, relative to irradiated or heat-sterilised soils, even when these had been reinoculated with native soil biotic assemblages. Another study that investigated whether plant–soil feedbacks contribute to the performance of invasive plant species in novel environments found that the addition of soil microorganisms and microarthropods exerted top-down control on plant parasitic nematodes in the root zone of both native and invasive species (Viketoft and van der Putten 2015). Similarly, the application of straw or compost mulch increases the abundance of natural enemies including surface-dwelling ground beetles, parasitoid Hymenoptera, and spiders and the abundance of earthworms in Australian vineyards (Thompson and Hoffmann 2007), which in turn could have negative impacts on potential pest species through suppression or positive effects on yield through improved soil quality (Baggen and Gurr 1998, Bengtsson et al. 2005).

Management practices that incorporate greater diversity of plant functional groups and impose less disturbance, such as agroforestry, crop rotation, inter-cropping, minimum-tillage with mulch additions, and integrated livestock-arable production systems, generally support more diverse soil communities (Swift et al. 2004). For example, no-till management when combined with mixed crop rotation, cover crops, integrated pest management practices (IPM), nutrient restoration, and conserved usage of agrochemicals (collectively referred to as Good Agricultural Practices or GAPs) increased the abundances of litter and soil fauna, particularly ants, earthworms, prostigmatid mites, and springtails relative to conventional no-till practices on two different soil types in the Argentine Pampas region (Bedano et al. 2016). Moreover, there were substantial shifts in assemblage structure for these taxa that are likely to reflect changes in ecosystem functioning. Importantly, these practices are known to support high productivity (Albertengo et al. 2011), which should aid in their implementation. Converting intensively managed arable fields to extensively managed grasslands by contrast generally have positive effects on soil biodiversity, including soil microarthropods (de Groot et al. 2016). However, this is not necessarily desirable given the increased need for greater crop production to feed our growing population.

Incorporation of trees in agricultural systems, i.e. agroforestry (Figure 6.2), generally have positive effects on soil biota (Martius et al.

Figure 6.2 An example of agroforestry in Ndindi, Malawi, where maize is cultivated in the presence of the leguminous tree *Faidherbia albida*. Courtesy of Johan Six.

2004, Pauli et al. 2011). In particular, trees may contribute to habitat modifications that are beneficial to soil fauna. For example, when comparing litter layer temperatures of native rainforests, secondary forest, and plantations it was found that increased canopy cover substantially reduced litter temperatures during hot days, with monthly average temperatures of 2–4°C, and up to 10°C on individual days, higher in the plantation (Martius et al. 2004). This in turn influenced soil macrofauna biomass that was positively related to canopy closure. Moreover, a recent literature review found that agroforestry increases earthworm, beetle, centipede, millipede, ant, collembolan, mite, and non-parasitic nematode abundances, but not the abundance of termites or plant parasitic nematodes relative to continuous cropping systems (Barrios et al. 2012). However, these results were derived from a limited selection of experiments, and more research is required to substantiate when and where agroforestry can benefit soil fauna assemblages and to what extent. Moreover, this should be linked to the health of the ecosystem and changes in yield or profitability to promote sustainable management of these systems. It is also important to consider the landscape matrix of land use types when managing soil fauna assemblages. In a survey of the controls on soil macroarthropod species diversity in low-input farming systems in Germany, it was shown that, although land use and habitat characteristics to a large extent govern the diversity of macroarthropods, the broader landscape characteristics are also important (Dauber et al. 2005). In some cases, the effect of landscape characteristics was even more important than land use or habitat characteristics, with millipede species richness strongly dependent on the presence of nearby forested habitats.

6.2 Fertilisation and Nitrogen Deposition

As mentioned earlier, the input of nitrogen, phosphorus, and other nutrients has increased substantially since the industrial revolution, particularly driven by the increasing demand for agricultural productivity, modifying global biogeochemical cycles (Vitousek et al. 1997b). The application of N and P in particular is likely to have significant impacts on the soil food web by influencing the environmental stoichiometry (Mulder et al. 2015) and reducing the reliance on microbial associates by plants (Aslam et al. 2015). An early meta-analysis involving data from 82 publications showed that N fertilisation resulted in decreased microbial biomass (−15%) and an associated reduction in soil respiration likely driven by the biomass responses given a strong correlation between the biomass and respiration response ratios (Treseder 2008). Moreover, the author found that the effects were more pronounced in studies of longer duration and increased with greater amounts of N additions. This could have important implications whereby fertilisation reduces the reliance of plants on belowground organisms for carbon and nutrient mineralization that is likely to have cascading effects on higher trophic levels. The nutrients are generally added to production systems to boost yields, but it has been estimated that only about 50% of the N applied as fertiliser is used by plants with a large proportion of the remaining N being stored in the soil, lost to the atmosphere as volatile compounds or leached to surface and groundwater reservoirs posing a significant threat to our ecosystems (Galloway et al. 2008). Most studies to date have focussed on the effects of N additions with limited knowledge of the impact of P and other nutrients. However, they are likely to have similar effects. The results of fertilisation studies have to be interpreted with care as recent work has found that the effect of P fertilisation on soil fauna was associated with indirect effects of the P addition due to changes in soil pH rather than an increase in P availability *per se* (Nielsen et al. 2015a).

A recent meta-analysis provided insight into the effect of fertiliser application on nematode assemblages (Liu et al. 2016). The authors canvassed the literature for studies that investigated the effect of inorganic and organic fertilisers on nematode assemblages resulting in 229 data points from 54 studies. These studies collectively provided strong evidence that the application of organic fertilisers with high-carbon contents have a positive effect on nematode abundances and species richness relative to unfertilised control plots, whereas the application of inorganic nitrogen-rich fertilisers negatively impacted nematode species richness and diversity, the abundance of omnivore-predatory nematodes and reduced the maturity index (MI). However, the organic fertilisers differed in their capacity to influence nematode assemblage structure in that carbon-rich organic fertilisers, such as crop residue, promoted nematode abundances and diversity, and the structure (SI) and enrichment (EI) indices, whereas the nitrogen-rich organic fertilisers such as animal manure reduced plant parasitic nematode abundances. The latter finding is likely because animal manure contains a large amount of labile material that benefits the bacterial-feeding nematodes in particular as observed elsewhere (Ponge et al. 2013). The study importantly highlights that the impact of fertilisers can be predicted relatively well, based on the type of fertiliser and its carbon and nutrient contents. Such information is critical to ensure that ecosystem functioning is promoted rather than impaired by fertilisation. Similarly, other studies have found that the application of organic fertilisers can have positive impacts on soil fauna biomass and modify belowground assemblages (Edwards and Lofty 1969, Treonis et al. 2010). Manning et al. (2006) observed an increase in collembolan abundances (e.g. bottom-up effects) through increased litter inputs associated with nitrogen addition. Similarly, the application of fertiliser in a nitrogen-limited tallgrass prairie ecosystem promoted herbivorous nematode populations (Todd et al. 1999). Such effects are only expected where nitrogen addition enhances resource availability and quality, i.e. plant inputs or microbial resources (Wardle 2002). However, more limited effects of nitrogen addition were observed in a long-term (13-year) grassland field experiment, except for an increase in fungal-feeding nematodes and a decrease in predatory nematodes, with no impacts on other nematodes or microarthropods (Eisenhauer et al. 2013).

More broadly, Earth's ecosystems, and by extension the soil fauna assemblages, are influenced by increased atmospheric nitrogen deposition. Most nitrogen deposition originates from the burning of biomass and fossil fuels, and volatilisation from production of fertilisers and livestock (Vitousek et al. 1997a), and is deposited mainly as either reduced (e.g. NH_4) or oxidised (e.g. NO, NO_2) forms with substantial variation in quantities deposited among different geographical regions ranging from

6.2 Fertilisation and Nitrogen Deposition

negligible amounts to over 30 kg N ha^{-1}. There is evidence that the long-term deposition of N has influenced soil C:N ratios, at least of (semi) natural ecosystems (Mulder et al. 2015), and there is concern that the soil acidification caused by N deposition may influence ecosystem function (Bowman et al. 2008). Nitrogen is limiting plant productivity in nearly every major biome (LeBauer and Treseder 2008), and while an increase in N *per se* is unlikely to directly influence soil fauna assemblages there might be significant indirect effects through changes in the plant assemblage (e.g. host plants), plant litter inputs and exudates, and microbial assemblages (resource quantity and quality, altered edaphic conditions). For example, N enrichment generally reduces plant species richness and diversity, often resulting in the extinction of locally rare plant species and N fixing plants (Bobbink et al. 2010, Suding et al. 2005), although the exact cause of this is yet to be established (Manning 2012). Moreover, it appears that the observed loss of plant species due to N addition is associated with an increase in plant primary productivity (Clark et al. 2007). The loss of plant species in response to N deposition could have cascading effects on soil fauna assemblages through the loss of suitable plant hosts for belowground herbivores, such as plant parasitic nematodes, but also through changes in the quality and quantity of resource inputs. In particular, the loss of legumes could result in more recalcitrant litter. By contrast, increased N availability is likely to promote primary productivity and through this the root exudation and input of organic matter to the soil, which could increase the population size of at least some soil fauna. Furthermore, increased N availability tends to promote plant N content (Xia and Wan 2008) and favours plant species with high-quality litters (Chapin 1980), which could compensate for the high-quality leaf litter lost due to suppression of legumes and other N-fixing plants. A study found that soil microarthropod communities in alpine ecosystems appeared to be indirectly impacted by N deposition through changes in habitat (moss cover and depth) and resource (plant C:N ratio) across the United Kingdom (Mitchell et al. 2016). In particular, the authors found that oribatid mites and springtail abundances increased at sites with higher N deposition where moss depth and plant C:N was lower and hypothesised that the increased abundances were associated with greater resource quality. By contrast, the predatory mesostigmatid mites were less impacted by habitat and resource quality and were also impacted by prey availability.

The effects of N deposition, fertilisers, and other agrochemicals on soil fauna assemblages are relatively easy to quantify but not necessarily that informative. A more interesting question might be what are the consequences for plant nutrient uptake, carbon, and nutrient cycling, and ecosystem functioning more broadly. For example, a study of the impact of fertiliser and irrigation on soil fauna assemblages in an experimental eucalyptus plantation showed that fertilisation in combination with irrigation have substantial negative impacts on mite and nematode abundances, but there were no changes in plant bioavailable nutrients (Aslam et al. 2015). This suggested that the ongoing fertiliser application in combination with irrigation were maintaining nutrient supply, with the soil fauna contributing less to ecosystem functioning. This indicates a trade-off between nutrients supplied via fertilisers and mineralization by soil fauna. While this is not necessarily a concern to the land manager in the short term, it does indicate that this system will require fertiliser application to maintain production in the longer term. However, because there is a negative trade-off between fertilisation and soil fauna, this could be less cost effective than better management of fertiliser inputs and promoting the service provision by soil fauna.

6.3 Agrochemicals and Other Pollutants

The impacts of pollutants, such as heavy metals and pesticides, on above- and belowground fauna can be substantial. They are particularly likely to impact organisms that are in direct contact with dissolved chemical compounds, such as the microfauna that lives in the water films and water-filled pores within the soil, but most soil fauna is at risk. The influence is likely to be related to the bioavailability of the compound, rather than the total amount, which is moderated by soil properties and the properties of the compound itself, and bioaccumulation may contribute to effects at higher trophic levels as contaminants get transferred through the food chain (Didden and Römbke 2001). Moreover, effects of changes in the plant assemblage due to the use of herbicides indirectly impact soil fauna assemblages due to altered resource (and habitat) availability (Prasse 1989). The detrimental impacts of industrial pollutants have long been known. For example, soils influenced by chlorine from industrial use were found to have reduced species richness and densities of mesofauna, with oribatid mite densities decreasing by 60%, and an associated shift in assemblage composition (Vanek 1967). Another early study found a reduction in nematode fauna in sulphur dioxide (SO_2)–impacted forests in Germany, with fewer semi-parasitic nematodes and more saprophagous and predatory species, likely associated with impacts on the vegetation (Bassus 1968). However, the impacts are highly dependent on the type of pollutant, the scale of impact, and chemical properties, and the taxon involved.

Nematode responses to pollution have been reasonably well examined given their reputation as bioindicators (see Chapter 3). This work has shown that nematode abundances are rarely strongly influenced by contamination, but effects are often observed in nematode assemblage structure. For example, Shao et al. (2008) found that the abundance of nematodes in the 3 to 5 coloniser-persister (c-p) categories (i.e. persisters or K-strategists), but not total abundances, were related to heavy metal contamination of zinc and lead mine tailings in China. Similarly, an earlier study found that nematode biomass, diversity, and species richness were negatively correlated with lead contamination, with particularly pronounced effects on Dorylaimina that are mostly classified as c-p 4 and c-p 5 (Zullini and Peretti 1986), and another study found negative effects of copper, nickel, and zinc additions to soil on omnivore and predatory nematodes (Korthals et al. 1996). While neither of these studies found substantial effects on nematode abundances of c-p 1 and c-p 2 (i.e. colonisers or r-strategists), earlier studies have found both positive (Georgieva et al. 2002) and negative (Sánchez-Moreno et al. 2006) effects of heavy metal on these groups. It seems likely that fast reproduction or smaller size of the lower c-p value species may in some cases compensate for the loss of larger-bodied and longer-lived species. Moreover, it appears that the effects of heavy metal contamination on nematodes is relatively predictable, with higher trophic levels and species classified as higher c-p value organisms are more sensitive to contamination. A lab incubation using small amounts of soils collected from an arable field and a nearby degraded soil showed that the soil nematode assemblages from the arable field (labelled restored in the publication) maintained higher abundances, species richness, and ecosystem function even following disturbances (heating, drying, copper, chloroform fumigation) (Liu et al. 2012). However, there were treatment-specific differences in the response of the nematode structural index, with greater stability in the degraded soil in response to heating and drying, largely due to the presence of tolerant omnivores and predators, indicating that not all high c-p nematodes are sensitive to disturbances. Still, the arable soil showed greater functional resilience, i.e. higher rates of soil processes, in response to the disturbances imposed than the degraded soil, which may have implications for functioning under global change.

The application of pesticides and agrochemicals generally has a negative impact on both soil microbes and fauna (Chelinho et al. 2011, Eisenhauer et al. 2009), promoting the reliance on external inputs because of the associated impacts on soil processes. There is even evidence that it can contribute to changes in aboveground–belowground interactions and reduce biological pest control (Birkhofer et al. 2008). Microarthropods show mostly short-term negative responses to pesticide application, but species-specific responses contribute to altered assemblage composition (Petersen and Krogh 1987). Longer-term pesticide application generally negatively impacts species richness of microarthropods, but can have positive effects on abundances (Larink 1997). Interestingly, the predatory mesostigmatid mites showed a negative response with a possible decrease in predation of the remaining species. Enchytraeids are known to be sensitive to environmental contaminants, ranging from pesticides to heavy metals to acid rain (Didden and Römbke 2001), and have been shown to respond negatively to a broad range of pesticides, even at concentrations well below those associated with common agricultural practices. The effects of heavy metal contamination appear to be more variable, while acid rain and the associated shift in pH can influence enchytraeids if they are exposed to levels outside of their required ranges.

The effect of mining can be detrimental to soil assemblages due to the disturbance caused by the mining activities and increased concentrations of pollutants. For example, a survey of 43 sites near past mining and smelting sites found that the abundance of enchytraeid densities were negatively impacted by heavy metal concentrations (Kapusta et al. 2011). By contrast, the higher concentration of exchangeable heavy metals had no effect on nematode or tardigrade densities. However, heavy metal concentrations were generally higher in habitats that had greater organic matter contents. Given the link between organic matter and soil fauna densities this could have interacted with the effects of heavy metal concentrations, particularly if nematodes and tardigrades are less sensitive than enchytraeids to pollution. Heavy metal contamination similarly had limited impact on oribatid mite densities among nine west European woodlands with varying levels of contamination, but there was substantial shift in assemblage structure among contamination levels, with heavy metals negatively impacting *Platynothrus peltifer* and *Hypochtonius rufulus*, both species that have been shown elsewhere to be sensitive to heavy metals (Khalil et al. 2009). Similarly, a comparison of shooting ranges contaminated by lead (Pb) and antimony (Sb) from pellets with control sites in Italy found limited impact on oribatid mite or springtail abundances (Migliorini et al. 2005). However, both springtail and oribatid mite assemblage composition was related to the level of contamination, with stronger shifts in assemblage composition observed for the oribatid mites compared with springtail assemblages. When comparing soil fauna densities of an active shooting range with an abandoned shooting range and a control site in a boreal forest, Selonen et al. (2014) found substantial impacts on enchytraeid, nematode, and microarthropod densities and assemblage composition. However, because of the increased release of lead from the pellets over time, the effects were most pronounced in the humus layer in the abandoned shooting range, with enchytraeids being completely absent from this layer. The effect was less pronounced in the fermentation layer, likely due to the deposition of new, uncontaminated organic material. There is therefore limited evidence for consistent effects of heavy metals on microarthropod densities, but strong support for consistent shifts in assemblage composition related to the sensitivity of individual species. Several of the studies outlined earlier indicate that oribatid mite assemblages are particularly sensitive to contamination, and they may be useful bioindicators. However, more work is required to validate the use of microarthropods as indicators of heavy metal contamination.

Few studies have investigated the effects of acid rain on soil fauna assemblages. Given the potential impact on soil pH and changes in the vegetation aboveground, it is highly likely that acid rain can have strong effects belowground, both on the organisms and ecosystem functioning. There is broad agreement that acid rain can cause changes in soil chemistry through adsorption and desorption processes (Qiu et al. 2015), aluminium toxicity (Zhang et al. 2014), and impacts on microbial assemblages and functioning (Wang et al. 2014). Few studies have assessed the impacts on soil fauna, but acid rain has been shown to suppress earthworm activity (Zhang et al. 2015) and enchytraeid assemblages (Didden and Römbke 2001). In many areas, acid rain may not be a prominent problem following greater industrial regulation, but there are still parts of the world where acid rain poses a significant threat. For example, it is estimated that acid rain is a substantial contemporary threat to ecosystems in China (Wei et al. 2017). The authors accordingly investigated the possible effects of acid rain by altering pH (creating a soil pH gradient from 2.5 to 7) on a broad range of soil fauna. The abundance and diversity of soil fauna decreased in the heavily impacted soils only (pH = 2.5 and 3.5) while at the same time causing significant shifts in assemblage composition, indicating that acid rain impacts will be moderated by the change in pH elicited by the acid rain.

6.4 Impacts of Invasive Species

One of the main threats to ecosystems is the increased dispersal of microbial, animal, and plant species, often facilitated by human activities, which may become invasive in a new habitat. This threat is further confounded by global changes and the ongoing disturbance of our ecosystems leaving them more vulnerable to invasion. The potential consequence of invasive species has been discussed in several excellent papers, but with a particular focus on invasive plant and animal species, and our understanding of the effect of belowground invasive species is more limited (but see Wardle and Peltzer 2017). There is substantial evidence that invasive plant species can influence belowground assemblages but that the effects depend on vegetation type, plant species, and litter quality (Belnap and Phillips 2001, Chen et al. 2007). There are fewer examples of the effects of invasive soil fauna, albeit with a few notable exceptions. The main focus of this section will be on invasive species in relation to soil fauna assemblages. This will include direct and indirect effects of invasive plants, and indirect effects of invasive animals, on soil fauna assemblages as well as the impacts of invasive soil fauna on other soil organisms, the vegetation, and the ecosystem more broadly.

6.4.1 Movement of Plants and Animals Aboveground

An early literature review highlighted that few studies have assessed the impacts of plant invasion on soil microbial assemblages and associated consequences for ecosystem functioning (van der Putten et al. 2007). They concluded that plant invasions were most likely to have significant impacts on specialist microbes, assemblage diversity, and ecosystem functioning, with limited impacts on generalist decomposer microbes. In turn, pathogenic and symbiotic soil microbes are more likely to influence the plant assemblage and ecosystem functioning than microbial decomposers. While none of these papers specifically assessed the effects on the soil fauna assemblages, the associated modifications to the plant and microbe assemblages and ecosystem functioning is likely to influence the soil fauna as well. Moreover, types of soil fauna that are specialists or associated with particular types of plants are more likely to be responsive than generalist decomposers as observed at the microbial level. Since the paper by van der Putten et al. (2007), there has been a significant increase in the available literature on this topic that has provided new insights.

McCary et al. (2016) surveyed the literature to assess the impacts of invasive plant species on primary and secondary consumers in both 'green' (grazer) and 'brown' (detrital) food webs in wetlands, grasslands, and forests. The authors conducted a meta-analysis to quantify the impacts based on 98 observations extracted from 32 papers. Because the focus of the book is on soil fauna, I will mention only that invasive plant species had a marginal negative effect on the abundance of primary consumers, but increased the abundance of secondary consumers, in detrital food webs in forests (in both cases $p < 0.1$ only), whereas no effects were observed in the grasslands. Moreover, the results showed a significant decrease in primary consumers in the green food web in the forest, with no effect in the grassland. These results indicate that forest ecosystems may be more sensitive to invasive species than grasslands. While most of the herbivores associated with the green food web in this meta-analysis are found aboveground, the impacts on belowground herbivores are likely to show a similar trajectory. It is, however, difficult from these results to draw broader conclusions about the potential impact of invasive plant species on key soil fauna taxa or feeding groups, and it highlights the lack of data to support these analyses. Moreover, the impacts are likely to be highly dependent on the type of plant invaders, as I will highlight below.

Invasive plant species can modify successional patterns by moderating belowground assemblages. For example, in a removal experiment it was shown that low-biomass non-native plant species had a disproportionally large impact on ecosystem structure during primary succession, enhancing soil carbon, microbial biomass, and altering composition, and increasing microbial feeding and predatory nematodes (Peltzer et al. 2009). These results indicate that the presence of low-biomass plant species can cause trophic cascades and substantially modify ecosystem functioning, here likely driven by their life history traits and higher leaf nitrogen content relatively to the dominant native species. Indeed, a meta-analysis of the effects of invasive plant species on C and N dynamics points to a substantial impact (Liao et al. 2008). In particular, invasive plant species are associated with greater plant C stocks, particularly aboveground, and increased fluxes of C and N due to greater productivity and increased decomposition rates. Moreover, invasive plants are associated with an increase in soil NH_4^+ and NO_3^- content as well as greater plant N concentrations. These effects are particularly pronounced for invasive woody plant species and N-fixing plants. The effect of invasive species is likely to be particularly important in some ecosystems. For example, invasive species, including plants, is one of the key threats to Antarctica's unique terrestrial ecosystems that currently only support

Figure 6.3 The only two native vascular plants, *Colobanthus quitensis* and *Deschampsia antarctica*, found in Antarctica.
Photo by the author.

two indigenous vascular plant species (Figure 6.3). A recent assessment of the risk of establishment indicates that human activities represent a significant vector of propagules, with the western Antarctic Peninsula being at greatest risk, coinciding with recent discoveries of alien species in this region (Chown et al. 2012). The establishment of alien plant species in Antarctica is likely to have profound impacts on the indigenous soil fauna, raising significant concerns for the future of the local ecosystems and the soil fauna assemblages.

There are fewer studies that report on the effects of invasive species of aboveground invertebrates and vertebrates. Large herbivores are likely to have substantial impacts belowground, both through their impact on vegetation composition, nutrient inputs via urine and faecal matter, and by modifying the physical environment by trampling and digging, but there are few studies on the effect of invasive large herbivores on soil fauna assemblages explicitly. More studies have investigated the effects of invasive terrestrial invertebrates. In an effort to assess the effect of invasive terrestrial invertebrates on plant productivity and vegetation composition, animal diversity and abundance, Cameron et al. (2016) conducted a meta-analysis using 710 individual cases reported in 112 articles. The authors grouped the impacts across all invasive terrestrial invertebrates and by trophic position. Overall, the presence of one or more invasive terrestrial invertebrates had a negative effect on plant fitness, animal density, and diversity, but increased litter decomposition. Most of the studies that assessed effects on litter decomposition rates involved the presence of invasive species in areas where no native invertebrate species were present, highlighting the likely impact of novel functional traits or ecosystem engineers. Moreover, there was strong evidence that the presence of invasive decomposers, again largely driven by studies of non-native earthworms, reduces the abundance of animals. The impacts of earthworms will be discussed in more detail in the next section.

The success and impact of non-native species are, however, likely in turn to be moderated by the native soil fauna. The effect of soil fauna on alien plant species is likely to be predominantly associated with negative plant–soil feedbacks because most direct soil fauna–plant interactions are negative. It has been proposed that species that rely on mutualistic belowground organisms are unlikely to be great colonisers. However, very few types of soil fauna can be considered host-specific mutualists that would differentially benefit non-native plant species. Hence, the ability of a given plant species to colonise a new location is more likely to be limited by belowground plant pests, such as plant parasitic nematodes or root-feeding insects, or be promoted by fewer potential pests in the ecosystem colonised. By contrast, indirect effects of invasive species could contribute to both positive and negative plant–soil feedbacks. For example, indirect positive plant–soil feedbacks mediated by the presence of ecosystem engineers or decomposers may benefit non-native plant species more than native species. There is some evidence that invasive plant species may experience 'enemy release' in their novel environments. For example, van der Putten et al. (2005) showed that *Ammophila arenaria* (Figure 6.4) have fewer specialist, but not generalist, plant parasitic nematodes in the southern hemisphere than within its natural distributional range. This pattern appears to be true at the global scale where *A. arenaria* is invasive (Reinhart and Callaway 2006). Similarly, four of six European perennial forbs showed substantial negative plant–soil feedbacks in their native soils, but not in North American grassland soils where they are introduced, indicating significant enemy release (Maron et al. 2014). By contrast, plant species that rely heavily on mutualistic associations are unlikely to become invasive, unless mutualists from their native range are transferred simultaneously or novel mutualistic associations can be formed with indigenous organisms (van der Putten et al. 2009). Novel

Figure 6.4 Ammophila arenaria is a common plant in European sand dune systems, including those pictured, where it helps stabilise the dunes. However, it has become invasive in many parts of the world, seemingly aided by a release from specialist nematode parasites.
Photo by the author.

mutualistic relationships are possible, but this is less likely to be a driver of soil fauna assemblages, although it could amplify the potential indirect impacts by promoting certain invasive plant species over native or other potential invasive species (Wardle and Peltzer 2017).

6.4.2 Invasive Soil Organisms

Invasions by soil fauna and its associated impact on ecosystems are not particularly well described, but it is known to occur and, in some cases, have substantial impact. A particularly great impact can be expected where new functional types are introduced. Reliably identifying the presence of non-native soil fauna is, however, limited by a lack of knowledge of species' natural distribution patterns, particularly for smaller taxa that are not well explored. Some of the best examples of the direct impacts of invasive soil organisms on ecosystems therefore involve macrofauna, such as ants, termites, and earthworms. For example, invasive ants often displace native ant species and substantially alter the entire ecosystem they colonise (O'Dowd et al. 2003). They reduce the richness of native ant species, alter the phylogenetic composition of the remaining assemblage through non-random species loss (Lessaard et al. 2009), and can through this alter ecosystem functioning. However, there are a few other illustrative examples of invasive soil fauna and their impact is described next.

Invasive earthworms can have a substantial impact on ecosystems, particularly when they colonise previously earthworm-free ecosystems (Hale et al. 2005, Hendrix et al. 2008). It has long been known that certain earthworms have a distribution that is well beyond that which would be expected (Beddard 1912, Eisen 1900), with more than 100 known species of invasive earthworms. This pattern is likely caused largely by unintentional human-assisted migration (Cameron et al. 2007, Lee 1987). An excellent overview of the origin and distribution of invasive earthworms is presented in Hendrix et al. (2008) and therefore I will not go into detail about this here. Instead, I will provide a few examples where the effects of invasive earthworms are well described. In particular, the ongoing invasion of European and Asian lumbricid earthworms of temperate forests in North America provides a good example of earthworm invasions and their impact on the ecosystems. Many North American temperate forests lack earthworms because they have not yet been able to colonise since the area was deglaciated (James 1995). However, in many areas non-native lumbricids have been introduced, intentionally or unintentionally. A review by Bohlen et al. (2004) discusses how the invasion generally reduces soil carbon storage and alters biogeochemical cycles, but highlights that there is also evidence for impacts on the soil food web structure more broadly and even the vegetation aboveground, leading to concerns about the extinction of rare native forb species. Moreover, the forests currently serves as a carbon sink, but the enhanced carbon cycling driven by earthworms may contribute to these forests becoming a carbon source in the future. Combined with the ongoing global change pressures, the effect of invasive earthworms on biogeochemical cycles, flora, and fauna raises uncertainties about the future of the temperate forest ecosystems in North America.

While many documented cases of the invasion of earthworms involve introductions where earthworms were previously missing due to glaciation or more recent disturbances, impacts of invasive earthworms have been documented in areas with native earthworm assemblages. Hendrix et al. (2006) reviewed the literature to assess the invasion success of non-native earthworms in ecosystems with and without native earthworms. They concluded that non-native earthworms were particularly successful in colonising disturbed habitats including those where native earthworms were not present. However, there were many cases where native and non-native earthworms managed to co-exist, at least in the short term, suggesting that there is limited competitive exclusion. Finally, they hypothesised that there might be some potential for native earthworm assemblages to resist an invasion of non-native earthworms but highlighted that there was not enough data to support this. However, it is not well understood what makes an earthworm likely to become invasive. Traits that are observed in highly invasive species are also found in non-invasive species, and close relatives of an invasive species are not necessarily likely to become invasive themselves (Hendrix et al. 2008). New molecular approaches may provide further insight into the distribution of native and non-native species. For example, Porco et al. (2013) compared the genetic structure of five non-native springtails and 10 non-native earthworms in North America with that of their native range in Europe using DNA barcoding (the 5' region of the mitochondrial cytochrome c oxidase subunit I, COI). Their results indicated 'massive and recurrent introduction' of most of the species surveyed. This was somewhat expected for the earthworms due to intentional human-assisted introductions but not for the springtails, suggesting that un-intentional introductions of at least smaller types of soil fauna occur frequently. Still, a few species of earthworms and springtails showed limited genetic diversity in North America, indicating population expansion from a small number of individuals, e.g. bottlenecks.

Exotic springtails have been shown to be present in several biogeographical regions, including Australia (Greenslade 2008, King et al. 1985, Womersley 1939), New Zealand (Salmon 1941), and the sub-Antarctic Islands (Gabriel et al. 2001, Greenslade and Convey 2012). There is broad agreement that invasive species are generally more tolerant to warming and may therefore be favoured by climate change (Janion et al. 2009, Slabber et al. 2007). A recent paper illustrated this well, providing strong evidence that non-native (alien) springtail species have a greater tolerance of climate warming than indigenous springtails (Janion-Scheepers et al. 2018) (Figure 6.5). The authors cultured 14 indigenous and 16 alien springtails from sites along a broad latitudinal gradient (16° S to 54° S) and investigated their critical thermal limits as well as warming tolerance. The alien springtails on average had a higher critical thermal limit than indigenous springtails from the same region. Moreover, the alien springtails also had a higher tolerance to warming (~3°C on average) across all sampling locations. Importantly, they also conducted an experiment to test whether the springtail thermal tolerance was plastic, which showed limited variation between generations. This suggests that it is unlikely that indigenous species will adapt to the new conditions. The authors therefore concluded that the predicted warming would be likely to benefit the alien springtail species over indigenous springtails across

6.4 Impacts of Invasive Species · 217

Figure 6.5 Examples of native and alien springtail species used to assess potential climate change impacts on springtail assemblages. Top panel: an indigenous temperate springtail of the genus *Lepidocyrtus* (left) and the alien species *Pogonognathellus flavescens* (right). Bottom panel: an indigenous tropical springtail of the genus *Triacanthella* (left) and an alien of the genus *Isotomurus* (right). Courtesy of Charlene Janion-Scheepers.

the climate gradient investigated because the alien species would be able to function throughout a larger proportion of the year. Moreover, invasive springtails are often more abundant in disturbed habitats, including those caused by land use changes, fertilisation, and high grazing intensity (Oliver et al. 2005, Yeates et al. 2000). Indeed, overgrazing can cause substantial changes in the plant assemblages, with corresponding effects belowground that may benefit invasive species. For example, it has been shown that the invasive springtail *Hypogastrura manubrialis* was more abundant under a grazing-tolerant plant species, yellow-bush (*Galenia africana*), than native springtail species in Renosterveld vegetation of the Western Cape, South Africa, exposed to high grazing pressures (Leinaas et al. 2015). Similarly, land use change often favour termite species likely to become invasive and could therefore promote the spread of invasive species (Leniaud et al. 2009). Disturbed coastal sand dune ecosystems in southern North America were also found to support greater abundance of the invasive ant species *Solenopsis invicta*, while several ant species known to be sensitive to disturbance were not found in disturbed sites (Chen et al. 2015). The key constraints of successful introduction to Antarctica beyond dispersal opportunities include being able to survive the harsh conditions and building up a viable population size despite limited resources. This suggests that at least some Antarctic ecosystems may not be in great risk of invasion by non-native species, with cold adapted species being the likely invaders. Still, even cold-adapted species may not become successful invaders. The springtail *Hypogastrura viatica* has a near 'cosmopolitan' distribution with sporadic occurrence at mid-high latitudes, but has not been found in the tropics. This springtail species has colonised several sub-Antarctic and maritime Antarctic sites. Although the populations at some of these sites appear to be doing well, that is not the case at all the sites where *H. viatica* has been recorded. The most southern record is from Léonie Island (~68° S) near British Antarctic Survey's Rothera Research Station on the Antarctic Peninsula that *H. viatica* colonised sometime before 1993. However, a substantial survey of sites on Léonie Island and other islands in the vicinity to substantiate the potential distribution of *H. viatica* found no evidence of the springtail in 2015 (Hughes et al. 2017), suggesting that the springtail has either not managed to establish in the long term or have a very restricted distribution in the area.

Another great example of the potential impacts of invasive soil fauna is the Argentine ant (*Linepithema humile*) that is native to South America, but is now found on all continents except Antarctica (Suarez et al. 2001), causing disruption to native invertebrate assemblages. For example, Sanders et al. (2003) describe how the presence of the Argentine ant at sites within the Jasper Ridge Biological Preserve in California dramatically moderate the assemblage composition of ground-foraging native ants. Specifically, Argentine ant invasion causes a decrease in biodiversity but also results in a shift in the spatial distribution of the other ant fauna. At sites outside the Argentine ant's range, the native ant fauna shows clear patterns of segregation, but following invasion the distribution of species shows random distribution to weak aggregation. This shift happens rapidly, with the pattern observed within a year of colonisation by the Argentine ant. Similarly, an invasive soil organism that has received a fair bit of attention is the predatory flatworm *Arthurdendyus triangulatus* originating from New Zealand. This flatworm has colonised several new locations, including the British Isles, where it is likely to establish and could have significant impacts on ecosystems. It is also likely to flourish in similar habitats in western and northern Europe if dispersal is achieved

6.4 Impacts of Invasive Species

(Boag and Yeates 2001). The flatworm is a predator of earthworms, and one of the concerns is that it will impact ecosystem functioning through suppression of earthworm populations. There is moreover concern that reduced earthworm population sizes will influence animals and birds that feed on earthworms. Indeed, the authors note that a negative correlation between flatworms and moles has been observed in fields in western Scotland.

It is well established that the presence or absence of specific root herbivores influence plant carbon and nutrient allocation, and production of secondary metabolites, in turn, impact the herbivore assemblages and their parasitoids aboveground (Masters et al. 2001, Soler et al. 2007, Soler et al. 2009). Two main hypotheses try to explain this response: the stress-response hypothesis (Masters et al. 1993) and the defence-induction hypothesis (Soler et al. 2005a). The stress-response hypothesis poses that the tissue damage caused by root herbivores illicit a stress response reducing plant root water and nutrient uptake, translocating this aboveground to the benefit of aboveground herbivores. By contrast, the defence-induction hypothesis proposes that the plant produces more phytotoxins following attack including in the aboveground biomass reducing the performance of aboveground herbivores and their parasitoids and predators. A meta-analysis mentioned earlier found that the effects can be both positive and negative depending on the situation, with the effects further depending on whether the belowground or aboveground herbivore arrives first (Johnson et al. 2012). Either way, invasive root herbivores are likely to have substantial impacts on their new environment through their interactions with the plant assemblage.

It is obvious that invasive species, aboveground and belowground, are major threats to the future of natural and managed ecosystems. Evidence is increasing of the impacts of invasive microbial, plant, and animal species on soil fauna assemblages, and there is some evidence of the impacts of invasive soil fauna on belowground communities and the vegetation aboveground. A key question is how large a problem will invasive species be in the future. Ongoing climate change pressures may contribute to broader ranges of invasive species opening up for further impacts at a larger scale, and increased human movement among continents and into more remote areas with limited past human presence opens up for more introductions of potentially invasive species. This may put particularly great risk on current isolated ecosystems with unique soil fauna assemblages, such as the isolated habitats of Antarctica. However, there is a clear need for more data to generalise these impacts, particularly from the soil fauna perspective. At the moment, all we have are a few examples of impacts of individual species across a broad range of taxa, albeit with a more succinct understanding of invasive earthworm impacts. One possible avenue to reduce the risk of biological invasions belowground is to focus on increasing soil biodiversity. While there is limited empirical evidence on the capacity of soil biodiversity to reduce the risk of soil fauna invasions, it has been shown that diverse bacterial assemblages provide protection against the establishment of a known bacterial pathogen (van Elsas et al. 2012). It appears likely that reductions in soil biodiversity across the soil food web may facilitate the establishment of invasive species both aboveground and belowground.

6.5 Summary

Global change is a major threat to Earth's ecosystems, including soils and its inhabitants. There is substantial evidence that the conversion of natural ecosystems to agro-ecosystems or other human uses have detrimental impacts on soil fauna communities, although not all taxa respond equally to the changes. Agricultural practices generally negatively influence soil fauna assemblage diversity and cause shifts in assemblage composition. In itself this may not appear to be a great concern unless one wishes to conserve belowground biodiversity, but the shift is accompanied with an increasing reliance on external inputs ranging from fertilisers to pesticides to provide the services otherwise supplied by healthy soils. However, there is great promise in optimising land use management practices to incorporate soil fauna diversity and harness the services they provide as discussed in Chapter 9. Pollutants often have detrimental impacts on the soil fauna through direct and indirect pathways that in turn can influence soil food web structure and ecosystem function with unknown consequences. Human activities further contribute to an increasing movement of microbes, animals, and plants that can become invasive in new environments. Such invasive species range from animals and plants aboveground to invasive soil fauna that can have large impacts through direct and indirect interactions with the native fauna and flora as well as habitat modifications. We presently have a reasonable understanding of the potential impacts of global changes belowground, but more data is needed to establish evidence-based management actions and policies to reduce the impacts and capitalise on the contributions of soil fauna to ecosystem functioning.

7 · Climate Change Impacts on Soil Fauna

It should come as no surprise that Earth's climate is undergoing dramatic changes that are primarily driven by human activities. Indeed, the report by the IPCC (2014) provides evidence for unequivocal warming of the atmosphere and other changes to the biosphere. Moreover, the best projections based on global circulation models using realistic increases in CO_2 concentrations indicate that the mean surface temperature is likely to increase by at least 1.5°C in most scenarios, and is likely to exceed 2.0°C in many scenarios, by 2100. There are also likely to be changes to rainfall regimes causing increased disparity between wet and dry regions, increased seasonality, and higher frequency of extreme events. The report further notes that sea levels are likely to continue to increase and that the snow cover and glacier volume of the northern hemisphere is likely to decrease. Climate change has accordingly been observed in many parts of the world, with particularly rapid changes occurring in the polar regions (Post et al. 2009, Turner et al. 2009). For example, at the Faraday/Vernadsky station on the Antarctic Peninsula, the mean surface air temperature increased by up to 0.56°C per decade during the second half of the twentieth century (Turner et al. 2005), while the temperature in parts of Greenland increased by 1.19°C per decade between 1982 and 2005 (Comiso 2006). The documented climate changes have already contributed to changes in ecosystems, including, for example, northward range shifts in Arctic vegetation (Callaghan et al. 2011, Serreze et al. 2000) and population increases in native grasses in Antarctica (Fowbert and Smith 1994, Parnikoza et al. 2009) following local warming. Climate change has been shown to have similar impacts elsewhere.

It is well established that elevated atmospheric carbon dioxide concentrations (eCO_2), warming, and altered precipitation influence terrestrial ecosystems. For example, a meta-analysis of observed ecosystem-level responses to warming and altered precipitation based on 85 publications found that warming and increased precipitation on average enhance plant growth and ecosystem carbon fluxes (Wu et al. 2011c). Reduced rainfall by contrast on average reduces plant growth and ecosystem carbon fluxes; however, ecosystem productivity and carbon fluxes were generally less responsive to reductions in rainfall than to increased precipitation. Such responses will have cascading effects belowground given strong aboveground–belowground linkages (see Chapter 2, Section 2.2), but will also in part be mediated by impacts on soil fauna assemblages themselves. This chapter will provide an overview of our current understanding of soil fauna responses to climate change, focussing on what these assemblages may look like in the future and how their contribution to ecosystem function might be modified by climate change. The three main climate change drivers are elevated atmospheric CO_2 concentrations (henceforth eCO_2), temperature, and rainfall that are in part driven by changes in CO_2 concentrations, and these will be the main focus of this chapter. However, I have included a section on elevated ozone concentrations (eO_3) given potential impacts belowground. It is beyond the scope of this book to discuss in detail climate change scenarios for different biomes and possible impacts on soil fauna assemblages. Rather, I will outline broad patterns of climate change responses and the potential longer-term impacts. It is worth noting here that experimental observations are not always robust proxies of responses to climate change occurring at natural scales (Bokhorst et al. 2011). Moreover, it is important to keep in mind that changes in mean temperature and rainfall may not have strong direct impacts. Instead, changes in the range associated with changes in mean conditions could induce novel climatic conditions possibly exceeding lethal thresholds, particularly if the variance around the mean increases (Gutt et al. 2018), with disproportionally large impacts. Finally, I will conclude the chapter with a section on interactions between global change drivers. This is of great importance because Earth's ecosystems are rarely impacted by only one global change driver and the interactions between these drivers may cancel each other out or, more likely, act synergistically with greater than expected effects.

7.1 Elevated CO_2

Soil fauna lives in an environment with higher CO_2 concentrations than that observed in the atmosphere (usually ranging between 0.3% and 3% relative to 0.04% in the current atmosphere), and are therefore well adapted to high CO_2 conditions. Hence, we can expect mostly indirect effects through plant assemblage responses, with modification of resource quantity and quality as well as changes in edaphic properties, such as soil water content. Indeed, an increase in soil water content is likely due to more efficient photosynthesis at eCO_2 conditions reducing plant water uptake (although this might be counteracted by increased plant productivity with no net effect on soil water content). Moreover, changes in the plant assemblage to include 'high-impact' functional types, such as nitrogen-fixing plants, may have particularly large impacts on soil biota, including the soil fauna and ecosystem functioning. By contrast, an increase in slower-growing plant species that produce recalcitrant litter may have negative effects on some soil biota and ecosystem functioning.

Elevated CO_2 has been found to increase photosynthesis and primary productivity, particularly in soils with high nutrient levels (Long et al. 2004), and to augment the transfer of photosynthetically derived carbon to microbial symbionts and the rhizosphere (Treseder 2004, Zak et al. 1993), which generally accelerates soil carbon and nutrient cycling (Phillips et al. 2011). Accordingly, a meta-analysis of free-air CO_2 enrichment (FACE, Figure 7.1) facilities found a general increase in diurnal

Figure 7.1 One of the arrays used to manipulate atmospheric carbon dioxide concentrations in the Eucalyptus Free Air Carbon Enrichment (EucFACE) facility in Richmond, New South Wales, Australia.
Photo by the author.

carbon assimilation, growth, and above ground biomass production, and a reduction in specific leaf area and stomatal conductance in response to eCO_2 (Ainsworth and Long 2005). This in turn may have cascading effects on soil fauna assemblages. The authors also highlighted a small, but significant, reduction in plant nitrogen content accounted for largely by reductions in rubisco, and that plant functional groups respond differentially to eCO_2. Later studies have accordingly found increased plant tissue carbon to nitrogen ratios in response to eCO_2 (Milchunas et al. 2005, Pendall et al. 2004b). Furthermore, several studies have shown that eCO_2 increases the production of fine roots (Curtis and Wang 1998, Pendall et al. 2004a, Rogers et al. 1996), which indicates possible changes in vegetation composition under future conditions that may impact soil organisms. Briefly, these changes are likely to influence belowground assemblages through the quantity and quality of organic matter inputs (root exudates, litter), altered vegetation composition (inputs, host plant species), and soil water content (reduced water uptake through reductions in stomatal conductivity). The main question is how large an effect this will have on the soil fauna at higher trophic levels.

One of the first meta-analyses of belowground responses to eCO_2, including both glasshouse and field experiments, provided insight into the possible impacts (Blankinship et al. 2011). The authors found that microfauna abundances generally increase, and mesofauna abundances decrease, in response to eCO_2. However, the effect size decreased with treatment duration, likely because the largest effects were observed in short-term experiments and were greater in glasshouse experiments than under field conditions. Indeed, when glasshouse and field experiments were analysed separately, treatment duration had no effect, indicating that this pattern is a legacy of experimental approaches. Finally, the authors found that eCO_2 increased only detritivore micro- and mesofauna densities, with no significant impact on herbivores or higher trophic levels, indicating limited trophic cascades. A more recent meta-analysis by A'Bear et al. (2014) also found limited evidence of eCO_2 impacts belowground, with only a decrease in nematode (except plant parasites) and mite abundances at eCO_2. These meta-analyses highlight that belowground soil fauna densities may respond to eCO_2, but the responses are generally limited to certain feeding groups, particularly lower trophic levels. Indeed, several studies have found limited evidence for strong eCO_2 effects on belowground assemblages. For example, a long-term experiment found only a slight decrease in the abundance of Thysanoptera and species richness of mesofauna overall (Eisenhauer et al. 2013). Similarly, no effect of elevated CO_2 on earthworm assemblage structure or abundance was found in an experimental grassland after three years (600 μL CO_2 L^{-1}) (Zaller and Arnone III 1999).

There is, however, evidence that eCO_2 can modify soil fauna assemblage composition. For example, eCO_2 had no effect on total plant parasitic nematode abundances in three grasslands, but the abundance of Hoplolaimidae decreased at one site, and the abundance of Anguinidea increased at another (Ayres et al. 2008), indicating changes in assemblage composition. Similarly, nine years exposure to eCO_2 (475 μL L^{-1}) was shown to increase the abundance of both plant parasitic and predatory nematodes in a New Zealand pasture with follow-up lab incubations suggesting that the increase in the dominant plant parasitic nematode *Longidorus elongates* and eCO_2 had additive negative effects on specific root length (Yeates and Newton 2009). Moreover, eCO_2 tended to increase total nematode abundances in a short-term FACE experiment during winter wheat and sugar beet rotation (Sticht et al. 2009). Interestingly, the effects differed between the two crops, with eCO_2 increasing the relative abundances of fungal feeders and bacterial feeders under winter wheat and sugar beet, respectively, indicating contrasting effects on soil food web structure. Other studies have similarly found that nematode genera respond differentially to eCO_2 (Neher and Weicht 2013) and molecular approaches show similar patterns. For example, Drigo et al. (2007) used a PCR-DGGE approach to assess the effect of eCO_2 on bacterial, fungal, and nematode assemblage structure in the rhizosphere of two plant species, *Carex arenaria* and *Festuca rubra*, grown in sand dune soils from three different locations. Their results showed consistent, but taxa-dependent, contributions of eCO_2, soil origin and plant species identity on assemblage structure, with eCO_2 explaining about 10% of the variation in nematode assemblage structure across all treatments. Finally, elevated CO_2 can also contribute to changes in ecosystem functioning mediated in part by soil fauna. For example, wheat litter grown under eCO_2 conditions was observed to decompose more slowly than that grown under ambient conditions (Frederiksen et al. 2001). This effect coincided with a decrease in bacterial-feeding soil fauna, including nematodes, indicating potential shifts in ecosystem functioning likely driven by changes in leaf C:N ratios (i.e. more recalcitrant when grown at eCO_2).

There is thus limited evidence that eCO_2 will have substantial effects on the density of soil fauna assemblages, particularly at higher trophic levels that are less strongly influenced by the plant community. Hence, the density of root associates and detritivores are most likely to be directly impacted through changes in root exudation and the quantity and quality of litter inputs. This can in turn contribute to modifications to the soil food web structure. More broadly, changes in soil fauna assemblage composition are most likely to reflect eCO_2 effects on plant assemblage composition. Hence, given that belowground responses to eCO_2 are mediated mostly via the plants, they are likely to be moderated by constraints on the resource availability for plants. Specifically, weaker responses are likely where plant growth is limited by nutrient availability or climatic conditions. Conversely, eCO_2 could have a more pronounced effect in biomes where plant growth is moderately constrained by soil water content whereby the more water use efficient uptake of carbon allows an enhanced plant growth response. However, this response appears unlikely in biomes where plants are severely water limited.

7.2 Warming

Increases in surface temperatures are not uniformly distributed across the globe, with some areas experiencing limited effects, while other regions have warmed considerably over the past five decades in particular. Similar differences are likely to present themselves in future climate scenarios, thus impacting Earth's biomes differentially. Moreover, impacts of climate changes are moderated by current abiotic conditions so that warming may have contrasting effects among various regions. Warming is likely to have strong direct effects on soil fauna, but the effect size will be moderated by altered soil water content and changes in vegetation. Indeed, temperature increases are likely to increase plant primary productivity, microbes, and animals due to enhanced metabolic and physiological processes because these processes are generally temperature sensitive (Ehnes et al. 2011, Gillooly et al. 2001). Conversely, metabolic processes may be detrimentally impacted if the organism is exposed to temperatures above their optimal temperature ranges. This is problematic because upper thermal lethal limits are more likely to be exceeded in a warmer world (Figure 7.2). Upper thermal limits are therefore critical to understand at a species level if we are to predict the (potential) future ranges of species. The effects of increased temperatures on soil fauna might be lesser than on the fauna aboveground because the soil temperature is buffered considerably relative to surface temperatures, with increasing buffering capacity at greater depth, under closed or compact vegetation cover, and with increasing soil water content. Similarly, snow cover contributes to buffering of soil temperatures during winter, with

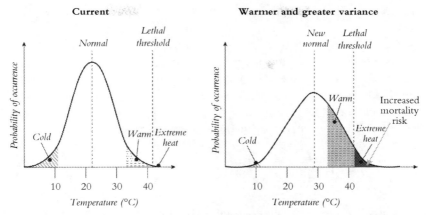

Figure 7.2 Schematic diagram illustrating the hypothetical consequences of an increase in mean temperature and greater variance in temperature around this mean. Under contemporary conditions (left panel), a given individual with a lethal threshold of 42°C will experience few events extreme enough to induce mortality. Under a future scenario with a higher mean annual temperature and greater variance (right panel), the same species will experience conditions that *can induce mortality more often.*
Based on Gutt et al. (2018) with permission from Elsevier Science Ltd.

possible negative impacts of warming due to loss of snow cover during cold snaps (Lavelle and Spain 2001).

The meta-analysis conducted by Blankinship et al. (2011) showed that warming only consistently influenced nematode abundances, with greater abundances observed at higher temperatures. However, the effects of warming were related to the contemporary climate, with negative responses at sites with low mean annual precipitation, switching to positive responses above an estimated 626 mm precipitation per year. Moreover, reductions in densities were more likely to be observed in longer-term experiments, indicating that responses may accumulate over time. No consistent effects were observed on the abundance of other soil fauna groups, including microarthropods and enchytraeids. The more recent meta-analysis by A'Bear et al. (2014) in contrast found no strong influence of warming on total nematode abundances, but instead found evidence for a decrease in plant parasites and an increase in fungal-feeding and predatory nematodes, indicating shifts in the assemblage and soil food web structure. Moreover, these authors found an increase in enchytraeid abundances at elevated temperatures. The results showed an interaction between temperature and precipitation, so that warming enhanced the negative effects of drought on mite densities, while warming and increased precipitation enhanced mite and springtail abundances. Several other studies provide evidence that warming contributes to changes in soil fauna assemblage composition. For example, in a warming study (ambient, +1.7°C, +3.4°C) in a temperate-boreal forest ecotone, no effects were observed on total nematode, but the relative abundance of nematode trophic groups shifted with more bacterial-feeding nematodes in the warmed plots at both a closed and open canopy site (Thakur et al. 2014). Moreover, the nematode plant parasite index (PPI), which was lower in the closed canopy site than in the open canopy site, decreased in response to warming. These results show that warming may not contribute to significant impacts on nematode abundances but can moderate assemblage composition, possibly causing long-term changes in ecosystem functioning. Similarly, warming of 1°C contributed to a decrease in nematode abundances and a shift to longer-lived species, in a heath (Stevnbak et al. 2012).

Warming is likely to be particularly important in ecosystems where biological activity is currently constrained by low temperatures. One study investigated the effects of short-term increases in temperature on testate amoeba assemblages in grasslands in Greenland (Tsyganov et al. 2011). A free-air temperature manipulation was used to increase soil temperatures over the growing season (roughly two months) and the effects on protozoan assemblages were assessed in upper (0–3 cm) and deeper (3–6 cm) soil horizons. The temperature manipulation contributed to an average increase of 2.6°C and 2.1°C at 2.5 cm and 7.5 cm, respectively, throughout the treatment duration and importantly had no impact on soil water content. The observed soil warming increased the abundance of living amoebae and empty shells in the upper soil horizon only, while species richness only increased in the deeper soil horizon. Interestingly, the proportion of shells of small-sized species increased. A recent synthesis of studies investigating the effects of warming on soil fauna in the polar regions found variable responses with negative, neutral, and positive responses observed (Nielsen and Wall 2013). However, it appeared that negative responses were generally due to reductions in the population size of organisms sensitive to low soil moisture contents (e.g. springtails) (Day et al. 2009), particularly where soil moisture was already limiting (Coulson et al. 1996). This was further supported by experimental studies that found water additions to ameliorate the negative effects of increased temperature (Day et al. 2009, Simmons et al. 2009). However, responses can be idiosyncratic, vegetation and taxa dependent. In a warming study including sites in the Falkland Islands, Signy Island, and Anchorage Island, representing a latitudinal gradient and several vegetation types, Bokhorst et al. (2008) found that warming had no effect on microarthropod diversity or abundance in the Falkland Islands or in Signy Island. However, a reduction in total springtail abundance, driven by a substantial decline in the dominant species *Cryptopygus antarcticus* (Figure 7.3) was observed in the lichen community at Anchorage Island after two seasons. Moreover, there was a shift in mite assemblage structure with fewer mesostigmatid mites (represented by the sole species *Gamasellus racovitzai*) and more prostigmatid mites. Warming is moreover likely to contribute to broader changes in soil fauna assemblage composition because polar region mites are generally more tolerant of high temperatures than collembolans (Block et al. 1994, Hodkinson et al. 1996). Finally, it appeared likely that warming will increase the abundance of nematodes and will impact nematode assemblage structure (Nielsen and Wall 2013, Nielsen et al. 2011b), although negative effects of warming have been observed. For example, Simmons et al. (2009) found that long-term warming reduced the population size of the dominant nematode in an experiment in the McMurdo Dry Valleys, Antarctica.

While warming can increase soil fauna density and diversity there is evidence that extreme events, including heatwaves, can have drastic impacts on the performance of soil fauna, may even cause mortality such as observed during a heatwave in the high Arctic (Coulson et al. 1996),

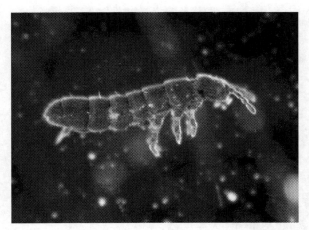

Figure 7.3 *Cryptopygus antarcticus* is the dominant springtail throughout much of maritime Antarctica.
Photo by the author.

and could impact soil fauna assemblages through cascading impacts driven by changes in soil water content or the vegetation aboveground. An experimental growing season heatwave imposed on a dry heath tundra in West Greenland, severe enough to cause significant leaf mortality of the vegetation (infrared radiation, ~7–9°C above ambient), had limited impacts on the abundance of testate amoeba (Beyens et al. 2009). However, the heatwave caused a shift in assemblage composition of the testate amoeba and an increase in population size of bacterivorous amoebae was observed weeks after the heatwave ended following a peak in bacterial population sizes in both layers, indicating a rapid but transient increase in population size of these species.

Warming could also influence soil fauna communities by altering snow cover depth and duration of cover. Snow acts as a buffer against low temperature during winter, with warmer and less variable temperatures observed under snow packs than in exposed soils (Walker et al. 1999), and alter soil properties, particularly soil water content (Gooseff et al. 2003), which in turn influences soil fauna assemblages. Winter warming can have substantial negative effects on microarthropod assemblages as observed in the Arctic either through direct effects of warming or due to decreased snow cover to buffer climate impacts (Bokhorst et al. 2012). In this study, the authors simulated weeklong extreme winter warming events in a sub-Arctic dwarf shrub heathland over two seasons. The extreme winter warming resulted in increased frequency of freeze–thaw cycles and reduced the minimum temperature observed in the soil. This in turn caused a reduction in microarthropod abundances, driven by a substantial impact on the smaller prostigmatid mites, mesostigmatid mite nymphs, and small springtail species. Indeed, the extreme events caused a shift in springtail assemblage structure favouring larger hemi-edaphic species over smaller euedaphic species that was not evident from abundance data alone. However, whether an increase in freeze–thaw cycles influence soil fauna positively or negatively appears to depend on the frequency of these events, with positive impacts observed in a study with a lower frequency (Konestabo et al. 2007) compared to a study where negative impacts were observed (Bokhorst et al. 2012). Positive responses to increased freeze–thaw cycles could be related to an increase in conditions favouring biological activity (Konestabo et al. 2007). In any case increased freeze–thaw cycles would likely cause soil fauna assemblage structural changes given that organisms differ in their sensitivity to these events. For example, oribatid mites appear to be more tolerant to freeze–thaw events than springtails (Coulson et al. 2000). Increases in freeze–thaw cycles were shown to have increasingly negative effects on nematode abundances in soils collected from two temperate grasslands with different climate regimes (Ireland, Poland), and there was a tendency for greater effects on the nematode assemblage that is not usually exposed to frost (i.e. Ireland) (Dam et al. 2012). Moreover, continuous freezing for 88 days at −6°C to −7°C had detrimental effects on nematode survival in both soils, particularly pronounced for early colonisers. This is problematic given that a warmer climate or changes in precipitation patterns might contribute to lower snow cover, which buffers the underlying soil from frost during the cold season and therefore provides some protection of the fauna within.

One of the important predicted consequences of elevated temperature is a net increase in the transfer of carbon from soils to the atmosphere due to greater temperature sensitivity of soil respiration to warming than primary production (Fisher et al. 2010). While this will to a great extent be driven by microbial responses, soil fauna may modify the outcome. For example, enchytraeids have been found to enhance the response of soil respiration to increases in temperature and at the same time promote the turnover of 'old' organic carbon (Briones et al. 2004). Similarly, an increased population size of enchytraeids in peatlands was correlated with accelerated rates of decomposition (Briones et al. 2007b). By contrast, no consistent effect of warming on enchytraeid abundances was observed following 13 years of simulated nighttime warming in either of three European heathland ecosystems (Holmstrup et al. 2012). The passive nighttime warming was imposed using high-density polyethylene mesh and was designed to increase minimum temperatures only. They resulted in an increase in mean annual soil temperature at 5 cm depth ranging from 0.3°C to 0.8°C only, which might have been too little to influence the enchytraeids. Climate is a strong driver of enchytraeid distribution (Briones et al. 2007a), indicating that climate change is likely to impact these assemblages, with implications for ecosystem functioning.

There is also evidence that changes in temperature modify predator–prey interactions with cascading impacts on the soil food web structure. In a microcosm study, Lang et al. (2014) manipulated soil food webs and investigated the effects of temperature and soil water content on trophic interactions. The authors used maize litter as a resource, fungi as decomposers, springtails as primary consumers, and mites or centipedes as secondary consumers (i.e. top predators). The top-down control of springtails by the top predators and that of fungi on litter decomposition increased with soil temperature and drier soils. There was therefore a trophic cascade in that the top predators exerted greater grazing pressures on the springtails that in turn impacted the fungi, and through this the top predators indirectly influenced litter decomposition processes. Changes in soil temperature and soil water contents associated with climate changes may therefore have important consequences for biogeochemical cycling in soils. Similarly, Thakur et al. (2017a) created litter-based mesocosms to assess the effect of predation on the co-existence of two springtail species under warming. Contrary to expectations, predation by predatory mites reduced springtail co-existence at elevated temperatures, constantly favouring the larger springtail, *Folsomia candida*, possibly because of this species' greater morphological trait plasticity (reduced body sizes were observed under warming). These results indicate that in some cases warming may contribute to greater predation effects with negative impacts on species co-existence; however, this is unlikely to be the case in all situations. Indeed, the effects of warming are complex and therefore not easily predicted. In a paper synthesising the effects of warming on soil food web structure from two related experiments in Minnesota, the authors found contrasting effects in a closed-canopy old growth forest relative to a clear-cut patch replanted with tree seedlings and following exposure to simultaneous drought (Schwarz et al. 2017). Warming had limited effects on energy fluxes to fauna in the closed canopy forest but contributed to enhanced fluxes in the disturbed vegetation. Warming also had a greater effect on fluxes to detritivores in the disturbed vegetation than the closed canopy forest (i.e. a warming by canopy interaction), and while warming increased energy fluxes to predators in the disturbed plots by 110%, there was a 30% reduction in fluxes in the closed canopy forest.

It is clear that warming has a great potential to impact soil fauna assemblages directly, both positively through enhanced metabolism and negatively by exceeding thermal lethal limits, and indirectly mediated by the vegetation and modifications to soil water contents. Moreover, a warmer climate is likely to increase soil fauna densities particularly in areas that are currently limited by cold climates, but this could come at an expense to the indigenous fauna by facilitating the establishment of non-native species. Increased temperatures are expected to extend the range sizes of organisms that are currently confined to warmer climates, such as termites. It has been suggested that the hindgut mutualistic system of termites may not be sufficiently efficient below 23°C to allow biomass production (Sugimoto et al. 2000). Higher temperatures would thus allow increased biomass production at sites where temperature is currently limiting biomass production, and allow termites to increase their ranges to areas currently too cold to support them. Similarly, as outlined earlier, ant species diversity and their role as predators are lower in colder climates (Jeanne 1979). An increase in temperatures could therefore increase the richness of ant assemblages and their impacts on the food web. Conversely, too high temperatures may impair metabolism. Hence, the effects of warming on soil fauna densities are highly context dependent but predictable. By contrast, warming may have negative effects on soil fauna densities where species are already living close to the upper thermal limit, or where warming contributes to significant reductions in soil water content. Finally, there is strong evidence that extreme temperature events (i.e. heatwaves) can have disproportionately great impact on the soil fauna (Bokhorst et al. 2012).

7.3 Altered Rainfall Regimes

Rainfall regimes are predicted to change globally, but predictions for local scenarios are highly variable. Global circulation models have indicated that wet and dry regions will become increasingly disparate under future climate scenarios (IPCC 2014), although recent predictions are more ambiguous. More broadly, the global circulation models predict more extreme events, both deluges and drought, increased and reduced rainfall, and altered seasonality. Altered rainfall regimes will indirectly influence the soil fauna assemblages via changes in the plant assemblage, while more direct impacts are expected through changes in soil water content in particular. Climate changes that reduce soil water contents are likely to reduce soil fauna density and biomass, whereas increases in soil water content are likely to have the opposite effects, except when they result in flooding or promote anoxic conditions through waterlogging. Moreover, changes in soil water content are likely to more substantially impact the microfauna, such as nematodes (Vandegehuchte et al. 2015), given that they are essentially aquatic organisms. Moreover, reduced soil water contents are likely to impact soil-dwelling herbivores, such as insect larvae, negatively, because their permeable cuticle makes them prone to desiccation (Brown and Gange 1990). A literature review accordingly highlights that reduced soil water content often has negative impacts on belowground herbivore densities (Staley and Johnson 2008). Some soil invertebrates show avoidance behaviour or physiological adaptions that can help alleviate drought impacts. For example, it has been shown that drought drives lumbricid earthworms deeper into the soil (Gerard 1967) and that drying of peat displaces enchytraeids to more favourable microhabitats (Briones et al. 1998). Some enchytraeids of the genera *Enchytraeus, Fridericia, Henlea* can, however, produce drought-resistant cocoons (O'Connor 1967) to cope with the unfavourable conditions. Still, changes in soil water content are likely to have substantial impacts belowground that in turn can have cascading impacts on ecosystem functioning. For example, a study of summer drought effects on a heath ecosystem over eight years showed a negative effect on decomposer biota, including nematodes, and an associated reduction in C flow indicating significant effects on ecosystem functioning (Stevnbak et al. 2012). Shifts in assemblage composition, and associated with this ecosystem functioning, are therefore likely under future rainfall scenarios, particularly where water is currently limited and where it becomes a limiting resource (Nielsen and Ball 2015).

There is substantial evidence that altered rainfall regimes impact soil fauna assemblages. The aforementioned meta-analysis by Blankinship et al. (2011) found that increased precipitation generally has a positive effect on soil fauna abundances, with greater abundances of springtails and enchytraeids with increasing rainfall. The effects were particularly pronounced for mesofauna densities and fungal feeders, but the effect size decreased with mean annual temperature. Hence, positive effects were observed in boreal forests and temperate deciduous and coniferous forests, whereas no effects were observed in tundra, heath, and grassland ecosystems. It should be noted that several studies were drought experiments, and that in those cases the 'ambient' condition represented the 'increased precipitation' treatment, whereas the 'drought' represented the control. In the forested ecosystems the largest effect sizes were indeed observed in the drought studies, indicating that a reduction in precipitation may be particularly important given that these conditions represent the anomaly. The more recent meta-analysis found that drought consistently reduced enchytraeid, mite, and springtail abundances as well as plant parasitic and bacterial-feeding nematode abundances (A'Bear et al. 2014). By contrast, increased rainfall generally had a positive effect on nematode abundances and, when combined with warming, contributed to greater densities of microarthropods. The effects of altered rainfall on nematodes are, however, moderated by ecosystem properties, such as vegetation composition, soil type, and nutrient levels (Klironomos et al. 1996, Niklaus et al. 2003, Smolik and Dodd 1983). Hence, the response to reduced rainfall is predicted to vary between ecosystems, ranging from potential positive effects in wet ecosystems such as peatlands to negative effects in ecosystems where water becomes the main limiting factor. Conversely, increased rainfall may increase soil fauna densities particularly in current water-limited ecosystems, while no or even reduced densities may be observed in ecosystems where water is not currently the main limiting factor. It is therefore predicted that deserts, hot and cold, will respond more strongly than wet temperate and tropical ecosystems. Moreover, changes in rainfall will differentially impact soil fauna depending on their sensitivity to low and high soil water contents. For example, an experiment that manipulated water content in soil monoliths showed that the density of protozoans decrease substantially in a non-linear response to reduced water availability over a couple of months, driven in large parts by a very strong response of amoeba (Geisen et al. 2014). Moreover, it was apparent that taxa with larger specimens were more strongly impacted, indicating that responses are not uniform among taxa. The authors found no strong pattern in evenness or diversity of protozoans in response to soil water content, but these might become apparent in longer-term studies. Similarly, a study that manipulated rainfall over a year (complete removal, 'ambient', and increased rainfall) in a sandy forest soil in New Jersey found substantial impacts on nematode abundances, with total nematode abundances increasing with precipitation (Landesman et al. 2011). Drought impacted certain bacterial-feeding nematode families more than others, with Plectidae showing strong responses, while Cephalobidae and Qudsianematidae were not affected. The authors speculated that the increase in bacterial-feeding nematodes might have contributed to the observed finding that microbial biomass was unaffected by altered rainfall in the same experiment. Similarly, irrigation that resulted in an approximate 15% increase in soil water content in a tallgrass prairie in Kansas, was found to increase the abundance of plant parasitic nematodes on average 90% relative to control plots across four years (Todd et al. 1999). By contrast, the effects on other trophic groups were limited and when present varied from reductions to increases. The authors also completed a reciprocal soil core transplant study that indicated that nematode assemblage responses to short-term increases in soil water content were not comparable with shifts in nematode assemblages observed between sites with contrasting rainfall levels, indicating that other variables are important in the longer term.

To better assess the potential implications of changes in rainfall regime on arid to semi-arid ecosystems, Nielsen and Ball (2015) conducted a literature review of observed responses to changes in rainfall regime focussing on the belowground assemblages and soil processes. They synthesised this information to provide a new framework for predicting potential ecosystem-level impacts of changes in rainfall whilst also highlighting areas where more information is needed. The literature strongly supports the hypothesis that belowground organisms in arid and semi-arid ecosystems are water limited. Therefore, increased rainfall will generally have a positive effect on soil fauna assemblage diversity and abundance that can further contribute to altered assemblage composition. Similarly, the relationship between mean annual precipitation and soil fauna assemblages suggest that reductions in rainfall are likely to have negative effects on densities and diversity of soil fauna. However, the experimental data is less supportive of this hypothesis. In many studies, even those that impose substantial rainfall reductions, soil fauna assemblages show very limited responses. Many dryland organisms are well adapted to drought, whether this is manifested as extended periods with below-average rainfall or a distinct period with no rainfall, which might explain the limited responses observed in the short term. It, however, still seems likely that longer-term changes in rainfall will eventually manifest belowground. Another complication is that many studies do not investigate soil fauna communities at the species level, thus likely reporting false negatives, i.e. there may well have been treatment effects, but they were not observed at the level of investigation. For example, Nielsen et al. (2016) investigated the effects of altered rainfall regimes on soil nematode assemblages in a modified pasture in Australia (Figure 7.4). The treatments included increased and reduced precipitation (150% and 50% relative to ambient rainfall, respectively), altered frequency (fewer events, same amount), and summer drought (all water removed three months during the growing season) and found no response of the soil nematode assemblage at the trophic level after three years rainfall manipulation. However, when the nematode assemblage was assessed at the species level the authors found a substantial difference between the summer drought and ambient treatments indicating strong changes in nematode assemblage structure. Moreover, the data indicated that nematode biomass was smaller in the summer drought treatment and that summer drought reduced nutrient cycling based on knowledge of nematode life history traits (Sieriebriennikov et al. 2014). Specifically, drought appears to favour nematode genera classified as c-p 2, i.e. colonisers or r-strategists, likely because they are very tolerant to environmental stress and recover quickly from disturbance (Ferris et al. 2001). For example, nematodes classified as colonisers tend to be more

7.3 Altered Rainfall Regimes

Figure 7.4 The rainfall manipulation facility Drought and Root Herbivore Interactions in a Grassland (DRI-Grass) in Richmond, New South Wales, Australia. The roofs remove all water, and irrigation is used to simulate ambient, increased precipitation (150% of ambient), reduced precipitation (50% of ambient), altered frequency (rain every three weeks), and summer drought (all water removed during the peak growing season). The facility has been operating since 2013.
Photo by the author.

prominent at sites where water is limited while persisters (e.g. c-p 4–5) are more abundant, at least relatively speaking, at wetter sites (Fraser et al. 2012). The literature review by Nielsen and Ball (2015) also highlighted that responses to altered rainfall regimes will depend on the historical rainfall regime, seasonality, and even event size (Figure 7.5). For example, a shift towards more small rainfall events may negatively impact biomass and diversity, whereas fewer but larger events are more likely to have neutral or even positive effects. The difference between the contrasting rainfall regimes lies in their controls on water availability and use by plants and biota. Small rainfall events may trigger a biotic response but may not be enough for plants to reach the carbon-compensation point, i.e. where carbon uptake from the atmosphere balances out metabolic processes, so that it is a net cost to the plant. Soil fauna may experience similar negative effects if it exits its resting stages only to immediately have to return to this state without being able to acquire new resources. Moreover, a larger proportion of the water delivered by small events is likely to evaporate compared with larger event sizes. Therefore, larger events contribute to greater water availability over longer time scales. Large events also allow for deeper water infiltration and greater biological responses. The time between events may be longer but because the organisms are well adapted to such 'droughts' they may not have large

238 · Climate Change Impacts on Soil Fauna

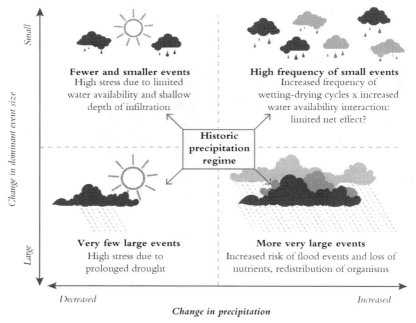

Figure 7.5 Conceptual diagram illustrating the likely effects of altered rainfall regimes on dryland ecosystems. It is expected that both changes in the amount of rainfall and its delivery (i.e. few large or many small events) will influence dryland ecosystems. However, the impacts will be modified by the historical rainfall regime.
Modified from Nielsen and Ball (2015) with permission from Elsevier Science Ltd.

effects on the biota or plants. It should be noted that these responses are applicable only to dryland ecosystems, whereas ecosystems that are not strongly water limited are unlikely to show similar responses.

Interestingly, there is also evidence that changes in rainfall regime may influence aboveground–belowground linkages in unexpected ways that could have unpredictable consequences. The presence of belowground root herbivores alters the response of aboveground herbivores to modified rainfall regimes mediated by impacts on host plants (Ryalls et al. 2016). Along the same lines, drought might modify interaction between aboveground and belowground herbivores, with an experimental summer drought found to disrupt a negative host plant-mediated interaction between the root-feeding wire worm larvae (*Agriotes* sp.) and the leaf-miner *Stephensia brunnichella* (Staley et al. 2007). Moreover, in a rainfall manipulation experiment in an Australian pasture several relationships between fauna aboveground and fauna belowground, including positive relationships between the abundance of Acari aboveground and Coleoptera belowground and between Collembola aboveground and Megadrilacea belowground, and a negative relationship between chewing herbivores aboveground and fungal-feeding nematodes belowground, were observed only under ambient rainfall conditions (Torode et al. 2016). In some cases, these relationships appeared to be related to similar resource uses and the discrepancy in effects of altered rainfall may be due to greater effects on the plant biomass aboveground than belowground. By contrast, the negative relationship between fungal-feeding nematodes and leaf-chewing herbivores may be facilitated by changes in plant physiology associated with mycorrhizal responses to altered rainfall. The authors termed this 'climatic decoupling', whereby climate impacts on host plant influence aboveground and belowground organisms differentially. While these hypotheses are highly speculative and the underlying mechanisms are not identified, the results do suggest that unexpected and different responses of aboveground versus belowground fauna may cause changes in aboveground–belowground linkages that could have longer-term impacts on ecosystem functioning.

Finally, there is evidence that drought effects on belowground organisms differ between plant assemblages. For example, in a drought experiment combined with the removal of subordinate plant species in a species-rich calcareous grassland in the Swiss Jura Mountains, the investigators found that summer drought in the previous year benefitted subordinate plant species (i.e. the dominant species were suppressed by the drought and the subordinate species increased in biomass relatively to the control), which in turn contributed to significantly higher earthworm densities, particularly due to an increase in anecic earthworms (Mariotte et al. 2016). The authors noted that the increase in earthworm densities observed following the drought in the plots with subordinate plant species present were likely caused by the litter of these species being more nutritious, specifically higher in nitrogen content. However, there is a great need for further data to generalise the responses to drought mediated by plant assemblage composition.

7.4 Elevated O_3

Another climate change–related global change driver is tropospheric ozone (O_3) concentration. Current O_3 levels are in the range of 25–40 ppb, up from pre-industrial concentrations estimated at around 10 ppb, and are expected to increase by a further 40%–70% by the end of the twenty-first century (Zeng et al. 2008). Ozone is known to be a powerful pollutant that can have strong effects on plant assemblages, including agricultural crops and forestry species, and is therefore likely to also influence belowground organisms. Very limited effort has, however, been vested in investigating the effects of O_3 belowground to date (Andersen 2003, Chen et al. 2009). Of the few studies that have investigated O_3 effects on soil fauna the results have been mixed. For example, one of the earliest studies using O_3 fumigation found greater damage by the plant parasitic nematode *Meloidogyne incognita* on tomato at elevated O_3 concentrations (Khan and Khan 1998), while soil O_3 fumigation caused a reduction in total nematode abundances, including plant parasites, in a sandy loam soil (Qiu et al. 2009). Another study found no impact of elevated O_3 concentrations on microarthropod or nematode densities in a chamber experiment (Tingey et al. 2006), whereas Schrader et al. (2009) found a decrease in microarthropods and enchytraeids. A more recent study investigated the effect of elevated O_3 concentrations on soil assemblages associated with O_3-tolerant and O_3-sensitive wheat cultivars in China (Li et al. 2012). Ozone had limited effects on nematode abundances and protozoan PLFA markers, but there were significant shifts in assemblage composition for both taxa. In particular, the abundance of bacterial-feeding nematodes classified as persisters (c-p 4) decreased in response to elevated O_3, whereas fungal-feeding nematodes classified as persisters (c-p 4) increased in response to elevated O_3. Moreover, the abundance of flagellates increased in response to elevated O_3 in the tolerant wheat cultivar, but showed the opposite response in the sensitive wheat cultivar. Similarly, a free-air enrichment facility that manipulated both CO_2 and O_3 found that CO_2 had a negative effect on both springtail and mite abundances, while O_3 negatively affected mite abundances only (−47%) (Loranger et al. 2004). Interestingly, the authors observed an interaction between elevated CO_2 and O_3 concentrations so that no net effects on microarthropods were observed when the concentration of both elements increased. Moreover, a related study found that aspen (*Populus tremuloides*) leaf litter grown at elevated O_3 concentrations had increased litter lignin and fibre concentration, which in turn supported greater population growth of the springtail *Sinella curviseta*, but not the earthworm *Lumbricus terrestris*, relative to litter in the control plots (Meehan et al. 2010). In comparison, eCO_2 increased the concentration of condensed-tannin in leaf litter and reduced N content, which was associated with lower population growth rates of both the earthworm and the springtail. These results indicate that there is a potential for complex belowground impacts of O_3 mediated by plants. More research is required to further elucidate the possible mechanisms through which these impacts are manifested, but the observed changes in plant chemistry indicate predictable impacts.

7.5 Global Change Interactions

As noted earlier, global change effects are rarely singular. Rather, multiple global change drivers combine to impact Earth's ecosystems and the interactions between climate change variables highlighted in this chapter are likely to be of greater importance than the effects of either in isolation (Figure 7.6). For example, there is evidence that the effects of eCO_2 is modified by climate and soil nutrient content, while warming and altered rainfall regimes will interact to impose negative to positive responses on soil fauna densities and diversity depending on future scenarios. Specifically, warming combined with reduced precipitation or drought is likely to have negative to neutral impacts on soil fauna densities depending on current conditions, whereas warming and increased

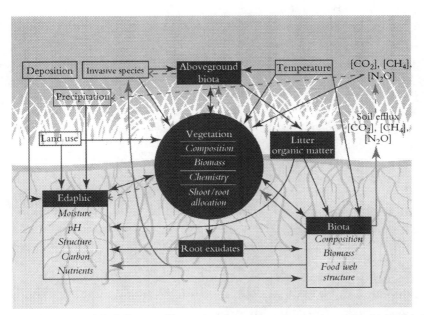

Figure 7.6 Simplified diagram illustrating the main pathways through which global change drivers will influence soil fauna assemblages (black arrows) and how soil fauna assemblages in turn will moderate the global change effects (grey arrows). Modified from Nielsen et al. (2015b) with permission from *Annual Reviews*.

precipitation are likely to increase soil fauna densities, with the effect size being moderated by contemporary climatic conditions. Moreover, there likely is significant climate change by land use change interactions, which have implications for how we manage production systems to maintain productivity in future climates.

Elevated CO_2 can interact with other climate change drivers to moderate soil fauna responses. Accordingly, there is evidence that eCO_2 can ameliorate negative warming effects by reducing plant transpiration, and eCO_2 may amplify positive effects of warming and increased precipitation (A'Bear et al. 2014). Moreover, there is evidence that the effect of eCO_2 is moderated by nutrient availability. For example, a study that manipulated atmospheric CO_2 concentrations in low and high nitrogen content soils found that nematode responses were strongly moderated by soil nitrogen concentrations (Hoeksema et al. 2000). The authors grew aspen seedlings in raised beds filled with two contrasting soil types and exposed the seedlings to ambient and twice-ambient CO_2 concentrations for two years before collecting soil samples for analyses of the nematode assemblages as indicators of belowground responses. In the low nitrogen soils, a doubling of CO_2 concentrations had a positive effect on the plant parasites in the family Trichodoridae but reduced the density of the bacterial-feeding Rhabditidae. The authors also found a decrease in the nematode assemblage evenness under eCO_2 in the low nitrogen soil. By contrast, eCO_2 had a positive effect on predatory and omnivore nematodes in the high nitrogen soil but reduced overall nematode diversity. Elevated CO_2 also increased the maturity index (MI, see Chapter 3 for a brief introduction), suggesting an increase in nutrient availability and a change in soil food web structure to greater dominance of the bacterial pathway.

The interactive effects of temperature and precipitation on soil fauna abundances appear relatively straightforward, with neutral or positive effects when both temperature and precipitation are increased and negative effects are more likely when temperature increases are not buffered by simultaneous increases in precipitation. Moreover, the effects are likely to be greater in ecosystems where water is already a limiting factor or where reduced water availability due to altered rainfall regimes or increased temperature creates a water deficit. For example, if the climate in the polar regions on average becomes warmer and wetter, it is likely to increase the biological activity, population sizes, and species richness in the Antarctic, whereas in the Arctic, biological activity may increase and assemblage composition is likely to change, but species richness may not increase given higher contemporary richness (Nielsen and Wall 2013). By contrast, warming in areas that are currently water limited may have less effect or even negatively impact soil fauna density and diversity. However, even where rainfall increases, the net effect of increased temperature and precipitation could cause reduced soil water availability due to increased evaporation with net negative effects on the vegetation and biota. One of the main concerns with this is the potential release of carbon bound up in permafrost soils, which is estimated to store approximately $1,672 \times 10^{15}$ g of carbon (Tarnokai et al. 2009), resulting in a positive feedback to climate change.

The consequences of global change interactions are, however, difficult to predict because shifts in biological interactions may contribute to unforeseen impacts or conversely alleviate the effects of global change. In a combined warming and nitrogen addition experiment at the Harvard Forest Long-Term Ecological Research site that manipulated soil assemblages *in situ* the authors found that top-down control might become more prominent under future conditions and modify the effect of the treatments (Crowther et al. 2015). The authors found that warming and nitrogen deposition combined to reduce the bottom-up control of fungal biomass, driven by cord-forming fungal responses, resulting in increased enzyme activity and wood decomposition. However, in treatments where isopods were present the increase in fungal cord consumption compensated for the positive effect of the global change drivers, effectively causing top-down control of fungal biomass, which in turn mediated the effects on soil enzyme activity and wood decomposition. Hence, biotic interactions can have unexpected effects that potentially have great implications for soil carbon-climate feedbacks. There is also evidence that eCO_2 may interact with potential invasive species through modification of the soil fauna assemblages. For example, when comparing soil nematode assemblages of two native and two invasive plant species grown at aCO_2 and eCO_2 in controlled conditions, it was found that the proportion of bacterial-feeding nematodes increased at eCO_2 under both invasive species, and the proportion of plant parasitic nematodes decreased under one of the invasive species (Xiao et al. 2013). In contrast, the proportion of bacterial-feeding nematodes and plant parasitic nematodes decreased and increased, respectively, in the presence of one of the native plant species. Thus, eCO_2 may increase the competitive ability of certain invasive plant species relative to native species due to reductions in belowground herbivory.

Global change drivers do, however, not always show strong interactive effects. For example, in a 13-year-long grassland experiment there were very few interactive effects of plant species richness, eCO_2 and nitrogen addition on soil biota (Eisenhauer et al. 2013). In fact, the only interactive effect the authors observed was between plant species richness and eCO_2, with greater positive effects of eCO_2 on microbial biomass observed at increased plant species richness. The increase in microbial biomass could propagate responses at higher trophic levels, but this was not observed. In another study that investigated the effects of water (+30% relative to ambient) and nitrogen (equivalent to 50 kg N ha^{-1} year^{-1}) additions on nematode assemblages over three years in a temperate old growth forest in China, the authors observed limited effects of nitrogen or water addition independently (Sun et al. 2013). However, when both water and nitrogen were added, there was a significant decrease in total nematode abundance, and in the abundance of plant parasitic nematodes, fungivores, and omnivore-predators, in the organic horizon, whereas the opposite pattern was observed in the mineral soil beneath. The authors did not quantify changes in belowground plant biomass, but it seems likely that this pattern would be driven by deeper rooting depth with greater resource availability at depth in the water and nitrogen addition treatment. Similarly, another study investigated the effects of eCO_2, warming and altered rainfall regime on microarthropods in an old field in Tennessee (Kardol et al. 2011). The authors collected soil samples in two seasons (June, November) after the treatments had been in place for approximately five years. The treatments included ambient and elevated CO_2 (ambient + 300 ppm), wet and dry (25 mm versus 2 mm water added weekly), and ambient and increased temperature (ambient + 3°C). Overall, the treatments had no effects on total microarthropod abundances, but there were differences in the microarthropod assemblage structure between treatments due to taxon-specific responses. In particular, microarthropod richness was lower in the reduced rainfall treatment than at ambient rainfall, while at ambient temperatures eCO_2 had a positive effect on microarthropod richness relative to ambient CO_2. Across all the treatments, precipitation and warming explained most of the variation in microarthropod assemblage structure. Moreover, springtail abundance and richness was positively related to soil moisture across all treatment plots. The authors found evidence that the negative effects of temperature on springtails were likely due to reduced soil moisture contents rather than increased temperature *per se*. In another recent study, Thakur et al. (2017b) assessed the effects of warming (ambient +3.4°C) and reduced summer precipitation (40% reduction) on soil detritivore feeding activity in two North American boreal forest experiments over four years. It was hypothesised that warming would increase feeding activities, but only under ambient precipitation. Contrary to this, the authors found that warming had minimal effects on the feeding activity of soil detritivores and, moreover, warming combined with reduced summer precipitation caused a roughly 14% decrease in feeding activity on average during the experiment. Hence, climate change drivers will interact to modify ecosystem functioning.

7.6 Summary

Climate change is likely to incur simultaneous alterations in temperature and rainfall driven at least in part by changes in CO_2 concentrations that will further moderate how ecosystems respond to these changes specifically through increased carbon availability to the plants aboveground. In very broad terms, elevated CO_2 concentrations are likely to somewhat moderate the effects of increased temperatures and reduced rainfall via increased water use efficiency of the plant thereby limiting the impacts on soil water content. Moreover, warming and increased precipitation is likely to cancel each other out, whereas warming in combination with reduced precipitation will have greater than expected effects because of the dual impacts on water use and availability. In comparison, our knowledge of how these effects will interact with other global change drivers, such as land use change and nitrogen deposition, is severely limited. The few studies that have investigated the interactive effects of multiple global change drivers often find unexpected outcomes that are strongly context dependent. Moreover, studies are understandably generally limited to two or three variables given logistical and economic constraints. Therefore, we might be able to fairly and reliably predict the consequences of global change when only one variable is changing, but it is much more difficult to predict the effects of multiple global change drivers. Our ability to predict the long-term effects are further limited by a lack of suitable long-term manipulations. There is therefore a great need for a systematic approach to assess the interactive effects of key global change drivers in more detail by establishing robust long-term experimental manipulations, preferably under field conditions. While it is virtually impossible to assess all global change drivers simultaneously, we can use existing data to identify key drivers likely to have particularly large effects in a given biome or ecosystem type, and set up hypothesis-driven experiments to evaluate their interactive effects over a climatic and environmental gradient relevant to the system being investigated. This will be of great importance for the future of our production systems and the provision of ecosystem services (see Chapter 9).

8 · Soil Fauna Assemblage Succession and Restoration

Ecosystems change over long timescales through the process of succession that is governed by a range of climatic, environmental, and biological mechanisms. In its purest form succession is considered as primary when new habitats are made available with no legacy of past microbial, animal, or plant assemblages. Over time colonisation occurs, first by a so-called pioneer species that can facilitate or inhibit later successional stage species from arriving. The aboveground and belowground assemblages then change relatively predictably through time. However, disturbance can 'reset' successional trajectories, effectively switching states from later successional stages to earlier successional stages, with the time of recovery increasing with the scale of disturbance. In very extreme cases, such as volcanic eruptions, this can result in restarting primary succession, but in most cases, propagules will be left behind, and recovery will proceed through what is known as secondary succession. A large proportion of Earth's terrestrial surface has been modified by human activities such as food production, resource extraction, and construction of infrastructure. Once the land has been deemed of limited value for these purposes or otherwise unfit for human occupation, it is often abandoned, which opens up opportunities to restore the ecosystems to their 'natural state' or a certain target type of vegetation likely to be found at the location. Fundamentally, ecosystems recover following human impacts through processes similar to those observed during succession, although the trajectory is not always as clear. Importantly, there is evidence that by facilitating succession, we can promote the rate of restoration and steer the trajectory of ecosystem recovery. Given the large contribution of soil fauna to biochemical processes and plant assemblage dynamics (Chapter 2), it follows that restoration can benefit from incorporating these organisms into restoration management practices to ensure the best possible outcomes. Moreover, there is also evidence that the addition of soil fauna can promote the rate and trajectory of ecosystem restoration. In this chapter, I will provide an overview of successional patterns in soil fauna assemblages and the role of soil fauna as modifiers of succession before discussing how soil fauna assemblages respond to, and may aid in, restoration projects.

8.1 Successional Patterns of Soil Fauna Assemblage Structure

Succession in the plant assemblage is generally characterised by a build-up phase (early to mid-successional stages), a climax stage with high biomass and species richness, and, in the absence of major disturbances, the ecosystem can enter a retrogression phase that is best described for plant communities (Figure 8.1). The build-up phase is generally characterised by an increase in plant biomass, soil nutrient availability, and organic matter content, whereas the retrogression phase is exemplified by a corresponding decrease in primary productivity, organic matter, and

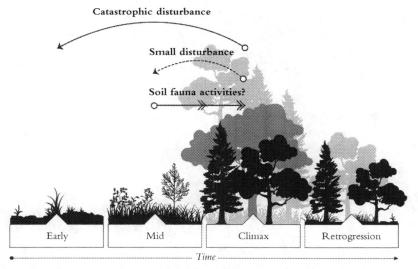

Figure 8.1 A simplified diagram illustrating successional patterns in plant assemblages. It is a well-established concept that the plant assemblage goes through a series of stages during primary succession: starting with an early stage with limited diversity and biomass, peaking at a climax stage with high diversity and biomass, and in some cases, entering a retrogression stage. The latter is signified by a decrease in primary productivity and nutrient limitation, particularly phosphorus. However, disturbances can reset successional patterns, with larger disturbances imposing a greater effect. Interestingly, there is increasing evidence that soil fauna activities, particularly that of plant herbivores and parasites, may promote succession in plant assemblages.

P availability (Peltzer et al. 2010). The main patterns of succession are well described, but our knowledge of succession in soil fauna assemblages is much more limited. Given the substantial changes in vegetation composition taking place during succession, it is, however, expected that soil fauna assemblages differ between different successional stages. Our capacity to investigate patterns of primary succession is limited by the long timescales involved. However, there are several significant papers on the development of soil fauna assemblages during succession based on chronosequences where the authors use a 'space for time' substitution by investigating patterns across ecosystems of different ages with otherwise similar climatic and environmental conditions. Common examples include a series of sand dunes with different ages or glacier foreland where glaciers are receding. These studies have collectively shown that soil fauna assemblages show substantial changes during succession. Moreover, secondary succession whereby soil fauna assemblages develop following disturbances, such as conversion to agriculture, have provided important insights into successional patterns belowground. However, the trajectory is generally influenced by a legacy of propagules from the previous occupants, both aboveground and belowground.

The investigation of successional patterns was initially focussed on the vegetation aboveground. However, a few researchers investigated the belowground patterns associated with the changes in vegetation relatively early on. For example, one study observed that there is a directional shift in springtail assemblages during bog soil succession from lime-rich aquatic fenland vegetation to *Sphagnum*-dominated vegetation to Calluna-Cladonia heathland (Murphy 1955). Specifically, the author noted that springtail assemblages change from *Tetracanthella brachyura*, *Isotomurus* sp., *Sminthurides malmgreni* to *Folsomia brevicauda*, *Friesea mirabilis*, *Isotoma sensibilis* to *Tetracanthella wahlgreni*, *Arrhopalites principalis* among the main successional stages. Similarly, Popp (1962) described directional changes in mite assemblages during hummock formation in Germany, and protozoan assemblages in Antarctic fellfield soils show relatively predictable successional patterns, going through a sequence from pioneer microflagellate colonisers to larger flagellates and ciliates, and finally testate amoeba (Smith 1996). Similarly, it has been shown that the relative abundance of omnivore nematodes increased progressively during succession across a Scottish sand dune chronosequence, going from a sandy beach to mature, heath-covered dunes, which appeared to be related to an increase in soil organic matter content (Wall et al. 2002). Such studies have promoted the interest in succession as a topic in soil ecology, and more recent studies provide substantial insight into the broader patterns observed belowground during succession.

The use of chronosequences to study primary and secondary succession has provided substantial insights. A study using two >1,900-year proglacial chronosequences in the high Arctic found strong evidence for deterministic successional patterns in invertebrate assemblages, including protozoans, insects, microarthropods, and spiders that contributed to progressive increases in species richness (Hodkinson et al. 2004). One of the key findings here was that certain groups arrived much earlier than other invertebrates, notably drought-resistant oribatid mites, surface-active springtails, and spiders. Indeed, these groups colonised the new habitats before vascular plants established and soils developed, while other groups needed to be facilitated by the presence of vascular plants and soil development. It was also noted that dispersal limitation was likely not a main driver of assemblage structure across the chronosequences, with only a few late successional species not observed. Similarly, rapid colonisation of recently exposed habitat at the Central Alpine glacier foreland in Austria by epigean invertebrates was dominated by predators, with herbivores and decomposers arriving later in the 140-year chronosequence (Kaufmann 2001, Kaufmann et al. 2002). Moreover, the succession of soil fauna assemblages progressed rapidly over the first 50 years, with more stable assemblage composition observed in the later stages. Other studies have reported similar rapid colonisation of glacier foreland by surface-dwelling springtails, spiders, and epigeal beetles (Matthews and Vater 2015). Moreover, the patterns of carabid beetles were studied along another ~150-year glacier foreland chronosequence in Switzerland (Schlegel and Riesen 2012). The carabid beetles colonised the newly exposed habitat rapidly, and there was a progressive increase in species richness and activity over the first 40 years, before a slight slump, and an increase again towards the older sites. Habitat characteristics, particularly plant cover and litter, explained part of the variation in carabid beetle assemblages, but age of the substrate was a better predictor of assemblage composition. Hence, the successional patterns differ somewhat predictably across taxa and life history traits.

By contrast, there was no directional change in mite species abundance, species richness, and diversity along a roughly 60–5,000 retrogressive chronosequence comprised of islands of various sizes in two Swedish lakes that are differentially exposed to fires started by lightning (Bokhorst et al. 2017a). However, there were directional shifts in springtail assemblages, with euedaphic species dominating the youngest islands where they may be better at utilising the resources in the soil. Hence, springtail functional traits can provide robust insight into shifts in assemblage structure that is related to changes in the environment. While mite assemblage composition showed limited correlation with island size or time since fire, there were mite and springtail species that were related to successional stages thus contributing to shifts in the assemblage composition. There is also mixed evidence for changes in nematode diversity during succession, with some studies indicating decreased (Sohlenius and Wasilewska 1984, Wall et al. 2002) and increased (Armendáriz et al. 1996, Freckman and Ettema 1993, Wardle et al. 1995) diversity, respectively, as succession progress. These discrepancies may be related to the widely different ecosystem types investigated, but this is yet to be substantiated.

There appears to be a general shift in soil food web structure during succession from predominantly bacterial-dominated to greater relative fungal influences at later successional stages (Bokhorst et al. 2017b). This in turn has predictable cascading effects on the soil fauna assemblages. In a study comparing soil food web structure across five successional stages, with the oldest representing a retrogression stage, at four sites in different climatic regions, Laliberté et al. (2017) indeed found that the fungal pathway became more important with successional stage age. The observed changes in microbial pathways in turn influenced bacterial- and fungal-feeding nematode assemblages (Figure 8.2). The abundances of carnivorous and omnivorous nematodes were positively related to the abundance of bacterial-feeding nematodes, while predatory mites were positively related to fungal-feeding mite abundances. Moreover, they found that the root pathway was most important at intermediate successional stages, with cascading effects on plant parasitic nematodes. It appears that basal resources, here measured as soil organic matter, is unimodally related to successional stage age with the greatest amounts found at intermediate ages. However, root biomass showed a different pattern increasing throughout successional progression and into the retrogression stages, possibly because plants allocate more C belowground to root growth and root exudates in an effort to compensate for the diminishing nutrient availability in the retrogression stages. The study also provides strong evidence for a greater influence of successional stage on soil food web structure than climate; however, this is not surprising from a theoretical point of view in that climate may direct succession rather than prevent certain vegetation from existing. Other studies have also observed a tendency for omnivorous soil fauna to become more abundant as succession progress (Goralczyk 1998, Procter 1984, Wall et al. 2002) indicating predictable

8.1 Successional Patterns of Soil Fauna Assemblage Structure · 251

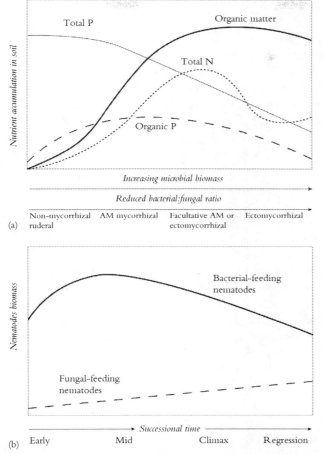

Figure 8.2 Our understanding of belowground patterns during succession is more limited than that of the vegetation aboveground. (a) The changes in soil organic matter, nitrogen, and phosphorus contents are relatively well described, with a general increase in nitrogen and organic matter content as succession progresses, except in the case of retrogression, and a steady decrease in total phosphorus content. Associated with these changes, there is a general increase in microbial biomass as succession progresses, with bacteria dominating at early successional stages and a relative increase in fungal dominance in the later successional stages (modified from Bardgett (2005) by permission of Oxford University Press, www.oup.com).
(b) The patterns in soil fauna assemblages are not yet clear, but an increase in fungal biomass suggests that the fungal pathway would become more important at later successional stages. Accordingly, there is evidence from a comparison of five chronosequences that the biomass of bacterial-feeding nematodes peaks at mid to climax successional stages, whereas there is a general increase in fungal-feeding nematodes as succession progress.
Based on Laliberté et al. (2017).

changes in soil food web structure across successional sequences. At longer timescales, ecosystems can enter retrogression after the climax stage where the ecosystem becomes less favourable to the soil fauna. For example, in a study investigating soil fauna and microbial changes across a *c.* 290,000-year chronosequence in New Zealand, Williamson et al. (2005) found that the abundance of enchytraeids and nematodes, both predatory and microbial feeders, decreased in the latter stages of succession. This appeared to be associated with a decrease in resource quality and quantity, due in part to increases in the C:N and C:P ratios, with a decrease in microbial and soil fauna activity and a more fungal-based food web as retrogression takes place. Similarly, nematode and macro-invertebrate richness has been found to decrease slightly during the retrogression phase (Doblas-Miranda et al. 2008).

While there are a few chronosequences that investigate primary succession, most chronosequences are based on secondary succession following human activities. A study of 27 sites representing a gradient from pasture to old growth forest in Brazil showed that the conversion of forests to pasture has detrimental impacts on ant assemblage richness. Following the establishment of secondary forests, the richness of ants increases incrementally, with the assemblage representing a subset of the species found in the old growth forest. However, the assemblage structure and richness of older secondary forests – 35–50 years following reforestation – was still substantially different from that of old growth forests. The pattern was particularly prominent in the epigeic ant assemblages, with hypogeic (soil-dwelling) ant assemblages showing no directional recovery towards old growth states. The lack of recovery in the hypogeic ant assemblage indicates that these may have low resilience to disturbance. The slow recovery of ant assemblages have implications for the conservation of ants and likely other soil fauna as only old growth forests will function as reservoirs of species diversity (Bihn et al. 2008). An earlier meta-analysis estimated that recovery of ant species richness in tropical forests would be completed in 20–40 years (Dunn 2004b), but the results presented by Bihn et al. (2008) highlight that this might not always be the case. They elaborate on this by presenting evidence that at least some genera of ants are more species diverse in old growth forests than disturbed habitats (Kalif et al. 2001) and that species recovery is often non-linear and asymptotic (Simberloff and Wilson 1970). The difference in recovery of litter (epigeic) and soil-dwelling (hypogeic) ant assemblages could be due to microhabitat differences. Once the canopy closes in secondary forests the litter layer rapidly recovers, providing a

8.1 Successional Patterns of Soil Fauna Assemblage Structure · 253

suitable habitat for the litter dwellers. By contrast, it may take longer for relevant soil microhabitats to develop or resource requirements to be fulfilled with hypogeic ants being considered dietary specialists (Delabie and Fowler 1995).

Similarly, it has been found that the species richness and biomass of springtails increase with beech forest age (16–130-year-old stands) in France, and there is a directional shift in springtail assemblage composition driven by changes in the relative abundances of individual species (Chauvat et al. 2011). By contrast, centipede assemblages showed a different pattern in managed beech forests in Slovenia. When comparing deforested, juvenile (~20-year-old trees), pole (~30–40-year-old trees), and timber (~60–80-year-old trees) phases, the highest species richness was observed in the juvenile forest and the lowest in the deforested plots, respectively (Grgič and Kos 2005). The authors note that this is likely because the young, ~2 m high trees, provide a suitable environment for this particular group of macrofauna. During the secondary succession from abandoned arable land to beechwood forest representing a 150-year chronosequence in Germany, Scheu and Schulz (1996) observed that saprophagous macro-invertebrate and oribatid mite assemblages differed across successional stages. While all the macro-invertebrates showed changes in assemblage structure and richness, with a considerable decrease in species following the establishment of woody species particularly for Diplopoda and Isopoda, the oribatid mite assemblages showed a continuous change across the successional sequence and the richness increased with succession. By contrast, earthworm assemblages showed less variability across the successional stages. The decrease in Diplopoda and Isopoda during succession appeared to be related to a more limited litter layer in the mid-successional ash-dominated stage. The changes in the oribatid mite assemblage structure and the observed increase in species richness appeared to be most strongly associated with the formation of a less-dense mineral soil rich in organic matter and greater soil water content. There is similarly a clear shift in mite assemblage structure following conversion from arable land to extensively managed grassland ecosystems, with a progressive increase in species richness and biomass driven in large parts by an increased presence of decomposer and predatory species (de Groot et al. 2016). This indicates there may be coinciding shifts in ecosystem functioning, particularly decomposition pathways and pest suppression.

Successional patterns have also been studied at shorter timescales and smaller spatial scales. Wallwork (1976) noted that there are clear patterns of succession in soil fauna assemblages on roots alongside the succession from young healthy roots through maturation to senescence, to disease and death, with a switch from specialised root feeders to more generalist forms, including nematodes, springtails, and others that feed on decaying root tissue. There are consistent, albeit weak, successional patterns in soil fauna assemblages during detritus decomposition. In particular, large litter transformers or shredders generally arrive earlier than soil-dwelling equivalents while microbivore species generally arrive later in the process, with a shift from bacterial feeders to fungal feeders over time as decomposition progresses (Bastow 2012). This is likely associated with a change in litter quality. Moreover, surface-dwelling springtails arrive earlier than soil-dwelling species possibly due to greater dispersal ability, with a switch from fungal feeders to detritivores over time, and the predators generally arrive after their microbivore prey increase in population size. Finally, it appears that certain oribatid mites are more common in early stages of litter decomposition than later, and other species are more common in later stages. We can therefore expect that individual microhabitats differ in soil fauna assemblage composition because they are at different successional patterns independent of the ecosystem-level successional stage.

8.2 Belowground Effects of Restoration Practices

There is relatively limited knowledge of the impact of restoration practices on soil fauna assemblages, with most studies focussing on the vegetation aboveground. While this is unfortunate, there is reason to expect that restoration practices that contribute to the recovery of the vegetation aboveground also help promote the recovery of belowground assemblages. Indeed, some restoration practices focus on improving soil conditions, including pH, C, and nutrient concentrations, etc., in an effort to facilitate vegetation restoration, and these practices are also likely to benefit indigenous soil fauna. Accordingly, the biomass and diversity of soil biota increase with the age of abandoned, non-reclaimed mining sites ranging from 1 to 41 years (Frouz et al. 2013). Similarly, there are clear but contrasting shifts in assemblage structure of oribatid mites and nematodes during secondary succession from former arable land to heath land (Kardol et al. 2009). In particular, nematode α-diversity was highest in the mid to late successional stages, with no change in γ-diversity along the chronosequence, while oribatid mite α-diversity and γ-diversity both increased since abandonment. Moreover, nematode β-diversity decreased and oribatid mite β-diversity initially increased and then decreased during succession. These contrasting patterns indicate that oribatid mite assemblages are primarily structured by dispersal limitation, whereas nematode assemblages are more strongly related to shifts in edaphic or biotic properties. There is also evidence for successional patterns in mesostigmatid mites following reclamation. For example, during secondary succession at two reclaimed electric power plant waste dumps in Poland there were clear shifts in mesostigmatid mite assemblage composition, primarily driven by shifts in the dominant species at different successional stages (Madej and Stodółka 2008). The authors found a clear directional successional pattern in one of the sites, with the mite assemblage structure approaching that of nearby reference sites; however, the pattern was less clear at the other site. Accordingly, mesostigmatid mite species associated with degraded habitats dominated the assemblages in the early successional stages. Hence, there is clear evidence that soil fauna assemblages respond to the cessation of both agricultural and industrial land use. However, it is less clear whether soil fauna assemblages develop at the same rate as the vegetation aboveground and if the trajectory aligns with target ecosystems.

There is evidence that ecological restoration can have positive impacts on soil assemblages. For example, a study that assessed the effects of woodland restoration and management on surface-active arthropods in the Chicago metropolitan area found promising results (McCary et al. 2015). The authors compared arthropod assemblages in degraded sites, sites undergoing active restoration (3–21 years), and restored sites considered 'reference sites' with 11–21 years' management. The results showed that the sites undergoing active restoration supported soil fauna assemblages that were different from the degraded sites, approaching those in the target reference sites. Moreover, there were fewer non-native isopods in the managed restoration woodlands and much greater springtail abundances in the reference sites. The authors conclude that practices that successfully restore woodland ecosystems in this area also restore soil fauna assemblages. One disclaimer that is worth highlighting here is the possible lack of 'true' reference sites that reflect the state of above- and belowground assemblages in the absence of anthropogenic disturbances that even the managed reference sites have experienced in this study. Similar difficulties in acquiring optimal reference sites are likely to occur where the native vegetation has been heavily impacted by human activities, including agricultural landscapes and metropolitan areas elsewhere.

An excellent recent study investigated the effects of restoration using a chronosequence representing recent, mid-, and long-term (up to 30 years) secondary succession stages following the cessation of agricultural practices (Morriën et al. 2017). The authors found that as secondary succession progressed the soil biotic network connectivity increased, reflecting more biotic interactions as would be expected in less disturbed food webs. This suggests that the soil biotic assemblages respond to restoration practices and may return to a state with greater connectivity, both of which are likely to benefit the resistance and resilience of the resulting ecosystems. By contrast, no increase in soil food web connectance was observed as succession progressed at 14 non-reclaimed post-mining sites in the Czech Republic, even though the oldest site was 41 years old and had secondary forest growth (Frouz et al. 2013). However, this could possibly be attributed to the likely large legacy of mining activities and that no post-heaping management had occurred. Interestingly though, the authors observed a switch from bacterial- to fungal-dominated food webs between the young and intermediate aged post-mining sites, and back again in the older forested sites, which the authors speculate could be due to an increase in earthworm presence. In particular, the study highlighted that fungal influences increased with the depth of the fermentation layer (i.e. the H layer as described in Chapter 1). The presence of earthworms in the older forested sites contributes to increased bioturbation and mixing of the organic and mineral horizons, thus negatively impacting the fungal-based food web, and earthworms are known to promote bacterial-based food webs more broadly (Bardgett and Wardle 2010).

There is also evidence that certain restoration practices positively affect leaf litter arthropods in tropical forests. For example, reforestation of former agricultural fields in the Atlantic Forest biome of two different regions in Brazil showed that the soil fauna communities of reforested patches progressively became more similar to remnant forests (Meloni and Varanda 2015). In particular, the soil fauna assemblages of 10–20-year-old reforested sites were more similar to the remnant forest, and the richness of the soil fauna assemblages increased with forest maturity. Reforestation age had limited effect on the abundance of soil fauna, although the abundance of Diplura, Protura, and Symphyla was positively related to forest age. Another noteworthy finding was that the assemblages showed much greater dissimilarity between patches of similar ages, suggesting highly stochastic colonisation patterns in the early years. Similarly, another study assessed the effects of restoration of tropical forests on former pastures in Costa Rica using the establishment of plantation, 'vegetation islands', and natural regeneration had differential

8.2 Belowground Effects of Restoration Practices · 257

effects on leaf litter arthropods (Cole et al. 2016). The plantation and vegetation islands approaches both used the same species of plants, namely two native timber species and two non-native legumes, but differed in the planting pattern. In the plantation treatment, trees were planted uniformly throughout the area, whereas in the treatment with vegetation islands, trees were planted in areas covering 4 m × 4 m, 8 m × 8 m, and 12 m × 12 m. These vegetation islands contributed to a canopy cover of roughly 20% initially, but the canopy cover increased to ~50% during the experiment as the trees grew and reproduced. After seven to eight years following restoration, the plots with vegetation islands had greater abundances and plot-level richness of arthropods than did plantations or natural regeneration, likely due to the creation of a greater range of habitats. Impressively, the arthropod richness, diversity, and number of functional groups in the plots with vegetation islands were often similar to, or even greater than, those in the reference forests nearby. This suggests that restoration can be achieved with less intensive management practices, and therefore lower cost. However, the assemblages were still different from the reference sites, indicating that ongoing management or more time is required to re-establish ecosystems similar to the reference forests. One possible extension of the vegetation island approach would be to include a greater level of plant species diversity to foster greater variability within and between the vegetation islands, with a specific focus on plant species associated with target vegetation types. This would likely further facilitate the establishment of other organisms including soil fauna. The use of such planting methods to facilitate the restoration of diversity soil fauna assemblages, however, requires further assessment, particularly if the goal is to restore assemblages similar to those found in native pristine ecosystems.

Ant assemblages have been used extensively to assess the recovery during restoration. For example, Andersen and Sparling (1997) studied ant communities at recovering mine sites in seasonal tropical ecosystems in Australia and compared these with more 'pristine' ecosystems in an effort to determine whether ants were useful bioindicators of restoration success. The authors found that ant species richness responded positively to restoration and concluded that ants are a good indicator of restoration success. However, possibly the best assessment of the effect of ecological restoration is based on projects taking place on abandoned bauxite mining sites in Western Australia in former Jarrah forests (*Eucalyptus marginata*). An overview of the effects based on 30 years' research is presented and discussed in Majer et al. (2007), with the objective of establishing self-sustaining ecosystems. In the early days the focus was on ant communities, and it was found that seeding mixed over- and understory plant communities had supported ant communities that were more similar to remnant reference sites than *E. marginata* monocultures and non-restored sites, and that the variability in ant species richness and diversity was best explained by plant species richness and diversity, respectively, time since restoration, plant cover, and the presence of logs. Follow-up studies later showed that restoration had similar effects on springtail (increased abundances associated with improved plant cover and richness), mite (increased oribatid mite density and richness with time since restoration), and termite (increased abundance and diversity with time since restoration comparable to that of remnants) communities, but that community composition was rarely identical to that of the remnant vegetation suggesting that restoration has not yet mirrored the lost habitat. This is one of the ongoing concerns of restoration – how do we quantify the success of restoration and what is it we want to restore? However, it is clear from this work that several soil fauna taxa may be very useful indicators of restoration success and trajectory, each providing different levels of information. There is great scope for incorporating soil fauna into restoration practices more broadly.

Establishing the vegetation aboveground is, however, not always a strong driver of belowground responses. A study that manipulated plant species diversity *in situ* in a short-term restoration experiment found very limited effects of increased addition of plant species diversity on plant biomass production or the soil fauna belowground (Hedlund et al. 2003). In this study, the authors constructed high- and low-species diversity plant assemblages on abandoned arable land by seeding with 15 and 4 mid-successional plant species mixes, respectively, and compared these treatments with control plots where plants were established from the seed bank at sites in five European countries with different climates and soil types. To avoid confounding species richness with sampling effects, the four species treatment were randomly drawn from the larger 15 species pool. All 15 species mixes were composed of five grasses, five legumes, and five forbs, while the four species mixes comprised two grasses, one legume, and one forb. After three years the high plant diversity plots had greater biomass production than the control plots. However, across all plots there was no correlation between plant species richness and biomass production at three sites, while the other two showed a positive and negative correlation, respectively. Accordingly, there were no generalisable effects on belowground microbial or soil fauna biomass. The only group that showed a response to the short-term restoration practices was the nematodes, which increased in abundance following cessation of agricultural practices from 1996 to 1998. Indeed, the abandonment of agricultural practices had a much greater effect on nematodes, mites, and earthworms over the first three years than the plant species richness treatments *per se* (Korthals et al. 2001). Similarly, a recent study found limited evidence that the successful restoration of the aboveground vegetation of varying complexity has corresponding effects on microbial communities, even after 16 years (e.g. Strickland et al. 2017). This would likely have direct knock-on effects on soil fauna assemblages given that microbial communities form a great part of their food source. These results highlight that increasing plant species richness may not be a useful tool for promoting the rate or steering the trajectory of secondary succession at least in the short term. This is particularly true if plant species arrival is not a random process during succession.

One concern mentioned earlier is that in many cases restoration efforts increase soil biodiversity, but the resulting assemblages do not necessarily resemble those found in the identified target sites, and it may take decades to foster the development of soil fauna assemblages. In particular, some soil fauna may be particularly slow to colonise following disturbances. For example, Scheu and Schulz (1996) found that while earthworms, isopods, and diplopods relatively quickly colonised abandoned arable land, the oribatid mite assemblage structure and diversity developed much more slowly with a continuous change in assemblage structure and increasing species richness throughout secondary succession until the expected beechwood forest climax stage. Promoting the species richness of fragmented ecosystems may be difficult due to spatial isolation (i.e. assisted migration may be required) and a higher risk of extinction (i.e. a given patch is unlikely to support as many species as a larger area simply due to low rates of immigration and high extinction rates as per the species-area relationship and island biogeography theory). Furthermore, the immigration of non-target species not native to the ecosystem may prevent the successful recovery of target soil fauna assemblages similar to those found in pristine examples of a given ecosystem. Moreover, the diversity of endemic New Zealand earthworms responded positively to restoration of former agricultural land into native vegetation through sequential replanting, quickly colonising the restored sites and dominating the earthworm biomass and abundance (Boyer et al. 2016). However, the authors noted that exotic earthworms were still present even after 30 years and that the proportion of biomass or abundance accounted for by endemics was a better proxy of restoration success than actual biomass or abundance of exotic or endemic species, *per se*. As highlighted in Chapter 6, some plant functional types have greater impacts on biogeochemical cycling and belowground communities including soil fauna and may be particularly important to consider in restoration projects. For example, the removal of a dominant nitrogen-fixing shrub had severe impacts on soil fauna diversity and abundance in a primary successional stage (St John et al. 2012). By extension, the inclusion of N-fixing plants in restoration plantings may be a useful tool for promoting belowground communities. However, this might also have unintended impacts and the choice of plants to include should be considered with care. The value of such manipulations will further depend on what the desired target is; for example, whether we try to replicate or re-create a target ecosystem or aim to create a functional ecosystem that support above- and belowground biodiversity.

8.3 Potential for Soil Fauna to Aid Remediation of Degraded Sites

One of the main principles of restoration is that the recovery of vegetation takes place through the process of succession. It follows then that restoration practices should focus on enhancing the rate of succession by modifying the environment to favour late successional species. There is evidence that this can be done both through manipulations of the physical environment as well as by modifying the biotic communities themselves. One of the potential limitations of past and ongoing restoration efforts of degraded ecosystems is that they generally focus almost exclusively on establishing or enhancing the native vegetation and creating habitat for rare or iconic animals (Ruiz-Jean and Aide 2005). Yet, ecosystem functioning is strongly moderated by aboveground–belowground interactions, particularly through plant–soil microbial interactions, but the soil fauna is a key component that is often overlooked. Indeed, a review written in 2008 highlighted this knowledge gap (Callaham et al. 2008). Although a few noteworthy papers illustrating the importance of soils in restoration ecology have been published since then, soil and its biology are still not fully taken into consideration in restoration projects. Throughout this book I have provided examples of the contribution of soil fauna to ecosystem functioning, both directly and through their interactions with the other organisms within the soil food web.

8.3 Potential for Soil Fauna to Aid Remediation of Degraded Sites

Therefore, ecosystems where only the plant community is restored may never reach a state that is functionally similar to the target, and even if it approaches the target state, the functional resistance and resilience may yet be compromised. Fortunately, there is evidence that appropriate management of soil fauna assemblages, such as through the introduction of single species or whole assemblages and implementing management regimes that benefit the soil fauna, can aid in the recovery of ecosystems (Carbajo et al. 2011, Wubs et al. 2016). However, we often lack a target example of a truly pristine assemblage for a given ecosystem making it difficult to set realistic, desirable end points for restoration practices. This is even more pronounced belowground given that soil organisms are less well catalogued compared to the vegetation aboveground.

Earthworms are ecosystem engineers that can substantially modify their environment, making them likely candidates to aid in the remediation of degraded sites, promote the rate of restoration, or steer the trajectory of ecosystem development. In particular, anecic earthworms may be of use in restoration practices given their vertical mixing of organic and mineral substrates combined with their impact on soil structure and biogeochemical cycling. Earthworm application can be highly advantageous under the right circumstances, but their introduction has to be justified (i.e. fit the target ecosystem), the right species for introduction has to be identified before application and then applied only if the soil conditions are amenable to support the species in question. A synthesis of four case studies of the contribution of earthworms to the restoration of reclaimed land in the United Kingdom highlighted that care should be taken when considering this as a management technique (Butt 2008). Similarly, earthworms have been applied to restore ecosystem services after opencast mining with varying degrees of success (Boyer and Wratten 2010). The goal is to promote the formation of a better soil structure, improved biogeochemical cycling, and stabilisation of organic wastes; however, a common issue with the reclamation of opencast mining sites is that the soil has been stored in large piles, with a substantial impact on the biota, organic matter content, and soil structure. It is therefore critical to a providing a suitable habitat for the earthworms often through improvements of the soil characteristics and to apply species appropriate to the conditions. One practice that appears to be of particular importance to promote the establishment of earthworms is the application of organic matter as a substrate. Other detritivore macrofauna such as millipedes and isopods have been considered as organisms to be applied in a restoration project, both to promote the restoration of ecosystem function and as bioindicators, but their potential contributions are less well described (Snyder and Hendrix 2008).

Several other studies have shown that introducing soil fauna can promote succession. Early work that used selective insecticides to suppress aboveground and belowground insects at different successional stages found evidence that root-feeding insects can promote early secondary succession by reducing the competitive dominance of annual forbs (Brown and Gange 1992). Similar results elsewhere highlight the significant role of belowground herbivores in promoting succession (Schädler et al. 2004). A more comprehensive study by De Deyn et al. (2003) provided strong evidence for the role of soil fauna in succession. The authors grew experimental mixed grassland plant communities with species representing early (pasture), mid (restored grassland, 20 years old), and late successional (species rich, natural grassland) stages in sterile soils inoculated with soil fauna from either the early, mid, or late successional stage. The addition of soil fauna always favoured the late successional plant species and promoted plant species diversity, whereas the sterile control soil favoured the mid-successional plant species. The effect on the early to mid-successional species appeared to be due to selective suppression of the dominant species by belowground soil herbivores. In short, soil fauna generally has greater antagonistic effects on early to mid-successional plant species and therefore promote late successional species (Figure 8.3). More recent work similarly suggests that inoculating whole soil communities including the soil fauna can be a powerful tool for promoting the recovery of ecosystems, and this can also be used to steer the direction of plant communities towards a target ecosystem type. For example, one study experimentally inoculated organic top soil and mineral soil collected from arable land with donor soils collected from restored grasslands ranging in age from 5 to 41 years as well as a donor reference to semi-natural grassland (Carbajo et al. 2011). The authors then grew late successional plant species in the arable soils with different volumes of donor soils (1:1 versus 1:5) to test how the inoculants influenced plant communities. They found that soil inoculants from restored grasslands promoted plant community biomass but not evenness, whereas inoculants from the semi-natural grassland promoted plant community evenness but not biomass. In both cases, the effects increased with increased volumes of inoculant, with the strongest effects observed in the mineral soil. Therefore, the authors concluded that soil inoculants from appropriate donor sites with whole soil communities promote

8.3 Potential for Soil Fauna to Aid Remediation of Degraded Sites · 263

Figure 8.3 A simplified diagram illustrating the possible effect of belowground herbivores on succession. There is recent evidence that shows preferential feeding on early successional plant species of root herbivores that promote the dominance of later successional stage plant species, thus effectively enhancing succession. Alternatively, later successional plant species may be more resistant to herbivores to the same effect.

the restoration of grasslands on ex-arable lands, particularly where the organic top soil has been removed. Importantly, a substantial part of the variation in plant community composition could be explained by the abundance of bacterial-feeding nematodes, highlighting the contribution of soil fauna to this pattern. However, the volumes of soils applied in this study (1:1; 1:5) are unlikely to be realistic for in-field applications. There is further evidence from field experiments that particularly late successional plant species benefit from whole soil inoculants. Middleton and Bever (2012) grew early to late successional plant species at various distances (0.25, 0.5, 1, or 2 m) from nurse plants, some of which had been inoculated with old prairie soils. The late successional plant species, particularly those planted close to nurse plants, generally benefited from the soil inoculants whereas inoculants had a negative effect on early successional plant species. However, all plant species were influenced by the soil inoculants across all distances from the nurse plants. This indicates that applying soil inoculants introduced with nurse plants may be a viable practice to establish belowground communities at a larger scale.

More recently, Wubs et al. (2016) inoculated former agricultural fields, with and without the top soil removed, with soils from two nearby contrasting ecosystem types, a restored grassland and a dry heathland, at a rate of 2.5 L m^{-2} to assess the impact on the plant and soil community recovery over time. Six years after the plots had been inoculated, the authors found a considerable impact of the inoculations with contrasting and directional changes in the soil communities and plant communities steered by the soil inoculum, particularly in the plots where the topsoil had been removed. This strongly indicates that soil microbial and faunal assemblage management can be used as a tool for directing the restoration of ecosystems, although the influence of the soil fauna is difficult to assess from this study (Figure 8.4). Moreover, the fact that this result was achieved with the application of 'only' 2.5 L soil per m^2 suggests that this is a feasible restoration practice provided that an appropriate inoculum can be obtained from the target ecosystem type. Given that there is limited evidence that managing the plant community only during restoration has any noticeable impacts on the belowground communities beyond the effects of cessation of intensive management practices (Strickland et al. 2017), it follows that both the above- and belowground communities should be managed in synchrony to direct and maximise the speed of restoration. In particular, the likely successional pattern needs to be considered to match target late successional plant species with optimal soil inoculants. The main limitations to this approach are the availability of useful inoculants and the feasibility of application

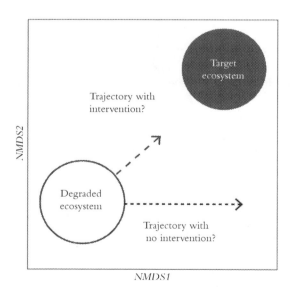

Figure 8.4 Conceptual diagram illustrating the possible effect of inoculation of soil biota on ecosystem development. If a suitable 'target' ecosystem can be identified, it may be possible to acquire soils for inoculation that can help promote the development of soil assemblages that are more similar to those in the target ecosystem. However, the application of such interventions should be considered carefully.

under field conditions. Moreover, the translocation of soil inoculum should be done with care to avoid moving potentially invasive harmful pests and pathogens to new restoration plots, but this could be secured by screening potential inoculums. However, native belowground pests and pathogens may be critical to progressing succession given evidence that they favour late successional species (De Deyn et al. 2003, Schädler et al. 2004).

8.4 Implications for Ecosystem Resistance and Resilience

There is clear evidence that restoration practices can promote the development of desirable soil fauna assemblages, that soil fauna can act as bioindicators of restoration trajectories, and that inoculating single species or whole assemblages of soil fauna may aid in restoration practices. However, our capacity to apply adaptive restoration practices that consider soil fauna assemblages explicitly is still in its infancy. Importantly, certain restoration practices appear to benefit soil fauna richness and diversity, which might be of great importance to the functional resistance and resilience of ecosystems in the longer term, particularly in the light of the ongoing global change pressures. While the biodiversity–ecosystem functioning relationship is still a somewhat contentious issue in ecology (Chapter 2; Section 2.4), it appears clear that both richness and assemblage composition are important to ecosystem functioning (Nielsen et al. 2011a). More recent work further provides evidence that the diversity–functioning relationship is stronger when multiple functions are considered (Wagg et al. 2014). However, the caveat is that the relationship depends on what functions are investigated. For example, carbon storage is a desirable outcome in agricultural systems depleted in organic matter and to counteract the increase in atmospheric CO_2 contents, but increased belowground diversity is often positively related to carbon cycling and respiration, creating a mismatch between our intended outcomes and biodiversity management. However, the restoration of ecosystems to a given target vegetation type has proven to be inherently difficult, expensive, and labour intensive, and restored ecosystems often require ongoing management. Moreover, as stated in the previous chapter, natural and managed ecosystems are continuously influenced by a combination of various global change drivers, including climate change, nitrogen deposition, and invasive species that could further hinder the successful restoration of degraded ecosystems, including former agricultural land and mining sites, and their persistence in the longer term.

Given the constraints on restoration, it is therefore imperative that appropriate actions are implemented to promote successful restoration projects, and it should be recognised that restoration is a long-term process, particularly in forested ecosystems (Chazdon 2008). The level of action required will be proportional to the level of habitat degradation, with less intensive actions and less time needed when sites have a relatively high level of biodiversity and limited degradation. However, adaptive management plans need to be developed to ensure that the restored sites are resilient in the longer term, particularly with the level of global change impacts in mind. Soil biodiversity may be of critical importance to the longer-term performance of ecological restoration projects given the biodiversity–functioning relationship described earlier. In particular, improved soil biodiversity may buffer ecosystems' responses to ongoing external pressures and disturbances, both natural and human caused. For example, as mentioned in Chapter 2, there is evidence that the rate of litter decomposition as well as the 'stability' of decomposition rates is impacted by decomposer assemblage diversity (Kitz et al. 2015). This finding suggests that biodiversity may both enhance and stabilise the rate of soil processes, which could be of substantial consequence under natural conditions where assemblages are constantly exposed to variation in environmental conditions. Indeed, such spatiotemporal biodiversity–ecosystem functioning relationships may be critical to maintaining functioning in the long term under fluctuating conditions. However, it may be more opportune to assess these relationships in terms of feeding guild (or functional group) diversity rather than species richness *per se* given the inherent link between feeding guilds and functioning.

8.5 Summary

It has long been observed that ecosystems develop through a directional pattern from early to late successional stages. Most of our knowledge of these patterns relies on changes in the plant assemblage aboveground, but there is an increasing number of studies that have investigated patterns belowground. It is still too early to describe successional patterns in soil fauna assemblages in detail, but some patterns are emerging. For example, there are clear examples of pioneer soil fauna that have functional traits that allow them to colonise rapidly following disturbance or the creation of a new habitat and exist in the harsher environmental conditions. It is also evident that soil fauna assemblage structure and composition shift as succession proceeds, seemingly governed by changes in vegetation aboveground and edaphic variables belowground, while the presence of certain soil fauna can influence successional trajectories. By contrast, it is less clear what the patterns in species richness and biomass are. Importantly, ecosystems recover following disturbance through the process of succession, and we can use these principles to speed up and steer the trajectory of restoration projects. A greater focus on belowground biota could improve restoration management practices. While the application of microbial associates of plants (symbiotic and otherwise) that improve plant health is an achievable and highly desirable target, there is also great potential in including soil fauna assemblages in restoration practices. Even plant parasitic nematodes and other belowground herbivores can play an important role by reducing the competitive ability of early successional-stage invasive plant species relative to later successional-stage native plant species. There is therefore much to be gained by further investigating the role of soil fauna in successional patterns.

9 · The Future of Soil Fauna Assemblages

Our understanding of soil fauna assemblages from the minute microfauna to mesofauna to macrofauna has improved substantially over the past few decades, spurred on by the recognition of the great diversity of organisms found belowground and their contributions to ecosystem functions. It is now clear that soil fauna assemblages are governed by multiple factors that exert their influence across broad spatial and temporal scales calling for a hierarchical approach to understanding the observed patterns of assemblage structure and composition observed at the finest scales. As outlined in the previous chapters, evolutionary and geological processes govern the possible distribution of soil fauna at continental to global scales, while climate, vegetation type, and soil type influence distribution at scales ranging from landscapes to global scales. However, the ability of organisms to disperse passively plays a key role in the observed differences in species distribution ranges. These processes thus modify the regional species pools from which soil fauna assemblages at smaller scales are ultimately derived. Within ecosystems, the spatial distribution of individual plant species, edaphic variables, active dispersal, behaviour, and biological interactions become more important, while at the finest scales the physical structure of the soil itself, the distribution of resources, and biological interactions are the key drivers. However, the relative influence of these forces differs substantially among soil fauna taxa due to difference in, for example, their evolutionary history, life history strategies and functional characteristics, dispersal abilities, and behaviour. Moreover, stochasticity associated with disturbances appears to play a critical role in soil fauna assemblage patterns even in relatively pristine ecosystems. This is likely why we can generally explain only a rather small proportion of the variation in soil fauna assemblages at smaller scales. Still, there are general patterns in belowground assemblages that suggest we will eventually be able to better explain the observed differences among sites. Indeed, there is clear evidence that soil fauna shows biogeographical and macroecological patterns that are at least in part similar to those aboveground promising that generalisations can be drawn once more data are acquired. However, there is still a substantial lack of information on the global distribution of soil fauna, the mechanisms that organise local assemblages, and the contributions of soil fauna to ecosystem functioning. Hence, there is a great need for studies that systematically address key knowledge gaps taking advantage of the increasingly sophisticated technologies available. Given the substantial contribution of soil fauna to ecosystems functioning, this is furthermore likely to be highly rewarding in terms of establishing and implementing better management practices.

It is increasingly clear that human activities have contributed substantially to alterations of soil fauna assemblage structure and composition, particularly through the conversion of natural ecosystems to production systems and other human uses, but also through modifications to the global climate and biogeochemical cycles more broadly. These modifications can have detrimental impacts on soil fauna assemblages, contributing to the homogenisation and simplification of local assemblages, and even cause local extinctions through displacement due to physical disturbance or loss of suitable habitat. Whether human activities have contributed to broader extinction of soil fauna is yet to be seen, but it appears unlikely that human activities have caused significant levels of extinctions belowground given the rather broad dispersal patterns observed for most soil fauna. Hence, possibly the greatest concern associated with the impacts of human activities on soil fauna assemblage structure and composition lie in the potential implications for ecosystem functioning. Indeed, there is substantial evidence that the negative impacts associated with land use management practices and pollution can compromise important ecosystem functions and the delivery of ecosystem services in part because of the impacts on soil fauna assemblages. On a more positive note, there is an ongoing movement striving to increase the focus on soil health given the importance of soil to the provision of ecosystem services fundamental to human well-being. Indeed, soil biodiversity, including the soil fauna, is likely to play a significant role in our quest to manage our ecosystems under future scenarios (Nielsen et al. 2015b) and make Earth's ecosystems resilient to global change (Willis et al. 2018). In this final chapter, I will provide a brief overview of the likely future of soil fauna assemblages, with a specific consideration of the benefits we can gain from an increased focus on soil fauna assemblages in our managed ecosystems.

9.1 The Future of Soil Fauna Assemblages

Soil fauna assemblages of the twenty-first century and beyond will be moderated by global changes ranging from the conversion of natural ecosystems to production systems and urban environments to climate changes and pollution to modifications of global biogeochemical cycles. Changes in land use will generally have detrimental impacts on soil fauna diversity and density, as well as soil food web complexity more broadly. Hence, the loss of natural ecosystems is a great concern for soil fauna assemblages because of the likely decreases in densities and possible local extinctions. The impacts of observed and predicted climate changes and shifts in biogeochemical cycles on soil fauna diversity and densities are more difficult to predict given the observed idiosyncratic responses belowground but are likely to contribute to shifts in soil fauna assemblage composition. Climate change in particular may result in novel assemblages if there is a mismatch between responses aboveground and belowground. Moreover, human activities contribute to the dispersal of species to new areas and the likelihood of these non-native species becoming invasive is enhanced by the disturbance of natural ecosystems caused by land use and climate changes that disrupt the indigenous assemblages. This may provide an opportunity for some types of soil fauna to increase their range sizes, but it is more likely to, on average, cause a homogenisation of soil fauna assemblages, contributing to the possible loss of soil fauna at a global scale. The consequences of invasive soil fauna are likely to be detrimental due to the spread of plant pests, particularly belowground root herbivores that include insect larvae and plant parasitic nematodes. However, broader impacts are also likely as invasive species may contribute to substantial modifications of the local environment they invade. These impacts are likely to be greatest associated with the invasion by ecosystem engineers, such as earthworms or termites, but species with novel functional traits may also impose considerable effects. As described in Chapter 6, there is substantial evidence that many species of earthworms have increased their ranges. There is less evidence for range expansion in soil fauna more broadly given a lack of knowledge of species distribution, particularly for smaller organisms.

This may paint a rather dire view of the future of soil fauna assemblages as a whole, but there is cause for optimism given recent trends. Specifically, the increasing focus on soil health to aid in sustainable land use management holds significant promise to promote soil fauna biodiversity in our managed ecosystems, and the ongoing efforts to conserve natural ecosystems and restore degraded ecosystems may contribute to the conservation of soil fauna species diversity. Soil health can be broadly defined as the ability of a soil to support a productive and diverse ecosystem with an emphasis on maintaining the broad range of soil processes (functions) that are required for this. Moreover, there has been a recent increase in the effort to inform the public about the value of soil biodiversity in our managed systems. This is inspiring a greater interest in soil fauna in and of itself, but there has been limited emphasis on taking measures that aim to conserve soil fauna to date. One way to approach this perceived gap is to focus on the possible conservation value of soil fauna assemblages both in terms of the intrinsic value of diversity of soil fauna in its own right, but also, and probably more relatable, fauna's contributions to ecosystem functioning and service delivery under the current and future scenarios as discussed throughout this book. This approach has been highlighted previously – see, for example, Decaëns et al. (2006) – but has not been successfully addressed in detail or used to guide the implementation of sustainable land use management, conservation of natural areas, restoration ecology, or policy development. Indeed, even when using the broadest possible definition of soil fauna, only around 100 species have been included on International Union for Conservation of Nature (IUCN) red lists of threatened species. The soil fauna entries on the IUCN list include the giant Gippsland earthworm, several species of ants, and a few spiders that could broadly be considered soil fauna (www.iucnredlist.org). There is therefore great potential to better incorporate soil fauna biodiversity conservation as a target in and of itself. While there is substantial evidence to guide this, there is still a need for further data to support the development of evidence-based approaches to soil biodiversity management and conservation. The successful conservation of soil fauna will thus require a robust approach to defining belowground biodiversity hotspots and biogeographical regions to capture the diversity of soil fauna on a global scale. Such an approach can be immensely powerful for identifying areas of particular interest and potential targets for conservation efforts. For example, a paper by Terauds et al. (2012) provides a great example of the value of taking this approach. The authors used known Antarctic physical parameters, expert knowledge, and terrestrial species records, ranging from soil fauna to plants, to identify 15 distinct bioregions. These bioregions provide a robust framework for identifying areas of high conservation value and potential risks of biodiversity losses, effectively identifying targets for conservation. Few attempts have been made at the global scale, although the Global Soil Biodiversity Initiative (www.globalsoilbiodiversity.org) provides a substantial step in the right direction.

Soil fauna assemblages will play a key role in maintaining soil health given their importance in ecosystem functioning. Indeed, it is well established that soil biodiversity, including that of soil fauna, is important to soil fertility and plant productivity, but the importance of these linkages under field conditions is still being discussed. In a recent study, the linkages between soil biodiversity, soil fertility, and plant productivity were assessed empirically from 289 samples representing a continental scale in Australia (Delgado-Baquerizo et al. 2017). The results showed a substantial positive tripartite feedback between soil biodiversity (microbial and invertebrate), soil fertility, and plant productivity in the top 0–10 cm soil. The feedback loop was further moderated by soil chemistry and properties, particularly pH and clay content, and was negatively and predictably impacted by aridity and mean annual temperature. Such studies provide great foundations to promote practices that support healthy ecosystems via management of soil biodiversity, soil fertility, and plant productivity to greater net benefits due to the positive feedbacks observed. Indeed, small increases in one or all of these components will have synergistic effects and greater-than-predicted net benefits on soil health and through this ecosystem functioning. It also highlights that any management action or disturbance to the ecosystem that compromises one or more of these components can have cascading negative impacts on the ecosystem as a whole. Soil fauna assemblages are also increasingly being used as potential indicators of soil health because of their rapid responses to land use management (Cardosa et al. 2013). However, there is a great need for further insight into the ecology of soil fauna to promote this more broadly. Maintaining soil health is an important goal to continue producing goods based on our lands and conserving natural to semi-natural functional and resilient ecosystems in the long term. The contribution of soil fauna to ecosystem processes that can support production systems including agro-ecosystems, forestry, and livestock production, is particularly relevant to the discussion of the value of conserving soil fauna diversity.

9.2 Managing Soil Fauna Biodiversity

The approach taken to manage soil fauna biodiversity depends fundamentally on the scale of operation. Our capacity for intervention at the global scale is mostly limited to the conservation and restoration of critical soil fauna habitat, minimising the impacts of global changes ranging from climate change to pollution and nutrient deposition to land use changes, and establishing biosecurity measures to reduce the dispersal of potentially invasive species. While these are wide-ranging targets, there is much to be gained from an increased emphasis on taking measures to protect soil fauna biodiversity at this level. We have much greater capacity to manage soil fauna biodiversity in production and urban landscapes by providing better conditions for the soil fauna, by establishing refugia where populations can be maintained and from which to disperse, and by restoring valuable habitats. For example, the restoration of degraded agricultural systems through land sharing (i.e. promoting biodiversity and ecosystem service provision of the farmed environment itself) or land sparing (i.e. incorporating separate non-farmed areas at the farm or landscape scale) has been shown to benefit both biodiversity aboveground and belowground and the provision of regulatory and supporting ecosystem services in agroecosystems. In particular, using a meta-analysis, Barral et al. (2015) found that restored agroecosystems, whether they were restored through land sharing or sparing, on average supported 78% higher levels of biodiversity, including microfauna and invertebrates, although this was based on only a few studies. Moreover, restored sites had higher levels of supporting (42%) and regulating (120%) ecosystem services. Hence, more environmentally friendly farming practices can have substantial benefits to soil biodiversity and ecosystem services more broadly.

There are several key entry points to the management of soil biodiversity in production landscapes ranging from the physical impacts of agricultural practices to the application of agrochemicals and management of plant species diversity (Figure 9.1). It is broadly desirable to reduce the disturbance of the soil structure caused by the management practices themselves to minimise the impacts on soil food webs to allow more sensitive organisms to colonise and build sustainable population sizes. This is particularly important to some ecosystem engineers, such as earthworms, and higher trophic levels that can have substantial effects on nutrient cycling and the suppression of plant pests and pathogens. Similarly, it is desirable to reduce the inputs of agrochemicals, including inorganic fertilisers and pesticides, that are likely to have harmful impacts on soil fauna assemblages. Importantly, the services provided by inorganic fertilisers can be replaced by a combination of organic fertilisers and a greater reliance on soil biodiversity to contribute to nutrient availability through mineralisation processes, while natural enemies of

274 · The Future of Soil Fauna Assemblages

Benefits of soil biodiversity

- Regional species pool from which beneficial organisms can disperse
- Improved broad-scale provision of services including regulation of soil erosion, nutrient dynamics, and water
- Adaptability, resistence, and resilience to environmental change

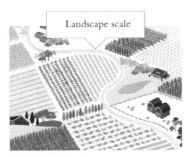
Landscape scale

Management practices

- Diversification of land use
- Mix of agricultural and natural ecosystems
- Increased landscape diversity, complexity, and connectivity between ecosystems
- Restoration of natural ecosystems

- Support of local populations of beneficial organisms
- Improved species diversity, including antagonists of plant pests and pathogens

Farm scale

- Adoption of low-impact management practices
- Strategic rotation
- Diversification of crop types
- Hedgerows
- Buffer strips
- Riparian zones
- Promote farm plant diversity
- Agroforestry

- Nutrient cycling and uptake
- Nutrient and water-use efficiency
- Plant growth, health, and stress tolerance
- Pest, pathogen, and disease supression
- Soil organic matter regulation
- Soil structure
- Water retention

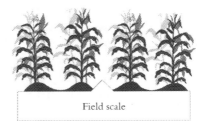
Field scale

- High precision management of nutrients, chemistry, water, pests, and pathogens
- Minimum tillage with residue retention
- Permanent plant cover
- Green manures
- Minimise chemical inputs

Figure 9.1 Diagram illustrating how soil biodiversity can benefit production systems at various spatial scales. In turn, management practices at the same spatial scales may enhance the potential benefit of soil biodiversity in said systems. Modified from Nielsen et al. (2015b) with permission from *Annual Reviews*.

pests and pathogens can take the place of most pesticides. Indeed, there is evidence that the use of pesticides has limited benefits because they negatively impact natural enemy populations, thereby increasing the likelihood of significant pest outbreaks that then require further pesticide application (Oerke 2006, van den Bosch and Stern 1962). Moreover, a more complex soil food web is likely to induce systemic plant responses that can increase their resistance to plant pests. The establishment of healthy, complex soil food webs in production landscapes requires better management of soil organic matter and plant species identity and diversity in rotations and the broader landscape. Maintaining soil fauna biodiversity will also require directed management at the landscape scale. While some extensive or low-impact management practices combined with increased crop diversity can increase the diversity and density of certain soil fauna in managed systems, individual fields are unlikely to support substantial populations of all soil fauna. For example, a study that assessed the diversity of ant assemblages in crop, pasture, and remnant native woodlands found that non-native systems contributed only a small proportion of ant diversity within the landscape matrix in eastern Australia (House et al. 2012). Instead, to promote the diversity of certain soil fauna one will need to incorporate habitat that can act as a reservoir of soil biodiversity, such as hedgerows, buffer strips, riparian zones, and forest. Indeed, several studies have shown that the presence of natural habitat increases the richness and abundance of natural enemies of soil pest and pathogens within fields. However, as outlined elsewhere, more data are required to guide such endeavours, but the potential benefits could be substantial.

Many agricultural systems suffer from a loss of soil organic matter, but improved management of plant diversity and organic inputs can contribute to re-establishing soil organic carbon. This in turn can promote water-holding capacity, infiltration capacity, macroporosity, and aggregation, and reduce surface crusting and bulk density (Haynes and Naidu 1998). One can also manage organic inputs to modify the C:N and lignin:nitrogen ratios, which in turn influence soil organic carbon pools (Paustian et al. 1997). Specifically, the C:N ratio controls decomposition during the early stages, while the lignin:nitrogen ratio modifies later stages of decomposition (Taylor et al. 1989). Moreover, there is evidence that the management of crop plant diversity is important to soil biodiversity. For example, increased plant diversity in rotations from one species to five crop species positively influenced microbial assemblage diversity and contributed to increased functioning, including organic carbon content, aggregation, total nitrogen, and microbial activity (Tiemann et al. 2015). Such effects are likely to have knock-on effects on the soil fauna assemblages and soil health more broadly.

The inclusion of cover crops in rotations with cash crops can be used to promote several ecosystem services, including biological nitrogen fixation, weed control, nutrient and carbon retention/management, soil water management, infiltration, reduction of water- and wind-driven erosion (Brandsæter and Netland 1999, Eviner and Chapin III 2001), as well as to manage soil biodiversity and soil food web structure (Buyer et al. 2010, Schutter et al. 2001). For example, the inclusion of cover crops in sorghum and garbanzo bean rotations has been shown to enhance nematode densities and biomass, the nematode metabolic footprint, and functional guilds related to soil fertility and important prey items (Zhang et al. 2017). The authors note that the presence of cover crops is important to create a continuous supply of carbon inputs and presence of roots in the soil. Similarly, intercropping cover crops might be considered a potential way to increase plant diversity of agricultural systems to provide indirect ecosystems services such as nitrogen fixation, weed suppression, and habitat for beneficial fauna, both aboveground and belowground (Bergkvist et al. 2010, Fiedler et al. 2008). Similarly, the identity of forage plant species influences soil fauna assemblages. In a four-year study, Crotty et al. (2015) found that soil fauna biomass and abundances differed substantially between four different forage crops (red clover, *Trifolium pretense*; white clover, *Trifolium repens*; chicory, *Chicorium intybus*; perennial ryegrass, *Lolium perenne*). Specifically, white clover supported greater abundances and biomass of earthworms, particularly anecic earthworms, while clover and chicory increase fungal-feeding nematode densities. There were also superfamily-specific differences in springtail abundances, with more detritivore Poduromorpha in clover and chicory treatments, and more herbivorous Symphypleona in the ryegrass treatments. These changes likely reflect changes in resource inputs and plant growth form. For example, the authors noted that the extensive root systems of the ryegrass likely had a positive influence on belowground herbivores, whereas plant species with greater mycorrhizal associates likely benefit fungal-feeding fauna. It therefore seems likely that belowground impacts of changes in the forage species can be relatively well predicted, but more knowledge is critical to understanding broader impacts. This could be highly valuable as it would allow us to construct species mixes for pastures that maximise soil processes that support the provision of ecosystem services required for sustainable land management. Choosing a good cover crop or forage crop to include in agroecosystems, however, requires extensive knowledge of its impact on the soil food web (Crotty et al. 2015). One approach is to focus on plant functional traits that are known to be related to desirable belowground impacts ranging from nutrient cycling to pest suppression mediated by the soil assemblage (Faucon et al. 2017).

One promising solution to increase the sustainable use of our land is through ecological intensification as discussed by Bommarco et al. (2016). In particular, the authors describe how an increased focus on promoting services provided by our ecosystems through biological mechanisms can help increase productivity, while at the same time (possibly) reduce the reliance on costly pesticides and large inputs of inorganic fertilisers. One of the main concerns is that agricultural production is currently limited by the degradation of most farmland, which, in turn, requires ever-greater inputs and is unlikely to maintain productivity in the long term. They highlight that management practices such as integrated pest management (IPM), conservation tillage, manure and residue incorporation, mixed or diversified crop rotations, fallows or set-asides, and increased quality or coverage of semi-natural habitat have all been shown to benefit the biological control of pests and weeds, soil formation, and nutrient cycling and, more broadly, even pollination. Bender et al. (2016) applied the concept of ecological intensification more specifically to soils to illustrate how we might be better able to harness the benefits provided by soil organisms in production systems to promote the use of sustainable land use management practices. While the emphasis was on soil microbes given that they are vital to many soil processes, it is clear that there are also substantial benefits that can be achieved through better management to promote the diversity of soil fauna. Several studies have shown that an increase in the diversity of soil fauna is likely to be particularly beneficial to soil processes in ecosystems where the diversity is low (e.g. Nielsen et al. 2011a). Given that the diversity of soil fauna is often highly suppressed in agricultural systems (e.g. Tsiafouli et al. 2015), incorporating measures that promote soil fauna diversity is therefore likely to contribute to improved functioning, such as greater rates of nutrient cycling. There is a general positive relationship between soil biodiversity and ecosystem multi-functionality, but it is not the whole story. Bender et al. (2016) re-analysed the results of three studies and showed that functional diversity played a key role in the contribution of soil biodiversity to multi-functionality. They therefore proposed that using soil ecological engineering to modify soil biotic assemblages has great potential to improve management of soils. Although these studies were mostly based on functional diversity of microbial communities, it seems very likely that the same principle can be used for soil fauna. It is worth keeping in mind that the legacy of land use may not be easily overcome, at least in the short term, by shifting to management regimes that promote more complex soil food webs (Liiri et al. 2012), thereby moderating the possible benefits of the enhanced soil biodiversity. A shift in management will have to overcome this implicit inertia before gains are realised. There is some merit in addressing the issue from a classical ecological economics approach, appointing direct and perceived monetary value to the services provided by soil fauna, and completing cost–benefit analyses to highlight best management practices (Huguenin et al. 2006). The direct value is achieved through on-farm savings or improved productivity that increases the net farm income, while perceived value based on the willingness of the farmer or community to pay for a given service can be gained through off-farm impacts, such as protecting or improving the provision of clean drinking water, climate regulation, or even benefits to human well-being. Any measure that directly enhances farm income will, however, be much easier to implement than off-farm perceived value, which has no inherent value to the individual farmer if the action increases production costs (Swift et al. 2004).

Our understanding of soil fauna's contribution to ecosystem function is accumulating rapidly, but it is generally difficult to provide evidence-based recommendations to implementing adaptive management regimes for a given system. Moreover, many farmers are progressive in trialling individual management regimes, but they are understandably more reluctant to make changes to management regimes more broadly without a high level of certainty of the benefits. This severely limits our capacity to move towards a more holistic approach to land use management that also incorporates soil fauna diversity. Finally, it can be difficult to persuade a farmer or other land use managers to pay for a given management action that might provide production stability (e.g. through reduced sensitivity to climate variability or pest outbreaks), even if the action is likely to provide greater yield over longer time scales. This is a hurdle that we will have to overcome to better manage soil fauna assemblages and the benefits they can provide, particularly in managed ecosystems. Still, there is substantial evidence that soil biodiversity, including that of soil fauna, can be of great benefit to sustainable land use and human well-being more broadly. This will be the focus of the next section.

9.3 Harnessing Soil Biodiversity for Sustainable Land Use and Human Well-Being

The ongoing degradation of soils is concerning given the potential impacts on agricultural productivity, particularly because the human population size is estimated to increase to 9.7 billion and 11.2 billion by 2050 and 2100, respectively (UN 2015). It has accordingly been estimated that food demand will increase by 70% over the next four decades (Godfray et al. 2010), putting enormous pressure on our ecosystems to deliver increased production. Moreover, it is estimated that pests cause a 30%–40% reduction in crop yield annually (Oerke 2006), making pest management in sustainable agroecosystem landscapes key to the future of food production to an ever-increasing human population. The application of pesticides is generally used to suppress pests and pathogens, but it is costly, environmentally harmful, and the efficacy is decreasing due to an increase in pesticide resistance in many target organisms (Heckel 2012). However, an increased focus on improving soil biodiversity and soil health more broadly holds great promise for more sustainable land use practices that reduce the degradation of soil and application of agrochemicals. Indeed, it is not difficult to demonstrate that an increase in soil biodiversity benefits agricultural productivity. For example, a well-designed study assessed the effects of low versus high soil biodiversity on soil nutrient dynamics and plant productivity using open top lysimeters inoculated with soil assemblages comprised of (1) only microbes by passing the inoculum through a 16 μm mesh or (2) more diverse assemblages representing organisms up to ~2 mm body width that included arbuscular mycorrhizal fungi over two years simulating a maize and wheat rotation (Bender and van der Heijden 2015). In the first year, the high biodiversity treatment promoted crop yield (22%), plant nutrient uptake (nitrogen by 29%; phosphorus by 110%), and reduced nitrogen leaching by 51%, equivalent to roughly 76 kg nitrogen per ha. The effects were smaller in the second year, but there was still a significant increase in wheat biomass production (17%) and phosphorus content (+80%). These results were linked to greater phosphorus mineralisation, reduced relative nitrogen and phosphorus leaching losses, indicating enhanced nutrient use efficiency in the high soil biodiversity treatment. Such results point to the substantial benefits soil biodiversity could bring to land use management practices. However, the low versus high biodiversity treatments compared in this study are unlikely to be representative of the true conditions found in the field, and the effects may therefore be of significantly lower magnitudes under field conditions.

There is an increased emphasis on reduced reliance on external inputs in agricultural practices. This needs to be compensated for by a greater reliance on the self-regulating processes found in ecosystems (van Eekeren et al. 2010). Importantly, there is evidence that soil biodiversity can improve these processes under the right circumstances. The capacity of soils to provide nitrogen for plant growth is, for example, strongly related to soil organic matter content, increasing by >3 kg nitrogen per ha with each additional gram of soil organic matter per gram dry soil. Moreover, potential nitrogen and carbon mineralisation is correlated with soil fauna assemblage composition in production grassland ecosystems (van Eekeren et al. 2010). A common tenet is that introducing diversity aboveground can promote the provision of ecosystem services. This includes a theoretical potential for greater suppression of pest and pathogens through the presence of top-down control by predators and parasitoids. There is limited data to support this theory belowground, but evidence from food webs aboveground provides some initial insight. In particular, a meta-analysis showed that a greater richness of predators and parasitoids on average contributed to the suppression of herbivores, particularly in agricultural systems (increased suppression observed in 185 of 266 comparisons), although reduced suppression was observed in several studies (80 of 266 comparisons). Intriguingly, the effect was not statistically significant in natural systems, indicating that other mechanisms may be involved here (Letourneau et al. 2009). Along the same lines, IPM strategies are based on achieving better pest management through integrated biological and chemical control as discussed by van den Bosch and Stern (1962) and Oerke (2006). IPM strategies can be as basic as using agrochemicals more sensibly to allow greater control by native organisms, but it can be more inclusive ranging from the use of semiochemicals (e.g., pheromones) to attract key predators, the addition of biological control agents such as entomopathogenic nematodes (EPNs; Figure 9.2), or management regimes that benefit natural enemies of key pest species. Indeed, EPNs are already used widely for biocontrol, and the efficacy can be improved by the simultaneous application of *Photorhabdus* and *Xenorhabdus* – the microbial symbionts of EPNs – as microbial insecticides. The combined application of the EPN genera *Heterorhabditis* and *Steinernema* carrying potent strains of the bacteria *Photorhabdus* and *Xenorhabdus*, respectively, has been applied in agricultural settings to suppress populations of damaging pests, including root weevils and fungus gnat, albeit to various degrees of success (Denno et al. 2008, Lacey and Shapiro-Ilan 2008). Similarly, the two genera can also be infected with the fungus *Metarhizium* and used to combat other insect pests (Petzold-Maxwell et al. 2013). There is still a substantial gap in our understanding of what structure EPN assemblages *in situ*, making it difficult to make informed decisions on management regimes that might enhance the native populations for improved pest suppression (Stuart et al. 2006).

Figure 9.2 Adult females and infective juveniles of an entomopathogenic nematode *Steinernema* spp. emerging from an infected host (*Galleria mellonella*). Courtesy of Byron J. Adams.

There is also substantial evidence that many soil arthropod predators found in natural and agroecosystems have a potential use in the control of pest organisms. The most abundant predators include certain species of mites (Acari), ants (Formicidae), carabid beetles (Carabidae), staphylinid beetles (Staphylinidae), and spiders (Aranea) (Toepfer et al. 2009). However, the contribution and application of soil invertebrates as biological control of pests and pathogens are still largely unexplored (Cock et al. 2012). A better understanding of their feeding ecology and habitat requirements would likely make it possible to benefit from their services in agroecosystems, particularly through the application of sustainable land use management practices. However, it is noteworthy that predatory mesostigmatid mites have found a place in biocontrol already. For example, at least seven native and three non-native species of Phytoseiidae have been used for biocontrol of crop pests in Australia, specifically phytophagous mites (Beaulieu and Weeks 2007). The introduced species are most commonly used to control spider mites, whereas the native species have a broader target range. There is also evidence that natural populations of predatory mites provide pest suppression under certain management practices that allow them to flourish. The potential for Phytoseiidae to control belowground pests is more uncertain.

Several studies provide strong evidence that the soil microbial assemblage can be modified to suppress potential soil fauna pests, and appropriate management practices that favour the right species could substantially reduce the reliance on pesticide use. One group of bacteria with entomopathogen properties, the pseudomonads, appears particularly promising. Some root-associated pseudomonads show great capacity to suppress root-feeding insects while also improving plant growth, providing protection against phytopathogens, and inducing systemic plant defences, and are therefore potential bioinsecticide agents (Kupferschmied et al. 2013). Other species of bacteria including, notably, *Bacillus thuringiensis* and species of *Photorhabdus* similarly suppress plant pathogens but have more limited persistence in soils, making pseudomonads a superior candidate for the development of a robust bioinsecticide. Of particular interest are *Pseudomonas protegens* and *P. chlororaphis*, which are known to be pathogenic to a broad range of known agricultural insect pests (Flury et al. 2016). Of course, the application of such bacterial entomopathogens will require vigorous testing to ensure there are no unforeseen harmful side effects, including non-target effects on beneficial soil fauna (Kupferschmied et al. 2013). There are also more than 700 known species of fungi with entomopathogen properties that occur naturally in soils that have potential benefits for land managers (Roberts and Humber 1981). Some species, including representatives of *Beauveria*, *Isaria*, *Lecanicillium*, and *Metarhizium*, are already commercially available and used for suppression of a broad range of root-feeding insects (Roberts and Humber 1981). A recent paper further provided evidence that the nematode trapping Orbiliomycete fungi may be involved in suppression of the plant parasitic nematode *Meloidogyne hapla* (Bell et al. 2016). Specifically, these fungi were more abundant in two New Zealand grassland soils that showed more nematode suppression than in eight other soils that did not show nematode suppression. Moreover, their abundances increased in follow-up experimental approaches where the nematodes were added to the soil, and irradiation enhanced nematode galling on white clover (*Trifolium repens*) in one of the otherwise suppressive soils. Nematode-trapping fungi may also present a viable biocontrol agent, but they are not yet used commercially (Degenkolb and Vilcinskas 2016). Another way to promote crop yield is through the application of, or creation of, more suitable habitats for plant growth promoting rhizobacteria and fungi (PGPR and PGPF, respectively). While these microbes promote plant health and stress tolerance very broadly (Pieterse et al. 2014), the main benefit related to soil fauna pest species would be through increased tolerance of, or resistance to, pest attack primarily achieved through microbe-induced systemic responses by the plant. However, the effect of microbe-induced systemic plant responses on soil faunal pest impacts is an area that requires further research. Moreover, the presence

9.3 Harnessing Soil Biodiversity · 283

of arbuscular mycorrhizal (AM) fungi may contribute to greater disease and pest resistance. For example, it has been shown that tomato roots upregulate the expression of genes known to be involved in defence, signal transduction, and protein synthesis when colonised by AM fungi, and that the effect is greater when the root parasite *Meloidogyne incognita* is also present (Vos et al. 2013). This in turn appeared to provide increased resistance to root-feeding nematodes as there was lower nematode infection of roots colonised by AM fungi. Similarly, chewing insect herbivores are usually negatively impacted by the presence of mycorrhizal colonisation of plant roots – a trait that should and could be incorporated into land management practices (Johnson and Rasmann 2015). Many crop cultivars have been bred to rely on the provision of nutrients through the application of inorganic fertilisers, with limited contributions of nutrient supply via microbial symbionts. To promote plant health through biological mechanisms and lower the reliance on pesticide and fertiliser applications a different tact will have to be applied in which crop cultivars are selected for their ability to form beneficial relationships with soil biodiversity.

Another approach that has recently been suggested is to focus more strongly on known plant–soil feedbacks to improve the productivity and sustainability of management practices (Mariotte et al. 2018). Conversely, the authors also highlight how agriculture and other production systems provide a great platform for undertaking novel plant–soil feedback research not currently fully used, particularly relevant to management and engineering of soil communities to target key outcomes. In brief, the authors highlight that promoting positive plant–soil feedbacks through management of organic inputs, such as stubble retention and manure, and steering soil assemblage developments provides a relatively easy approach to improving agricultural productivity by enhancing nutrient availability. There is also much evidence that developing and integrating practices that enhance soil biodiversity can promote other functions essential to the long-term sustainability. Similarly, novel approaches, such as inoculation of beneficial microbes and plant breeding or gene editing, that enhance positive plant–soil feedbacks provide great opportunities, in particular because many currently grown crop varieties have reduced, or completely lost, the capacity to form beneficial symbiotic relationships with the microbial partners on which they rely in natural or more complex ecosystems. However, a substantial knowledge gap needs to be bridged before such technologies can be applied under field conditions.

A recent paradigm shift in the management of soil food webs through inputs in agricultural ecosystems has been driven by the finding that microbial processes are largely controlled by the availability of dissolved organic matter that in turn can fuel the breakdown of more stable organic matter (Lehmann and Kleber 2015). Accordingly, it can be hypothesised that ongoing additions of labile organic matter will promote microbial activity and drive soil processes underlying agricultural productivity and also soil organic matter formation because their residue breakdown processes leave behind recalcitrant matter. Putting this into practice could fundamentally change how agro-ecosystems are managed for greater reliance on biotic processes over pesticide and inorganic fertiliser inputs. This in turn is likely to also impact soil fauna assemblages more broadly, likely allowing these to contribute progressively more to ecosystem processes as the negative impacts of intensive agricultural management practices are abated. A key aspect of implementing soil management regimes that focus on improving soil biodiversity is that it requires a holistic approach with a broad shift in management regimes whereby a fully functional soil food web is established (Nielsen et al. 2015b, Wall et al. 2015). Indeed, management regimes that make only small steps towards increasing soil biodiversity may have negative consequences because they allow more pests and pathogens to flourish in the absence of natural enemies. Several of the steps described in this section could substantially contribute to more sustainable farming practices that ensure productive and profitable outcomes in the long term. However, the need for substantial modifications to management regimes is somewhat of an impediment as the farmer is unlikely to make the switch without strong evidence that it will be economically profitable. Hence, there is a great need for further insight into the contributions of the soil food web to ecosystem functioning and service provision in managed landscapes to further the incorporation of more biologically sound and evidence-based, adaptive management practices.

9.4 Critical Knowledge Gaps and Research Directions

While our understanding of soil fauna assemblages has improved substantially over the past few decades, there are still knowledge gaps that require our attention to further progress soil fauna ecology as a field of research and to aid in establishing generalisations for patterns in assemblage structure and composition. A great framework for the future direction of soil ecological research was provided by Eisenhauer et al. (2017), including several key areas that relate directly to the distribution and diversity of soil fauna and its role in ecosystem functioning. The

9.4 Critical Knowledge Gaps and Research Directions · 285

authors conducted a survey of 32 editors of *Pedobiologia* to identify critical research priorities formulated as questions broadly assigned to four themes: (1) soil biodiversity and biogeography; (2) interactions and the functioning of ecosystems; (3) global change and land management; and (4) new directions. I would encourage the interested reader to consult the paper for a broader consideration of knowledge gaps in soil ecology but will here briefly expand on some of the key areas of interest to soil fauna ecology specifically.

There are clear gaps in our knowledge of soil fauna biodiversity and biogeography. These knowledge gaps are currently limiting our ability to identify the drivers of soil fauna assemblage structure and composition, and to draw robust conclusions on biogeography and macroecology of soil fauna. There is, therefore, a great need for an increased effort to assess soil fauna diversity and distribution among biomes at a global scale using systematic approaches ideally combining morphological and molecular techniques. Specifically, the utilisation of both morphological and molecular tools would allow us to build better databases that may allow us to rely more on molecular techniques to characterise soil fauna assemblages in the future, which is currently restricted by the limited representation of soil fauna in existing databases. It is, moreover, desirable to establish standard operating protocols that allow the results of individual studies to be compared with greater ease, and data should be openly shared to facilitate such comparisons. Ideally, existing frameworks such as the Biodiversity Database managed by the Australian Antarctic Data Centre would be expanded to collate records for soil fauna and other organisms at a global scale and linked to key climatic and environmental properties. An increased knowledge of soil fauna biodiversity would further provide insights into whether there is a risk of a substantial extinction crisis in soil fauna similar to that observed elsewhere. Indeed, data-driven guidance for the conservation of soil fauna to ensure healthy ecosystems now and in the future is highly a desirable goal (Decaëns et al. 2006, Veresoglou et al. 2015, Wolters 2001).

The importance of soil fauna in our natural and managed landscapes has long been acknowledged, but there have been limited efforts to include soil fauna in conservation frameworks, likely driven by the substantial gap in knowledge relating to the possible status of individual soil fauna species. In particular, because we have limited knowledge of the actual distribution of most known soil fauna species and there are many species yet to be described, it is difficult to assess whether individual species may be at risk. Moreover, the perceived high-functional redundancy among soil fauna taxa has provided less incentive to protect them. Given the rapid increase in knowledge of soil fauna distribution and high likelihood of at least local scale extinctions it appears timely to set such actions in motion. One potential option is to look for possible 'umbrella' species belowground that are indicators of certain ecosystem characteristics valuable for the protection of soil fauna diversity more broadly, ecosystem functioning, and provision of ecosystem services. Another option is to focus on species known to be sensitive to ecological degradation and disturbance that can indicate possible shifts in ecosystem state.

Our understanding of the mechanisms that structure soil fauna assemblages is still somewhat limited. It is of great importance to consolidate existing information to identify and address current knowledge gaps. A better understanding of large-scale patterns would be greatly progressed by establishing current distributional patterns, which would be facilitated by the actions outlined in the previous paragraph. In particular, this would provide insight into the mechanisms that control organismal distribution at the global scale and the patterns of endemism in soil fauna. However, a better understanding of the evolutionary history of soil fauna will be critical to tease apart geological and ecological influences. This would also allow us to better examine other biogeographical and macroecological patterns, such as latitudinal and altitudinal gradients, species-area and distance-decay relationship, and why some species are more broadly distributed than others. At smaller scales, there is a great need for further investigation of the mechanisms that govern soil fauna assemblages, ranging from neutral processes to niche differentiation and biotic interactions. Similarly, we are yet to establish the importance of trophic interactions, such as predator–prey relationships, and whether soil fauna assemblages are influenced by top-down and/or bottom-up controls. Finally, the use of chemical cues in the quest for resources, predatory avoidance, and patterns of species aggregation is intriguing and deserves further recognition given the potential influences on soil fauna assemblages.

An enhanced capability to describe quantitatively soil fauna assemblages would improve our ability to better link soil fauna assemblage structure and composition with ecosystem functioning. Indeed, quantifying the role of key soil fauna in ecosystem functioning is of utmost importance if we are to more accurately provide evidence-based recommendations to land management. Some of the key questions relate to the potential consequences of species loss, including rare species, caused by global change impacts and how we can manage soil food webs using this

9.4 Critical Knowledge Gaps and Research Directions · 287

knowledge. One possible way to simplify how we study and quantify the contribution of soil fauna to ecosystem function is to increase the focus on functional traits. However, it is critical to assess whether soil fauna displays significant functional redundancy across spatial and temporal scales before relying solely on functional groupings. Early evidence indicated that the addition of just one or a few species could establish functioning, but later studies have indicated that there is considerable variation in the contributions to functioning among species. Indeed, increased richness of fauna with seemingly equal contributions to a given function can help stabilise the rate of that function over time and in some cases further enhance the rate of the function. This indicates that increased species richness of soil fauna with similar functional characteristics may yet be important to ecosystem functioning in a changing environment. Indeed, greater insight into the biodiversity-ecosystem functioning (BEF) and biodiversity-ecosystem multifunctionality (BEMF) relationships, discussed in Chapter 2, is worth pursuing. In particular, it is unlikely that the studies undertaken to date realistically represent soil communities because of their inherent random assembly achieved through the experimental approaches. In most cases, assemblages are created using dilution approaches, removal of target taxa using biocides, or additions of known species from cultures. All of these approaches have their own shortcomings (i.e. limited control using dilution, non-target effects of biocides, limits to which species can be cultured) that make it unlikely that the assemblages constructed are comparable to those in the field. Such studies can provide insight into the species diversity effects *per se*, but are less likely to provide much insight into the working of the more self-organised assemblages found in both managed and natural ecosystems. Investigating natural diversity gradients, whether created by environmental and climatic gradients or through management, present an opportune setting for *in situ* studies of these relationships, although the complexity of belowground assemblages can be cumbersome to investigate effectively. Moreover, many experimental studies are confounded by limitations in the diversity gradients that can be realistically managed, and problems associated with influences of species versus functional trait impacts that can only be overcome through unfeasibly large experimental treatment replication. One way to approach this is to focus more on the minimum diversity required to maintain ecosystem functioning as suggested by some (Swift et al. 2004). This approach might be particularly relevant in production systems where specific functions are sought, such as mineralisation processes underlying plant growth through the release of essential nutrients. Even so, greater soil diversity may be beneficial because multiple functions are generally required to sustain a healthy soil, and not all organisms will contribute to functioning at any given time. This topic can be further expanded to include biodiversity–ecosystem stability and biodiversity–ecosystem resilience relationships. One option is to further investigate and quantify links between above- and belowground food webs in models. Along the same line, the involvement of soil fauna in plant–soil feedbacks should be investigated in more detail given the potential implications for ecosystem functioning under current conditions and in response to global changes (Mariotte et al. 2018, van der Putten et al. 2013).

There is rapidly accumulating evidence that soil biodiversity contributes to human well-being (Wall et al. 2015). Some aspects of this are relatively easy to quantify, such as supporting sustainable production systems, whereas other pathways are less quantifiable. There is, for example, evidence that soil biodiversity broadly may contribute to the suppression of human pest and pathogen prevalence and distribution, reduce concentrations of particles in the air that can cause health issues, and that access to healthy ecosystems that support high biodiversity above- and belowground improves human immune systems resulting in less allergies. While these linkages have been established, they are poorly explored, and there is a great need for further insight, particularly in regard to the involvement of soil fauna. Hence, the potential health benefits of improved management practices should be assessed and used for evidence-based policy making that incorporates the possible costs of allowing suboptimal management practices. An example is how possible global changes impact human well-being through changes in soil-transmitted diseases. Soil-transmitted helminths are the largest parasitic burden on humans and are particularly prevalent in some of the world's poorest countries. There is increasing evidence that climate change will influence the life history and fitness of the soil-transmitted Helminths, with warming generally increasing developmental and reproductive rates, and higher soil water content increasing their survival in the soil. By contrast, warming and reduced water availability can negatively impact survival when this causes significant stress (Weaver et al. 2010). Fortunately, there is evidence that managing soil for biodiversity could aid in reducing the impact of soil-transmitted diseases. For example, the infection risk of the human and animal nematode parasite *Strongyloides stercoralis* was found to be higher in agricultural land with low organic carbon contents than forested land, indicating that better management can help alleviate the

9.4 Critical Knowledge Gaps and Research Directions · 289

impact of this parasite (Wall et al. 2015). The same paper provides strong evidence that management practices that promote soil biodiversity offer much broader benefits to human well-being, ranging from providing for our basic needs through food, fuel, and fibre provision to clean air and water to reduced incidence of allergies. Hence, promoting healthy soils that support high levels of biodiversity, including soil fauna, may have far-reaching benefits to the provision of essential ecosystem services and, by extension, human well-being.

With all of this in mind, there is a great need for an improved focus on fundamental and applied hypothesis-driven research that focusses more explicitly on the soil fauna, and there is much to gain from such insight. However, this would benefit substantially from improving existing technologies or developing new technologies to better address the issues. For example, there is a need for developing better protocols for high-throughput molecular approaches adapted to investigate soil fauna diversity and distribution. And this should be combined with taxonomical expertise based on morphological characteristics; there is also a need for more taxonomists to be trained to support this. Similarly, more sensitive analytical tools, such as equipment to measure stable isotopes or gut content analyses, would allow us to work at scales more relevant to the soil fauna, possibly even processing individual specimens. Furthermore, there is a need for large-scale, long-term observational and experimental studies that monitor soil fauna assemblages in detail to assess temporal trends under both contemporary and possible future global change scenarios. Finally, the themes discussed so far cover most of the research-oriented perspectives of soil ecology that still need to be addressed, but another essential task is the dissemination of the importance of soil fauna to land use managers and policy makers so that appropriate measures and guidelines can be put in place to integrate soil fauna into evidence-based adaptive land use management, from local to global scales. The establishment of key initiatives such as the *Global Soil Biodiversity Atlas* can provide platforms to further this and provide insight into ways to address the aims of the Global Soil Biodiversity Initiative (https://globalsoilbiodiversity.org) and the Convention on Biological Diversity Aichi Biodiversity Targets (www.cbd.int/sp/targets/). Similarly, the successful delivery on the UN Sustainable Development Goals (UN 2014) will require the incorporation of more sustainable land use practices. The protection and conservation of soil biodiversity is fundamental to achieving these targets (Wall et al. 2015). Increasing the public awareness of soil fauna and its contribution to ecosystem functioning through outreach and education may aid in these endeavours. Indeed, many people are likely to be fascinated by the diversity of organisms found in soil if the information is presented to them in a manageable form.

9.5 Summary

Soil ecologists have long been intrigued by the diversity of organisms found belowground. Indeed, even before the advent of the microscope there was great interest in the larger types of soil fauna and their interactions with the soil matrix. With the advent of the early microscopes, it was soon discovered that the diversity of organisms in soils was much greater than previously thought. This ongoing interest in soil organisms has contributed to a continuing expansion of our knowledge of the world belowground, the distribution of soil fauna, and its contribution to ecosystem functioning. With the more recent developments in molecular tools, more sophisticated and more sensitive analytical equipment, and new statistical and modelling approaches combined with increasingly powerful processors, we are making great strides towards a holistic understanding of soil fauna assemblages and the role they play in our ecosystems. We are already at a point where we can feasibly begin to manage our soil fauna assemblages to promote the health and sustainability of our ecosystems, including agro-ecosystems. Importantly, there are substantial benefits to be gained in more holistic management practices that explicitly incorporate soil fauna biology and ecology. Indeed, sustainable land use practices will gain from, and fundamentally rely on, the activities of soil fauna. However, there is still much to discover, particularly if we are to harness the contributions that soil fauna can provide in our production systems. Still, the current focus on promoting soil health is very encouraging, given the potential for the conservation of soil fauna including its positive contributions to ecosystem functioning.

Bibliography

A'Bear A. D., Crowther T. W., Ashfield R., et al. (2013) Localised invertebrate grazing moderates the effect of warming on competitive fungal interactions. *Fungal Ecology*, **6**, 137–140.

A'Bear A. D., Jones T. H., Boddy L. (2014) Potential impacts of climate change on interactions among saprotrophic cord-forming fungal mycelia and grazing soil invertebrates. *Fungal Ecology*, **10**, 34–43.

Acosta-Mercado D., Lynn D. H. (2002) A preliminary assessment of spatial patterns of soil ciliate diversity in two subtropical forests in Puerto Rico and its implications for designing an appropriate sampling approach. *Soil Biology & Biochemistry*, **34**, 1517–1520.

Adams B. J., Wall D. H., Gozel U., et al. (2007) The southernmost worm, *Scottnema lindsayae* (Nematoda): Diversity, dispersal and ecological stability. *Polar Biology*, **30**, 809–815.

Adams B. J., Wall D. H., Virginia R. A., Broos E., Knox M. A. (2014) Ecological biogeography of the terrestrial nematodes of Victoria Land, Antarctica. *ZooKeys*, **419**, 29–71.

Addison J. A. (1977) Population dynamics and biology of Collembola at Truelove lowland. In: *Truelove Lowland, Devon Island, Canada: A High Arctic Ecosystem* (ed. Bliss L. C.) pp. 363–382. Edmonton, University of Alberta Press.

Adl S. M., Simpson A. G., Farmer M. A., et al. (2005) The new higher level classification of eukaryotes with emphasis on the taxonomy of protists. *Journal of Eukaryotic Microbiology*, **52**, 399–451.

Agosti D., Johnson N. F. (2010) *Antbase*. World Wide Web electronic publication. www.antbase.org.

Ainsworth E. A., Long D. J. (2005) What have we learned from 15 years of free-air CO_2 enrichment (FACE)? A meta-analytic review of the responses of photosynthesis, canopy properties and plant production to rising CO_2. *New Phytologist*, **165**, 351–372.

Albertengo J., Bianchini A., Sylvestre Begnis A., et al. (2011) Sustainable certified agriculture: The farmer's production alternative. In: *World Congress on Conservation Agriculture (WCCA), Australia*. www.aciar.gov.au/wccaposters.

Ali F., Wharton D. A. (2014) Intracellular freezing in the infective juveniles of *Steinernema feltiae*: An entomopathogenic nematode. *PloS ONE*, **9**, e94179. doi: 10.1371/journal.pone.0094179.

Ali J. G., Alborn H. T., Stelinski L. L. (2011) Constitutive and induced subterranean plant volatiles attract both entomopathogenic and plant parasitic nematodes. *Journal of Ecology*, **99**, 26–35.

Allegrucci G., Carchini G., Convey P., Sbordino V. (2012) Evolutionary geographic relationships among orthocladine chironomid midges from maritime Antarctic and sub-Antarctic islands. *Biological Journal of the Linnean Society*, **106**, 258–274.

Alphey T. J. W. (1985) Study of spatial distribution and population dynamics of two sympatric species of trichodorid nematodes. *Annals of Applied Biology*, **107**, 497–509.

Alroy J. (2017) Effects of habitat disturbance on tropical forest biodiversity. *Proceedings of the National Academy of Sciences of the United States of America*, **114**, 6065–6061.

Alvarez T., Frampton G. K., Goulson D. (2001) Epigeic Collembola in winter wheat under organic, integrated and conventional farm management regimes. *Agriculture, Ecosystems & Environment*, **83**, 95–110.

Andersen A. N., Del Toro I., Parr C. L. (2015) Savanna ant species richness is maintained along a bioclimatic gradient of increasing latitude and decreasing rainfall in northern Australia. *Journal of Biogeography*, **42**, 2313–2322.

Andersen A. N., Sparling G. P. (1997) Ants as indicators of restoration success: Relationship with soil microbial biomass in the Australian seasonal tropics. *Restoration Ecology*, **5**, 109–114.

Andersen C. P. (2003) Source-sink balance and carbon allocation below ground in plants exposed to ozone. *New Phytologist*, **157**, 213–228.

Anderson J. M. (1975) The enigma of soil animal species diversity. In: *Progress in Soil Zoology* (ed. Vanek J.) pp. 51–58. Prague, Academia.

Anderson J. M. (1978a) Inter- and intra-habitat relationships between woodland Cryptostigmata species diversity and the diversity of soil and litter microhabitats. *Oecologia*, **32**, 341–348.

Anderson J. M. (1978b) A method to quantify soil-microhabitat complexity and its application to a study of soil animal species diversity. *Soil Biology & Biochemistry*, **10**, 77–78.

Anderson J. M. (1995) Soil organisms as engineers: Microsite modulation of macroscale processes. In: *Linking Species to Ecosystems* (eds. Jones C. G., Lawton J. H.) pp. 94–106. New York, Chapman & Hall.

Andrássy I. (1964) Süsswasser-Nematoden aus den grossen Gebirgsgegenden Ostafricas. *Acta Zoologica*, **10**, 1–59.

André H. M., Noti M.-I., Lebrun P. (1994) The soil fauna: The other last biotic frontier. *Biodiversity and Conservation*, **3**, 45–56.

Andriuzzi W. S., Wall D. H. (2017) Responses of belowground communities to large aboveground herbivores: Meta-analysis reveals biome-dependent patterns and critical research gaps. *Global Change Biology*, **23**, 3857–3868.

Andújar C., Arribas P., Ruzicka F., et al. (2015) Phylogenetic community ecology of soil biodiversity using mitochondrial metagenomics. *Molecular Ecology*, **24**, 3603–3617.

Aoki Y., Hoshino M., Matsubara T. (2007) Silica and testate amoebae in a soil under pine-oak forest. *Geoderma*, **142**, 29–35.

Armendáriz I., Hernández M. A., Jordana R. (1996) Temporal evolution of soil nematode communities in *Pinus nigra* forests of Navarra, Spain. *Fundamental and Applied Nematology*, **19**, 561–577.

Bibliography · 293

Arrhenius O. (1921) Species and area. *Journal of Ecology*, **9**, 95–99.
Aslam T. J., Benton T. G., Nielsen U. N., Johnson S. N. (2015) Impacts of eucalypt plantation management on soil faunal communities and nutrient bioavailability: Trading function for dependence? *Biology and Fertility of Soils*, **51**, 637–644.
Atkin L., Proctor J. (1988) Invertebrates in the litter and soil on Volcan Barva, Costa Rica. *Journal of Tropical Ecology*, **4**, 307–310.
Aubert M., Hedde M., Decaëns T., et al. (2003) Effects of tree canopy composition on earthworms and other macroinvertebrates in beech forests of Upper Normandy (France). *Pedobiologia*, **47**, 904–912.
Ayarbe J. P., Kieft T. L. (2000) Mammal mounds stimulate microbial activity in a semiarid shrubland. *Ecology*, **81**, 1150–1154.
Ayres E., Dromph K. M., Cook R., Ostle N., Bardgett R. D. (2007) The influence of below-ground herbivory and defoliation of a legume on nitrogen transfer to neighbouring plants. *Functional Ecology*, **21**, 256–263.
Ayres E., Heath J., Possell M., et al. (2004) Tree physiological responses to aboveground herbivory directly modify below-ground processes of soil carbon and nitrogen cycling. *Ecology Letters*, **7**, 469–479.
Ayres E., Wall D. H., Simmons B. L., et al. (2008) Belowground nematode herbivores are resistant to elevated atmospheric CO_2 concentrations in grassland ecosystems. *Soil Biology & Biochemistry*, **40**, 978–985.
Ayuke F. O., Pulleman M. M., Vanlauwe B., et al. (2011) Agricultural management affects earthworm and termite diversity across humid to semi-arid tropical zones. *Agriculture, Ecosystems & Environment*, **140**, 148–154.
Baas Becking L. G. M. (1934) *Geobiologie of inleiding tot de milieukunde*, The Hague, Van Stockum and Zoon.
Baermann G. (1917) Eine Einfache Methode zur Auffindung vor Ankylostomum (Nematoden). *Larven in Erdproben*, pp. 41–47. Batavia, Genesk Lab Feestbundel.
Baggen L. R., Gurr G. M. (1998) The influence of food on *Copidosoma koehleri* (Hymenoptera: Encyrtidae), and the use of flowering plants as a habitat management tool to enhance biological control of potato moth, *Phthorimaea operculella* (Lepidoptera: Gelechiidae). *Biological Control*, **11**, 9–17.
Bamforth S. S, Wall D. H., Virginia R. A. (2005) Distribution and diversity of soil protozoa in the McMurdo Dry Valleys of Antarctica. *Polar Biology*, **28**, 756–762.
Bardgett R. D. (2002) Causes and consequences of biological diversity in soil. *Zoology*, **105**, 367–374.
Bardgett R. D. (2005) *The Biology of Soils: A Community and Ecosystem Approach*, Oxford, Oxford University Press.
Bardgett R. D., Bowman W. D., Kaufman R., Schmidt S. K. (2005a) A temporal approach to linking aboveground and belowground ecology. *Trends in Ecology and Evolution*, **20**, 634–641.
Bardgett R. D., Chan K. F. (1999) Experimental evidence that soil fauna enhance nutrient mineralization and plant nutrient uptake in montane grassland ecosystems. *Soil Biology & Biochemistry*, **31**, 1007–1014.
Bardgett R. D., Cook R. G., Yeates W., Denton C. S. (1999a) The influence of nematodes on below-ground processes in grassland ecosystems. *Plant and Soil*, **212**, 23–33.
Bardgett R. D., Denton C. S., Cook R. (1999b) Belowground herbivory promotes soil nutrient transfer and root growth in grassland. *Ecology Letters*, **2**, 357–360.

Bibliography

Bardgett R. D., van der Putten W. H. (2014) Belowground biodiversity and ecosystem functioning. *Nature*, 515, 505–511.

Bardgett R. D., Wardle D. A. (2003) Herbivore-mediated linkages between aboveground and belowground communities. *Ecology*, 84, 2258–2268.

Bardgett R. D., Wardle D. A. (2010) *Aboveground–Belowground Linkages: Biotic Interactions, Ecosystem Processes, and Global Change*, New York, Oxford University Press.

Bardgett R. D., Yeates G. W., Anderson J. M. (2005b) Patterns and determinants of soil biological diversity. In: *Biological Diversity and Function in Soils* (eds. Bardgett R. D., Usher M. B., Hopkins D. W.) pp. 100–118. Cambridge, Cambridge University Press.

Barker G. M., Mayhill P. C. (1999) Patterns of diversity and habitat relationships in terrestrial mollusc communities of the Pukeamaru Ecological District, northeastern New Zealand. *Journal of Biogeography*, 26, 215–238.

Barral M. P., Benayas J. M. R., Meli P, Maceira N. O. (2015) Quantifying the impacts of ecological restoration on biodiversity and ecosystem services in agroecosystems: A global meta-analysis. *Agriculture, Ecosystems and Environment*, 202, 223–231.

Barrett J. E., Virginia R. A., Wall D. H., et al. (2008) Persistent effects of a discrete climate event on a polar desert ecosystem. *Global Change Biology*, 14, 2249–2261.

Barrios E. (2007) Soil biota, ecosystem services and land productivity. *Ecological Economics*, 64, 269–285.

Barrios E., Sileshi G. W., Shephard K., Sinclair F. (2012) Agroforestry and soil health: Linking trees, soil biota, and ecosystem services. In: *Soil Ecology and Ecosystem Services* (ed. Wall D. H.) pp. 315–330. Oxford, Oxford University Press.

Bass D., Thomas T. A., Matthai L., Marsh V., Cavalier-Smith T. (2007) DNA evidence for global dispersal and probable endemicity of protozoa. *BMC Evolutionary Biology*, 7, 162.

Bassus W. (1968) Über Einflüsse von Industrieexhalaten auf den Nematodenbesatz im Boden von Kiefernwäldern. *Pedobiologia*, 8, 289–295.

Bastow J. (2012) Succession, resource processing, and diversity in detrital food webs. In: *Soil Ecology and Ecosystem Services* (ed. Wall D. H.) pp. 117–135. Oxford, Oxford University Press.

Bates S. T., Clemente J. C., Flores G. E., et al. (2013) Global biogeography of highly diverse protistan communities in soil. *The ISME Journal*, 7, 652–659.

Battigelli J. P., Spence J. R., Langor D. W., Berch S. M. (2004) Short-term impact of forest soil compaction and organic matter removal on soil mesofauna density and oribatid mite diversity. *Canadian Journal of Forest Research*, 34, 1136–1149.

Beare M. H., Coleman D. S., Crossley D. A., Jr, Hendrix P. F., Odum E. P. (1995) A hierarchical approach to evaluating the significance of soil biodiversity to biogeochemical cycling. *Plant and Soil*, 170, 5–22.

Beare M. H., Hu S., Coleman D. C., Hendrix P. F. (1997) Influences of mycelia fungi on soil aggregation and organic matter storage in conventional and no-tillage soils. *Applied Soil Ecology*, 5, 211–219.

Beare M. H., Parmelee R. W., Hendrix P. F., et al. (1992) Microbial and faunal interactions and effects on litter nitrogen and decomposition in agroecosystems. *Ecological Monographs*, 62, 569–591.

Beaulieu F., Weeks A. R. (2007) Free-living mesostigmatic mites in Australia: Their roles in biological control and bioindication. *Australian Journal of Experimental Agriculture*, **47**, 460–478.
Bedano J. C., Domínguez A., Arolfo R., Wall L. G. (2016) Effect of good agricultural practices under no-till on litter and soil invertebrates in areas with different soil types. *Soil & Tillage Research*, **158**, 100–109.
Beddard F. E. (1912) *Earthworms and Their Allies*, Cambridge, Cambridge University Press.
Behan-Pelletier V. M. (1999) Oribatid mite biodiversity in agroecosystems: Role for bioindication. *Agriculture, Ecosystems & Environment*, **74**, 411–423.
Bell N. L., Adam K. H., Jones R. J., et al. (2016) Detection of invertebrate suppressive soils, and identification of a possible biological control agent for *Meloidogyne* nematodes using high resolution rhizosphere microbial community analysis. *Frontiers in Plant Science*, **7**, 1946.
Belnap J., Phillips S. L. (2001) Soil biota in an ungrazed grassland: Response to annual grass (*Bromus tectorum*) invasion. *Ecological Applications*, **11**, 1261–1275.
Bender S. F., van der Heijden M. G. A. (2015) Soil biota enhance agricultural sustainability by improving crop yield, nutrient uptake and reducing nitrogen leaching losses. *Journal of Applied Ecology*, **52**, 228–239.
Bender S. F., Wagg C., van der Heijden M. A. (2016) An underground revolution: Biodiversity and soil ecological engineering for agricultural sustainability. *Trends in Ecology and Evolution*, **31**, 440–452.
Bengtsson G., Rundgren S. (1983) Respiration and growth of a fungus, *Mortierella isabellina*, in response to grazing by *Onychiurus armatus* (Collembola). *Soil Biology & Biochemistry*, **15**, 469–473.
Bengtsson J. (2002) Disturbance and resilience in soil animal communities. *European Journal of Soil Biology*, **387**, 119–125.
Bengtsson J., Ahnström J., Weibull A. C. (2005) The effects of organic agriculture on biodiversity and abundance: A meta-analysis. *Journal of Applied Ecology*, **42**, 261–269.
Benoit J. B., Elnitsky M. A., Schulte G. G., Lee Jr. R. E., Denlinger D. L. (2009) Antarctic collembolans use chemical signals to promote aggregation and egg laying. *Journal of Insect Behaviour*, **22**, 121–133.
Berg M. P. (2012) Patterns of biodiversity at fine and small spatial scales. In: *Soil Ecology and Ecosystem Services* (ed. Wall D. H.) pp. 136–152. Oxford, Oxford University Press.
Berg M. P., Bengtsson J. (2007) Spatial and temporal variation in food web composition. *Oikos*, **116**, 1789–1804.
Berg M. P., Kneise J. P., Bedaux J. J. M., Verhoef H. A. (1998) Dynamics and stratification of functional groups of micro- and mesoarthropods in the organic layer of a Scots pine forest. *Biology and Fertility of Soils*, **26**, 268–284.
Berg M. P., Stoffer M., van den Heuvel H. H. (2004) Feeding guilds in Collembola based on digestive enzymes. *Pedobiologia*, **48**, 589–601.
Bergkvist G., Stenberg M., Wetterlind J., Bâth B., Elfstrand S. (2010) Clover cover crops under-sown in winter wheat increase yield of subsequent spring barley – Effect of N dose and companion grass. *Field Crop Research*, **120**, 292–298.

Beyens L., Ledeganck P., Graae B. J., Nijs I. (2009) Are soil biota buffered against climatic extremes? An experimental test on testate amoebae in arctic tundra (Qeqertarsuaq, West Greenland). *Polar Biology*, **32**, 453–462.
Bezemer T. M., De Deyn G. B., Bossinga T. M., et al. (2005) Soil community composition drives aboveground plant–herbivore–parasitoid interactions. *Ecology Letters*, **8**, 652–661.
Bezemer T. M., Fountain M. T., Barea J. M., et al. (2010) Divergent composition but similar function of soil food webs of individual plants: Plant species and community effects. *Ecology*, **91**, 3027–3036.
Bezemer T. M., Wagenaar R., van Dam N. M., Wäckers F. L. (2003) Interactions between above- and belowground insect herbivores as mediated by the plant defense system. *Oikos*, **101**, 555–562.
Bignell D. E. (2000) Introduction to symbiosis. In: *Termites: Evolution, Sociality, Symbioses, Ecology* (eds. Abe T., Bignell D. E., Higashi M.) pp. 189–208. Dordrecht, Kluwer Academic.
Bignell D. E. (2006) Termites as soil engineers and soil processors. In: *Soil Biology* (eds. König H., Varma A.) pp. 183–220. Berlin, Springer-Verlag.
Bignell D. E., Eggleton P. (2000) Termites in ecosystems. In: *Termites, Evolution, Sociality, Symbioses, Ecology* (eds. Abe T., Bignell D. E., Higashi M.) pp. 363–387. Dordrecht, Kluwer Academic Press.
Bihn J. H., Verhaagh M., Brändle M., Brandl R. (2008) Do secondary forests act as refuges for old growth forest animals? Recovery of ant diversity in the Atlantic forest of Brazil. *Biological Conservation*, **141**, 733–743.
Bik H. M., Porazinska D. L., Creer S., et al. (2012) Sequencing our way towards understanding global eukaryotic biodiversity. *Trends in Ecology and Evolution*, **27**, 233–243.
Binet F., Trehen P. (1992) Experimental microcosm study of the role of *Lumbricus terrestris* (Oligochaeta: Lumbricidae) on nitrogen dynamics in cultivated soils. *Soil Biology & Biochemistry*, **24**, 1501–1506.
Birkhofer K., Bezemer T. M., Bloem J., et al. (2008) Long-term organic farming fosters below and aboveground biota: Implications for soil quality, biological control and productivity. *Soil Biology & Biochemistry*, **40**, 2297–2308.
Birkhofer K., Diekötter T., Boch S., et al. (2011) Soil fauna feeding activity in temperate grassland soils increases with legume and grass species richness. *Soil Biology & Biochemistry*, **43**, 2200–2207.
Bishop T. R., Robertson M. P., Van Rensburg B. J., Parr C. L. (2014) Exploring variation in ant diversity through space and time: An elevational study in the Maloti-Drakensberg Mountains of South Africa. *Journal of Biogeography*, **41**, 2256–2268.
Blankinship J. C., Niklaus P. A., Hungate B. A. (2011) A meta-analysis of responses of soil biota to global change. *Oecologia*, **165**, 553–565.
Block W. (1983) Low temperature tolerance of soil arthropods – Some recent advances. In: *New Trends in Soil Biology* (eds. Lebrun P., André H. M., De Medts A., Wauthy G.) pp. 427–431. Ottignies, Diey-Brichart.
Block W., Webb N. R., Coulson S. J., Hodkinson I. D. (1994) Thermal adaptation in a high arctic collembolan *Onychiurus arcticus*. *Journal of Insect Physiology*, **40**, 715–722.

Bloemers G. F., Hodda M., Lambshead P. J. D., Lawton J. H., Wanless F. R. (1997) The effects of forest disturbance on diversity of tropical soil nematodes. *Oecologia*, **111**, 575–582.

Blomqvist M. M., Olff H., Blaauw M. B., Bongers T., van der Putten W. (2000) Interactions between above- and belowground biota: Importance for small-scale vegetation mosaics in a grassland ecosystem. *Oikos*, **90**, 582–598.

Blouin M., Hodson E., Delgado E. A., et al. (2013) A review of earthworm impact on soil function and ecosystem services. *European Journal of Soil Science*, **64**, 161–182.

Boag B., Yeates G. W. (1998) Soil nematode biodiversity in terrestrial ecosystems. *Biodiversity and Conservation*, **7**, 617–630.

Boag B., Yeates G. W. (2001) The potential impact of the New Zealand flatworm, a predator of earthworms, in western Europe. *Ecological Applications*, **11**, 1276–1286.

Bobbink R., Hicks K., Galloway J. N., et al. (2010) Global assessment of nitrogen deposition effects on terrestrial plant diversity: A synthesis. *Ecological Applications*, **20**, 30–59.

Bohlen P. J., Scheu S., Hale C. M., et al. (2004) Non-native invasive earthworms as agents of change in northern temperate forests. *Frontiers in Ecology and the Environment*, **2**, 427–435.

Bokhorst S., Berg M. P., Wardle D. A. (2017a) Micro-arthropod community responses to ecosystem retrogression in boreal forest. *Soil Biology & Biochemistry*, **110**, 79–86.

Bokhorst S., Huiskes A., Convey P., et al. (2011) Microclimate impacts of passive warming methods in Antarctica: Implication for climate change studies. *Polar Biology*, **34**, 1421–1435.

Bokhorst S., Huiskes A., Convey P., Van Bodegom P. M., Aerts R. (2008) Climate change effects on soil arthropod communities from the Falkland Islands and the Maritime Antarctic. *Soil Biology & Biochemistry*, **40**, 1547–1556.

Bokhorst S., Kardol P., Bellingham P. J., et al. (2017b) Response of communities of soil organisms and plants to soil aging at two contrasting long-term chronosequences. *Soil Biology & Biochemistry*, **106**, 69–79.

Bokhorst S., Phoenix G. K., Bjerke J. W., et al. (2012) Extreme winter warming events more negatively impact small rather than large soil fauna: Shift in community composition explained by traits not taxa. *Global Change Biology*, **18**, 1152–1162.

Bommarco R., Kleijn D., Potts S. J. (2016) Ecological intensification: Harnessing ecosystem services for food security. *Trends in Ecology and Evolution*, **28**, 230–238.

Bongers T. (1990) The maturity index: An ecological measure of environmental disturbance based on nematode species composition. *Oecologia*, **83**, 14–19.

Bongers T. (1999) The maturity index, the evolution of nematode life history traits, adaptive radiation and cp-scaling. *Plant and Soil*, **212**, 13–22.

Bonkowski M. (2004) Soil protozoa and plant growth: The microbial loop in soil revisited. *New Phytologist*, **162**, 617–631.

Bonkowski M., Brandt F. (2002) Do soil protozoa enhance plant growth by hormonal effects? *Soil Biology & Biochemistry*, **34**, 1709–1715.

Bonkowski M., Geoghegan I. E., Birch A. N. E., Griffiths B. S. (2001) Effects of soil decomposer invertebrates (protozoa and earthworms) on an above-ground phytophagous insect (cereal aphid), mediated through changes in the host plant. *Oikos*, **95**, 441–450.

Bonkowski M., Griffiths B. S., Scrimgeour C. (2000) Substrate heterogeneity and microfauna in soil organic 'hotspots' as determinants of nitrogen capture and growth of rye-grass. *Applied Soil Ecology*, **14**, 37–53.

Bonkowski M., Roy J. (2012) Decomposer community complexity affects plant competition in a model early successional grassland community. *Soil Biology & Biochemistry*, **46**, 41–48.

Bonkowski M., Scheu S. (2004) Biotic interactions in the rhizosphere: Effects on plant growth and herbivore development. In: *Insects and Ecosystem Functioning* (eds. Weisser W., Sieman E.) pp. 71–91. Heidelberg, Germany, Ecological Studies: Springer Verlag.

Bonkowski M., Villenave C., Griffiths B. (2009) Rhizosphere fauna: The functional and structural diversity of intimate interactions of soil fauna with plant roots. *Plant and Soil*, **321**, 213–233.

Borcard D., Legendre P. (2002) All-scale spatial analysis of ecological data by means of principal coordinates of neighbour matrices. *Ecological Modelling*, **153**, 51–68.

Borcard D., Legendre P., Drapeau P. (1992) Partialling out the spatial component of ecological variation. *Ecology*, **73**, 1045–1055.

Borcard D., Matthey M. (1995) Effect of a controlled trampling of sphagnum mosses on their oribatid mite assemblages (Acari, Oribatei). *Pedobiologia*, **39**, 219–230.

Borgonie G., Garcia-Moyano A., Litthauer D., et al. (2011) Nematoda from the terrestrial deep subsurface of South Africa. *Nature*, **474**, 79–82.

Bornebusch C. H. (1930) The fauna of forest soil. *Forst. Fors Vaes. Danm.*, **11**, 1–224.

Bouché M. B. (1983) The establishment of earthworm communities. In: *Earthworm Ecology: From Darwin to Vermiculture* (ed. Satchell J. E.) pp. 431–448. London, Chapman and Hall.

Bouwman L. A., Zwart K. B. (1994) The ecology of bacterivorous protozoans and nematodes in arable soil. *Agriculture, Ecosystems & Environment*, **51**, 145–160.

Bowman W. D., Cleveland C. C., Halada Ĺ., Hresko J., Baron J. S. (2008) Negative impact of nitrogen deposition on soil buffering capacity. *Nature Geoscience*, **1**, 767–770.

Boyd J. N. (1958) The ecology of earthworms in cattle-grazed machair in Tiree, Argyll. *Journal of Animal Ecology*, **27**, 147–157.

Boyer S., Blakemore R. J., Wratten S. D. (2011) An integrative taxonomic approach to the identification of three new New Zealand endemic earthworm species (Acanthodrilidae, Octochaetidae: Oligochaeta). *Zootaxa*, **2994**, 21–32.

Boyer S., Kim Y.-N., Bowie M. H., Lefort M.-C., Dickinson N. M. (2016) Response of endemic and exotic earthworm communities to ecological restoration. *Restoration Ecology*, **24**, 717–721.

Boyer S., Wratten S. D. (2010) The potential of earthworms to restore ecosystem services after opencast mining – A review. *Basic and Applied Ecology*, **11**, 196–203.

Brady S. G. (2003) Evolution of the army ant syndrome: The origin and long-term evolutionary stasis of a complex of behavioural and reproductive adaptations. *Proceedings of the National Academy of Sciences of the United States of America*, **100**, 6575–6579.

Brady S. G., Schultz T. R., Fisher B. L., Ward P. S. (2006) Evaluating alternative hypotheses for the early evolution and diversification of ants. *Proceedings of the National Academy of Sciences of the United States of America*, **103**, 18172–18177.

Brandl R., Topp W. (1985) Size structure of *Pterostichus* spp. (Carabidae): Aspects of competition. *Oikos*, **44**, 234–238.

Brandsæter L. O., Netland J. (1999) Winter annual legumes for use as cover crops in row crops in northern regions: I. Field experiments. *Crop Science*, **39**, 1369–1379.

Brennan A., Fortune T., Bolger T. (2006) Collembola abundances and assemblage structures in conventionally tilled and conservation tillage arable systems. *Pedobiologia*, **50**, 135–145.

Bretherton S., Tordoff G. M., Jones T. H., Boddy L. (2006) Compensatory growth of *Phanerochaete velutina* mycelial systems grazed by *Folsomia candida* (Collembola). *FEMS Microbiology Ecology*, **58**, 33–40.

Breznak J. A., Brune A. (1994) Role of microorganisms in the digestion of lignocellulose by termites. *Annual Review of Entomology*, **39**, 453–487.

Bridges E. M. (1997) *World Soils*, Cambridge, Cambridge University Press.

Bridges E. M., Oldeman L. R. (1999) Global assessment of human-induced soil degradation. *Arid Soil Research and Rehabilitation*, **13**, 319–325.

Briones M. I., Garnett M. H., Piearce T. G. (2005) Earthworm ecological groupings based on ^{14}C analysis. *Soil Biology & Biochemistry*, **37**, 2145–2149.

Briones M. J. I. (2009) Uncertainties related to the temperature sensitivity of soil carbon decomposition. In: *Uncertainties in Environmental Modelling and Consequences for Policy Making* (eds. Baveye P., Mysiak J., Laba M.) pp. 317–335. New York, Springer.

Briones M. J. I., Ineson P. (2002) Use of ^{14}C carbon dating to determine feeding behaviour of enchytraeids. *Soil Biology & Biochemistry*, **34**, 881–881.

Briones M. J. I., Ineson P., Heinemeyer A. (2007a) Predicting potential impacts of climate change on the geographical distribution of enchytraeids: A meta-analysis approach. *Global Change Biology*, **13**, 2252–2269.

Briones M. J. I., Ineson P., Poskitt J. (1998) Climate change and *Cognettia sphagnetorum*: Effects on carbon dynamics in organic soil. *Functional Ecology*, **12**, 528–535.

Briones M. J. I., Ostle N., Garnett M. H. (2007b) Invertebrates increase the sensitivity of non-labile soil carbon to climate change. *Soil Biology & Biochemistry*, **39**, 8169–8818.

Briones M. J. I., Poskitt J., Ostle N. (2004) Influence of warming and enchytraeid activities on soil CO_2 and CH_4 fluxes. *Soil Biology & Biochemistry*, **36**, 1851–1859.

Brown J. (1984) On the relationship between abundance and distribution of species. *American Naturalist*, **124**, 255–279.

Brown V. K., Gange A. C. (1990) Insect herbivory below ground. *Advances in Ecological Research*, **20**, 1–58.

Brown V. K., Gange A. C. (1992) Secondary plant succession – how is it modified by insect herbivory? *Vegetatio*, **101**, 3–13.

Brown W. L. (1973) A comparison of the Hylean and Congo-West African rain forest ant faunas. In: *Tropical Forest Ecosystems in Africa and South America: A Comparative Review* (eds. Meggers B. J., Ayensu E. S., Duckworth W. D.) pp. 161–185. Washington, DC, Smithsonian Institute Press.

Brückner A., Hilpert A., Heethoff M. (2017) Biomarker function and nutritional stoichiometry of neutral lipid fatty acids and amino acids in oribatid mites. *Soil Biology & Biochemistry*, **115**, 35–43.

Brühl C. A., Mohamed M., Linsenmair K. E. (1999) Altitudinal distribution of leaf litter ants along a transect in primary forests on Mount Kinabalu, Malaysia. *Journal of Tropical Ecology*, **15**, 265–277.

Brussaard L., Aanen D. K., Briones M. J. I., et al. (2012) Biogeography and phylogenetic community structure of soil invertebrate ecosystem engineers: Global to local patterns, implications for ecosystem functioning and services and global environmental change impacts. In: *Soil Ecology and Ecosystem Services* (ed. Wall D. H.) pp. 201–232. Oxford, Oxford University Press.

Brussaard L., Behan-Pelletier V. M., Bignell D. E., et al. (1997) Biodiversity and ecosystem functioning in soil. *Ambio*, 26, 563–570.

Buchowski R. W., Bradford M. A., Grandy A. S., Schmitz O. J., Wieder W. R. (2017) Applying population and community ecology theory to advance understanding of belowground biogeochemistry. *Ecology Letters*, **20**, 231–245.

Butt K. R. (2008) Earthworms in soil restoration: Lessons learned from United Kingdom case studies of land reclamation. *Restoration Ecology*, **16**, 637–641.

Buyer J. S., Teasdale J. R., Roberts D. P., Zasada I. A., Maul J. E. (2010) Factors affecting soil microbial community structure in tomato cropping systems. *Soil Biology & Biochemistry*, **42**, 831–841.

Callaghan T. V., Tweedie C. E., Akerman J., et al. (2011) Multi-decadal changes in tundra environments and ecosystems: Synthesis of the International Polar Year-Back to the Future Project (IPY-BTF). *Ambio*, **40**, 705–716.

Callaham M. A., Rhoades C. C., Heneghan L. (2008) A striking profile: Soil ecological knowledge in restoration management and science. *Restoration Ecology*, **16**, 604–607.

Cameron E. K., Bayne E. M., Clapperton M. J. (2007) Human-facilitated invasion of exotic earthworms into northern boreal forests. *Ecoscience*, **14**, 482–490.

Cameron E. K., Vilà M., Cabeza M. (2016) Global meta-analysis of the impacts of terrestrial invertebrate invaders on species, communities and ecosystems. *Global Ecology and Biogeography*, **25**, 596–606.

Carbajo V., den Braber B., van der Putten W. H., De Deyn G. B. (2011) Enhancement of late successional plants on ex-arable land by soil inoculations. *PloS ONE*, **6**, e21943. doi:10.1371/journal.pone.0021943.

Cardosa E. J. B. N., Vasconcellas R. L. F., Bini D., et al. (2013) Soil health: Looking for suitable indicators. What should be considered to assess the effects of use and management on soil health? *Acientia Agricola*, **70**, 274–289.

Caro G., Decaëns T., Lecarpentier C., Mathieu J. (2013) Are dispersal behaviours of earthworms related to their functional group? *Soil Biology & Biochemistry*, **58**, 181–187.

Carpenter D., Hodson M. E., Eggleton P., Kirk C. (2007) Earthworm induced mineral weathering: Preliminary results. *European Journal of Soil Biology*, **43**, S176–S183.

Carrillo C., Ball B. A., Bradford M. A., Jordan C. F., Molina M. (2011) Soil fauna alter the effects of litter composition on nitrogen cycling in a mineral soil. *Soil Biology & Biochemistry*, **43**, 1440–1449.

Caruso T., Hogg I. D., Carapelli A., Frati F., Bargagli R. (2009) Large-scale spatial patterns in the distribution of Collembola (Hexapoda) species in Antarctic terrestrial ecosystems. *Journal of Biogeography*, **36**, 879–886.

Caruso T., Trokhymets V., Bargagli R., Convey P. (2013) Biotic interactions as a structuring force in soil communities: Evidence from the micro-arthropods of an Antarctic moss model system. *Oecologia*, **172**, 495–503.

Caruso T., Taormina M., Migliorini M. (2012) Relative role of deterministic and stochastic determinants of soil animal community: A spatially explicit analysis of oribatid mites. *Journal of Animal Ecology*, **81**, 214–221.

Chahartaghi M., Langel R., Scheu S., Ruess L. (2005) Feeding guilds in Collembola based on nitrogen stable isotope ratios. *Soil Biology & Biochemistry*, **37**, 1718–1725.

Chaladze G. (2012) Climate-based model of spatial pattern of the species richness of ants in Georgia. *Journal of Insect Conservation*, **16**, 791–800.

Chamberlain P., Mcnamara N., Chaplow J., Stott A., Black H. (2006) Translocation of surface litter carbon into soil by Collembola. *Soil Biology & Biochemistry*, **38**, 2655–2664.

Chao A., Li P. C., Agatha S., Foissner W. (2006) A statistical approach to estimate soil ciliate diversity and distribution based on data from five continents. *Oikos*, **114**, 479–493.

Chapin F. S. (1980) The mineral nutrition of wild plants. *Annual Review of Ecology and Systematics*, **11**, 233–260.

Chauvat M., Trap J., Perez G., Delporte P., Aubert M. (2011) Assemblages of Collembola across a 130-year chronosequence of beech forest. *Soil Organisms*, **83**, 405–418.

Chauvat M., Wolters V., Dauber J. (2007) Response of collembolan communities to land-use change and grassland succession. *Ecography*, **30**, 183–192.

Chauvel A., Grimaldi M., Barros E., et al. (1999) Pasture damage by an Amazonian earthworm. *Nature*, **398**, 32–33.

Chazdon R. L. (2008) Beyond deforestation: Restoring forests and ecosystem services on degraded lands. *Science*, **320**, 1458–1460.

Chelinho S., Sautter K. D., Cachada A., et al. (2011) Carbofuran effects in soil nematode communities: Using trait and taxonomic based approaches. *Ecotoxicology and Environmental Safety*, **74**, 2002–2012.

Chen D., Cheng J., Chu P., et al. (2016) Effect of diversity on biomass across grasslands on the Mongolian Plateau: Contrasting effects between plants and soil nematodes. *Journal of Biogeography*, **43**, 955–966.

Chen H. L., Li B., Fang C. M., Chen J. K., Wu J. H. (2007) Exotic plant influences soil nematode communities through litter input. *Soil Biology & Biochemistry*, **39**, 1782–1793.

Chen X., Adams B., Bergeron C., Sabo A., Hooper-Bùi L. (2015) Ant community structure and response to disturbances on coastal dunes of Gulf of Mexico. *Journal of Insect Conservation*, **19**, 1–13.

Chen Z., Wang X. K., Feng Z. Z., Xiao Q., Duan X. (2009) Impact of elevated O_3 on soil microbial community function under wheat crop. *Water, Air, & Soil Pollution*, **198**, 189–198.

Chernova N. M., Potapov M. B., Savenkova Y.Y., Bokova A. I. (2009) Ecological significance of parthenogenesis in collembola. *Zoologichesky Zhurnal*, **88**, 1455–1470.

Chown S. L., Huiskes A. H. L., Gremmen N. J. M., et al. (2012) Continent-wide risk assessment for the establishment of nonindigenous species in Antarctica. *Proceedings of the National Academy of Sciences of the United States of America*, **109**, 4938–4943.

Christensen B. (1956) Studies on Enchytraeidae 6. Technique for culturing Enchytraeidae, with notes on cocoon types. *Oikos*, **7**, 303–307.

Christensen B., Dózka-Farkas K. (2006) Invasion of terrestrial enchytraeids into two postglacial tundras: North-eastern Greenland and the Arctic archipelago of Canada (Enchytraeidae, Oligochaeta). *Polar Biology*, **29**, 454–466.

Christensen B., Glenner H. (2010) Molecular phylogeny of Enchytraeidae (Oligochaeta) indicates separate invasions of the terrestrial environment. *Journal of Zoological Systematics and Evolutionary Research*, **48**, 208–212.

Christensen S., Griffiths B. S., Ekelund F., Rønn R. (1992) Huge increase in bacterivores on freshly killed barley roots. *FEMS Microbiology Ecology*, **86**, 303–310.

Chust G., Pretus J. L., Ducrot D., Bedòs A., Deharveng L. (2003) Response of soil fauna to landscape heterogeneity: Determining optimal scales for biodiversity. *Conservation Biology*, **17**, 1712–1723.

Clarholm M. (1981) Protozoan grazing of bacteria in soil – Impact and importance. *Microbial Ecology*, **7**, 343–350.

Clarholm M. (1985) Interactions of bacteria, protozoa and plants leading to mineralization of soil nitrogen. *Soil Biology & Biochemistry*, **17**, 181–187.

Clarholm M. (1989) Effects of plant–bacterial–amoebal interactions on plant uptake of nitrogen under field conditions. *Biology and Fertility of Soils*, **8**, 373–378.

Clark C. M., Cleland E. E., Collins S. L., et al. (2007) Environmental and plant community determinants of species loss following nitrogen enrichment. *Ecology Letters*, **10**, 596–607.

Cobb N. A. (1915) *Nematodes and Their Relationships*, Washington, DC, U.S. G.P.O.

Cock M. J. W., Biesmeijer J. C., Cannon R. J. C., et al. (2012) The positive contribution of invertebrates to sustainable agriculture and food security. *CAB Reviews*, **7**, 1–27.

Cohn E., Koltai H., Sharon E., Spiegel Y. (2002) Root-nematode interactions: Recognition and pathogenicity. In: *Plant Roots – The Hidden Half* (eds. Waisel J., Eshel A., Kalkaf U.) pp. 783–796. New York, Marcel Dekker.

Čoja T., Bruckner A. (2003) Soil microhabitat diversity of a temperate Norway spruce (*Picea abies*) forest does not influence the community composition of gamasid mites (Gamasida, Acari). *European Journal of Soil Biology*, **39**, 79–84.

Cole A. C. J. (1940) A guide to the ants of the Great Smoky Mountains National Park, Tennessee. *The American Midland Naturalist*, **24**, 1–88.

Cole L., Bardgett R. D., Ineson P. (2000) Enchytraeid worms (Oligochaeta) enhances mineralization of carbon in organic upland soils. *European Journal of Soil Science*, **51**, 185–192.

Cole R. J., Holl K. D., Zahawi R. A., Wickey P., Townsend A. R. (2016) Leaf litter arthropod responses to tropical forest restoration. *Ecology and Evolution*, **6**, 5158–5168.

Coleman D. C. (1994) The microbial loop concept as used in terrestrial soil ecology studies. *Microbial Ecology*, **28**, 245–250.

Coleman D. C. (2008) From peds to paradoxes: Linkages between soil biota and their influences on ecological processes. *Soil Biology & Biochemistry*, **40**, 271–289.

Coleman D. C., Callaham Jr M. A., Crossley Jr D. A. (2018) *Fundamentals of Soil Ecology*, 3rd edn, London, Academic Press.

Coleman D. C., Crossley Jr D. A., Hendrix P. F. (2004) *Fundamentals of Soil Ecology*, 2nd edn, San Diego, CA, Academic Press.

Coleman D. C., Ingham R. E., Mcclellan J. F., Trofymow J. A. (1984) Soil nutrient transformations in the rhizosphere via animal–microbial interactions. In: *Invertebrates–Microbial Interactions* (eds. Anderson J. M., Rayner A. D. M., Walton D. W. H.) pp. 35–58. Cambridge, Cambridge University Press.

Coleman D. C., Macfadyen A. (1966) The recolonization of gamma-irradiated soil by small arthropods. *Oikos*, **17**, 62–70.

Coleman D. C., McGinnis J. T. (1970) Quantification of fungus – Small arthropod food chains in the soil. *Oikos*, **21**, 134–137.

Coleman D. C., Whitman W. B. (2005) Linking species richness, biodiversity and ecosystem function in soil systems. *Pedobiologia*, **49**, 479–497.

Collins N. M. (1980) The distribution of soil macrofauna on the West Ridge of Gunung (Mount) Mulu, Sarawak. *Oecologia*, **44**, 263–275.

Collison E. J., Ruitta T., Slade E. M. (2013) Macrofauna assemblage composition and soil moisture interact to affect soil ecosystem functions. *Acta Oecologica*, **47**, 30–36.

Colwell R. K., Coddington J. A. (1994) Estimating terrestrial biodiversity through extrapolation. *Philosophical Transactions of the Royal Society B: Biological Sciences*, **345**, 101–118.

Comiso J. C. (2006) Arctic warming signals from satellite observations. *Weather*, **61**, 70–76.

Convey P., Chown S. L., Clarke A., et al. (2014) The spatial structure of Antarctic biodiversity. *Ecological Monographs*, **84**, 203–244.

Convey P. A., McInnis S. J. (2005) Exceptional tardigrade-dominated ecosystems in Ellsworth Land, Antarctica. *Ecology*, **86**, 519–527.

Costa S. R., Kerry B. R., Bardgett R. D., Davies K. G. (2012) Interactions between nematodes and their microbial enemies in coastal sand dunes. *Oecologia*, **170**, 1053–1066.

Cotrufo M. F., Soong J., Vandegehuchte M. L., et al. (2014) Naphthalene addition to soil surfaces: A feasible method to reduce soil micro-arthropods with negligible direct effects on soil C dynamics. *Applied Soil Ecology*, **74**, 21–29.

Coulson J. C., Whittaker J. B. (1978) The ecology of moorland animals. In: *Production Ecology of British Moors and Montane Grasslands* (eds. Heal O. W., Perkins D. F.) pp. 52–93. Berlin, Springer.

Coulson S. J., Hodkinson I. D., Webb N. R. (2003) Microscale distribution patterns in high arctic soil arthropod communities: The influence of plant species within the vegetation mosaic. *Ecography*, **26**, 801–809.

Coulson S. J., Hodkinson I. D., Webb N. R. et al. (1996) Effects of experimental temperature elevation on high arctic soil microarthropod populations. *Polar Biology*, **16**, 147–153.

Coulson S. J., Leinaas H. P., Ims R. A., Sovik G. (2000) Experimental manipulation of the winter surface ice layer: The effects on a high Arctic soil microarthropod community. *Ecography*, **23**, 299–306.

Bibliography

Cox B., Moore P. D., Ladle R. (2016) *Biogeography: An Ecological and Evolutionary Approach*, Chichester, UK, Wiley-Blackwell.
Cox G. W., Mills J. N., Ellis B. A. (1992) Fire ants (Hymenoptera: Formicidae) as major agents of landscape development. *Environmental Entomology*, **21**, 281–286.
Cragg J. B. (1961) Some aspects of the ecology of moorland animals. *Journal of Ecology*, **49**, 477–506.
Creamer R. E., Hannula S. E., Van Leeuwen J. P., et al. (2016) Ecological network analysis reveals the inter-connection between soil biodiversity and ecosystem function as affected by land use across Europe. *Applied Soil Ecology*, **97**, 112–124.
Creevy A. L., Fisher J., Puppe D., Wilkinson D. A. (2016) Protist diversity on a nature reserve in NW England – With particular reference to their role in soil biogenic silicon pools. *Pedobiologia*, **59**, 51–59.
Crist T. O. (1998) The spatial distribution of termites in shortgrass steppe – A geostatistical approach. *Oecologia*, **114**, 410–416.
Crotty F.V., Adl S. M., Blackshaw R. P., Murray P. J. (2012a) Protozoan pulses unveil their pivotal position within the soil food web. *Microbial Ecology*, **63**, 905–918.
Crotty F. V., Adl S. M., Blackshaw R. P., Murray P. J. (2012b) Using stable isotopes to differentiate trophic feeding channels within soil food webs. *Journal of Eukaryotic Microbiology*, **59**, 520–526.
Crotty F.V., Fychan R., Scullion J., Sanderson R., Marley C. L. (2015) Assessing the impact of agricultural forage crops on soil biodiversity and abundance. *Soil Biology & Biochemistry*, **91**, 119–126.
Crowther T. W., A'Bear A. D. (2012) Impacts of grazing soil fauna on decomposer fungi are species-specific and density-dependent. *Fungal Ecology*, **5**, 277–281.
Crowther T. W., Boddy L., Jones T. H. (2011a) Outcomes of fungal interactions are determined by soil invertebrate grazers. *Ecology Letters*, **14**, 1134–1142.
Crowther T. W., Hefin Jones H., Boddy L., Baldrian P. (2011b) Invertebrate grazing determines enzyme production by basidiomycete fungi. *Soil Biology & Biochemistry*, **43**, 2060–2068.
Crowther T. W., Jones T. H., Boddy L. (2011c) Species-specific effects of grazing invertebrates on mycelial emergence and growth from woody resources into soil. *Fungal Ecology*, **5**, 333–341.
Crowther T. W., Stanton D. W. G., Thomas S. M., et al. (2013) Top-down control of soil fungal community composition by a globally distributed keystone consumer. *Ecology*, **94**, 2518–2528.
Crowther T. W., Thomas S. M., Maynard D. S., et al. (2015) Biotic interactions mediate soil microbial feedbacks to climate change. *Proceedings of the National Academy of Sciences of the United States of America*, **112**, 7033–7038.
Culman S. W., Young-Mathews A., Hollander A. D., et al. (2010) Biodiversity is associated with indicators of soil ecosystem functions over a landscape gradient of agricultural intensification. *Landscape Ecology*, **25**, 1333–1348.
Cunha A., Azevedo R. B. R., Emmons S. W., Leroi A. M. (1999) Variable cell numbers in nematodes. *Nature*, **402**, 253.
Curtis P. S., Wang X. (1998) A meta-analysis of elevated CO_2 effects on woody plant mass, form, and physiology. *Oecologia*, **113**, 299–313.
Cushman J. H., Lawton J. H., Manly B. F. J. (1993) Latitudinal patterns in European ant assemblages: Variation in species richness and body size. *Oecologia*, 95, 30–37.

Czechowski P., Clarke L. J., Breen J., Cooper A., Stevens M. I. (2016) Antarctic eukaryotic soil diversity of the Prince Charles Mountains revealed by high-throughput sequencing. *Soil Biology & Biochemistry*, **95**, 112–121.

Dam M., Vestergård M., Christensen S. (2012) Freezing eliminates efficient colonizers from nematode communities in frost-free temperate soils. *Soil Biology & Biochemistry*, **48**, 167–174.

Darwin C. (1859) *On the Origin of Species by Means of Natural Selection, Or the Preservation of Favoured Races in the Struggle for Life*, London, Murray.

Darwin C. (1881) *The Formation of Vegetable Mould, through the Action of Worms, with Observations of Their Habits*, London, Murray.

Dash M. C. (1990) Enchytraeidae. In: *Soil Biology Guide* (ed. Dindal D. L.) pp. 311–340. New York, John Wiley.

Dauber J., Purtauf T., Allspach A., et al. (2005) Local vs. landscape controls on diversity: A test using surface-dwelling soil macroinvertebrates of differing mobility. *Global Ecology and Biogeography*, **14**, 213–221.

Davidson D. A., Bruneau P. M. C., Grieve I. C., Young I. M. (2002) Impacts of fauna on an upland grassland soil as determined by micromorphological analysis. *Applied Soil Ecology*, **20**, 133–143.

Davis E. L., Hussey R. S., Baum T. J. (2004) Getting to the root of parasitism by nematodes. *Trends in Parasitology*, **20**, 134–141.

Day T. A., Ruhland C. T., Strauss S. L., et al. (2009) Response of plants and the dominant microarthropod, *Cryptopygus antarcticus*, to warming and contrasting precipitation regimes in Antarctic tundra. *Global Change Biology*, **15**, 1640–1651.

De Deyn G. B., Raaijmakers C. E., van Ruijven J., Berendse F., van der Putten W. H. (2004) Plant species identity and diversity effects on different trophic levels of nematodes in the soil food web. *Oikos*, **106**, 576–586.

De Deyn G. B., Raaijmakers C. E., Zoomer H. R., et al. (2003) Soil invertebrate fauna enhances grassland succession and diversity. *Nature*, **422**, 711–713.

De Deyn G. B., van der Putten W. H. (2005) Linking aboveground and belowground diversity. *Trends in Ecology and Evolution*, **20**, 625–633.

de Graaff M.-A., Adkins J., Kardon P., Throop H. L. (2015) A meta-analysis of soil biodiversity impacts on the carbon cycle. *Soil*, **1**, 257–271.

de Groot G. A., Jagers Op Akkerhuis G. A. J. M., Dimmers W. J., Charrier X., Faber J. H. (2016) Biomass and diversity of soil mite functional groups respond to extensification of land management, potentially affecting soil ecosystem services. *Frontiers in Environmental Science*, **4**, 15.

De Ruiter P. C., Moore J. C., Zwart K. B., et al. (1993) Simulation of nitrogen mineralization in the below-ground food webs of two winter wheat fields. *Journal of Applied Ecology*, **30**, 95–106.

de Vries F. T., Bloem J., Quirk H., et al. (2012a) Extensive management promotes plant and microbial nitrogen retention in temperate grassland. *PloS ONE*, **7**, e51201.

de Vries F. T., Liiri M., Bjørnlund L., et al. (2012b) Land use alters the resistance and resilience of soil food webs to drought. *Nature Climate Change*, **2**, 276–280.

Decaëns T. (2010) Macroecological patterns in soil communities. *Global Ecology and Biogeography*, **19**, 287–302.

Decaëns T., Bureau F., Margerie P. (2003) Earthworm communities in a wet agricultural landscape of the Seine Valley (Upper Normandy, France). *Pedobiologia*, **47**, 479–489.

Decaëns T., Jiménez J. J., Barros A. E., et al. (2004) Soil macrofaunal communities in permanent pastures derived from tropical forest or savanna. *Agriculture, Ecosystems and Environment*, **103**, 301–312.

Decaëns T., Jiménez J. J., Gioia C., Measey G. J., Lavelle P. (2006) The values of soil animals for conservation biology. *European Journal of Soil Biology*, **42**, S23–S38.

Decaëns T., Jiménez J. J., Rossi J. P. (2009) A null-model analysis of the spatio-temporal distribution of earthworm communities in Colombian grasslands. *Journal of Tropical Ecology*, **25**, 415–427.

Decaëns T., Lavelle P., Jiménez J. J., Escobar G., Rippstein G. (1994) Impact of land management on soil macrofauna in the Oriental Llanos of Colombia. *European Journal of Soil Biology*, **30**, 157–168.

Decaëns T., Margerie P., Aubert M., Hedde M., Bureau F. (2008) Assembly rules within earthworm communities in north-western France: A regional analysis. *Applied Soil Ecology*, **39**, 321–335.

Decaëns T., Mariani L., Lavelle P. (1999) Soil surface macrofaunal communities associated with earthworm casts in grasslands of the Eastern Plains of Colombia. *Applied Soil Ecology*, **13**, 87–100.

Decaëns T., Rossi J. P. (2001) Spatio-temporal structure of earthworm community and soil heterogeneity in a tropical pasture. *Ecography*, **24**, 671–682.

Degenkolb T., Vilcinskas A. (2016) Metabolites from nematophagous fungi and nematicidal natural products from fungi as an alternative for biological control. Part I: Metabolites from nematophagous ascomycetes. *Applied Microbiology and Biotechnology*, **100**, 3799–3812.

Delabie J. H. C., Fowler G. W. (1995) Soil and litter cryptic ant assemblages of Bahian cocoa plantations. *Pedobiologia*, **39**, 423–433.

Delaville L., Rossi J.-P., Quénéhervé P. (1996) Plant row and soil factors influencing the microspatial patterns of plant parasitic nematodes on sugarcane in Martinique. *Fundamental and Applied Nematology*, **19**, 321–328.

Delgado-Baquerizo M., Powell J. R., Hamonts K., et al. (2017) Circular linkages between soil biodiversity, fertility and plant productivity are limited to topsoil at the continental scale. *New Phytologist*, **215**, 1186–1196.

Denno R. F., Gruner D. S., Kaplan I. (2008) Potential for entomopathogenic nematodes in biological control: A meta-analytical synthesis and insights from trophic cascade theory. *Journal of Nematology*, **40**, 61–72.

Devetter M., Háněl L., Řeháková K., Doležal J. (2017) Diversity and feeding strategies of soil microfauna along elevation gradients in Himalayan cold deserts. *PloS ONE*, **12**, e0187646.

Diamond J. M. (1975) Assembly of species communities. In: *Ecology and Evolution of Communities* (eds. Cody M. L., Diamond J. M.) pp. 342–444. Cambridge, MA, Harvard University Press.

Didden W., Römbke J. (2001) Enchytraeids as indicator organisms for chemical stress in terrestrial ecosystems. *Ecotoxicology and Environmental Safety*, **50**, 25–43.

Didden W. A. M. (1990) Involvement of Enchytraeidae (Oligochaeta) in soil structure evolution in agricultural fields. *Biology and Fertility of Soils*, **9**, 152–158.

Didden W. A. M. (1993) Ecology of terrestrial Enchytraeidae. *Pedobiologia*, **37**, 2–29.
Dijkstra P., Ishizu A., Doucett R., et al. (2006) ^{13}C and ^{12}N natural abundance of soil microbial biomass. *Soil Biology & Biochemistry*, **38**, 3257–3266.
Dindal D. L. (1980) *Soil Biology Guide*, New York, John Wiley & Sons.
Dirilgen T., Jucevia E., Melecis V., Querner P., Bolger T. (2018) Analysis of spatial patterns informs community assembly and sampling requirements for Collembola in forest soils. *Acta Oecologica*, **86**, 23–30.
Doblas-Miranda E., Wardle D. A., Peltzer D. A., Yeates G. W. (2008) Changes in the community structure and diversity of soil invertebrates across the Franz Josef Glacier chronosequence. *Soil Biology & Biochemistry*, **40**, 1069–1081.
Domínguez A., Bedano J. C., Becker A. R. (2014) Organic farming fosters agroecosystem functioning in Argentinian temperate soils: Evidence from litter decomposition and soil fauna. *Applied Soil Ecology*, **83**, 170–176.
Donner J. (1966) *Rotifers*. London, Warne.
Dósza-Farkas K. (1996) Reproduction strategies in some enchytraeid species. In: *Newsletter on Enchytraeidae No. 5* (ed. Dósza-Farkas K.) pp. 25–33. Budapest, Hungary, Eötvös Loránd University.
Dray S., Legendre P., Peres-Neto P. R. (2006) Spatial modelling: A comprehensive framework for principal coordinate analysis of neighbor matrices (PCNM). *Ecological Modelling*, **196**, 483–493.
Drigo B., Kowalchuk G. A., Yergeau E., et al. (2007) Impact of elevated carbon dioxide on the rhizosphere communities of *Carex arenaria* and *Festuca rubra*. *Global Change Biology*, **13**, 2396–2410.
Dromph K. M., Cook R., Ostle N. J., Bardgett R. D. (2006) Root parasite induced nitrogen transfer between plants is density dependent. *Soil Biology & Biochemistry*, **38**, 2495–2498.
Ducarme X. D., André H. M., Wauthy G., Lebrun P. (2004) Are there real endogeic species in temperate forest mites? *Pedobiologia*, **48**, 139–147.
Dunn R. R. (2004a) Managing the tropical landscape: A comparison of the effects of logging and forest conversion to agriculture on ants, birds, and lepidoptera. *Forest Ecology and Management*, **191**, 215–224.
Dunn R. R. (2004b) Recovery of faunal communities during tropical forest regeneration. *Conservation Biology*, **18**, 302–309.
Dunn R. R., Agosti D., Andersen A. N., et al. (2009) Climatic drivers of hemispheric asymmetry in global patterns of ant species richness. *Ecology Letters*, **12**, 324–333.
Edgecombe G. D., Giribet G. (2007) Evolutionary biology of centipedes (Myriapoda: Chilopoda). *Annual Review of Entomology*, **52**, 151–170.
Edwards C. A., Lofty J. R. (1969) The influence of agricultural practices on soil micro-arthropod populations. In: *The Soil Ecosystem* (ed. Sheals J. G.) pp. 237–248. London, Publs. Syst. Assoc.
Edwards C. A., Lofty J. R. (1977) *Biology of Earthworms*, 2nd edn, London, Chapman and Hall.
Edwards C. A., Reichle D. E., Crossley Jr. D. A. (1970) The role of soil invertebrates in turnover of organic matter and nutrients. *Ecological Studies – Analysis and Synthesis*, **1**, 147–172.
Eggleton P. (1994) Termites live in a pear-shaped world: A response to Platnik. *Journal of Natural History*, **28**, 1209–1212.

Eggleton P. (2000) Global patterns of termite diversity. In: *Termites: Evolution, Sociality, Symbioses, Ecology* (eds. Abe T., Bignell D. E., Higashi M.) pp. 25–51. Dordrecht, Kluwer Academic Press.

Eggleton P., Bignell D. E. (1995) Monitoring the response of tropical insects to changes in the environment: Troubles with termites. In: *Insects in a Changing Environment* (eds. Harrington R., Stork N. E.) pp. 473–497. London, Academic Press.

Eggleton P., Bignell D. E., Sands W. A., et al. (1996) The diversity, abundance and biomass of termites under differing levels of forest disturbance in the Mbalmayo Forest Reserve, southern Cameroon. *Philosophical Transactions of the Royal Society B: Biological Sciences*, **351**, 51–68.

Eggleton P., Vanbergen A. J., Jones D. T., et al. (2005) Assemblages of soil macrofauna across a Scottish land-use intensification gradient: Influences of habitat quality, heterogeneity and area. *Journal of Applied Ecology*, **42**, 1153–1164.

Ehnes R. B., Rall B. C., Brose U. (2011) Phylogenetic grouping, curvature and metabolic scaling in terrestrial invertebrates. *Ecology Letters*, **14**, 993–1000.

Eisen G. (1900) Researches in American Oligochaeta, with especial reference to those of the Pacific Coast and adjacent islands. *Proceedings of the California Academy of Sciences 3rd Series: Zoology*, **2**, 85–276.

Eisenhauer N. (2010) The action of an animal ecosystem engineer: Identification of the main mechanisms of earthworm impacts on soil microarthropods. *Pedobiologia*, **53**, 343–352.

Eisenhauer N., Antunes P. M., Bennett A. E., et al. (2017) Priorities for research in soil ecology. *Pedobiologia – Journal of Soil Ecology*, **63**, 1–7.

Eisenhauer N., Bowker M. A., Grace J. B., Powell J. R. (2015) From patterns to causal understanding: Structural equation modeling (SEM) in soil ecology. *Pedobiologia*, **58**, 65–72.

Eisenhauer N., Dobies T., Cesarz S., et al. (2013) Plant diversity effects on soil food webs are stronger than those of elevated CO_2 and N deposition in a long-term grassland experiment. *Proceedings of the National Academy of Sciences of the United States of America*, **110**, 6889–6894.

Eisenhauer N., Klier M., Partsch S., et al. (2009) No interactive effects of pesticides and plant diversity on soil microbial biomass and respiration. *Applied Soil Ecology*, **42**, 31–36.

Eisenhauer N., Milcu A., Sabais A. C. W., et al. (2011a) Plant diversity surpasses plant functional groups and plant productivity as drivers of soil biota in the long term. *PloS ONE*, **6(1)**, e16055. doi:10.1371/journal.pone.0016055.

Eisenhauer N., Reich P. B. (2012) Above- and below-ground plant inputs both fuel soil food webs. *Soil Biology & Biochemistry*, **45**, 156–160.

Eisenhauer N., Sabais A. C. W., Scheu S. (2011b) Collembola species composition and diversity effects on ecosystem functioning vary with plant functional group identity. *Soil Biology & Biochemistry*, **43**, 1697–1704.

Eisenhauer N., Schädler M. (2011) Inconsistent impacts of decomposer diversity on the stability of aboveground and belowground ecosystem functions. *Oecologia*, **165**, 403–415.

Eisenhauer N., Scheu S., Reich P. B. (2012) Increasing plant diversity effects on productivity with time due to delayed soil biota effects on plants. *Basic and Applied Ecology*, **13**, 571–578.

Ekelund F., Rønn R. (1994) Notes on protozoa in agricultural soil with emphasis on heterotrophic flagellates and naked amoebae and their ecology. *FEMS Microbiology Reviews*, **15**, 321–353.
Ekelund F., Rønn R., Christensen S. (2001) Distribution with depth of protozoa, bacteria and fungi in soil profiles from three Danish forest sites. *Soil Biology & Biochemistry*, **33**, 475–481.
Eldridge D. J., Koen T. B. (2008) Formation of nutrient-poor soil patches in a semi-arid woodland by the European rabbit (*Oryctolagus cuniculus* L.). *Austral Ecology*, **33**, 88–98.
Emerson B. C., Cicconardi F., Fanciulli P. P., Shaw P. J. A. (2011) Phylogeny, phylogeography, phylobetadiversity and the molecular analysis of biological communities. *Philosophical Transactions of the Royal Society B: Biological Sciences*, **366**, 2391–2402.
Endlweber K., Ruess L., Scheu S. (2009) Collembola switch diet in presence of plant roots thereby functioning as herbivores. *Soil Biology & Biochemistry*, **41**, 1151–1154.
Endlweber K., Scheu S. (2006) Effects of Collembola on root properties of two competing ruderal plant species. *Soil Biology & Biochemistry*, **38**, 2025–2031.
Erséus C. (2005) Phylogeny of Oligochaetous Clitellata. *Hydrobiologia*, **535**, 357–372.
Escobar F., Lobo J. M., Halffter G. (2005) Altitudinal variation of dung beetle (Scarabaeidae: Scarabaeinae) assemblages in the Colombian Andes. *Global Ecology and Biogeography*, **14**, 327–337.
Ettema C. H. (1998) Soil nematode diversity: Species coexistence and ecosystem function. *Journal of Nematology*, **30**, 159–169.
Ettema C. H., Coleman C. D., Vellidis G., Lowrance R., Rathbun S. L. (1998) Spatiotemporal distributions of bacterivorous nematodes and soil resources in a restored riparian wetland. *Ecology*, **79**, 2721–2734.
Ettema C. H., Rathbun S. L., Coleman D. C. (2000) On spatiotemporal patchiness and the coexistence of five species of *Chronogaster* (Nematoda: Chronogasteridae) in a riparian wetland. *Oecologia*, **125**, 444–452.
Ettema C. H., Wardle D. A. (2002) Spatial soil ecology. *Trends in Ecology and Evolution*, **17**, 177–183.
Eviner V. T., Chapin III F. S. (2001) Plant species provide vital ecosystem functions for sustainable agriculture, rangeland management and restoration. *California Agriculture*, **55**, 54–59.
Faber J. H. (1991) Functional classification of soil fauna. A new approach. *Oikos*, **62**, 110–117.
Fanin N., Gundale M. J., Farrell M., et al. (2018) Consistent effects of biodiversity loss on multifunctionality across contrasting ecosystems. *Nature Ecology & Evolution*, **2**, 269–278.
Fattorini S. (2009) On the general dynamic model of oceanic island biogeography. *Journal of Biogeography*, **36**, 1100–1110.
Faucon M. P., Houben D., Lambers H. (2017) Plant functional traits: Soil and ecosystem services. *Trends in Plant Science*, **22**, 385–394.
Fayle T. M., Turner E. C., Snaddon J. L. (2010) Oil palms expansion into rain forest greatly reduces ant biodiversity in canopy, epiphytes and leaf-litter. *Basic and Applied Ecology*, **11**, 337–345.

Feldman L. J. (1988) The habits of roots. *Bioscience*, **38**, 612–618.
Feller C., Brown G. G., Blanchart E., Deleporte P., Chernyanskii S. S. (2003) Charles Darwin, earthworms and the natural sciences: Various lessons from past to future. *Agriculture, Ecosystems & Environment*, **99**, 29–49.
Ferris H., Bongers T., De Goede R. G. M. (2001) A framework for soil food web diagnostics: Extension of the nematode faunal analysis concept. *Applied Soil Ecology*, **18**, 13–29.
Ferris H., Venette R. C., Lau S. S. (1997) Population energetics of bacterial-feeding nematodes: Carbon and nitrogen budgets. *Soil Biology & Biochemistry*, **29**, 1183–1194.
Ferris V. R., Ferris J. M., Goseco C. G. (1981) Phylogenetic and biogeographic hypotheses in Leptonchidae (Nematoda: Dorylaimida) and a new classification. In: *Proceedings of the Helminthological Society*. pp. 163–171. Washington.
Ferris V. R., Goseco C. G., Ferris J. M. (1976) Biogeography of free-living soil nematodes from the perspective of plate tectonics. *Science*, **193**, 508–510.
Fiedler A. K., Landis D. A., Wratten S. D. (2008) Maximizing ecosystem services from conservation biological control: The role of habitat management. *Biological Control*, **45**, 254–271.
Fiera C. (2014) Application of stable isotopes and lipid analysis to understand trophic interactions in springtails. *North-western Journal of Zoology*, **10**, 227–235.
Fierer N., Strickland M. S., Litzin D., Bradford M. A., Cleveland C. C. (2009) Global patterns in belowground communities. *Ecology Letters*, **12**, 1238–1249.
Filser J. (2003) The role of Collembola in carbon and nitrogen cycling in soil. *Pedobiologia*, **46**, 234–245.
Finlay B. G. (2002) Global dispersal of free-living microbial eukaryote species. *Science*, **296**, 1061–1063.
Finlay B. J., Fenchel T. (1999) Divergent perspectives on protist species richness. *Protist*, **150**, 229–233.
Fisher B. L. (1999a) Ant diversity patterns along an elevational gradient in the reserve Naturelle Integrale d'Andohahela, Madagascar. *Fieldiana Zoology*, **94**, 129–147.
Fisher B. L. (1999b) Improving inventory efficiency: A case study of leaf-litter ant diversity in Madagascar. *Ecological Applications*, **9**, 714–731.
Fisher R., Mcdowell N., Purvis D., et al. (2010) Assessing uncertainties in a second-generation dynamic vegetation model caused by ecological scale limitations. *New Phytologist*, **187**, 666–681.
Floren A., Freking A., Biehl M., Linsenmair K. E. (2001) Anthropogenic disturbance changes the structure of arboreal tropical ant communities. *Ecography*, **24**, 547–554.
Flury P., Aellen N., Ruffner B., et al. (2016) Insect pathogenicity in plant-beneficial pseudomonads: Phylogenetic distribution and comparative genomics. *The ISME Journal*, **10**, 2527–2542.
Foissner W. (1987) Soil protozoa: Fundamental problems, ecological significance, adaptations in ciliates and testaceans, bioindicators, and guide to the literature. *Progress in Protistology*, **2**, 69–212.
Foissner W. (1999a) Protist diversity: Estimates of the near-imponderable. *Protist*, **150**, 363–368.
Foissner W. (1999b) Soil protozoa as bioindicators: Pros and cons, methods, diversity, representative examples. *Agriculture, Ecosystems and Environment*, **74**, 95–112.

Foissner W. (2006) Biogeography and dispersal of micro-organisms: A review emphasizing protists. *Acta Protozoologica*, **45**, 111–136.

Foley J., Ramankutty N., Brauman K., et al. (2011) Solutions for a cultivated planet. *Nature*, **478**, 337–342.

Fontaneto D., Ricci C. (2006) Spatial gradients in species diversity of microscopic animals: The case of bdelloid rotifers at high altitude. *Journal of Biogeography*, **33**, 1305–1313.

Fontaneto D., Westberg M., Hortal J. (2011) Evidence of weak habitat specialisation in microscopic animals. *PloS ONE*, **6**, e23969. doi:10.1371/journal.pone.0023969.

Forey E., Barot S., Decaëns T., et al. (2011) Importance of earthworm seed interactions for the composition and structure of plant communities: A review. *Acta Oecologica*, **37**, 594–603.

Fortin M.-J., Dale M. (2005) *Spatial Ecology: A Guide for Ecologists*. Cambridge, UK, Cambridge University Press.

Fowbert J. A., Smith R. I. L. (1994) Rapid population increases in native vascular plants in the Argentine islands, Antarctic Peninsula. *Arctic and Alpine Research*, **26**, 290–296.

Fox C. A., Fonseca E. J. A., Miller J. J., Tomlin A. D. (1999) The influence of row position and selected soil attributes on Acarina and Collembola in no-till and conventional continuous corn on a clay loam soil. *Applied Soil Ecology*, **13**, 1–8.

Francini G., Hui N., Jumpponen A., et al. (2018) Soil biota in boreal urban greenspace: Responses to plant type and age. *Soil Biology & Biochemistry*, **118**, 145–155.

Francl L. J. (1993) *Interactions of Nematodes with Mycorrhizae and Mycorrhizal Fungi*. New York, Chapman & Hall.

Fraser C. I., Terauds A., Smellie J., Convey P., Chown S. L. (2014) Geothermal activity helps life survive glacial cycles. *Proceedings of the National Academy of Sciences of the United States of America*, **111**, 5634–5639.

Fraser P. M., Schon N. L., Piercy J. E., Mackay A. D., Minor M. A. (2012) Influence of summer irrigation on soil invertebrate populations in a long-term sheep irrigation trial at Winchmore (Canterbury). *New Zealand Journal of Agricultural Research*, **55**, 165–180.

Freckman D. W. (1988) Bacterivorous nematodes and organic matter decomposition. *Agriculture, Ecosystems & Environment*, **24**, 195–217.

Freckman D. W., Ettema C. H. (1993) Assessing nematode communities in agroecosystems of varying human intervention. *Agriculture, Ecosystems & Environment*, **45**, 239–261.

Freckman D. W., Virginia R. A. (1989) Plant-feeding nematodes in deep-rooting desert ecosystems. *Ecology*, **70**, 1665–1678.

Frederiksen H. B., Rønn R., Christensen S. (2001) Effect of elevated atmospheric CO_2 and vegetation type on microbiota associated with decomposing straw. *Global Change Biology*, **7**, 313–321.

Frew A., Barnett K., Riegler M., Nielsen U. N., Johnson S. N. (2016) Belowground ecology of scarabs feeding on grass roots: Current knowledge and future directions for management in Australasia. *Frontiers in Plant Science*, **7**, 321. doi: 10.3389/fpls.2016.00321.

Fromm H., Winter K., Filser J., Hantschel R., Beese F. (1993) The influence of soil type and cultivation system on the spatial distributions of the soil fauna and microorganisms and their interactions. *Geoderma*, **60**, 109–118.

Frostegård Å., Petersen S., Bååth E., Nielsen T. (1997) Dynamics of a microbial community associated with manure hot spots as revealed by phospholipid fatty acid analyses. *Applied and Environmental Microbiology*, **63**, 2224–2231.

Frouz J., Thébault E., Pižl V., et al. (2013) Soil food web changes during spontaneous succession at post mining sites: A possible ecosystem engineering effect on food web organization? *PloS ONE*, **8**, e79694.

Fukima T., Nakajima M. (2013) Complex plant–soil interactions enhance plant species diversity by delaying community convergence. *Journal of Ecology*, **101**, 316–324.

Gabbutt P. D. (1967) Quantitative sampling of the pseudoscorpion *Chthonius ischnocheles* from beech litter. *Journal of Zoology, London*, **151**, 469–478.

Gabriel A. G. A., Chown S. L., Barendse J., et al. (2001) Biological invasions of Southern Ocean islands: The Collembola of Marion Island as a test of generalities. *Ecography*, **24**, 421–430.

Galloway J. N., Townsend A. R., Erisman J. W., et al. (2008) Transformation of the nitrogen cycle: Recent trends, questions and potential solutions. *Science*, **320**, 889–892.

Gange A. C., Stagg P. G., Ward L. K. (2002) Arbuscular mycorrhizal fungi affect phytophagous insect specialism. *Ecology Letters*, **5**, 11–15.

Gao M., He P., Zhang X., Liu D., Wu D. (2014) Relative roles of spatial factors, environmental filtering and biotic interactions in fine-scale structuring of a soil mite community. *Soil Biology & Biochemistry*, **79**, 68–77.

Garćia-Palacios P., Maestre F. T., Kattge J., Wall D. H. (2013) Climate and litter quality differently modulate the effects of soil fauna on litter decomposition across biomes. *Ecology Letters*, **16**, 1045–1053.

Gaston K. J. (2000) Global patterns in biodiversity. *Nature*, **405**, 220–227.

Gaston K. J., Blackburn T., Lawton J. H. (1997) Interspecific abundance range size relationships: An appraisal of mechanisms. *Journal of Animal Ecology*, **66**, 579–601.

Geisen S. (2016) The bacterial–fungal energy channel concept challenged by enormous functional versatility of soil protists. *Soil Biology & Biochemistry*, **102**, 22–25.

Geisen S., Cornelia B., Römbke J., Bonkowski M. (2014) Soil water availability strongly alters the community composition of soil protists. *Pedobiologia*, **57**, 205–213.

Geisen S., Koller R., Hünninghaus M., Dumack K., Bonkowski M. (2016) The soil food web revisited: Diverse and widespread mycophagous soil protists. *Soil Biology & Biochemistry*, **94**, 10–18.

Geisen S., Mitchell E. A. D., Wilkinson D. M., et al. (2017) Soil protistology rebooted: 30 fundamental questions to start with. *Soil Biology & Biochemistry*, **111**, 94–103.

Geisen S., Rosengarten J., Koller R., et al. (2015a) Pack hunting by a common soil amoeba on nematodes. *Environmental Microbiology*, **17**, 4538–4546.

Geisen S., Viscaíno A., Bonkowski M., De Groot G. A. (2015b) Not all are free-living: High-throughput DNA metabarcoding reveals a diverse community of protists parasitizing soil metazoa. *Molecular Ecology*, **24**, 4556–4569.

George P. B. L., Keith A. M., Creer S., et al. (2017) Evaluation of mesofauna communities as soil quality indicators in a national-level monitoring programme. *Soil Biology & Biochemistry*, **115**, 537–546.
Georgieva S. S., Mcgrath S. P., Hooper D. J., Chambers B. S. (2002) Nematode communities under stress: The long-term effects of heavy metals in soil treated with sewage sludge. *Applied Soil Ecology*, **20**, 27–42.
Gerard B. M. (1967) Factors affecting earthworms in pastures. *Journal of Animal Ecology*, **36**, 235–252.
Gilbert O. W. (1956) The natural histories of four species of *Calathus* (Coleoptera, Carabidae) living in sand dunes in Anglesey, N. Wales. *Oikos*, **7**, 22–47.
Gill R. W. (1969) Soil microarthropod abundance following old-field litter manipulation. *Ecology*, **50**, 805–816.
Giller K. E., Beare M. H., Lavelle P., Izac A. M. N, Swift M. J. (1997) Agricultural intensification, soil biodiversity and agroecosystem function. *Applied Soil Ecology*, **6**, 3–16.
Giller P. S. (1996) The diversity of soil communities, the 'poor man's tropical rainforest'. *Biodiversity and Conservation*, **5**, 135–168.
Gillison A. N., Jones D. T., Susilo F.-X., Bignell D. E. (2003) Vegetation indicates diversity of soil macroinvertebrates: A case study with termites along a land-use intensification gradient in lowland Sumatra. *Organisms, Diversity and Evolution*, **3**, 111–126.
Gillooly J. F., Brown J. H., West G. B., Savage V. B., Charnov E. L. (2001) Effects of size and temperature on metabolic rate. *Science*, **293**, 2248–2251.
Godfray H. C. J., Beddington J. R., Crute I. R., et al. (2010) Food security: The challenge of feeding 9 billion people. *Science*, **327**, 812–818.
González G., García E., Cruz V., et al. (2007) Earthworm communities along an elevation gradient in northeastern Puerto Rico. *European Journal of Soil Biology*, **43**, S24–S32.
Gooseff M. N., Barrett J. E., Doran P. T., et al. (2003) Snowpack influence on soil biogeochemical processes and invertebrate distribution in the McMurdo Dry Valleys, Antarctica. *Arctic, Antarctica and Alpine Research*, **35**, 91–99.
Goralczyk K. (1998) Nematodes in a coastal dune succession: Indicators of soil properties? *Applied Soil Ecology*, **9**, 465–469.
Görres J. H., Dichiaro M. J., Lyons J. B., Amador J. A. (1998) Spatial and temporal patterns of soil biological activity in a forest and an old field. *Soil Biology & Biochemistry*, **30**, 219–230.
Gossner M. M., Lewinsohn T. M., Kahl T., et al. (2016) Land-use intensification causes multitrophic homogenization of grassland communities. *Nature*, **540**, 266–269.
Gotelli N. J., Ellison A. M. (2002) Biogeography at a regional scale: Determinants of ant species density in New England bogs and forests. *Ecology*, **83**, 1604–1609.
Gotelli N. J., Graves G. R. (1996) *Null Models in Ecology*, Washington, DC, Smithsonian Institution Press.
Grace J. B. (2006) *Structural Equation Modeling and Natural Systems*, Cambridge, Cambridge University Press.
Graham J. H. (2001) What do root pathogens see in mycorrhizas? *New Phytologist*, **149**, 357–359.

Grandy A. S., Wieder W. R., Wickings K., Kyker-Snowman E. (2016) Beyond microbes: Are fauna the next frontier in soil biogeochemical models? *Soil Biology & Biochemistry*, **102**, 40–44.

Greenslade P. (2008) Has survey effort of Australia's islands reflected conservation and biogeographical significance? An assessment using Collembola. *European Journal of Soil Biology*, **44**, 458–462.

Greenslade P., Convey P. (2012) Exotic Collembola on subantarctic islands: Pathways, origins and biology. *Biological Invasions*, **14**, 405–417.

Greenstone M. H., Weber D. C., Coudron T. A., Payton M. E., Hu J. S. (2012) Removing external DNA contamination from arthropod predators destined for molecular gut-content analysis. *Molecular Ecology Resources*, **12**, 464–469.

Grgič T., Kos I. (2005) Influence of forest development phase on centipede diversity in managed beech forests in Slovenia. *Biodiversity and Conservation*, **14**, 1841–1862.

Griffiths B. S. (1989) Enhanced nitrification in the presence of bacteriophagous protozoa. *Soil Biology & Biochemistry*, **21**, 1045–1051.

Griffiths B. S. (1990) A comparison of microbial-feeding nematodes and protozoa in the rhizosphere of different plants. *Biology and Fertility of Soils*, **9**, 83–88.

Griffiths B. S. (1994) Soil nutrient flow. In: *Soil Protozoa* (ed. Darbyshire J. F.) pp. 65–91. Wallingford, CAB International.

Griffiths B. S., Caul S. (1993) Migration of bacterial-feeding nematodes, but not protozoa, to decomposing grass residues. *Biology and Fertility of Soils*, **15**, 201–207.

Grime J. P. (1973) Control of species diversity in herbaceous vegetation. *Journal of Environmental Management*, **1**, 151–167.

Gunnarson T., Tunlid A. (1986) Recycling of fecal pellets in isopods: Microorganisms and nitrogen compounds as potential food for *Oniscus asellus* L. *Soil Biology & Biochemistry*, **18**, 595–600.

Gutt J., Isla E., Bertler N., et al. (2018) Cross-disciplinarity in the advance of Antarctic ecosystem research. *Marine Genomics*, **37**, 1–17.

Haase S., Ruess L., Neumann G., Marhan S., Kandeler E. (2007) Low-level herbivory by root-knot nematodes (*Meloidogyne incognita*) modifies root hair morphology and rhizodeposition in host plants (*Hordeum vulgare*). *Plant and Soil*, **301**, 151–164.

Hågvar S. (1998) The relevance of the Rio-Convention on biodiversity to conserving the biodiversity of soils. *Applied Soil Ecology*, **9**, 1–7.

Hågvar S., Klanderud K. (2009) Effect of simulated environmental change on alpine soil arthropods. *Global Change Biology*, **15**, 2972–2980.

Haimi J., Huhta V. (1990) Effects of earthworms on decomposition processes in a raw humus soil: A microcosm study. *Biology and Fertility of Soils*, **10**, 178–183.

Hale C. M., Frelich L. E., Reich P. B., Pastor J. (2005) Effects of European earthworm invasion on soil characteristics in northern hardwood forests of Minnesota, USA. *Ecosystems*, **8**, 911–927.

Hamilton W. E., Dindal D. L. (1983) The vermisphere concept: Earthworm activity and sewage sludge. *Biocycle*, **24**, 54–55.

Handa I. T., Aerts R., Berendse F., et al. (2007) Consequences of biodiversity loss for litter decomposition across biomes. *Nature*, **509**, 218–221.

Hanlon R. D. G., Anderson J. M. (1979) The effects of Collembola grazing on microbial activity in decomposing leaf litter. *Oecologia*, **38**, 93–99.

Bibliography · 315

Hanlon R. D. G., Anderson J. M. (1980) Influence of macroarthropod feeding activities on microflora in decomposing oak leaves. *Soil Biology & Biochemistry*, **12**, 255–261.

Hansen R. (2000) Effects of habitat complexity and composition on a diverse litter microarthropod assemblage. *Ecology*, **81**, 1120–1132.

Hansen R. A., Coleman D. C. (1998) Litter complexity and composition are determinants of the diversity and species composition of oribatid mites (Acari: Oribatida) in litterbags. *Applied Soil Ecology*, **9**, 17–23.

Harris J. (2009) Soil microbial communities and restoration ecology: Facilitators or followers? *Science*, **325**, 573–575.

Hart S. P., Usinowicz J., Levine J. M. (2017) The spatial scales of species coexistence. *Nature Ecology & Evolution*, **1**, 1066–1073.

Hassall M., Turner J. G., Rands M. R. W. (1987) Effects of terrestrial isopods on the decomposition of woodland leaf litter. *Oecologia*, **72**, 597–604.

Hassink J., Bouwman L. A., Zwart K. B., Brussard L. (1993) Relationship between habitable pore space, soil biota and mineralization rates in grassland soil. *Soil Biology & Biochemistry*, **25**, 47–55.

Hättenschwiler S., Tiunov A. V., Scheu S. (2005) Biodiversity and litter decomposition in terrestrial ecosystems. *Annual Review of Ecology, Evolution and Systematics*, **36**, 191–218.

Haynes R. J., Naidu R. (1998) Influence of lime, fertilizer and manure applications on soil organic matter content and soil physical conditions: A review. *Nutrient Cycling in Agroecosystems*, **51**, 123–137.

Heckel D. G. (2012) Insecticide resistance after Silent spring. *Science*, **337**, 1612–1614.

Hedlund K., Boddy L., Preston C. M. (1991) Mycelial responses of the soil fungus, *Mortierella isabellina*, to grazing by *Onychiurus armatus* (Collembola). *Soil Biology & Biochemistry*, **23**, 361–366.

Hedlund K., Öhrn O. (2000) Tritrophic interactions in a soil community enhance decomposition rates. *Oikos*, **88**, 585–591.

Hedlund K., Santa Regina I., van der Putten W. H., et al. (2003) Plant species diversity, plant biomass and responses of the soil community on abandoned land across Europe: Idiosyncracy or above-belowground time lags. *Oikos*, **103**, 45–58.

Heemsbergen D. A., Berg M. P., Loreau M., et al. (2004) Biodiversity effects on soil processes explained by interspecific functional dissimilarity. *Science*, **306**, 1019–1020.

Heger T. J., Lara E., Mitchell E. A. D. (2011) Arcellinida testate amoebae (Amoebozoa: Arcellinida): Model of organisms for assessing microbial biogeography. In: *Biogeography of Microscopic Organisms* (ed. Fontaneto D.) pp. 111–129. Cambridge, Cambridge University Press.

Heidemann K., Scheu S., Ruess L., Maraun M. (2011) Molecular detection of nematode predation and scavenging in oribatid mites: Laboratory and field experiments. *Soil Biology & Biochemistry*, **43**, 2229–2236.

Heisler C., Kaiser E.-A. (1995) Influence of agricultural traffic and crop management on collembolan and microbial biomass in arable soil. *Biology and Fertility of Soils*, **19**, 159–165.

Helmus M. R., Savage K., Diebel M. W., Maxted J. T., Ives A. R. (2007) Separating the determinants of phylogenetic community structure. *Ecology Letters*, **10**, 917–925.

Bibliography

Hendrix P. F., Baker G. H., Callaham Jr M. A., et al. (2006) Invasion of exotic earthworms into ecosystems inhabited by native earthworms. *Biological Invasions*, **8**, 1287–1300.

Hendrix P. F., Callaham M. A. J., Drake J. M., et al. (2008) Pandora's box contained bait: The global problem of introduced earthworms. *Annual Review of Ecology, Evolution and Systematics*, **39**, 593–613.

Heneghan L., Coleman C. D., Zou X., Crossley Jr. D. A., Haines B. L. (1998) Soil microarthropod community structure and litter decomposition dynamics: A study of tropical and temperate sites. *Applied Soil Ecology*, **9**, 33–38.

Hillebrand H. (2004) On the generality of the latitudinal diversity gradient. *American Naturalist*, **163**, 192–211.

Hillebrand H., Blenckner T. (2002) Regional and local impact on species diversity – From pattern to processes. *Oecologia*, **132**, 479–491.

Hillebrand H., Watermann F., Karez R., Berninger U.-G. (2001) Differences in species richness patterns between unicellular and multicellular organisms. *Oecologia*, **126**, 114–124.

HilleRisLambers J., Adler P. B., Harpole W. S., Levine J. M., Mayfield M. M. (2012) Rethinking community assembly through the lens of coexistence theory. *Annual Review of Ecology, Evolution, and Systematics*, **43**, 227–248.

Hiltner L. (1904) Über neue Erfahrungen und Probleme auf dem Gebiet der Bodenbakteriologie unter besonderer Berücksichtigung der Gründüngung und Brache. *Arbeiten der Deutschen Landwirtschaftlichen Gesellschaft*, **98**, 59–78.

Hobbs R. J., Mooney H. A. (1985) Community and population dynamics of serpentine grassland annuals in relation to gopher disturbance. *Oecologia*, **67**, 342–351.

Hodda M. (2007) Phylum Nematoda. *Zootaxa*, **1668**, 265–293.

Hodda M., Nobbs J. (2008) A review of current knowledge on particular taxonomic features of the Australasian nematode fauna, with special emphasis on plant feeders. *Australasian Plant Pathology*, **37**, 308–317.

Hodkinson I. D., Coulson S. J., Webb N. R. (2004) Invertebrate community assembly along proglacial chronosequences in the high Arctic. *Journal of Animal Ecology*, **73**, 556–568.

Hodkinson I. D., Coulson S. J., Webb N. R., Block W. (1996) Can Arctic soil microarthropods survive elevated summer temperatures? *Functional Ecology*, **10**, 314–321.

Hoeksema J. D., Lussenhop J., Teeri J. A. (2000) Soil nematodes indicate food web responses to elevated atmospheric CO_2. *Pedobiologia*, **44**, 725–735.

Hofmann J., El Ashry A., Anwar S., et al. (2010) Metabolic profiling reveals local and systemic responses of host plants to nematode parasitism. *The Plant Journal*, **62**, 1058–1071.

Hole D. G., Perkins A. J., Wilson J. D., et al. (2005) Does organic farming benefit biodiversity? *Biological Conservation*, **122**, 113–130.

Holmstrup M., Sørensen J. G., Maraldo K., et al. (2012) Increased frequency of drought reduces species richness of enchytraeid communities in both wet and dry heathland soils. *Soil Biology & Biochemistry*, **53**, 43–49.

Holt J. A., Lepage M. (2000) Termites and soil properties. In: *Termites: Evolution, Sociality, Systematics, Symbioses, Ecology* (eds. Abe T., Bignell D. E., Higashi M.) pp. 389–407. Dordrecht, Kluwer Academic Press.

Holterman M., Karegar A., Mooijman P., et al. (2017) Disparate gain and loss of parasitic abilities among nematode lineages. *PloS ONE*, **12**, e0185445.

Hooper D. U., Adair C. E., Cardinale B. J., et al. (2012) A global synthesis reveals biodiversity loss as a major driver of ecosystem change. *Nature*, **486**, 105–108.

Hooper D. U., Chapin F. S. I., Ewel J. J., et al. (2005) Effects of biodiversity on ecosystem functioning: A consensus of current knowledge. *Ecological Monographs*, **75**, 3–35.

Hopkin S. P. (1997) *Biology of the Springtails (Insecta: Collembola)*, Oxford, Oxford University Press.

Hopkin S. P. (2007) *A Key to the Collembola (Springtails) of Britain and Ireland*, Shropshire, FSC Publications.

House A. P. N., Burwell C. J., Brown S. D., Walters B. J. (2012) Agricultural matrix provides modest habitat value for ants on mixed farms in eastern Australia. *Journal of Insect Conservation*, **16**, 1–12.

Howe A. T., Bass D., Vickerman K., Chao E. E., Cavalier-Smith T. (2009) Phylogeny, taxonomy, and astounding genetic diversity of Glissomonadida ord. nov., the dominant gliding zooflagellates in soil (Protozoa: Cercozoa). *Protist*, **160**, 159–189.

Hughes K. A., Greenslade P., Convey P. (2017) The fate of the non-native Collembolon, *Hypogastrura viatica*, at the southern extent of its introduced range in Antarctica. *Polar Biology*, **40**, 2127–2131.

Huguenin M. T., Leggett C. G., Paterson R. W. (2006) Economic valuation of soil fauna. *European Journal of Soil Biology*, **42**, S16–S22.

Huhta V. (2007) The role of soil fauna in ecosystems: A historical review. *Pedobiologia*, **50**, 489–495.

Huhta V., Persson T., Setälä H. (1998) Functional implications of soil fauna diversity in boreal forests. *Applied Soil Ecology*, **10**, 277–288.

Hunt H. W., Coleman D. C., Ingham E. R., et al. (1987) The detrital food web in a shortgrass prairie. *Biology and Fertility of Soils*, **3**, 57–68.

Hunt H. W., Wall D. H. (2002) Modelling the effects of loss of soil biodiversity on ecosystem function. *Global Change Biology*, **8**, 33–50.

Huston M. A. (1994) *Biological Diversity*, Cambridge, Cambridge University Press.

Hyodo F., Tayasu I., Konate S., et al. (2008) Gradual enrichment of ^{15}N with humification of diets in a below-ground food web: Relationship between ^{15}N and diet age determined using ^{14}C. *Functional Ecology*, **22**, 513–522.

Hyvönen R., Persson T. (1996) Effects of fungivorous and predatory arthropods on nematodes and tardigrades in microcosms with coniferous forest soil. *Biology and Fertility of Soils*, **21**, 121–127.

Ingham R. E. (1988) Interactions between nematodes and vesicular-arbuscular mycorrhizae. *Agriculture, Ecosystems and Environment*, **24**, 169–182.

Ingham R. E., Detling J. K. (1984) Plant–herbivore interactions in a North American mixed-grass prairie. III. Soil nematode populations and root biomass on *Cynomys ludovicianus* colonies and adjacent uncolonized areas. *Oecologia*, **63**, 307–313.

Ingham R. E., Trofymow J. A., Ingham E. R., Coleman D. C. (1985) Interactions of bacteria, fungi, and their nematode grazers: Effects on nutrient cycling and plant growth. *Ecological Monographs*, **55**, 119–140.

Ingimarsdóttir M., Caruso T., Ripa J., et al. (2012) Primary assembly of soil communities: Disentangling the effect of dispersal and local environment. *Oecologia*, **170**, 745–754.

IPCC (2014) Climate Change 2014 – Impacts, Adaptation and Vulnerability. *Part A: Global and Sectoral Aspects. Contribution of Working Group II to the Fifth Assessment Report of the Intergovernmental Panel on Climate Change*, Cambridge and New York, Cambridge University Press.

James S. W. (1995) Systematics, biogeography, and ecology of nearctic earthworms from eastern, central, southern and southwestern United States. In: *Earthworm Ecology and Biogeography in North America* (ed. Hendrix P. F.). Boca Raton, FL, Lewis Publishers.

Janion-Scheepers C., Phillips L., Sgrò C. M., et al. (2018) Basal resistance enhances warming tolerance of alien over indigenous species across latitude. *Proceedings of the National Academy of Sciences of the United States of America*, **115**, 145–150.

Janion C., Worland M. R., Chown S. L. (2009) Assemblage level variation in springtail lower lethal temperature: The role of invasive species on sub-Antarctic Marion Island. *Physiological Entomology*, **34**, 284–291.

Janssen M. P. M., Heijmans G. J. S. M. (1998) Dynamics and stratification of protozoa in the organic layer of a Scots pine forest. *Biology and Fertility of Soils*, **26**, 285–292.

Jeanne R. L. (1979) A latitudinal gradient in rates of ant predation. *Ecology*, **60**, 1211–1224.

Jeffery S., Gardi C., Jones A., et al. (2010) *European Atlas of Soil Biodiversity*, Luxembourg, European Commission, Publications Office of the European Union.

Jenkins C. N., Sanders N. J., Andersen A. N., et al. (2011) Global diversity in light of climate change: The case of ants. *Diversity and Distributions*, **17**, 652–662.

Jenny H. (1941) *Factors of Soil Formation: A System of Quantitative Pedology*, New York, McGraw-Hill.

Jensen T. C., Leinaas H. P., Hessen D. O. (2006) Age-dependent shift in response to food element composition in Collembola: Contrasting effects of dietary nitrogen. *Oecologia*, **149**, 583–592.

Jentschke G., Bonkowski M., Godbold D. L., Scheu S. (1995) Soil protozoa and forest tree growth: Non-nutritional effects and interaction with mycorrhizas. *Biology and Fertility of Soils*, **20**, 263–269.

Jiménez J. J., Decaëns T., Rossi J. P. (2006) Stability of the spatio-temporal distribution and niche overlap in Neotropical earthworm assemblages. *Acta Oecologica*, **30**, 299–311.

Jiménez J. J., Rossi J. P. (2006) Spatial dissociation between two endogeic earthworms in the Colombian 'Llanos'. *European Journal of Soil Biology*, **42**, S218–S224.

Johns A. D. (1992) Species conservation in managed tropical forests. In: *Tropical Deforestation and Species Extinction* (eds. Whitmore T. C., Sayer J. A.) pp. 15–50. London, Chapman & Hall.

Johnson A. W., Nusbaum C. J. (1968) The activity of *Tylenchorhynchus claytoni*, *Trichodorus christiei*, *Pratylenchus brachyurus*, *P. zeae*, and *Helicotylenchus dihystera* in single and multiple inoculations on corn and soybean. *Nematologica*, **14**, 9.

Johnson D., Krsek M., Wellington E. M. H., et al. (2003) Soil invertebrates disrupt carbon flow through fungal networks. *Science*, **309**, 1047.

Johnson S. N., Clark K. E., Hartley S. E., et al. (2012) Aboveground–belowground herbivore interactions: A meta-analysis. *Ecology*, **93**, 2208–2215.

Johnson S. N., Rasmann S. (2015) Root-feeding insects and their interactions with organisms in the rhizosphere. *Annual Review of Entomology*, **60**, 517–535.

Jones C. G., Lawton J. H., Shachak M. (1997) Positive and negative effects of organisms as physical ecosystem engineers. *Ecology*, **78**, 1946–1957.

Jonsson M., Yeates G. W., Wardle D. A. (2009) Patterns of invertebrate density and taxonomic richness across gradients of area, isolation, and vegetation diversity in a lake–island system. *Ecography*, **32**, 963–972.

Jørgensen H. B., Canbäck B., Hedlund K., Tunlid A. (2005) Selective foraging of fungi by collembolans in soil. *Biology Letters*, **1**, 243–246.

Jouquet P., Dauber J., Lagerlöf J., Lavelle P., Lepage M. (2006) Soil invertebrates as ecosystem engineers: Intended and accidental effects on soil and feedback loops. *Applied Soil Ecology*, **32**, 153–164.

Judas M. (1988) The species–area relationship of European Lumbricidae (Annelida, Oligochaeta). *Oecologia*, **76**, 579–587.

Juen A., Traugott M. (2006) Amplification facilitators and multiplex PCR: Tools to overcome PCR-inhibition in DNA-gut-content analysis of soil-living invertebrates. *Soil Biology & Biochemistry*, **38**, 1872–1879.

Kalif K. A. B., Azevedo-Ramos C., Moutinho P., Malcher S. A. O. (2001) The effect of logging on the ground-foraging ant community in Eastern Amazonia. *Studies on Neotropical Fauna and Environment*, **36**, 215–219.

Kambhampati S., Eggleton P. (2000) Taxonomy and phylogeny of termites. In: *Termites: Evolution, Sociality, Symbioses, Ecology* (eds. Abe T., Bignell D. E., Higashi M.) pp. 1–24. Dordrecht, Kluwer Academic.

Kampichler C., Bruckner A. (2009) The role of microarthropods in terrestrial decomposition: A meta-analysis of 40 years of litterbag studies. *Biological Reviews*, **84**, 375–389.

Kaneda S., Kaneko N. (2004) The feeding preference of a collembolan (*Folsomia candida* Willem) on ectomycorrhiza (*Pisolithus tinctorius* (Pers.)) varies with the mycelial growth condition and vitality. *Applied Soil Ecology*, **27**, 1–5.

Kaneko N. (1988) Feeding habits and cheliceral size of oribatid mites in cool temperate forest soils in Japan. *Revue d'Ecologie et de Biologie du Sol*, **25**, 353–363.

Kaneko N., Salamanca E. F. (1999) Mixed leaf litter effects on decomposition rates and soil microarthropod communities in an oak-pine stand in Japan. *Ecological Research*, **14**, 131–138.

Kapusta P., Sobczyk L., Rozen A., Weiner J. (2003) Species diversity and spatial distribution of enchytraeid communities in forest soils: Effects of habitat characteristics and heavy metal contamination. *Applied Soil Ecology*, **23**, 187–198.

Kapusta P., Szarek-Łukaszewska G. S., Stefanowicz A. M. (2011) Direct and indirect effects of metal contamination on soil biota in a Zn–Pb post-mining and smelting area (S Poland). *Environmental Pollution*, **159**, 1516–1522.

Karban P. (1980) Periodical cicada nymphs impose periodical oak tree wood accumulation. *Nature*, **287**, 326–327.

Kardol P., Bezemer T. M., van der Putten W. H. (2006) Temporal variation in plant–soil feedback controls succession. *Ecology Letters*, **9**, 1080–1088.

Kardol P., Newton J. S., Bezemer T. M., Maraun M., van der Putten W. H. (2009) Contrasting diversity patterns of soil mites and nematodes in secondary succession. *Acta Oecologica*, **35**, 603–609.

Kardol P., Reynolds W. N., Norby R. J., Classen A. T. (2011) Climate change effects on soil microarthropod abundance and community structure. *Applied Soil Ecology*, **47**, 37–44.

Kardol P., Throop H. L., Adkins J., de Graaff M.-A. (2016) A hierarchical framework for studying the role of biodiversity in soil food web processes and ecosystem services. *Soil Biology & Biochemistry*, **102**, 33–36.

Kardol P., Wardle D. A. (2010) How understanding aboveground–belowground linkages can assist restoration ecology. *Trends in Ecology and Evolution*, **25**, 670–679.

Kaspari M., Ward P. S., Yuan M. (2004) Energy gradients and the geographic distribution of local ant diversity. *Oecologia*, **140**, 407–413.

Kaspari M., Yuan M., Alonso L. (2003) Spatial grain and the causes of regional diversity gradients in ants. *The American Naturalist*, **161**, 459–477.

Kaufmann R. (2001) Invertebrate succession on an alpine glacier foreland. *Ecology*, **82**, 2261–2278.

Kaufmann R., Fuchs M., Gosterxeier N. (2002) The soil fauna of an alpine glacier foreland: Colonization and succession. *Arctic, Antarctic, and Alpine Research*, **34**, 242–250.

Kaya M., De Smet W. H., Fontaneto D. (2010) Survey of moss-dwelling bdelloid rotifers from middle Arctic Spitsbergen (Svalbard). *Polar Biology*, **33**, 833–842.

Keilin D. (1959) The problem of anabiosis or latent life: History and current concept. *Proceedings of the Royal Society B*, **150**, 167–173.

Keith A. M., Brooker R. W., Ostler G. H. R., et al. (2009) Strong impacts of belowground tree inputs on soil nematode trophic composition. *Soil Biology & Biochemistry*, **41**, 1060–1065.

Kerfahi D., Tripathi B. M., Porazinska D. L., et al. (2016) Do tropical rain forest soils have greater nematode diversity than High Arctic tundra? A metagenetic comparison of Malaysia and Svalbard. *Global Ecology and Biogeography*, **25**, 716–728.

Kerry B. R. (2000) Rhizosphere interactions and the exploitation of microbial agents for the biological control of plant-parasitic nematodes. *Annual Review of Phytopathology*, **38**, 423–441.

Khalil M. A., Janssens T. K. S., Berg M. P., van Straalen N. M. (2009) Identification of metal-responsive oribatid mites in a comparative survey of polluted soils. *Pedobiologia*, **52**, 207–221.

Khan M. R., Khan M. W. (1998) Interactive effects of ozone and root-knot nematode on tomato. *Agriculture, Ecosystems and Environment*, **70**, 97–107.

King K. L., Greenslade P., Hutchinson K. J. (1985) Collembolan associations in natural versus improved pastures of the New England tableland, NSW: Distribution of native and introduced species. *Australian Journal of Ecology*, **10**, 421–427.

Kitz F., Steinwandter M., Traugott M., Seeber J. (2015) Increased decomposer diversity accelerates and potentially stabilizes litter decomposition. *Soil Biology & Biochemistry*, **83**, 138–141.

Klironomos J. N. (2002) Feedback with soil biota contributes to plant rarity and invasiveness in communities. *Nature*, **417**, 67–70.
Klironomos J. N., Rillig M. C., Allen M. F. (1996) Below-ground microbial and microfauna response to *Artemisia tridentata* grown under elevated atmospheric CO_2. *Functional Ecology*, **10**, 527–534.
Klironomos J. N., Rillig M. C., Allen M. F. (1999) Designing belowground field experiments with the help of semi-variance and power analyses. *Applied Soil Ecology*, **12**, 227–238.
Konestabo H. S., Michelsen A., Holmstrup M. (2007) Responses of springtail and mite populations to prolonged periods of soil freeze–thaw cycles in a subarctic ecosystem. *Applied Soil Ecology*, **36**, 136–146.
Korthals G.W., Smilauer P.,Van Dijk C., van der Putten W. H. (2001) Linking above- and below-ground biodiversity: Abundance and trophic complexity in soil as a response to experimental plant communities on abandoned arable land. *Functional Ecology*, **15**, 506–514.
Korthals G.W., van de Ende A., van Megen H., et al. (1996) Short-term effects of cadmium, copper, nickel and zinc on soil nematodes from different feeding and life-history strategy groups. *Applied Soil Ecology*, **4**, 107–117.
Krantz G. W., Walter D. E. (2009) *A Manual of Acarology*, 3rd edn, Lubbock, TX, Texas Tech University Press.
Kuikman P. J., Jansen A. G., van Veen J. A., Zehnder A. J. B. (1990) Protozoan predation and the turnover of soil organic carbon and nitrogen in the presence of plants. *Biology and Fertility of Soils*, **10**, 22–28.
Kulmatiski A., Beard K. H., Stevens J. R., Cobbold S. M. (2008) Plant–soil feedbacks: A meta-analytical review. *Ecology Letters*, **11**, 980–992.
Kuntz M., Berner A., Gattinger A., et al. (2013) Influence of reduced tillage on earthworm and microbial communities under organic arable farming. *Pedobiologia*, **56**, 251–260.
Kupferschmied P., Maurhof M., Keel C. (2013) Promise for plant pest control: Root-associated pseudomonads with insecticidal activities. *Frontiers in Plant Science*, **4**, 287.
Kusnezov N. (1957) Numbers of species of ants in faunae of different latitudes. *Evolution*, **11**, 298–299.
Kwon T.-S., Kim S.-S., Chun J. H. (2014) Pattern of ant diversity in Korea: An empirical test of Rapoport's altitudinal rule. *Journal of Asia-Pacific Entomology*, **17**, 161–167.
Laakso J., Setälä H. (1999a) Population- and ecosystem-level effects of predation on microbial-feeding nematodes. *Oecologia*, **120**, 279–286.
Laakso J., Setälä H. (1999b) Sensitivity of primary production to changes in the architecture of belowground food webs. *Oikos*, **87**, 57–64.
Laakso J., Setälä H., Palojärvi A. (2000) Influence of decomposer food web structure and nitrogen availability on plant growth. *Plant and Soil*, **225**, 153–165.
Lacey L. A., Shapiro-Ilan D. I. (2008) Microbial control of insect pests in temperate orchard systems: Potential for incorporation into IPM. *Annual Review of Entomology*, **53**, 121–144.
Lal R. (2004) Soil carbon sequestration to mitigate climate change. *Geoderma*, **123**, 1–22.

Bibliography

Laliberté E., Kardol P., Didham R. K., et al. (2017) Soil fertility shapes belowground food webs across a regional climate gradient. *Ecology Letters*, **20**, 1273–1284.

Lambshead P. J. D. (1993) Recent developments in marine benthic biodiversity research. *Oceanis*, **19**, 5–24.

Landesman W. J., Treonis A. T., Dighton J. (2011) Effects of a one-year rainfall manipulation on soil nematode abundances and community composition. *Pedobiologia*, **54**, 87–91.

Lang B., Rall B. C., Scheu S., Brose U. (2014) Effects of environmental warming and drought on size-structured soil food webs. *Oikos*, **123**, 1224–1233.

Langford E. A., Nielsen U. N., Johnson S. N., Riegler M. (2014) Susceptibility of Queensland fruit fly, *Bactrocera tryoni* (Froggatt) (Diptera:Tephritidae), to entomopathogenic nematodes. *Biological Control*, **69**, 34–39.

Lara E., Heger T. J., Ekelund F., Lamentowicz M., Mitchell E. A. D. (2008) Ribosomal RNA genes challenge the monophyly of the Hyalospheniidae (Amoebozoa: Arcellinida). *Protist*, **159**, 165–176.

Larink O. (1997) Springtails and mites: Important knots in the food web of soils. In: *Fauna in Soil Ecosystems: Recycling Processes, Nutrient Fluxes, and Agricultural Production* (ed. Benckiser G.) pp. 225–264. New York, Marcel Dekker.

Lavelle P. (1983) *The Structure of Earthworm Communities*, London, Chapman & Hall.

Lavelle P., Blanchart E., Martin A., Spain A.V., Martin S. (1992) *Impact of Soil Fauna on the Properties of Soils in the Humid Tropics*, Madison, Soil Science Society of America.

Lavelle P. Decaëns T., Aubert M., et al. (2006) Soil invertebrates and ecosystem services. *European Journal of Soil Biology*, **42**, S3–S15.

Lavelle P., Lapied E. (2003) Endangered earthworms of Amazonia: And homage to Gilberto Righi. *Pedobiologia*, **47**, 419–427.

Lavelle P., Lattaud C., Trigo D., Barois I. (1995) Mutualism and biodiversity in soils. *Plant and Soil*, **170**, 23–33.

Lavelle P., Pashanasi B., Charpentier F., et al. (1998) Influence of earthworms on soil organic matter dynamics, nutrient dynamics and microbiological ecology. In: *Earthworm Ecology* (ed. Edwards C. A.) pp. 103–122. Boca Raton, FL, CRC Press.

Lavelle P., Spain A.V. (2001) *Soil Ecology*, Amsterdam, Kluwer Scientific.

Lebauer D.W., Treseder K. K. (2008) Nitrogen limitation of net primary productivity in terrestrial ecosystems is globally distributed. *Ecology*, **89**, 371–379.

Lee K. E. (1987) Peregrine species of earthworms. In: *On Earthworms* (eds. Pagliai A. M. B., Omodeo P.) pp. 315–328. Modena, Mucchi Editore.

Lee K. E., Foster R. C. (1991) Soil fauna and soil structure. *Australian Journal of Soil Research*, **29**, 745–775.

Legendre P., De Cáceres M. (2013) Beta diversity as the variance of community data: Dissimilarity coefficients and partitioning. *Ecology Letters*, **16**, 951–963.

Lehmann J., Kleber M. (2015) The contentious nature of soil organic matter. *Nature*, **60**, 60–68.

Lehmitz R., Russell D., Hohberg K., Christian A., Xylander W. E. R. (2012) Active dispersal of oribatid mites into young soils. *Applied Soil Ecology*, **55**, 10–19.

Leinaas H. P. (1983) Synchronized molting controlled by communication in group-living Collembola. *Science*, **219**, 193–195.

Leinaas H. P., Bengtsson J., Janion-Scheepers C., Chown S. L. (2015) Indirect effects of habitat disturbance on invasion: Nutritious litter from a grazing resistant plant favors alien over native Collembola. *Ecology and Evolution*, **5**, 3462–3471.

Leinaas H. P., Fjellberg A. (1985) Habitat structure and life-history strategies of two partly sympatric and closely related, lichen feeding Collembolan species. *Oikos*, **44**, 448–458.

Leniaud L., Dedeine F., Pichon A., Dupont S., Bagneres A. G. (2009) Geographical distribution, genetic diversity and social organization of a new European termite, *Reticulitermes urbis* (Isoptera: Rhinotermitidae). *Biological Invasions*, **12**, 1389–1402.

Lenoir L., Persson T., Bengtsson J., Wallander H., Wirén A. (2007) Bottom-up or top-down control in forest soil microcosms? Effects of soil fauna on fungal biomass and C/N mineralisation. *Biology and Fertility of Soils*, **43**, 281–294.

Lessaard J. P., Fordyce J. A., Gotelli N. J., Sanders N. J. (2009) Invasive ants alter the phylogenetic structure of ant communities. *Ecology*, **90**, 2664–2669.

Letourneau D. K., Jedlicka J. A., Bothwell S. G., Moreno C. R. (2009) Effects of natural enemy biodiversity on the suppression of arthropod herbivores in terrestrial ecosystems. *Annual Review of Ecology, Evolution and Systematics*, **40**, 573–592.

Li Q., Bao X., Lu C., et al. (2012) Soil microbial food web responses to free-air ozone enrichment can depend on the ozone-tolerance of wheat cultivars. *Soil Biology & Biochemistry*, **47**, 27–35.

Liang W., Jiang Y., Liu Q. L. Y., Wen D. (2005) Spatial distribution of bacterivorous nematodes in a Chinese Ecosystem Research Network (CERN) site. *Ecological Research*, **20**, 491–486.

Liao C., Peng R., Luo Y., et al. (2008) Altered ecosystem carbon and nitrogen cycles by plant invasion: A meta-analysis. *New Phytologist*, **177**, 706–714.

Liiri M., Häsä M., Haimi J., Setälä H. (2012) History of land-use intensity can modify the relationship between functional complexity of the soil fauna and soil ecosystem services – A microcosm study. *Applied Soil Ecology*, **55**, 53–61.

Liiri M., Setälä H., Haimi J., Pennanen T., Fritze H. (2002) Relationship between soil microarthropod species diversity and plant growth does not change when the system is disturbed. *Oikos*, **96**, 137–149.

Lindo Z., Winchester N. N. (2009) Spatial and environmental factors contributing to patterns in arboreal and terrestrial oribatid mite diversity across spatial scales. *Oecologia*, **160**, 817–825.

Liu M., Chen X., Griffiths B. S., et al. (2012) Dynamics of nematode assemblages and soil function in adjacent restored and degraded soils following disturbance. *European Journal of Soil Biology*, **49**, 37–46.

Liu T., Chen X., Ran W., Shen Q., Li H. (2016) Carbon-rich organic fertilizers to increase soil biodiversity: Evidence from a meta-analysis of nematode communities. *Agriculture, Ecosystems and Environment*, **232**, 199–207.

Lobry de Bruyn L., Conacher A. J. (1990) The role of termites and ants in soil modification: A review. *Australian Journal of Soil Research*, **28**, 55–93.

Long S. P., Ainsworth E. A., Rogers A., Ort D. R. (2004) Rising atmospheric carbon dioxide: Plants face the future. *Annual Review of Plant Biology*, **55**, 591–628.

Loof P. A. A. (1971) Freeliving and plant parasitic nematodes from Spitzbergen, collected by H. van Rossen. *Meded. Landbouwhogeschool Wageningen*, **71**, 1–86.

Loranger G., Bandyopadhyaya I., Razaka B., Ponge J. F. (2001) Does soil acidity explain altitudinal sequences in collembolan communities? *Soil Biology & Biochemistry*, **33**, 381–393.

Loranger G., Ponge J. F., Blanchart E., Lavelle P. (1998) Impact of earthworms on the diversity of microarthropods in a vertisol (Martinique). *Biology and Fertility of Soils*, **27**, 21–26.

Loranger G. I., Pregitzer K. S., King J. S. (2004) Elevated CO_2 and O_{3t} concentrations differentially affect selected groups of the fauna in temperate forest soils. *Soil Biology & Biochemistry*, **36**, 1521–1524.

Loreau M. (1987) Vertical distribution of activity of carabid beetles in a beech forest floor. *Pedobiologia*, **30**, 173–178.

Loreau M., Naeem S., Inchausti P., et al. (2001) Biodiversity and ecosystem functioning: Current knowledge and future challenges. *Science*, **294**, 804–808.

Luxton M. (1967) The zonation of saltmarsh Acarina. *Pedobiologia*, **7**, 257–277.

Luxton M. (1972) Studies on the oribatid mites of a Danish beech wood soil. I. Nutritional biology. *Pedobiologia*, **12**, 434–463.

Luxton M. (1982) The biology of mites from beech woodland soil. *Pedobiologia*, **23**, 1–8.

Lyford W. H. (1975) Overland migration of Collembola (*Hypogastrura nivicola* Fitch) colonies. *American Midland Naturalist*, **94**, 205–209.

Lynch J. M., Whipps J. M. (1990) Substrate flow in the rhizosphere. *Plant and Soil*, **129**, 1–10.

Maaß S., Caruso T., Rillig M. C. (2015) Functional role of microarthropods in soil aggregation. *Pedobiologia*, **58**, 59–63.

Maaß S., Migliorini M., Rillig M. C., Caruso T. (2014) Disturbance, neutral theory, and patterns of beta diversity in soil communities. *Ecology and Evolution*, **4**, 4766–4774.

Maboreke H. R., Graf M., Grams T. E. E., et al. (2017) Multitrophic interactions in the rhizosphere of a temperate forest tree affect plant carbon flow into the belowground food web. *Soil Biology & Biochemistry*, **115**, 526–536.

Macarthur R. H., Wilson E. O. (1967) *The Theory of Island Biogeography*, Princeton, NJ, Princeton University Press.

Macfadyen A. (1962) Soil arthropod sampling. *Advances in Ecological Research*, **1**, 1–34.

Macfadyen A. (1963) The contribution of the fauna to the total soil metabolism. In: *Soil Organisms* (eds. Doeksen J., Van Der Drift J.) pp. 3–17. Amsterdam, North Holland Publishing.

Macnamara C. (1924) The food of Collembola. *Canadian Entomology*, **56**, 99–105.

Madej G., Stodółka A. (2008) Successional changes and diversity of mesostigmatid mite communities (Acari: Mesostigmata) on reclaimed power plant waste dumps. *Annales Zoologici*, **58**, 267–278.

Magurran A. E. (2004) *Measuring Biological Diversity*, Oxford, Blackwell.

Majer J. D., Brennan K. E. C., Moir M. L. (2007) Invertebrates and the restoration of a forest ecosystem: 30 years of research following bauxite mining in Western Australia. *Restoration Ecology*, **15**, S104–S115.

Mando A., Brussaard L., Stroosnijder L. (1999) Termite- and mulch-mediated rehabilitation of vegetation on crusted soil in West Africa. *Restoration Ecology*, **7**, 33–41.

Mando A., Stroosnijder L., Brussaard L. (1996) Effects of termites on infiltration into crusted soil. *Geoderma*, **74**, 107–113.

Manning P. (2012) The impact of nitrogen enrichment on ecosystems and their services. In: *Soil Ecology and Ecosystem Services* (ed. Wall D. H.) pp. 256–269. Oxford, Oxford University Press.

Manning P., Newington J. E., Robson H. R., et al. (2006) Decoupling the direct and indirect effects of nitrogen deposition on ecosystem function. *Ecology Letters*, **9**, 1015–1024.

Maraun M., Alphei J., Bonkowski M., et al. (1999) Middens of the earthworm *Lumbricus terrestris* (Lumbricidae): Microhabitats for micro- and mesofauna in forest soil. *Pedobiologia*, **43**, 276–287.

Maraun M., Schatz H., Scheu S. (2007) Awesome or ordinary? Global diversity patterns of oribatid mites. *Ecography*, **30**, 209–216.

Marichal R., Grimaldi M., Feijoo M. A., et al. (2014) Soil macroinvertebrate communities and ecosystem services in deforested landscapes of Amazonia. *Applied Soil Ecology*, **83**, 177–185.

Mariotte P., Le Bayon R.-C., Eisenhauer N., Guenat C., Buttler A. (2016) Subordinate plant species moderate drought effects on earthworm communities in grasslands. *Soil Biology & Biochemistry*, **96**, 119–127.

Mariotte P., Mehrabi Z., Bezemer T. M., et al. (2018) Plant–soil feedback: Bridging natural and agricultural sciences. *Trends in Ecology and Evolution*, **33**, 129–142.

Maron J. L., Klironomos J. N., Waller L., Callaway R. A. (2014) Invasive plants escape from suppressive soil biota at regional scales. *Journal of Ecology*, **102**, 19–27.

Marshall D. J., Pugh P. J. A. (1996) Origin of the inland Acari of Continental Antarctica with particular reference to Dronning Maud Land. *Zoological Journal of the Linnean Society*, **118**, 101–118.

Martius C., Höfer H., Garcia M. V. B., et al. (2004) Microclimate in agroforestry systems in central Amazonia: Does canopy closure matter to soil organisms? *Agroforestry Systems*, **60**, 291–304.

Masters G. J., Brown V. K., Gange A. C. (1993) Plant mediated interactions between above- and below-ground insect herbivores. *Oikos*, **66**, 148–151.

Masters G. J., Jones T. H., Rogers M. (2001) Host-plant mediated effects of root herbivory on insect seed predators and their parasitoids. *Oecologia*, **127**, 246–250.

Mathieu J., Davies T. J. (2014) Glaciation as an historical filter of below-ground biodiversity. *Journal of Biogeography*, **41**, 1204–1214.

Mathieu J., Grimaldi M., Jouquet P., et al. (2009) Spatial patterns of grasses influence soil macrofauna biodiversity in Amazonian pastures. *Soil Biology & Biochemistry*, **41**, 586–593.

Mathieu J., Rossi J. P., Mora P., et al. (2005) Recovery of soil macrofauna communities after forest clearance in Eastern Amazonia, Brazil. *Conservation Biology*, **19**, 1598–1605.

Matthews J. A., Vater A. E. (2015) Pioneer zone geo-ecological change: Observations from a chronosequence on the Storbreen glacier foreland, Jotunheimen, southern Norway. *Catena*, **135**, 219–230.

McCary M. A., Martínez J.-C., Umek L., Heneghan L., Wise D. H. (2015) Effects of woodland restoration and management on the community of surface-active arthropods in the metropolitan Chicago region. *Biological Conservation*, **190**, 154–166.

McCary M. A., Mores R., Farfan M. A., Wise D. H. (2016) Invasive plants have different effects on trophic structure of green and brown food webs in terrestrial ecosystems: A meta-analysis. *Ecology Letters*, **19**, 328–335.
McGaughran A., Stevens M. I., Holland B. A. (2010) Biogeography of circum-Antarctic springtails. *Molecular Phylogenetics and Evolution*, **57**, 48–58.
McGill B. J., Enquist B. J., Weiher E., Westoby M. (2006) Rebuilding community ecology from functional traits. *Trends in Ecology and Evolution*, **21**, 178–185.
McInnis S. J., Pugh P. J. A. (2007) An attempt to revisit the global biogeography of limno-terrestrial Tardigrada. *Journal of Limnology*, **66 (Suppl. 1)**, 90–96.
Meehan T. D., Crossley M. S., Lindroth R. L. (2010) Impacts of elevated CO_2 and O_3 on aspen leaf litter chemistry and earthworm and springtail productivity. *Soil Biology & Biochemistry*, **42**, 1132–1137.
Meloni F., Varanda E. M. (2015) Litter and soil arthropod colonization in reforested semi-deciduous seasonal Atlantic forests. *Restoration Ecology*, **23**, 690–697.
Middleton E. L., Bever J. D. (2012) Inoculation with a native soil community advances succession in a grassland restoration. *Restoration Ecology*, **20**, 218–226.
Migliorini M., Pigino G., Caruso T., et al. (2005) Soil communities (Acari Oribatida; Hexapoda Collembola) in a clay pigeon shooting range. *Pedobiologia*, **49**, 1–13.
Mikola J., Bardgett R. D., Hedlund K. (2002) Biodiversity, ecosystem functioning and soil decomposer food webs. In: *Biodiversity and Ecosystem Functioning – Synthesis and Perspectives* (eds. Loreau M., Naeem S., Inchausti P.) pp. 169–180. Oxford, Oxford University Press.
Mikola J., Setälä H. (1998) No evidence of trophic cascades in an experimental microbial-based soil food web. *Ecology*, **79**, 153–164.
Milchunas D. G., Mosier A. R., Morgan J. A., et al. (2005) Root production and tissue quality in a shortgrass steppe exposed to elevated CO_2: Using a new ingrowth method. *Plant and Soil*, **268**, 111–122.
Milcu A., Manning P. (2011) All size classes of soil fauna and litter quality control the acceleration of litter decay in its home environment. *Oikos*, **120**, 1366–1370.
Minor M. A., Cianciolo J. M. (2007) Diversity of soil mites (Acari: Oribatida, Mesostigmata) along a gradient of land use types in New York. *Applied Soil Ecology*, **35**, 140–153.
Mitchell E. A. D., Borcard D., Buttler A. J., et al. (2000) Horizontal distribution patterns of testate amoeba (Protozoa) in a *Sphagnum magellanicum* carpet. *Microbial Ecology*, **39**, 290–300.
Mitchell E. A. D., Meisterfeld R. (2005) Taxonomic confusion blurs the debate on cosmopolitanism versus local endemism of free-living protists. *Protist*, **156**, 263–267.
Mitchell R. J., Urpeth H. M., Britton A. J., Black H., Taylor A. R. (2016) Relative importance of local- and large-scale drivers of alpine soil microarthropod communities. *Oecologia*, 913–924.
Mittelbach G. G., Steiner C. F., Scheiner S. M., et al. (2001) What is the observed relationship between species richness and productivity? *Ecology*, **82**, 2381–2396.
Monroy F., van der Putten W. H., Yergeau E., et al. (2012) Community patterns of soil bacteria and nematodes in relation to geographic distance. *Soil Biology & Biochemistry*, **45**, 1–7.

Moreau C. S., Bell C. D., Vila R., Archibald S. B., Pierce N. E. (2006) Phylogeny of the ants: Diversification in the age of angiosperms. *Science*, **312**, 101–104.

Moroenyane I., Dong K., Singh D., Chimphango S. B. M., Adams J. M. (2016) Deterministic processes dominate nematode community structure in the Fynbos Mediterranean heathland of South Africa. *Evolutionary Ecology*, **30**, 685–701.

Morriën E., Hannula S. E., Snoek L. B., et al. (2017) Soil networks become more connected and take up more carbon as nature restoration progresses. *Nature Communications*, **8**, 14349, doi: 10.1038/ncomms14349.

Mulder C., Ahrestani F. S., Bahn M., et al. (2013) Connecting the green and brown worlds: Allometric and stoichiometric predictability of above- and belowground networks. *Advances in Ecological Research*, **49**, 69–175.

Mulder C., Baerselman R., Posthuma C. (2007) Empirical maximum lifespan of earthworms is twice that of mice. *Age (Dordr)*, **29**, 229–231.

Mulder C., Boit A., Bonkowski M., et al. (2011) A belowground perspective on Dutch agroecosystems: How soil organisms interact to support ecosystem services. *Advances in Ecological Research*, **44**, 277–357.

Mulder C., Hettelingh J.-P., Montanarella L., et al. (2015) Chemical footprints of anthropogenic nitrogen deposition on recent soil C:N ratios in Europe. *Biogeosciences*, **12**, 4113–4119.

Murphy D. H. (1955) Long-term changes in collembolan populations with special reference to moorland soils. In: *Soil Zoology* (ed. Kevan D. K. McE) pp. 157–166. London, Buttersworth.

Murray P. J., Hatch D. J. (1994) Sitona weevils (Coleoptera, Curculionidae) as agents for rapid transfer of nitrogen from white clover (*Trifolium repens* L.) to perennial ryegrass (*Lolium perenne* L.). *Annals of Applied Biology*, **125**, 29–33.

Neher D. A., Weicht T. R. (2013) Nematode genera in forest soil respond differentially to elevated CO_2. *Journal of Nematology*, **45**, 214–222.

Neidig N., Jousset A., Nunes F., et al. (2010) Interference between bacterial feeding nematodes and amoebae relies on innate and inducible mutual toxicity. *Functional Ecology*, **24**, 1133–1138.

Neufeld J. D., Wagner M., Murrell J. C. (2009) Who eats what, where and when? Isotope-labelling experiments are coming of age. *The ISME Journal*, **1**, 103–110.

Newington J. E., Setälä H., Bezemer T. M., Jones T. H. (2004) Potential effects of earthworms on leaf-chewer performance. *Functional Ecology*, **18**, 746–751.

Ngosong C., Gabriel E., Ruess L. (2014) Collembola grazing on arbuscular mycorrhiza fungi modulates nutrient allocation in plants. *Pedobiologia*, **57**, 171–179.

Ngosong C., Raupp J., Richnow H.-H., Ruess L. (2011) Tracking Collembola feeding strategies by the natural C-13 signal of fatty acids in an arable soil with different fertilizer regimes. *Pedobiologia*, **54**, 225–233.

Nicholas W. L., Viswanathan S. (1975) A study of the nutrition of *Caenorhabditis briggsae* (Rhabditidae) fed Oo ^{14}C and ^{32}P-labelled bacteria. *Nematologica*, **21**, 385–400.

Nielsen U. N., Ayres E., Wall D. H., Bardgett R. D. (2011a) Soil biodiversity and carbon cycling: A synthesis of studies examining diversity–function relationships. *European Journal of Soil Science*, **62**, 105–116.

Nielsen U. N., Ayres E., Wall D. H., et al. (2014) Global-scale patterns of assemblage structure of soil nematodes in relation to climate and ecosystem properties. *Global Ecology and Biogeography*, **23**, 968–978.

Nielsen U. N., Ball B. A. (2015) Impacts of altered precipitation regimes on soil communities and biogeochemistry in arid and semi-arid ecosystems. *Global Change Biology*, **21**, 1407–1421.

Nielsen U. N., Gilarte P., Ochoa-Hueso R., et al. (2016) Effects of altered precipitation patterns on soil fauna in an Australian grassland. In: *Invertebrate Ecology of Australasian Grasslands. Proceedings of the Ninth ACGIE* (ed. Johnson S. N.). Penrith, Western Sydney University.

Nielsen U. N., Osler G. H. R., Campbell C. D., Burslem D. F. R. P., van der Wal R. (2010a) The influence of vegetation type, soil properties and precipitation on the composition of soil mite and microbial communities at the landscape scale. *Journal of Biogeography*, **37**, 1317–1328.

Nielsen U. N., Osler G. H. R., Campbell C. D., Burslem D. F. R. P., van der Wal R. (2012a) Predictors of fine-scale spatial variation in soil mite and microbe community composition differ between biotic groups and habitats. *Pedobiologia*, **55**, 83–91.

Nielsen U. N., Osler G. H. R., Campbell C. D., et al. (2010b) The enigma of soil animal species diversity revisited: The role of small-scale heterogeneity. *PloS ONE*, **5**, e11567.

Nielsen U. N., Osler G. H. R., van der Wal R., Campbell C. D., Burslem D. F. R. P. (2008) Soil pore volume and the abundance of soil mites in two contrasting habitats. *Soil Biology & Biochemistry*, **40**, 1538–1541.

Nielsen U. N., Prior S., Delroy B., et al. (2015a) Response of belowground communities to short-term phosphorus addition in a phosphorus-limited woodland. *Plant and Soil*, **391**, 321–331.

Nielsen U. N., Wall D. H. (2013) The future of soil invertebrate communities in polar regions: Different climate change responses in the Arctic and Antarctic? *Ecology Letters*, **16**, 409–419.

Nielsen U. N., Wall D. H., Adams B. J., Virginia R. A. (2011b) Antarctic nematode communities: Observed and predicted responses to climate change. *Polar Biology*, **34**, 1701–1711.

Nielsen U. N., Wall D. H., Adams B. J., et al. (2012b) The ecology of pulse events: Insights from an extreme climatic event in a polar desert ecosystem. *Ecosphere*, **3**, Article 17.

Nielsen U. N., Wall D. H., Li G., Toro M., Adams B. J., Virginia R. A. (2011c) Nematode communities of Byers Peninsula, Livingston Island, maritime Antarctica. *Antarctic Science*, **23**, 349–357.

Nielsen U. N., Wall D. H., Six J. (2015b) Soil biodiversity and the environment. *Annual Review of Environment and Resources*, **40**, 63–90.

Niemelä J., Haila Y., Halme E., Pajunen T., Punttila P. (1992) Small-scale heterogeneity in the spatial distribution of carabid beetles in the southern Finnish taiga. *Journal of Biogeography*, **19**, 173–181.

Niklaus P. A., Alphei J., Ebersberger D., et al. (2003) Six years of in situ CO_2 enrichment evoke changes in soil structure and soil biota of nutrient-poor grassland. *Global Change Biology*, **9**, 585–600.

Nkem J. N., Wall D. H., Virginia R. A., et al. (2006) Wind dispersal of soil invertebrates in the McMurdo Dry Valleys, Antarctica. *Polar Biology*, **29**, 346–352.

Noble J. C., Whitford W. G., Kaliszweski M. (1996) Soil and litter microarthropod populations from two contrasting ecosystems in semi-arid eastern Australia. *Journal of Arid Environments*, **32**, 329–346.

Norton D. C. (1978) *Ecology of Plant-Parasitic Nematodes*, New York, John Wiley.

Nowak E. (2001) Enchytraeid communities in successional habitats (from meadow to forest). *Pedobiologia*, **45**, 497–508.

Nowrouzi S., Andersen A. N., Macfadyen S., et al. (2016) Ant diversity and distribution along elevation gradients in the Australian wet tropics: The importance of seasonal moisture stability. *PloS ONE*, **11(4)**, e0153420, doi:10.1371/journal.pone.0153420

O'Connor F. B. (1967) The Enchytraeidae. In: *Soil Biology* (eds. Burges A., Raw F.) pp. 213–257. London and New York, Academic Press.

O'Dowd D. J., Green P. T., Lake P. S. (2003) Invasional meltdown on an oceanic island. *Ecology Letters*, **6**, 812–817.

Oerke E.-C. (2006) Crop losses to pests. *Journal of Agricultural Science*, **144**, 31–43.

Oliver I., Garden D., Greenslade P. J., et al. (2005) Effects of fertilizer and grazing on the arthropod communities of a native grassland in South-Eastern Australia. *Agriculture, Ecosystems & Environment*, **109**, 323–334.

Orgiazzi A., Bardgett R. D., Barrios E., et al. (2016) *Global Soil Biodiversity Atlas*, Luxembourg, Publications Office of the European Union.

Orgiazzi A., Dunbar M. B., de Groot G. A., Lemanceau P. (2015) Soil biodiversity and DNA barcodes: Opportunities and challenges. *Soil Biology & Biochemistry*, **80**, 244–250.

Osler G. H. R., Beattie A. J. (1999) Taxonomic and structural similarities in soil oribatid communities. *Ecography*, **22**, 567–574.

Osler G. H. R., Beattie A. J. (2001) Contribution of oribatid and mesostigmatid soil mites in ecologically based estimates of global species richness. *Austral Ecology*, **26**, 70–79.

Osler G. H. R., Sommerkorn M. (2007) Toward a complete soil C and N cycle: Incorporating the soil fauna. *Ecology*, **88**, 1611–1621.

Ostle N., Briones M. J. I., Ineson P., et al. (2007) Isotopic detection of recent photosynthate carbon flow into grassland rhizosphere fauna. *Soil Biology & Biochemistry*, **39**, 768–777.

Ostle N. J., Smith P., Fisher R., et al. (2009) Integrating plant–soil interactions into global carbon cycle models. *Journal of Ecology*, **97**, 851–863.

Ouédraogo E., Mando A., Brussaard L. (2006) Soil macrofauna affect crop water and nitrogen use efficiencies in semi-arid West Africa. *European Journal of Soil Biology*, **42 (Suppl. 1)**, S275–S277.

Paoletti M. G. (1999) The role of earthworms for assessment of sustainability and as bioindicators. *Agriculture, Ecosystems and Environment*, **74**, 137–155.

Parmelee R. W., Bohlen P. J., Blair J. M. (1998) Earthworms and nutrient cycling processes: Integrating across the ecological hierarchy. In: *Earthworm Ecology* (ed. Edwards C. A.) pp. 123–143. Boca Raton, FL, St. Lucie Press.

Parnikoza I., Convey P., Dykyy I., et al. (2009) Current status of the Antarctic herb tundra formation in the Central Argentine Islands. *Global Change Biology*, **15**, 1685–1693.

Parr C. L., Robertson H. G., Biggs H. C., Chown S. L. (2004) Response of African savanna ants to long-term fire regimes. *Journal of Applied Ecology*, **41**, 630–642.

Patten B. C., Witkamp M. (1967) Systems analysis of ^{134}cesium kinetics in terrestrial microcosms. *Ecology*, **48**, 813–824.

Pauli N., Barrios E., Conacher A. J. (2011) Soil macrofauna in agricultural landscapes dominated by the Quesungual slash-and mulch agroforestry system, western Honduras. *Applied Soil Ecology*, **47**, 119–132.

Paustian K., Collins H. P., Paul E. A. (1997) Management controls on soil carbon. In: *Soil Organic Matter in Temperate Agroecosystems* (ed. Paul E. A.) pp. 15–49. Boca Raton, FL, CRC Press.

Pavao-Zuckerman M. A., Sookhdeo C. (2017) Nematode community response to green infrastructure design in a semiarid city. *Journal of Environmental Quality*, **46**, 687–694.

Peltzer D. A., Bellingham P. J., Kurokawa H., et al. (2009) Punching above their weight: Low-biomass non-native plant species alter soil properties during primary succession. *Oikos*, **118**, 1001–1014.

Peltzer D. A., Wardle D. A., Allison V. J., et al. (2010) Understanding ecosystem retrogression. *Ecological Monographs*, **80**, 509–529.

Pendall E., Bridgham S., Hanson P. J., et al. (2004a) Below-ground process responses to elevated CO_2 and temperature: A discussion of observations, measurement methods, and models. *New Phytologist*, **162**, 311–322.

Pendall E., Mosier A. R., Morgan J. A. (2004b) Rhizodeposition stimulated by elevated CO_2 in a semiarid grassland. *New Phytologist*, **162**, 447–458.

Penev L. D. (1992) Qualitative and quantitative spatial variation in soil wire-worm assemblages in relation to climate and habitat factors. *Oikos*, **63**, 180–192.

Peñuelas J., Sardans J., Rivas-Ubach A., Janssens I. A. (2012) The human-induced imbalance between C, N and P in Earth's life system. *Global Change Biology*, **18**, 3–6.

Perry R. N. (1996) Chemoreception in plant parasitic nematodes. *Annual Review of Phytopathology*, **34**, 181–199.

Persson T., Bååth E., Clarholm M., et al. (1980) Trophic structure, biomass dynamics and carbon metabolism in a Scots pine forest. *Ecological Bulletins*, **32**, 419–459.

Petersen H., Krogh P. H. (1987) Effects of perturbing microarthropod communities of a permanent pasture and a rye field by an insecticide and a fungicide. In: *Soil Fauna and Soil Fertility* (ed. Strignova B. R.) pp. 217–229. Moscow, Proceedings of the 9th International Colloquium on Soil Zoology.

Petersen H., Luxton M. (1982) A comparative-analysis of soil fauna populations and their role in decomposition processes. *Oikos*, **39**, 287–388.

Petzold-Maxwell J. L., Jaronski S. T., Clifton E. H., et al. (2013) Interactions among Bt maize, entomopathogens, and rootworm species (Coleoptera: Chrysomelidae) in the field: Effects on survival, yield, and root injury. *Journal of Economic Entomology*, **106**, 622–632.

Pey B., Nahmani J., Auclerc A., et al. (2014) Current use of and future needs for soil invertebrate functional traits in community ecology. *Basic and Applied Ecology*, **15**, 194–206.

Pfeiffer M., Chimedregzen L., Ulykpan K. (2003) Community organization and species richness of ants (Hymenoptera/Formicidae) in Mongolia along an ecological gradient from steppe to Gobi desert. *Journal of Biogeography*, **30**, 1921–1935.

Bibliography · 331

Phillips R. P., Finzi A. C., Bernhardt E. S. (2011) Enhanced root exudation induces microbial feedbacks to N cycling in a pine forest under long-term CO_2 fumigation. *Ecology Letters*, **14**, 187–194.

Pieterse C. M. J., Zamioudis R. L. B., Weller D. M., Van Wees S. C. M., Bakker P. A. H. M. (2014) Induced systemic resistance by beneficial microbes. *Annual Review of Phytopathology*, **52**, 347–375.

Pilato G., Binda M. G. (2001) Biogeography and limno-terrestrial tardigrades: Are they truly incompatible binomials? *Zoologisher Anzeigler*, **240**, 511–516.

Poff N. (1997) Landscape filters and species traits: Towards mechanistic understanding and prediction in stream ecology. *Journal of the North American Benthological Society*, **16**, 391–409.

Poll J., Marhan S., Haase S., et al. (2007) Low amounts of herbivory by root-knot nematodes affect microbial community dynamics and carbon allocation in the rhizosphere. *FEMS Microbiology Ecology*, **62**, 268–279.

Pollierer M. M., Langel R., Körner C., Maraun M., Scheu S. (2007) The underestimated importance of belowground carbon input for forest soil animal food webs. *Ecology Letters*, **10**, 729–736.

Pollierer M. M., Langel R., Scheu S., Maraun M. (2009) Compartmentalization of the soil animal food web as indicated by dual analysis of stable isotope ratios ($^{15}N/^{14}N$ and $^{13}C/^{12}C$). *Soil Biology & Biochemistry*, **41**, 1221–1226.

Ponge J.-F. (2003) Humus forms in terrestrial ecosystems: A framework to biodiversity. *Soil Biology & Biochemistry*, **35**, 935–945.

Ponge J.-F., Dubs F., Gillet S., Sousa J. P., Lavelle P. (2006) Decreased biodiversity in soil springtail communities: The importance of dispersal and landuse history in heterogeneous landscapes. *Soil Biology & Biochemistry*, **38**, 1158–1161.

Ponge J.-F., Pérès G., Guernion M., et al. (2013) The impact of agricultural practices on soil biota: A regional study. *Soil Biology & Biochemistry*, **67**, 271–284.

Pop V. V. (1998) Earthworm biology and ecology – A case study: The genus *Octodrilus omodeo*, 1956 (Oligochaeta, Lumbricidae), from the Carpathians. In: *Earthworm Ecology* (ed. Edwards C. A.) pp. 65–103. Boca Raton, FL, St. Lucie Press.

Popp E. (1962) Semiaquatile Lebensräume (Bülten) im Hoch- und Niedermooren II. *Internationale Revue der gesamten Hydrobiologie*, **47**, 533–579.

Porazinska D. L., Giblin-Davis R. M., Faller L., et al. (2009) Evaluating high-throughput sequencing as a method for metagenomic analysis of nematode diversity. *Molecular Ecology Resources*, **9**, 1439–1450.

Porazinska D. L., Giblin-Davis R. M., Sequivel A., et al. (2010) Ecometagenetics confirm high tropical rainforest nematode diversity. *Molecular Ecology*, **19**, 5521–5530.

Porco D., Decaëns T., Deharveng L., et al. (2013) Biological invasions in soil: DNA barcoding as a monitoring tool in a multiple taxa survey targeting European earthworms and springtails in North America. *Biological Invasions*, **15**, 899–910.

Post E., Forchhammer M. C., Bret-Harte M. S., et al. (2009) Ecological dynamics across the Arctic associated with recent climate change. *Science*, **325**, 1355–1358.

Postma-Blaauw M. B., Bloem J., Faber J. H., et al. (2006) Earthworm species composition affects the soil bacterial community and net nitrogen mineralization. *Pedobiologia*, **50**, 243–256.

Postma-Blaauw M. B., de Goede R. G. M., Bloem J., Faber J. H., Brussaard L. (2010) Soil biota community structure and abundance under agricultural intensification and extensification. *Ecology*, **91**, 460–473.

Postma-Blaauw M. B., de Goede R. G. M., Bloem J., Faber J. H., Brussaard L. (2012) Agricultural intensification and de-intensification differentially affect taxonomic diversity of predatory mites, earthworms, enchytraeids, nematodes and bacteria. *Applied Soil Ecology*, **57**, 39–49.

Postma-Blaauw M. B., deVries F.T., de Goede R. G. M., et al. (2005) Within-trophic group interactions of bacterivorous nematode species and their effects on the bacterial community and nitrogen mineralization. *Oecologia*, **142**, 428–439.

Poveda K., Steffan-Dewenter I., Scheu S., Tscharntke T. (2005) Effects of decomposers and herbivores on plant performance and aboveground plant–insect interactions. *Oikos*, **108**, 503–510.

Poveda K., Steffan-Dewenter I., Scheu S., Tscharntke T. (2006) Belowground effects of organic and conventional farming on aboveground plant–herbivore and plant–pathogen interactions. *Agriculture, Ecosystems & Environment*, **113**, 162–167.

Powers L. E., Ho M. C., Freckman D.W., Virginia R. A. (1998) Distribution, community structure, and microhabitats of soil invertebrates along an elevational gradient in Taylor Valley, Antarctica. *Arctic and Alpine Research*, **30**, 133–141.

Prasse I. (1989) Indications of structural changes in the communities of microarthropods of the soil in an agro-ecosystem after applying herbicides. *Agriculture, Ecosystems & Environment*, **13**, 205–215.

Procter D. L. C. (1984) Towards a biogeography of free-living soil nematodes. 1. Changing species richness, diversity and densities with latitude. *Journal of Biogeography*, **11**, 103–117.

Procter D. L. C. (1990) Global overview of the functional roles of soil-living nematodes in terrestrial communities and ecosystems. *Journal of Nematology*, **22**, 1–7.

Prot J.-C. (1980) Migration of plant parasitic nematodes toward plant roots. *Revue Nématology*, **3**, 305–318.

Puppe D., Ehrmann O., Kaczorek D., Wanner M., Sommer M. (2015) The protozoic Si pool in temperate forest ecosystems – Quantification, abiotic controls and interactions with earthworms. *Geoderma*, **243–244**, 196–204.

Purtauf T., Roschewitz I., Dauber J., et al. (2005) Landscape context of organic and conventional farms: Influences on carabid beetle diversity. *Agriculture, Ecosystems & Environment*, **108**, 165–174.

Qiu J. J., Westerdahl B. B., Pryor A. (2009) Reduction of root-knot nematode, *Meloidogyne javanica*, and ozone mass transfer in soil treated with ozone. *Journal of Nematology*, **41**, 241–246.

Qiu Q., Wu J., Liang G., et al. (2015) Effects of simulated acid rain on soil and soil solution chemistry in a monsoon evergreen broadleaved forest in southern China. *Environmental Monitoring and Assessment*, **187**, 272.

Quist C. W., Gort G., Mulder C., et al. (2017) Feeding preference as a main determinant of microscale patchiness among terrestrial nematodes. *Molecular Ecology Resources*, **17**, 1257–1270.

Quist C.W., Smant G., Helder J. (2015) Evolution of plant parasitism in the Phylum Nematoda. *Annual Review of Phytopathology*, **53**, 289–310.

Rahbek C. (1995) The elevational gradient of species richness: A uniform pattern? *Ecography*, **18**, 200–205.

Rahbek C. (2005) The role of spatial scale and the perception of large-scale species-richness patterns. *Ecology Letters*, **8**, 224–239.
Rahman L., Whitelaw-Weckert M. A., Orchard B. (2014) Impact of organic soil amendments, including poultry-litter biochar, on nematodes in a Riverina, New South Wales, vineyard. *Soil Research*, **52**, 604–619.
Raw F. (1967) Arthropods (except Acari and Collembola). In: *Soil Biology* (eds. Burges A., Raw F.) pp. 323–362. London and New York, Academic Press.
Reay F., Wallace H. R. (1981) Plant nematodes associated with native vegetation in South Australia. *Nematologica*, **27**, 319–329.
Reinhart K. O., Callaway R. A. (2006) Soil biota and invasive plants. *New Phytologist*, **170**, 445–457.
Reynolds H. L., Packer A., Bever J. D., Clay K. (2003) Grassroots ecology: Plant–microbe–soil interactions as drivers of plant community structure and dynamics. *Ecology*, **84**, 2281–2291.
Reynolds J. F., Smith D. M., Lambin E. F., et al. (2007) Global desertification: Building a science for dryland development. *Science*, **316**, 847–851.
Ritz K., Black H. I. J., Campbell C. D., Harris J. A., Wood C. (2009) Selecting biological indicators for monitoring soils: A framework for balancing scientific and technical opinion to assist policy development. *Ecological Indicators*, **9**, 1212–1221.
Roberts D. W., Humber R. A. (1981) Entomogenous fungi In: *Biology of Conidial Fungi* (eds. Cole G. T., Kendrick W. B.) pp. 201–236. New York, Academic.
Robertson G. P., Freckman D. W. (1995) The spatial distribution of nematode trophic groups across a cultivated ecosystem. *Ecology*, **76**, 1425–1432.
Robeson M. S., King A. J., Freeman K. R., et al. (2011) Soil rotifer communities are extremely diverse globally but spatially autocorrelated locally. *Proceedings of the National Academy of Sciences of the United States of America*, **108**, 4406–4410.
Roger-Estrade J., Anger C., Bertrand M., Richard G. (2010) Tillage and soil ecology: Partners for sustainable agriculture. *Soil Tillage Research*, **111**, 33–40.
Rogers H. H., Prior S. A., Runion G. B., Mitchell R. J. (1996) Root to shoot ratio of crops as influenced by CO_2. *Plant and Soil*, **187**, 229–248.
Rønn R., Griffiths B. S., Ekelund F., Christensen S. (1996) Spatial distribution and successional pattern of microbial activity and micro-faunal populations on decomposing barley roots. *Journal of Applied Ecology*, **33**, 662–672.
Rønn R., Mccaig A., Griffiths B. S., Prosser I. (2002) Impact of protozoan grazing on bacterial community structure in soil microcosms. *Applied and Environmental Microbiology*, **68**, 6094–6105.
Rouatt J. W., Katznelson H., Payne T. M. B. (1960) Statistical evaluation of the rhizosphere effect. *Proceedings – Soil Science Society of America*, **24**, 271–273.
Ruess L., Chamberlain P. M. (2010) The fat that matters: Soil food web analysis using fatty acids and their carbon stable isotope signature. *Soil Biology & Biochemistry*, **42**, 1898–1910.
Ruf A., Beck L. (2005) The use of predatory soil mites in ecological soil classification and assessment concepts, with perspectives for oribatid mites. *Ecotoxicology and Environmental Safety*, **62**, 290–299.
Ruiz-Jean M. C., Aide T. M. (2005) Restoration success: How is it being measured? *Restoration Ecology*, **13**, 569–577.

Rusek J. (1985) Soil microstructures – Contributions on specific soil organisms. *Quaestiones Entomologicae*, **21**, 497–514.
Rusek J. (1998) Biodiversity of the Collembola and their functional role in ecosystems. *Biodiversity and Conservation*, **7**, 1207–1219.
Rusek J., Úlehlová B., Unar J. (1975) Soil biological features of some alpine grasslands in Czechoslovakia. In: *Progress in Soil Zoology* (ed. Vanek J.) pp. 199–215. Praha, Academia.
Rusek J., Weyda F. (1981) Morphology, ultrastructure and function of pseudocelli in *Onychiurus armatus* (Collembola, Onychiuridae). *Revue d'Écologie et de Biologie du Sol*, **18**, 127–133.
Rutgers M., Orgiazzi A., Gardi C., et al. (2014) Mapping earthworm communities in Europe. *Applied Soil Ecology*, **97**, 98–111.
Ryalls J. M. W., Moore B. D., Riegler M., Johnson S. N. (2016) Above-belowground herbivore interactions in mixed plant communities are influenced by altered precipitation patterns. *Frontiers in Plant Science*, **7**, Article 345.
Sackett T. E., Classen A. T., Sanders N. S. (2010) Linking soil food web structure to above- and belowground ecosystem processes: A meta-analysis. *Oikos*, **119**, 1984–1992.
Saetre P. (1998) Decomposition, microbial community structure, and earthworm effects along a birch-spruce soil gradient. *Ecology*, **79**, 834–846.
Sala O. E., Chapin F. S. I., Armesto J. J., et al. (2000) Global biodiversity scenarios for the year 2100. *Science*, **287**, 1770–1774.
Salmon J. T. (1941) The collembolan fauna of New Zealand, including a discussion of its distribution and affinities. *Transactions of the Royal Society of New Zealand*, **70**, 282–431.
Salmon S., Ponge J.-F., Gachet S., et al. (2014) Linking species, traits and habitat characteristics of Collembola at European scale. *Soil Biology & Biochemistry*, **75**, 73–85.
San-Blas E. (2013) Progress on entomopathogenic nematology research: A bibliometric study of the last three decades; 1980–2010. *Biological Control*, **66**, 102–124.
Sánchez-Moreno S. (2010) Suppressive service of the soil food web: Effects of environmental management. *Agriculture, Ecosystems & Environment*, **119**, 75–87.
Sánchez-Moreno S., Camargo J. A., Navas A. (2006) Ecotoxicological assessment of the impact of residual heavy metals on soil nematodes in the Guadiamar River Basin (Southern Spain). *Environmental Monitoring and Assessment*, **116**, 245–262.
Sanders N. J., Gotelli N. J., Gordon D. M. (2003) Community disassembly by an invasive species. *Proceedings of the National Academy of Sciences of the United States of America*, **100**, 2474–2477.
Sanders N. J., Lessard J.-P., Fitzpatrick M. C., Dunn R. R. (2007) Temperature, but not productivity or geometry, predicts elevational diversity gradients in ants across spatial grains. *Global Ecology and Biogeography*, **16**, 640–649.
Sanderson R. A., Rushton S. P., Cherrill A. J., Byrne J. P. (1995) Soil, vegetation and space: An analysis of their effects on the invertebrate communities of a moorland in north-east England. *Journal of Applied Ecology*, **32**, 506–518.
Santos P. F., Phillips J., Whitford W. G. (1981) The role of mites and nematodes in early stages of buried litter decomposition in a desert. *Ecology*, **62**, 664–669.

Satchell J. E. (1967) Lumbricidae. In: *Soil Biology* (eds. Burges A., Raw F.) pp. 259–322. London and New York, Academic Press.
Schädler M., Jung G., Brandl R., Auge H. (2004) Secondary succession is influenced by belowground insect herbivory on a productive site. *Oecologia*, **138**, 242–252.
Schaefer M., Schauermann J. (1990) The soil fauna of beech forests: Comparison between a mull and a moder soil. *Pedobiologia*, **34**, 299–314.
Scherber C., Eisenhauer N., Weisser W. W., et al. (2010) Bottom-up effects of plant diversity on multitrophic interactions in a biodiversity experiment. *Nature*, **468**, 553–556.
Scheu S., Albers D., Alphei J., et al. (2003) The soil fauna community in pure and mixed stands of beech and spruce of different age: Trophic structure and structuring forces. *Oikos*, **101**, 225–238.
Scheu S., Ruess L., Bonkowski M. (2005) Interactions between microorganisms and soil micro- and mesofauna. In: *Soil Biology, Microorganisms in Soils: Roles in Genesis and Functions* (eds. Buscot F., Varma A.) pp. 253–275. Berlin, Springer-Verlag.
Scheu S., Schulz E. (1996) Secondary succession, soil formation and development of a diverse community of oribatids and saprophagous soil macro-invertebrates. *Biodiversity and Conservation*, **5**, 235–250.
Scheu S., Theenshaus A., Hefin Jones T. (1999) Links between the detritivore and the herbivore system: Effects of earthworms and Collembola on plant growth and aphid development. *Oecologia*, **119**, 541–551.
Schlegel J., Riesen M. (2012) Environmental gradients and succession patterns of carabid beetles (Coleoptera: Carabidae) in an Alpine glacier retreat zone. *Journal of Insect Conservation*, **16**, 657–675.
Schmelz R. M., Niva C. C., Römbke J., Collado R. (2013) Diversity of terrestrial Enchytraeidae (Oligochaeta) in Latin America: Current knowledge and future research potential. *Applied Soil Ecology*, **69**, 13–20.
Schmidt M. H., Roschewitz I., Theis C., Tscharntke T. (2005) Differential effects of landscape and management on diversity and density of ground-dwelling farmland spiders. *Journal of Applied Ecology*, **42**, 281–287.
Schneider K., Migge S., Norton R. A., et al. (2004) Trophic niche differentiation in soil microarthropods (Oribatida, Acari): Evidence from stable isotope ratios ($^{15}N/^{14}N$). *Soil Biology & Biochemistry*, **36**, 1769–1774.
Schoener T. W. (1974) Resource partitioning in ecological communities. *Science*, **185**, 27–39.
Schon N. L., Mackay A. D., Gray R. A., van Koten C., Dodd M. B. (2017) Influence of earthworm abundance and diversity on soil structure and the implications for soil services throughout the season. *Pedobiologia – Journal of Soil Ecology*, **62**, 41–47.
Schrader S., Bender J., Weigel H. J. (2009) Ozone exposure of field-grown winter wheat affects soil mesofauna in the rhizosphere. *Environmental Pollution*, **157**, 3357–3362.
Schuldt A., Assmann T. (2009) Environmental and historical effects on richness and endemism patterns of carabid beetles in the western Palaearctic. *Ecography*, **32**, 705–714.
Schultz J. C., Appel H. M., Ferrieri A. P., Arnold T. M. (2013) Flexible resource allocation during plant defense responses. *Frontiers in Plant Science*, **4**, 324.

Schultz T. R., Brady S. G. (2008) Major evolutionary transitions in ant agriculture. *Proceedings of the National Academy of Sciences of the United States of America*, **105**, 5435–5440.

Schutter M. E., Sandeno J. M., Dick R. P. (2001) Seasonal, soil type, and alternative management influences on microbial communities of vegetable cropping systems. *Biology and Fertility of Soils*, **34**, 397–410.

Schuurman G.W. (2012) Ecosystem influences of fungus-growing termites in the dry paleotropics. In: *Soil Ecology and Ecosystem Services* (ed. Wall D. H.) pp. 173–188. Oxford, Oxford University Press.

Schwarz B., Barnes A. D., Thakur M. P., et al. (2017) Warming alters energetic structure and function but not resilience of soil food webs. *Nature Climate Change*, **7**, 895–900.

Scott W. A., Anderson R. (2003) Temporal and spatial variation in carabid assemblages from the United Kingdom Environmental Change Network. *Biological Conservation*, **110**, 197–210.

Seastedt T. (1984) The role of microarthropods in decomposition and mineralization processes. *Annual Review of Entomology*, **29**, 25–46.

Segers H. (2008) Global diversity of rotifers (Rotifera) in freshwater. *Hydrobiologia*, **595**, 49–59.

Segers H., De Smet W. H. (2008) Diversity and endemism in Rotifera: A review, and Keratella Bory de St Vincent. *Biodiversity Conservation*, **17**, 303–316.

Sell P., Kuo-Sell H. L. (1990) Influence of infestation of oats by root-knot nematodes (*Meloidogyne* sp.) on the performance of the cereal aphid, *Metopolophium dirhodum* (Walk) (Hom Aphididae). *Journal of Applied Entomology*, **109**, 37–43.

Selonen S., Liiri M., Setälä H. (2014) Can the soil fauna of boreal forests recover from lead-derived stress in a shooting range area? *Ecotoxicology*, **23**, 437–448.

Serreze M. C., Walsh J. E., Chapin F. S. I., et al. (2000) Observational evidence of recent changes in the northern high-latitude environment. *Climate Change*, **46**, 159–207.

Setälä H. (2000) Reciprocal interactions between Scots pine and soil food web structure in the presence and absence of ectomycorrhiza. *Oecologia*, **125**, 109–118.

Shao Y., Zhang W., Shen J., et al. (2008) Nematodes as indicators of soil recovery in tailings of a lead/zinc mine. *Soil Biology & Biochemistry*, **40**, 2040–2046.

Sharpley A. N., Syers J. K., Springett J. A. (1979) Effect of surface-casting earthworms on the transport of phosphorus and nitrogen in surface runoff from pasture. *Soil Biology & Biochemistry*, **11**, 459–462.

Shaw A. E., Adams B. J., Barrett J. E., et al. (2018) Stable C and N isotope ratios reveal soil food web structure and identify the nematode *Eudorylaimus antarcticus* as an omnivore-predator in Taylor Valley, Antarctica. *Polar Biology*, **41**, 1013–1018.

Sherlock E. (2012) *Key to the Earthworms of the UK and Ireland*, Shrewsbury, Field Studies Council.

Shmida A., Wilson M. V. (1985) Biological determinants of species diversity. *Journal of Biogeography*, **12**, 1–20.

Siepel H. (1994) Life history tactics of microarthropods. *Biology and Fertility of Soils*, **18**, 263–278.

Siepel H., de Ruiter-Dijkman E. M. (1993) Feeding guilds of oribatid mites based on their carbohydrase activities. *Soil Biology & Biochemistry*, **25**, 1491–1497.

Siepel H., Maaskamp F. (1994) Mites of different feeding guilds affect decomposition of organic matter. *Soil Biology & Biochemistry*, **26**, 1389–1394.

Sieriebriennikov B., Ferris H., De Goede R. G. M. (2014) NINJA: An automated calculation system for nematode-based biological monitoring. *European Journal of Soil Biology*, **61**, 90–93.

Sikora R. A., Malek R. B., Taylor D. P., Edwards D. I. (1979) Reduction of *Meloidogyne naasi* infection of creeping bentgrass by *Tylenchorhynchus agri* and *Paratrichodorus minor*. *Nematologica*, **25**, 179–183.

Sileshi G., Kenis M., Ogol C. K. P. O., Sithanantham S. (2001) Predators of *Mesoplatys ochroptera* Stål in sesbania-planted fallows in eastern Zambia. *BioControl*, **46**, 289–310.

Simaiakis S. M., Tjørve E., Gentile G., Minelli A., Mylonas M. (2012) The species–area relationship in centipedes (Myriapoda: Chilopoda): A comparison between Mediterranean island groups. *Biological Journal of the Linnean Society*, **105**, 146–159.

Simberloff D. S., Wilson E. O. (1970) Experimental zoogeography of islands: A two year record of colonization. *Ecology*, **51**, 934–937.

Simmons B. L., Wall D. H., Adams B. J., et al. (2009) Long-term experimental warming reduces soil nematode populations in the McMurdo Dry Valleys, Antarctica. *Soil Biology & Biochemistry*, **41**, 2052–2060.

Six J., Frey S. D., Thiet R. K., Batten K. M. (2006) Bacterial and fungal contributions to carbon sequestration in agroecosystems. *Soil Science Society of America Journal*, **70**, 555–569.

Slabber S., Worland M. R., Leinaas H. P., Chown S. L. (2007) Acclimation effects on thermal tolerances of springtails from sub-Antarctic Marion Island: Indigenous and invasive species. *Journal of Insect Physiology*, **53**, 113–125.

Smith H. G. (1996) Diversity of Antarctic terrestrial protozoa. *Biodiversity and Conservation*, **5**, 1379–1394.

Smith H. G., Bobrov A., Lara E. (2008a) Diversity and biogeography of testate amoebae. *Biodiversity and Conservation*, **17**, 329–343.

Smith H. G., Wilkinson D. M. (2007) Not all free-living microorganisms have cosmopolitan distributions – The case of *Nebela* (*Apodera*) *vas* Certes (Protozoa: Amoebozoa: Arcellinida). *Journal of Biogeography*, **34**, 1822–1831.

Smith R. G., Mcswiney C. P., Grandy A. S., et al. (2008b) Diversity and abundance of earthworms across an agricultural land-use intensity gradient. *Soil & Tillage Research*, **100**, 83–88.

Smolik J. D., Dodd J. L. (1983) Effect of water and nitrogen, and grazing on nematodes in a shortgrass prairie. *Journal of Range Management*, **36**, 744–748.

Snyder B. A., Hendrix P. F. (2008) Current and potential roles of soil macroinvertebrates (earthworms, millipedes, and isopods) in ecological restoration. *Restoration Ecology*, **16**, 629–636.

Sohlenius B. (1980) Abundance, biomass and contribution to energy flow by nematodes in terrestrial ecosystems. *Oikos*, **34**, 186–194.

Sohlenius B., Boström S. (2005) The geographic distribution of metazoan microfauna on East Antarctic nunataks. *Polar Biology*, **28**, 439–448.

Sohlenius B., Wasilewska L. (1984) Influence of irrigation and fertilization on the nematode community in a Swedish pine forest soil. *Journal of Applied Ecology*, **21**, 327–342.

338 · Bibliography

Soininen J. (2012) Macroecology of unicellular organisms – Patterns and processes. *Environmental Microbiology Reports*, **4**, 10–22.

Soininen J., Heino J. (2005) Relationships between local population persistence, local abundance and regional occupancy of species: Distribution patterns of diatoms in boreal streams. *Journal of Biogeography*, **32**, 1971–1978.

Soininen J., Korhonen J. J., Karhu J., Vetterli A. (2011) Disentangling the spatial patterns in community composition of prokaryotic and eukaryotic lake plankton. *Limnology & Oceanography*, **56**, 508–520.

Soler R., Bezemer T. M., van der Putten W. H., Vet L. E. M., Harvey J. A. (2005a) A multitrophic approach linking below and aboveground insects: The effects of root herbivory on the performance of an aboveground herbivore, its parasitoid and hyperparasitoid. *Journal of Animal Ecology*, **74**, 1121–1130.

Soler R., Bezemer T. M., van der Putten W. H., Vet L. E. M., Harvey J. A. (2005b) Root herbivore effects on above-ground herbivore, parasitoid and hyperparasitoid performance via changes in plant quality. *Journal of Animal Ecology*, **74**, 1121–1130.

Soler R., Harvey J. A., Kamp A. F. D., et al. (2007) Root herbivores influence the behaviour of an aboveground parasitoid through changes in plant volatile signals. *Oikos*, **116**, 367–376.

Soler R., Schaper S., Harvey J. A., et al. (2009) Influence of presence and spatial arrangement of belowground insects on host-plant selection of aboveground insects: A field study. *Ecological Entomology*, **34**, 339–345.

Sommer M., Jochheim H., Höhn A., et al. (2013) Si cycling in a forest biogeosystem – The importance of transient state biogenic Si pools. *Biogeosciences*, **10**, 4991–5007.

Soong J., Nielsen U. N. (2016) The role of microarthropods in emerging models of soil organic matter. *Soil Biology & Biochemistry*, **102**, 37–39.

Soong J. L., Vandegehuchte M. L., Horton A J., et al. (2016) Soil microarthropods support ecosystem productivity and soil C accrual: Evidence from a litter decomposition study in the tallgrass prairie. *Soil Biology & Biochemistry*, **92**, 230–238.

Spain A.V., McIvor J. G. (1988) The nature of herbaceous vegetation associated with termitaria in north-eastern Australia. *Journal of Ecology*, **76**, 181–191.

St John M. G., Bellingham P. J., Walker L. R., et al. (2012) Loss of a dominant nitrogen-fixing shrub in primary succession: Consequences for plant and belowground communities. *Journal of Ecology*, **100**, 1074–1084.

Staley J.T., Johnson S. N. (2008) Climate change impacts on root herbivores. In: *Root Feeders – An Ecosystem Perspective* (eds. Johnson S. N., Murray P. J.) pp. 192–213. Wallingford, CABI Publishing.

Staley J. T., Mortimer S. R., Morecroft M. D., Brown V. K., Masters G. J. (2007) Summer drought alters plant-mediated competition between foliar- and root-feeding insects. *Global Change Biology*, **13**, 866–877.

Standen V. (1978) The influence of soil fauna of decomposition by micro-organisms in blanket bog litter. *Journal of Animal Ecology*, **47**, 25–38.

Standen V. (1984) Production and diversity of enchytraeids, earthworms and plants in fertilized hay meadow plots. *Journal of Applied Ecology*, **21**, 293–312.

Stanton N. L. (1979) Patterns of species diversity in temperate and tropical litter mites. *Ecology*, **60**, 295–304.

Stanton N. L., Tepedino V. J. (1977) Island habitats in soil communities. *Ecological Bulletins*, **25**, 511–514.
Stary J., Block W. (1998) Distribution and biogeography of oribatid mites (Acari: Oribatida) in Antarctica, the sub-Antarctic islands and nearby land areas. *Journal of Natural History*, **32**, 861–894.
Steinacker D. F., Wilson S. D. (2008) Scale and density dependent relationship among roots, mycorrhizal fungi and collembola on grassland and forest. *Oikos*, **117**, 703–710.
Stevens G. C. (1989) The latitudinal gradient in geographical range: How so many species coexist in the tropics. *American Naturalist*, **133**, 240–256.
Stevnbak K., Maraldo K., Georgieva S., et al. (2012) Suppression of soil decomposers and promotion of long-lived, root herbivorous nematodes by climate change. *European Journal of Soil Biology*, **52**, 1–7.
Sticht C., Schrader S., Geisemann A., Weigel H.-J. (2009) Sensitivity of nematode feeding types in arable soil to free air CO_2 enrichment (FACE) is crop specific. *Pedobiologia*, **52**, 337–349.
Stirling G. R. (2011) Suppressive biological factors influence populations of root lesion nematode (*Pratylenchus thornei*) on wheat in vertosols from the northern grain-growing region of Australia. *Australasian Plant Pathology*, **40**, 416–429.
Stout J. D. (1963) Some observations on the Protozoa of soil beechwood soils on the Chiltern Hills. *Journal of Animal Ecology*, **32**, 281–287.
   (1968) The significance of the protozoan fauna in distinguishing mull and mor of beech (*Fagus sylvatica* L.). *Pedobiologia*, **8**, 387–400.
Stout J. D., Heal O. W. (1967) Protozoa. In: *Soil Biology* (eds. Burges A., Raw F.) pp. 149–195. London, Academic Press.
Strickland M. S., Callaham Jr. M. A., Gardiner E. S., et al. (2017) Response of soil microbial community composition and function to bottomland forest restoration. *Applied Soil Ecology*, **119**, 317–326.
Strickland M. S., Wickings K., Bradford M. A. (2012) The fate of glucose, a low molecular weight compound of root exudates, in the belowground foodweb of forests and pastures. *Soil Biology & Biochemistry*, **49**, 23–29.
Strong D. T., De Wever H., Merckx R., Recous S. (2004) Spatial location of carbon decomposition in the soil pore system. *European Journal of Soil Science*, **55**, 739–750.
Stuart R. J., Barbercheck M. E., Grewal P. S., Taylor R. A. J., Hoy C. W. (2006) Population biology of entomopathogenic nematodes: Concepts, issues, and models. *Biological Control*, **38**, 80–102.
Suarez A. V., Holway D. A., Case T. J. (2001) Patterns of spread in biological invasions dominated by long-distance jump dispersal: Insights from Argentine ants. *Proceedings of the National Academy of Sciences of the United States of America*, **98**, 1095–1100.
Suding K. N., Collins S. L., Gough L., et al. (2005) Functional- and abundance-based mechanisms explain diversity loss due to N fertilization. *Proceedings of the National Academy of Sciences of the United States of America*, **102**, 4387–4392.
Sugimoto A., Bignell D. E., MacDonald J. A. (2000) Global impact of termites on the carbon cycle and atmospheric trace gases. In: *Termites: Evolution, Sociality, Symbioses, Ecology* (eds. Abe T., Bignell D. E., Higashi M.) pp. 409–435. Dordrecht, Kluwer Academic Press.

Sun X., Zhang X., Zhang S., et al. (2013) Soil nematode responses to increases in nitrogen deposition and precipitation in a temperate forest. *PloS ONE*, **8**, e82468.
Susilo F. X., Neutel A. M., van Noordwijk M., et al. (2004) Soil biodiversity and food webs. In: *Below-ground Interactions in Tropical Agroecosystems* (eds. van Noordwijk M., Cadisch G., Ong C. K.) pp. 285–302. Wallingford, CAB International.
Susoy V., Sommer R. J. (2016) Stochastic and conditional regulation of nematode mouth-form dimorphisms. *Frontiers in Ecology and Evolution*, **4**, 23. doi: 10.3389/fevo.2016.00023.
Swift M. J., Heal O. W., Anderson J. M. (1979) *Decomposition in Terrestrial Ecosystems*, Berkeley, University of California Press.
Swift M. J., Izac A. M. N., van Noordwijk M. (2004) Biodiversity and ecosystem services in agricultural landscapes – Are we asking the right questions? *Agriculture, Ecosystems & Environment*, **104**, 113–134.
Tarnokai C., Canadell J. G., Schuur E. A. G., et al. (2009) Soil organic carbon pools in the northern circumpolar permafrost region. *Global Biogeochemical Cycles*, **23**, GB2023, doi:10.1029/2008GB003327.
Taylor B. R., Parkinson D., Parsons W. F. J. (1989) Nitrogen and lignin content as predictors of litter decay rates: A microcosm test. *Ecology*, **70**, 97–104.
Terauds A., Chown S. L., Fraser M., et al. (2012) Conservation biogeography of the Antarctic. *Diversity and Distribution*, **18**, 726–741.
Teuben A., Roelofsma T. A. P. J. (1990) Dynamic interactions between functional groups of soil arthropods and microorganisms during decomposition of coniferous litter in microcosm experiments. *Biology and Fertility of Soils*, **9**, 145–151.
Teuben A., Verhoef H. A. (1992) Direct contribution by soil arthropods to nutrient availability through body and faecal nutrient content. *Biology and Fertility of Soils*, **15**, 71–75.
Thakur M. P., Könne T., Griffin J. N., Eisenhauer N. (2017a) Warming magnifies predation and reduces prey coexistence in a model litter arthropod system. *Proceedings of the Royal Society B*, **284**, 2016–2570.
Thakur M. P., Reich P. B., Fisichelli N. A., et al. (2014) Nematode community shifts in response to experimental warming and canopy conditions are associated with plant community changes in the temperate–boreal forest ecotone. *Oecologia*, **175**, 713–723.
Thakur M. P., Reich P. B., Hobbie S. E., et al. (2017b) Reduced feeding activity of soil detritivores under warmer and drier conditions. *Nature Climate Change*, **8**, 75–78.
The *C. elegans* Sequencing Consortium (1998) Genome sequence of the nematode *C. elegans*: A platform for investigating biology. *Science*, **282**, 2012–2018.
Thoden T. C., Korthals G. W., Termorshuizen A. J. (2011) Organic amendments and their influences on plant-parasitic and free-living nematodes: A promising method for nematode management. *Nematology*, **13**, 133–153.
Thompson L. J., Hoffmann A. A. (2007) Effects of ground cover (straw and compost) on the abundance of natural enemies and soil macro invertebrates in vineyards. *Agricultural and Forest Entomology*, **9**, 173–179.
Thorne B. L., Grimaldi D. A., Krishna K. (2000) Early fossil history of the termites. In: *Termites: Evolution, Sociality, Symbioses, Ecology* (eds. Abe T., Bignell D. E., Higashi M.) pp. 77–94. Dordrecht, Kluwer Academic.

Tiemann L. K., Grandy A. S., Atkinson E. E., Marin-Spiotta E., Mcdaniel M. D. (2015) Crop rotational diversity enhances belowground communities and functions in an agroecosystem. *Ecology Letters*, **18**, 761–771.

Tietze F. (1968) Untersuchungen über die Beziehungen zwischen Bodenfeuchte und Carabiden-besiedlung in Wiesengesellschaften. *Pedobiologia*, **8**, 50–58.

Tilman D. (1982) *Resource Competition and Community Structure*, Princeton, NJ, Princeton University Press.

Tingey D. T., Johnson M. G., Lee E. H., et al. (2006) Effects of elevated CO_2 and O_3 on soil respiration under ponderosa pine. *Soil Biology & Biochemistry*, **38**, 1764–1778.

Tixier M.-S., Kreiter S., De Moraes G. J. (2008) Biogeographic distribution of the Phytoseiidae (Acari: Mesostigmata). *Biological Journal of the Linnean Society*, **93**, 845–856.

Todd T. C., Blair J. M., Milliken G. A. (1999) Effects of altered soil–water availability on a tallgrass prairie nematode community. *Applied Soil Ecology*, **13**, 45–55.

Toepfer S., Haye T., Erlandson M., et al. (2009) A review of the natural enemies of beetles in the subtribe Diabroticina (Coleoptera: Chrysomelidae): Implications for sustainable pest management. *Biocontrol Science and Technology*, **19**, 1–65.

Topoliantz S., Ponge J. F., Viaux P. (2000) Earthworm and enchytraeid activity under different arable farming systems, as exemplified by biogenic structures. *Plant and Soil*, **225**, 39–51.

Torode M. D., Barnett K. L., Facey S. L., et al. (2016) Altered precipitation impacts on above and below-ground grassland invertebrates: Summer drought leads to outbreaks in spring. *Frontiers in Plant Science*, **7**, 1468.

Traniello J. F. A., Levings S. C. (1986) Intra- and intercolony patterns of nest dispersion in the ant *Lasius neoniger*. Correlations with territoriality and foraging ecology. *Oecologia*, **69**, 413–419.

Trap J., Bonkowski M., Plassard C., Villenave C., Blanchart E. (2016) Ecological importance of soil bacterivores for ecosystem functions. *Plant and Soil*, **398**, 1–24.

Traunspurger W., Reiff N., Krashevska V., Majdi N., Scheu S. (2017) Diversity and distribution of soil micro-invertebrates across an altitudinal gradient in a tropical montane rainforest of Ecuador, with focus on freeliving nematodes. *Pedobiologia*, **62**, 28–35.

Treonis A. M., Austin E. E., Buyer J. S., et al. (2010) Effects of organic amendment and tillage on soil microorganisms and microfauna. *Applied Soil Ecology*, **46**, 103–110.

Treseder K. K. (2004) A meta-analysis of mycorrhizal responses to nitrogen, phosphorus, and atmospheric CO_2 in field studies. *New Phytologist*, **164**, 347–355.

Treseder K. K. (2008) Nitrogen additions and microbial biomass: A meta-analysis of ecosystem studies. *Ecology Letters*, **11**, 1111–1120.

Tsiafouli M. A., Bhusal D. R., Sgardelis S. P. (2017) Nematode community indices for microhabitat type and large scale landscape properties. *Ecological Indicators*, **73**, 472–479.

Tsiafouli M. A., Thébault E., Sgardelis S. P., et al. (2015) Intensive agriculture reduces soil biodiversity across Europe. *Global Change Biology*, **21**, 973–985.

Bibliography

Tsyganov A. N., Nijs I., Beyens L. (2011) Does climate warming stimulate or inhibit soil protist communities? A test on testate Amoebae in high-Arctic tundra with free-air temperature increase. *Protist*, **162**, 237–248.

Tuck S. L., Winqvist C., Mota F., et al. (2014) Land-use intensity and the effects of organic farming on biodiversity: A hierarchical meta-analysis. *Journal of Applied Ecology*, **51**, 746–755.

Tullgren A. (1918) Ein sehr einfacher Ausleseapparat für terricole Tierfaunen. *Zeitschrift für angewandte Entomologie*, **4**, 149–150.

Turner J., Bindschadler R., Convey P., et al. (2009) *Antarctic Climate Change and the Environment*, Cambridge, Scientific Committee for Antarctic Research.

Turner J., Colwell S. R., Marshall G. J., et al. (2005) Antarctic climate change during the last 50 years. *International Journal of Climatology*, **25**, 279–294.

Tyler A. N., Carter S., Davidson D. A., Long D. J., Tipping R. (2001) The extent and significance of bioturbation on ^{137}Cs distributions in upland soils. *Catena*, **43**, 81–99.

Ulrich W., Fiera C. (2009) Environmental correlates of species richness of European springtails (Hexapoda: Collembola). *Acta Oecologica*, **35**, 45–52.

Ulyshen M. D. (2016) Wood decomposition as influenced by invertebrates. *Biological Reviews*, **91**, 70–85.

UN (2014) *United Nations Sustainable Development Goals. Open Working Group Proposal for Sustainable Development Goals.* www.sustainabledevelopment.un.org/focussdgs.html.

UN (2015) *World Population Prospects: The 2015 Revision, Volume I: Comprehensive Tables (ST/ESA/SER.A/379)*. New York, Population Division of the Department of Economic and Social Affairs of the United Nations Secretariat.

Urbášek F., Chalupský J. (1992) Effects of artificial acidification and liming on biomass and on the activity of digestive enzymes in Enchytraeidae (Oligochaeta): Results of an ongoing study. *Biology and Fertility of Soils*, **14**, 67–70.

Urbášek F., Rusek J. (1994) Activity of digestive enzymes in seven species of Collembola (Insecta, Entognatha). *Pedobiologia*, **38**, 400–406.

Urich T., Lanzén A., Qi J., Huson D. H., Schleper C., Schuster C. H. (2008) Simultaneous assessment of soil microbial community structure and function through analysis of the meta-transcriptome. *PloS ONE*, **3**, e2527.

Usher M. B., Davis P., Harris J., Longstaff B. (1979) A profusion of species? Approaches towards understanding the dynamics of the populations of microarthropods in decomposer communities. In: *Population Dynamics* (eds. Anderson R. M., Turner B. D., Taylor L. R.) pp. 359–384. Oxford, Blackwell Scientific.

van den Bosch R., Stern V. M. (1962) The integration of chemical and biological control of arthropod pests. *Annual Review of Entomology*, **7**, 367–386.

van der Putten W. H. (2003) Plant defense belowground and spatiotemporal processes in natural vegetation. *Ecology*, **84**, 2269–2280.

van der Putten W. H., Bardgett R. D., Bever J. D., et al. (2013) Plant–soil feedbacks: The past, the present and future challenges. *Journal of Ecology*, **101**, 265–276.

van der Putten W. H., Bardgett R. D., De Ruiter P. C., et al. (2009) Empirical and theoretical challenges in aboveground–belowground ecology. *Oecologia*, **161**, 1–14.

van der Putten W. H., Klironomos J. N., Wardle D. A. (2007) Microbial ecology of biological invasions. *The ISME Journal*, **1**, 28–37.
van der Putten W. H., Yeates G. W., Duyts H., Reis C. S., Karssen G. (2005) Invasive plants and their escape from root herbivory: A worldwide comparison of the root-feeding nematode communities of the dune grass *Ammophila arenaria* in natural and introduced ranges. *Biological Invasions*, **7**, 733–746.
van Dooremalen C., Berg M. P., Ellers J. (2013) Acclimation responses to temperature vary with vertical stratification: Implications for vulnerability of soil-dwelling species to extreme temperature events. *Global Change Biology*, **19**, 975–984.
van Eekeren N., de Boer H., Hanegraaf M., et al. (2010) Ecosystem services in grassland associated with biotic and abiotic soil parameters. *Soil Biology & Biochemistry*, **42**, 1491–1504.
van Elsas J. D., Chiurazzi M., Mallon C. A., et al. (2012) Microbial diversity determines the invasion of soil by a bacterial pathogen. *Proceedings of the National Academy of Sciences of the United States of America*, **109**, 1159–1164.
van Groeningen J. W., Lubbers I. M., Vos H. M. J., et al. (2014) Earthworms increase plant production: A meta-analysis. *Scientific Reports*, **4**, 6365.
Van Gundy S. D., Stolzy L. H. (1961) Influence of soil oxygen concentrations on the development of *Meloidogyne javanica*. *Science*, **134**, 665–666.
van Vliet P. C. J. (1998) Hydraulic conductivity and pore size distribution in small microcosms with and without enchytraeids (Oligochaeta). *Applied Soil Ecology*, **9**, 277–282.
Van Wensem J., Verhoef H. A., Van Straalen N. M. (1993) Litter degradation stage as a prime factor for isopod interaction with mineralization processes. *Soil Biology & Biochemistry*, **25**, 1175–1183.
Vanbergen A. J., Watt A. D., Mitchell R., et al. (2007) Scale-specific correlations between habitat heterogeneity and soil fauna diversity along a landscape structure gradient. *Oecologia*, **153**, 713–725.
Vandegehuchte M. L., Sylvain Z. A., Reichmann L. G., et al. (2015) Responses of a desert nematode community to changes in water availability. *Ecosphere*, **6**, e44.
Vanek J. (1967) Industrie exhalate und Moosmilben gemeinschaften in Nordböhmen. In: *Progress in Soil Biology* (eds. Graff O., Satchell J. E.) pp. 331–339. North Holland, Amsterdam.
Vanfleteren J. R., Blaxter M. L., Tweedie S. A. R., et al. (1994) Molecular genealogy of some nematode taxa as based on cytochrome c and globin amino acid sequences. *Molecular Phylogenetics and Evolution*, **3**, 92–101.
Vannier G. (1987) The porosphere as an ecological medium emphasized in Professor Ghilarov's work on soil animal adaptations. *Biology and Fertility of Soils*, **3**, 39–44.
Vasconcelos H. L., Maravalhas J. B., Feitosa R. M., et al. (2018) Neotropical savanna ants show a reversed latitudinal gradient of species richness, with climatic drivers reflecting the forest origin of the fauna. *Journal of Biogeography*, **45**, 259–268.
Vegter J. J., Huyer-Brugman F. A. (1983) Comparative water relations in Collembola: Transpiration, desiccation tolerance and effects of body size. In: *New Trendsin Soil Biology* (eds. Lebrun P., André H. M., De Medts A., Wauthy G.) pp. 411–416. Ottignies, Diet-Brichart.

Bibliography

Velasco-Castrillón A., Page T. J., Gibson J. A. E., Stevens M. I. (2014a) Surprisingly high levels of biodiversity and endemism amongst Antarctic rotifers uncovered with mitochondrial DNA. *Biodiversity*, **15**, 130–142.

Velasco-Castrillón A., Schultz M. B., Colombo F., et al. (2014b) Distribution and diversity of soil microfauna from East Antarctica: Assessing the link between biotic and abiotic factors. *PloS ONE*, **9**, e87529. doi:10.1371/journal.pone.0087529.

Veresoglou S. D., Halley J. M., Rillig M. C. (2015) Extinction risk of soil biota. *Nature Communications*, **6**,8862, doi: 10.1038/ncomms9862.

Verhoef H. A., Brussaard L. (1990) Decomposition and nitrogen mineralization in natural and agri-ecosystems: The contribution of soil animals. *Biogeochemistry*, **11**, 175–211.

Verhoef H. A., Nagelkerke C. J., Joose E. N. G. (1977) Aggregation pheromones in Collembola. *Journal of Insect Physiology*, **23**, 1009–1013.

Verschoor B. C., Pronk T. E., de Goede R. G. M, Brussaard L. (2002) Could plant-feeding nematodes affect the competition between grass species during succession in grasslands under restoration management? *Journal of Ecology*, **90**, 753–761.

Vervoort M. T. W., Vonk J. A., Mooijman P. J. W., et al. (2012) SSU ribosomal DNA-based monitoring of nematode assemblages reveals distinct seasonal fluctuations within evolutionary heterogeneous feeding guilds. *PloS ONE*, **7(10)**, e47555. doi:10.1371/journal.pone.0047555.

Viketoft M., Bengtsson J., Sohlenius B., et al. (2009) Long-term effects of plant diversity and composition on soil nematode communities in model grasslands. *Ecology*, **90**, 90–99.

Viketoft M., van der Putten W. (2015) Top-down control of root-feeding nematodes in range-expanding and congeneric native plant species. *Basic and Applied Ecology*, **16**, 260–268.

Virginia R. A., Wall D. H. (1999) How soils structure communities in the Antarctic Dry Valleys. *Bioscience*, **49**, 973–983.

Vitousek P. M., Aber J. D., Howarth R. W., et al. (1997a) Human alteration of the global nitrogen cycle: Sources and consequences. *Ecological Applications*, **7**, 737–750.

Vitousek P. M., Mooney H. A., Lubchenco J., Melillo J. M. (1997b) Human domination of earth's ecosystems. *Science*, **277**, 494–499.

Vos C., Schouteden N., van Tuinen D., et al. (2013) Mycorrhiza-induced resistance against the rooteknot nematode *Meloidogyne incognita* involves priming of defense gene responses in tomato. *Soil Biology & Biochemistry*, **60**, 45–54.

Vreeken-Bruijs M. J., Hassink J., Brussaard L. (1998) Relationships of soil microarthropod biomass with organic matter and pore size distribution in soils under different land use. *Soil Biology & Biochemistry*, **30**, 97–106.

Wagg C., Bendera S. F., Widmerc F., van der Heijden M. G. A. (2014) Soil biodiversity and soil community composition determine ecosystem multifunctionality. *Proceedings of the National Academy of Sciences of the United States of America*, **111**, 5266–5270.

Walker M. D., Walker D. A., Welker J. M., et al. (1999) Long-term experimental manipulation of winter snow regime and summer temperature in arctic and alpine tundra. *Hydrological Processes*, **13**, 2315–2330.

Wall D. H. (2007) Global change tipping points: Above- and belowground biotic interactions in a low diversity ecosystem. *Philosophical Transactions of the Royal Society B: Biological Sciences*, **362**, 2291–2306.
Wall D. H., Bradford M. A., St John M. G., et al. (2008) Global decomposition experiment shows soil animal impacts on decomposition are climate-dependent. *Global Change Biology*, **14**, 2661–2677.
Wall D. H., Nielsen U. N., Six J. (2015) Soil biodiversity and human health. *Nature*, **528**, 69–76.
Wall J.W., Skene K. R., Neilson R. (2002) Nematode community and trophic structure along a sand dune succession. *Biology and Fertility of Soils*, **35**, 293–301.
Wallace A. R. (1853) On the insects used for food in the Indians of the Amazon. *Transactions of the Royal Entomological Society of London*, **2**, 241–244.
Wallace R. L., Snell T. W., Ricci C., Nogrady T. (2006) *Rotifera Volume 1: Biology, Ecology and Systematics*, 2nd edn, Gent: Kenobi Productions and The Hague: Backhyus Academic Publishing BV.
Wallwork J. A. (1970) *Ecology of Soil Animals*, New York, McGraw-Hill.
Wallwork J. A. (1976) *The Diversity and Distribution of Soil Fauna*, London, Academic Press.
Walsh C. L., Johnson-Maynard J. L. (2016) Earthworm distribution and density across a climatic gradient within the Inland Pacific Northwest cereal production region. *Applied Soil Ecology*, **104**, 104–110.
Wang J. G., Bakken L. R. (1997) Competition for nitrogen during decomposition of plant residues in soil: Effect of spatial placement of N-rich and N-poor plant residues. *Soil Biology & Biochemistry*, **29**, 153–162.
Wang L., Chen Z., Shang H., Wang J., Zhang P.Y. (2014) Impact of simulated acid rain on soil microbial community function in Masson pine seedlings. *Electronic Journal of Biotechnology*, **17**, 199–203.
Wang X., Nielsen U. N., Yang X., et al. (2018) Grazing induces direct and indirect shrub effects on soil nematode communities. *Soil Biology & Biochemistry*, **121**, 193–201.
Wardle D. A. (1992) A comparative assessment of factors which influence microbial biomass carbon and nitrogen levels in soil. *Biology Reviews*, **67**, 321–358.
Wardle D. A. (2002) *Communities and Ecosystems: Linking the Aboveground and Belowground Components*, Princeton, NJ, Princeton University Press.
Wardle D. A. (2006) The influence of biotic interactions on soil biodiversity. *Ecology Letters*, **9**, 870–886.
Wardle D. A., Giller K. E. (1996) The quest for a contemporary ecological dimension to soil biology. *Soil Biology & Biochemistry*, **28**, 1549–1554.
Wardle D. A., Peltzer D. A. (2017) Impacts of invasive biota in forest ecosystems in an aboveground–belowground context. *Biological Invasions*, **19**, 3301–3316.
Wardle D. A., Yeates G. W., Baker G. M., Bonner K. I. (2006) The influence of plant litter diversity on decomposer abundance and diversity. *Soil Biology & Biochemistry*, **38**, 1052–1062.
Wardle D. A., Yeates G. W., Watson R. N., Nicholson K. S. (1995) Development of the decomposer food-web, trophic relationships, and ecosystem properties during a three-year primary succession in sawdust. *Oikos*, **73**, 155–166.
Wasilewska L., Bienkowski P. (1985) Experimental study on the occurrence and activity of soil nematodes in decomposition of plant material. *Pedobiologia*, **28**, 41–57.

Watanabe H., Tokuda G. (2010) Cellulolytic systems in insects. *Annual Review of Entomology*, **55**, 609–632.
Wauthy G. (1982) Synecology of forest soil oribatid mites of Belgium (Acari, Oribatida). III. Ecological groups. *Acta Oecologia*, **3**, 469–494.
Wauthy G., Noti M.-I., Dufrêne M. (1989) Geographic ecology of soil oribatid mites in deciduous forests. *Pedobiologia*, **33**, 399–416.
Weaver H. J., Hawdon J. M., Hoberg E. P. (2010) Soil-transmitted helminthiases: Implications of climate change and human behavior. *Trends in Parasitology*, **26**, 574–581.
Webb C. O. (2000) Exploring the phylogenetic structure of ecological communities: An example for rain forest trees. *American Naturalist*, **156**, 145–155.
Webb N. R., Hoeting J. A., Ames G. M., Pyne M. I., Poff N. L. (2010) A structured and dynamic framework to advance traits-based theory and prediction in ecology. *Ecology Letters*, **13**, 267–283.
Wei H., Liu W., Zhang J., Qin Z. (2017) Effects of simulated acid rain on soil fauna community composition and their ecological niches. *Environmental Pollution*, **220**, 460–468.
Weis-Fogh T. (1948) Ecological investigations on mites and collemboles in the soil. *Natura Jutlandica*, **1**, 309–330.
Weiser M. D., Michaletz S. T., Buzzard V., et al. (2018) Toward a theory for diversity gradients: The abundance–adaptation hypothesis. *Ecography*, **41**, 255–264.
Wells T. C. E., Sheail J., Ball D. F., Ward L. K. (1976) Ecological studies in the Porton Ranges. Relationships between vegetation, soils and land-use history. *Journal of Ecology*, **64**, 589–624.
Weronika E., Łukasz K. (2017) Tardigrades in space research – Past and future. *Astrobiology*, **47**, 545–533.
Wertheim B., van Baalen E.-J. A., Dicke M., Vet L. E. M. (2005) Pheromone-mediated aggregation in nonsocial arthropods: An evolutionary ecological perspective. *Annual Review of Entomology*, **50**, 321–346.
Wharton D. A. (1986) *A Functional Biology of Nematodes*, Baltimore, MD, The Johns Hopkins University Press.
Wharton D.A., Fern D.J. (1995) Survival of intracellular freezing by the Antarctic nematode *Panagrolaimus davidi*. *The Journal of Experimental Biology*, **198**, 1381–1387.
Wickings K., Grandy A. S. (2011) The oribatid mite *Scheloribates moestus* (Acari: Oribatida) alters litter chemistry and nutrient cycling during decomposition. *Soil Biology & Biochemistry*, **43**, 351–358.
Wickings K., Grandy A. S., Reed S. C. (2012) The origin of litter chemical complexity during decomposition. *Ecology Letters*, **15**, 1180–1188.
Widenfalk L. A., Bengtsson J., Berggren Å., et al. (2015) Spatially structured environmental filtering of collembolan traits in late successional salt marsh vegetation. *Oecologia*, **179**, 537–549.
Widenfalk L. A., Leinaas H. P., Bengtsson J., Birkemoe T. (2018) Age and level of self-organization affect the small-scale distribution of springtails (Collembola). *Ecosphere*, **9**, e02058.
Widenfalk L. A., Malmström A., Berg M. P., Bengtsson J. (2016) Small-scale Collembola community composition in a pine forest soil – Overdispersion in functional traits indicates the importance of species interactions. *Soil Biology & Biochemistry*, **103**, 52–62.

Wilkinson D. M. (2001) What is the upper size limit for cosmopolitan distribution in free living microorganisms? *Journal of Biogeography*, **28**, 285–291.

Wilkinson D. M., Creevy A. L., Valentine J. (2012) The past, present and future of soil protist ecology. *Acta Protozoologica*, **51**, 189–199.

Wilkinson D. M., Mitchell E. A. D. (2010) Testate amoebae and nutrient cycling with particular reference to soils. *Geomicrobiology Journal*, **27**, 520–533.

Williams B. L., Griffiths B. S. (1989) Enhanced nutrient mineralization and leaching from decomposing Sitka spruce litter by enchytraeid worms. *Soil Biology & Biochemistry*, **21**, 1883–1888.

Williamson W. M., Wardle D. A., Yeates G. W. (2005) Changes in soil microbial and nematode communities during ecosystem decline across a long-term chronosequence. *Soil Biology & Biochemistry*, **37**, 1289–1301.

Willis K. J., Jeffers E. S., Tovar C. (2018) What makes a terrestrial ecosystem resilient? *Science*, **359**, 988–989.

Wilson E. O. (1974) *The Insect Societies*, Cambridge, MA, Belknap Press of Harvard University Press.

Wissuwa J., Salamon J.-A., Frank T. (2012) Effects of habitat age and plant species on predatory mites (Acari, Mesostigmata) in grassy arable fallows in Eastern Austria. *Soil Biology & Biochemistry*, **50**, 96–107.

Wolters V. (2000) Invertebrate control of soil organic matter stability. *Biology and Fertility of Soils*, **31**, 1–19.

Wolters V. (2001) Biodiversity of soil animals and its function. *European Journal of Soil Biology*, **37**, 221–227.

Womersley H. (1939) *Primitive Insects of South Australia: Silverfish, Springtails and their Allies*, Adelaide, Government Printer.

Wood T. G. (1971) The distribution and abundance of *Folsomides deserticola* (Collembola: Isotomidae) and other micro-arthropods in arid and semi-arid soils in southern Australia, with a note on nematode populations. *Pedobiologia*, **11**, 446–468.

Wood T. G. (1976) The role of termites (Isoptera) in decomposition processes. In: *The Role of Terrestrial and Aquatic Organisms in Decomposition Processes* (eds. Anderson J. M., Macfadyen A.) pp. 145–168. Oxford, Blackwell Scientific.

Wood T. G. (1978) Food and feeding habits of termites. In: *Production Ecology of Ants and Termites* (ed. Brian M.V.) pp. 55–80. Cambridge, Cambridge University Press.

Wood T. G., Sands W. A. (1978) The role of termites in ecosystems. In: *Production Ecology of Ants and Termites* (ed. Brian M. V.) pp. 245–293. Cambridge, Cambridge University Press.

Woods L. E., Cole C.V., Elliott E.V., Anderson R.V., Coleman D. C. (1982) Nitrogen transformation in soils as affected by bacterial–microfaunal interaction. *Soil Biology & Biochemistry*, **14**, 93–98.

Wu T., Ayres E., Bardgett R. D., Wall D. H., Garey J. R. (2011a) Molecular study of worldwide distribution and diversity of soil animals. *Proceedings of the National Academy of Sciences of the United States of America*, **108**, 17720–17725.

Wu X., Duffy J. E., Reich P. B., Sun S. (2011b) A brown-world cascade in the dung decomposer food web of an alpine meadow: Effects of predator interactions and warming. *Ecological Monographs*, **81**, 313–328.

Wu Z., Dijkstra P., Koch G. W., Peñuelas J., Hungate B. A. (2011c) Responses of terrestrial ecosystems to temperature and precipitation change: A meta-analysis of experimental manipulation. *Global Change Biology*, **17**, 927–942.

Bibliography

Wubs E. R. J., van der Putten W. H., Bosch M., Bezemer T. M. (2016) Soil inoculation steers restoration of terrestrial ecosystems. *Nature Plants*, **2**,16107, doi: 10.1038/NPLANTS.2016.1107.

Wurst S., Gebhardt K., Rillig M. C. (2011) Independent effects of arbuscular mycorrhiza and earthworms on plant diversity and newcomer plant establishment. *Journal of Vegetation Science*, **22**, 1021–1030.

Wurst S., Langel R., Reineking A., Bonkowski M., Scheu S. (2003) Effects of earthworms and organic litter distribution on plant performance and aphid reproduction. *Oecologia*, **137**, 90–96.

Wurst S., Ohgushi T. (2015) Do plant- and soil-mediated legacy effects impact future biotic interactions? *Functional Ecology*, **29**, 1373–1382.

Wurst S., van Dam N. M., Monroy F., Biere A., Van Der Putten W. H. (2008) Intraspecific variation in plant defense alters effects of root herbivores on leaf chemistry and aboveground herbivore damage. *Journal of Chemical Ecology*, **34**, 1360–1367.

Wurst S., van der Putten W. H. (2007) Root herbivore identity matters in plant-mediated interactions between root and shoot herbivores. *Basic and Applied Ecology*, **8**, 491–499.

Wurst S., Wagenaar R., Biere A., van der Putten W. H. (2010) Microorganisms and nematodes increase levels of secondary metabolites in roots and root exudates of *Plantago lanceolata*. *Plant and Soil*, **329**, 117–126.

Xia J. Y., Wan S. Q. (2008) Global response patterns of terrestrial plant species to nitrogen addition. *New Phytologist*, **179**, 428–439.

Xiao H. F., Schaefer D. A., Lei Y. B., et al. (2013) Influence of invasive plants on nematode communities under simulated CO_2 enrichment. *European Journal of Soil Biology*, **58**, 91–97.

Yamada A., Inoue T., Wiwatwitaya D., et al. (2005) Carbon mineralization by termites in tropical forests, with emphasis on fungus combs. *Ecological Research*, **20**, 453–460.

Yeates G. W. (1974) Studies on a climosequence of soils in tussock grasslands. *New Zealand Journal of Zoology*, **1**, 171–177.

Yeates G. W. (1998) Soil nematode assemblages: Regulators of ecosystem productivity. *Phytoparasitica*, **26**, 97–100.

Yeates G. W., Bongers T., De Goede R. G. M., Freckman D. W., Georgieva S. S. (1993) Feeding habits in soil nematode families and genera – An outline for soil ecologists. *Jounal of Nematology*, **25**, 315–331.

Yeates G. W., Hawke M. F., Rijkse W. C. (2000) Changes in soil fauna and soil conditions under *Pinus radiata* agroforestry regimes during a 25-year tree rotation. *Biology and Fertility of Soils*, **31**, 391–406.

Yeates G. W., Newton P. C. D. (2009) Long-term changes in topsoil nematode populations in grazed pasture under elevated atmospheric carbon dioxide. *Biology and Fertility of Soils*, **45**, 799–808.

Yeates G. W., Saggar S., Denton C. S., Mercer C. F. (1998) Impact of clover cyst nematode (*Heterodera trifolia*) infection on soil microbial activity in the rhizophere of white clover (*Trifolium repens*) – A pulse-labelling experiment. *Nematologica*, **44**, 81–90.

Yeates G.W., Wardle D.A. (1996) Nematodes as predators and prey: Relationships to biological control and soil processes. *Pedobiologia*, **40**, 43–50.
Young I. M., Crawford J.W. (2004) Interactions and self-organization in the soil–microbe complex. *Science*, **304**, 1634–1637.
Young I. M., Ritz K. (2000) Tillage, habitat space and function of soil microbes. *Soil & Tillage Research*, **53**, 201–213.
Young M. R., Behan-Pelletier V. M., Hebert P. D. N. (2012) Revealing the hyperdiverse mite fauna of subarctic Canada through DNA barcoding. *PloS ONE*, **7**, e48755. doi: 10.1371/journal.pone.0048755.
Zak D. R., Pregitzer K. S., Curtis P. S., et al. (1993) Elevated atmospheric CO_2 and feedback between carbon and nitrogen cycles. *Plant and Soil*, **151**, 105–117.
Zaller J. G., Arnone III J. A. (1999) Earthworm responses to plant species' loss and elevated CO_2 in calcareous grassland. *Plant and Soil*, **208**, 1–8.
Zeng G., Pyle J. A., Young P. J. (2008) Impact of climate change on tropospheric ozone and its global budgets. *Atmospheric Chemistry and Physics*, **8**, 369–387.
Zhang J., Yu J., Ouyang Y. (2015) Activity of earthworm in latosol under simulated acid rain stress. *Bulletin of Environmental Contamination and Toxicology*, **94**, 108–111.
Zhang J. E., Yu J.Y., Ouyang Y., Xu H. Q. (2014) Impact of simulated acid rain on trace metals and aluminum leaching in latosol from Guangdong Province, China. *International Journal of Soil and Sediment Contamination*, **23**, 725–735.
Zhang X., Ferris H., Mitchell J., Liang W. (2017) Ecosystem services of the soil food web after long-term application of agricultural management practices. *Soil Biology & Biochemistry*, **111**, 36–43.
Zhao C., Griffin J. N., Wu X., Sun S. (2013) Predatory beetles facilitate plant growth by driving earthworms to lower soil layers. *Journal of Animal Ecology*, **82**, 749–758.
Zhu T., Yang C., Wang J., et al. (2018) Bacterivore nematodes stimulate soil gross N transformation rates depending on their species. *Biology and Fertility of Soils*, **54**, 107–118.
Zullini A., Peretti E. (1986) Lead pollution and moss-inhabiting nematodes of an industrial area. *Water, Air, & Soil Pollution*, **27**, 403–410.
Zwart K. B., Kuikman P. J., vanVeen J. A. (1994) Rhizosphere protozoa: Their significance in nutrient dynamics. In: *Soil Protozoa* (ed. Darbyshire J. F.) pp. 93–122. Wallingford, CAB International.

Index

aboveground-belowground linkages
  altered rainfall regime, 238
  ecosystem function, 74
  spatial and temporal scales, 77
abundance-adaptation hypothesis,
  latitudinal patterns, 144
Acanthamoeba castellanii
  biotic interactions, 52
  suppression of *Caenorhabditis elegans*, 187
Acanthamoeba, biogeography, 126
Acari. *See* mites
Acariformes, 28
acid rain, effect of, 208, 209
Acutuncus antarcticus, feeding preference, 53
Adineta cf. gracilis, endemism, 130
Aenictinae, biogeography, 133
aggregatusphere, biological activity, 9, 10
agrochemicals, management of soil fauna, 274
agroecosystems, effect of restoration, 273
agroforestry, effect on soil fauna, 201
Agropyron cristatum, decomposition, 102
Allocasuarina torulosa, mite assemblage structure, 162
Allolobophora rosea, effect of vegetation composition, 165
allometric scaling, use in soil ecology, 99
altered rainfall regime
  aboveground-belowground linkages, 238
  ecosystem function, 236, 237
  ecosystem responses, 221
  vegetation composition, 239
Alternaria alternate, trophic cascades, 72
aluminum toxicity, interaction with acid rain, 209
Alveolata, RNA approaches, 94
amino acids, as biomarkers, 108
Ammophila arenaria, enemy-release, 213
Amoebozoa, 18

Amphimallon solstitiale, detection in gut contents, 108
Amynthas mekongianus, 37
Andropogon gerardii, litter decomposition, 109
anecic, definition, 15
Anguinidea, effect of elevated CO_2 concentration, 225
anhydrobiosis
  nematodes, 21, 128
  springtails, 32
Annelida. *See* earthworms
Antarctica
  anti-freeze proteins, 32
  assemblage structure, 186
  biogeography, 124
  climate change, 221
  edaphic influences, 168
  global chance, interaction among drivers, 242
  indigenous insects, 134
  invasive species, 211, 219
  latitudinal patterns, 140
  nematodes, 127
  Protozoa, 46
  rotifers, 25
  springtails, 30, 159
  survival strategies, 21
  tardigrades, 25
antifreeze protein, in springtails, 32
Antonie van Leeuwenhoek, 4, 27
ants
  agroforestry, 202
  altitudinal patterns, 146
  as biocontrol agents, 281
  biogeography, 133
  climatic influences, 153
  competition for resources, 186
  diversity and abundance, 35
  ecosystem function, 63

ants (*cont.*)
  feeding activities, 35
  invasive species, 214, 217, 218
  land use change, 194
  latitudinal patterns, 137, 142
  local and regional species richness relationships, 148
  management practices, 201
  restoration, 257
  species-area relationships, 136
  successional patterns, 252
  vegetation composition, 157
  vegetation structure, effect on, 161
  warming, effect on distribution, 233
Anurophorus subpolaris, survival in Antarctica, 32
Aphelenchoides, trophic cascades, 71
Aphodius erraticus, predator-prey interactions, 72
Apicomplexa, 18
  edaphic influences, 168
Apodera vas, biogeography, 125
Araneida, management practices, 198
Archegozetes longisetosus, feeding preference, 108
Archispirostreptus gigas, length, 40
Arrhopalites principalis, succession, 248
Arthropleona, 30
Arthurdendyus triangulates, distribution and impact, 218
Ascaris, molecular clock, 127
Ascidae, biogeography, 132
assemblage structure
  aboveground herbivory, 165
  aggregation pheromones, 170
  altered rainfall regime, 233, 236
  anthropogenic influences, 269
  biogeographical patterns, 121, 128
  biological processes, influence of, 160
  biotic interactions, 182, 184, 185
  characterization, 91
  climatic influences, 153
  deterministic versus stochastic influences, 187
  DNA barcoding, 94, 95
  edaphic influences, 153, 156, 160, 166, 167, 168, 177
  elevated CO_2 concentration, 225
  functional traits, 97, 99
  global change, interaction among multiple drivers, 241
  high throughput sequencing, 95

  human activities, 192
  knowledge gaps, 284
  leaf litter composition, 163
  macroecological patterns, 121
  metabarcoding, challenges, 93
  molecular sequencing approaches, constraints, 92
  predator-prey interactions, 184
  quantitative PCR, 93, 94
  restoration, 254
  RNA approaches, 93
  successional patterns, 153, 247
  vegetation composition, 153, 156, 163, 165
  vertical stratification, 16, 180, 182

Bacillus thuringiensis, suppression of plant pathogens, 282
bacterivores, effect on ecosystem function, 52
Baermann funnel, microfauna extraction, 87
Bdelloidea, 25
Beauveria, suppression of plant pathogens, 282
beetles
  aboveground-belowground linkages, 239
  agroforestry, 202
  altitudinal patterns, 147
  as biocontrol agents, 281
  competition for resources, 187
  edaphic influences, 157, 173
  land use change, 194
  management practices, 197
  organic farming, 200
  soil amendments, 201
  spatial patterns, 170, 173
  species-area relationships, 137
  successional patterns, 249
  vegetation composition, 157
  vertical stratification, 180
  wood decomposition, effect on, 65
Belgica albipes, biogeography, 134
Belgica antarctica, biogeography, 134
Benhamiinae, biogeography, 133
beta-diversity, insights from, 189
β-glucosidase, effect of fungal grazing, 66
biocides, use in soil ecology, 7
biocontrol
  contribution of soil fauna, 43
  entomopathogenic nematodes, 54, 280
biogeochemical cycling, influence of altered, 203

Index · 353

biogeography
  biological processes, 152
  biotic interactions, 152
  continental drift, 6
  cosmopolitan hypothesis, 124
  ecological biogeography theory, 6
  environmental filter, 152
  flagship species, 125, 129
  historical biogeography theory, 6
  knowledge gaps, 286
  Moderate Endemicity Model, 124
  origin as a field of research, 5
  Rapaport's rule, 140
  regional species pool, 152
  species filtering, 122
  the role of evolutionary history, 122
bioregions, contribution to conservation, 271
Blaniulus guttulatus, fungal grazing, 66
body size, latitudinal patterns, 143
bottom-up control, 70, 71
  global change effects, 243
  soil food web structure, 163, 164
Bromus sterilis, effect on mesostigmatid mite assemblages, 161
buffer strips, contribution to soil biodiversity, 275

Caecilians, 41
Caenorhabditis briggsae, carbon and phosphorus retention, 107
Caenorhabditis elegans
  as a model organism, 20
  biotic interactions, 52, 187
  trophic cascades, 71
Caenorhabditis, molecular clock, 127
calcium cycling, effect of millipedes, 67
Carabidae, 39
  competition, 186
Carex arenaria, effect of elevated CO_2 concentration, 225
Carmichaelia odorata, effect on soil fauna assemblage structure, 162
Catenaria, negative biotic interactions, 73
cellobiohydrolase, effect of fungal grazing, 66
cellulase, 21
cellulose
  as biomarker, 99
  production of, 64
centipedes
  agroforestry, 202
  biogeography, 135
  diversity and abundance, 40
  successional patterns, 253
  warming, 231
Cephalobidae, effect of altered rainfall regime, 235
Cercozoa, 18
  biogeography, 126
  edaphic influences, 168
  RNA approaches, 94
Chelonethi. *See* pseudoscorpions
Chicorium intybus, role as forage crop, 276
Chilopoda. *See* centipedes
Chironomidae, 39
chitinase, 21
chlorine, effect of, 206
chronosequences, use in ecology, 247
ciliates, 18
  edaphic influences, 160
Ciliophora, 18
  edaphic influences, 168
Cladocera, distribution, 159
Coleoptera. *See* beetles
Collembola. *See* springtails
collophore, springtail morphology, 30
Convention on Biological Diversity Aichi Biodiversity Targets, 289
Copepoda, distribution, 159
coprophagous, 72, 73
Coriolus versicolor, effect of grazing by springtails, 56
cover crops, contribution to ecosystem service provision, 275
crop plant diversity, management of, 275
crop rotation, influence of, 201
cryptic species complexes, insight from molecular techniques, 8
cryptobiosis, 27
Cryptodifflugia operculate, as predator of nematodes, 47
Cryptopygus antarcticus, effect of warming, 229
Cryptopygus, biogeography, 132
Ctenizidae, 40

Dasiphora fruticose, belowground effect of grazing, 166
decomposers
  altered rainfall regime, 234
  ecosystem function, 7, 83
  interspecific plant interactions, effect on, 69
  warming, 231

354 · Index

defense-induction hypothesis, influence of herbivores, 219
denaturing gradient gel electrophoresis, as biomarker, 46
detritusphere, biological activity, 9, 10
Dinophyceae, edaphic influences, 168
Diplopoda. *See* millipedes
Diplura, 28
   diversity and abundance, 34
   restoration, 256
Diptera, 39
dipterans
   altitudinal patterns, 147
   influence on aboveground assemblages, 76
dispersal rates, influence on distribution, 171
distance-decay relationships, 138
disturbance, influence on soil fauna diversity, 180
Ditylenchus, 22
diversity indices, assemblage structure, 92
DNA metabarcoding, insights into assemblage structure, 92
Dolichopodidae, 39
Dorylaimina
   heavy metals, 207
Dorylinae, biogeography, 133
drilosphere, biological activity, 9
dung beetles, effect on ecosystem function, 39, 65

earthworms
   aboveground herbivory, 165
   aboveground-belowground linkages, 76, 77, 239
   acid rain, 209
   agroforestry, 202
   altered rainfall regime, 239
   altitudinal patterns, 147
   as ecosystem engineers, 38
   biogeography, 133, 134
   climatic influences, 156
   competition for resources, 186
   density dependent effects, 184
   dispersal, 171
   distribution, 5
   disturbance, influence of, 187
   diversity and abundance, 37
   ecosystem engineers, effect as, 12
   ecosystem function, 4, 38, 60, 62
   edaphic influences, 38
   elevated CO_2 concentration, 225, 240
   endemism, 135
   environmental filtering, 189
   forage crops, 276
   invasive species, 215, 270
   latitudinal patterns, 140, 143
   life cycle, 38
   life history traits, 38
   litter decomposition, effect on, 103
   litter quality, 163
   local and regional species richness relationships, 149
   management practices, 196, 197, 198, 201
   organic farming, 200
   restoration, 256, 259
   role in restoration ecology, 261
   soil amendments, 201
   soil biodiversity, influence on, 183
   spatial patterns, 170, 189
   species-area relationships, 137
   successional patterns, 253
Ecdysozoa, 26
Ecitioninae, biogeography, 133
EcoFINDERS, 119, 157
ecological economics, role in agriculture, 278
ecological intensification, role in agriculture, 277
ecosystem engineers, effect of, 12, 15, 43, 59
ecosystem services, delivery of, 2
Eisenia andrei, life cycle, 39
Eisenia veneta, effect on weathering, 61
Elateridae, 43, 156
elevated CO_2 concentration, 221
   vegetation, effect on, 223
Enchytraeidae. *See* potworms
Enchytraeus, effect of altered rainfall regime, 234
endogeic, definition, 15
Enterobacteriaceae, endosymbiotic bacteria, 24
Entomobryomorpha, 30
entomopathogenic nematodes, as biocontrol agents, 20, 24, 43, 54, 280
environmental filtering, effect on phylogenetic clustering, 190
enzyme activity, as a biomarker, 31
epigeic, definition, 15
Escherichia coli, as bacterial prey, 107
Eucalyptus marginata, rehabilitation of mining sites, 257

Index · 355

Eucalyptus pilularis, mite assemblage structure, 162
Eucalyptus propiqua, mite assemblage structure, 162
Eucalyptus tereticornus, effect of fertilization, 118
Eudorylaimus antarcticus
  feeding preference, 53
Eudrilidae, 37
  biogeography, 133
euedaphic, definition, 15
Eutardigrada, 26
eutely, definition, 20
evenness indices, assemblage structure, 92

false scorpions. *See* pseudoscorpions
fecal pellets
  biogeochemical cycling, 73
  nutrient utilization, 73
  soil structure, 31, 58, 59, 64, 73
Fergusobia, biogeography, 127
fermentation layer, definition, 12
Festuca rubra, effect of elevated CO_2 concentration, 225
flagellates, 18
Folsomia brevicauda, succession, 248
Folsomia candida
  fungal grazing, 56, 66
  tillage, effect of, 198
  warming, 232
Folsomia fimetaria, trophic cascades, 72
Folsomia quadrioculata, spatial patterns, 174
Folsomides deserticola, distribution, 159
food demand, increase in, 279
Formicidae. *See* ants
free air carbon dioxide enrichment, use in soil ecology, 106
freeze-thaw cycles, effect of, 230
Fridericia, effect of altered rainfall regime, 234
Friesea grisea, distribution in Antarctica, 159
Friesea mirabilis, succession, 248
Friesea, feeding preferences, 31
functional traits, spatial patterns, 174
fungal feeders, ecosystem function, 68, 69, 74
furcular, springtail morphology, 30, 32, 97, 98
Fusarium oxysporum, trophic cascades, 72

Galenia africana, springtail abundance, 217
Gamasellus racovitzai, effect of warming, 229

Giant Gippsland Earthworm. *See Megascolides australis*
glacial refugia, potworms, 133
global change, 221
  ecosystems, impact on, 192
  multiple drivers, interaction among, 241, 243
  soil fauna assemblages, the future of, 270
Global Soil Biodiversity Atlas, 96, 289
Global Soil Biodiversity Initiative, 272, 289
Globodera, 23
Glomeris marginata, fungal grazing, 69
Glossoscolecidae, 37
  biogeography, 133
Gomphiocephalus hodgsoni, distribution in Antarctica, 159
gophers, effect on vegetation structure, 161
Gressittacantha terranova, distribution in Antarctica, 159
gut content DNA, as a biomarker, 31
gut content enzymatic activity, as indicator, 98

habitat loss, influence of, 192
Halicephalus mephisto, presence in deep soil, 181
Hartmannella, biogeography, 126
heat waves, effect on soil fauna, 229
heavy metals, effect of, 206
hedgerows, contribution to soil biodiversity, 275
hemiedaphic, definition, 15
Henlea, effect of altered rainfall regime, 234
herbivores
  altered rainfall regime, 233
  ecosystem function, 68
  invasive species, 212
herbivory, cascading effects belowground, 76
Heterodera, 22, 23
Heterodera trifolii, effect on *Trifolium repens*, 50
Heteroderidae, biogeography, 127
Heterorhabditidae, 24
Heterorhabditis, 24, 25
  as biocontrol agents, 280
Heterotardigrada, 26
Hoplolaimidae, effect of elevated CO_2 concentration, 225
humus layer, definition, 12
hydrobionts, definition, 17

hydrocarbon floatation, soil fauna quantification, 90
Hymenoptera, influence of soil amendments, 201
Hypoaspis aculeifer, trophic cascades, 72
Hypochtonius rufulus, effect of heavy metals, 208
Hypogastrura manubrialis, distribution, 217
Hypogastrura tullbergi, spatial patterns, 174
Hypogastrura viatica, distribution, 218

Illacme plenipes, number of legs, 40
insects
   as soil fauna, 39
   successional patterns, 249
integrated livestock-arable production, influence of, 201
integrated pest management
   agricultural practices, 201
   pest and pathogen suppression, 280
inter-cropping, influence of, 201
International Biological Program, contributions to soil ecology, 7
invasive plant species, effect of, 210
invasive soil fauna, effect of, 210, 270
irrigation, influence of, 206
Isaria, suppression of plant pathogens, 282
Isopoda. *See* isopods
isopods
   diversity and abundance, 39
   ecosystem function, 40, 65
   restoration, 255, 259
   role in restoration ecology, 261
   successional patterns, 253
   trophic cascades, 72
Isoptera. *See* termites
Isotoma sensibilis, succession, 248
Isotoma, feeding preferences, 31
Isotomurus, succession, 248
Ixodida, 28

keystone species, 8

Lamyctes emarginatus, 135
land use change, impact of, 193
land use, legacies of, 277
Lasius flavus, mounds, 63
latitudinal patterns, drivers of, 140
leaf litter, effect on assemblage structure, 177
Lecanicillium, suppression of plant pathogens, 282

Lepidium sativum, effects of Protozoa, 47
Lepidoptera, 39
Liacarus subterraneus, consumption of nematodes, 54
Linepithema humile, distribution and impact, 218
litter bag studies
   contribution of soil fauna, 65, 101, 103
   criticisms, 102
   early applications, 7
litter decomposition, effect of soil fauna, 42
litter layer, definition, 12
litter stoichiometry, role in decomposition, 104
litter transformers, successional patterns, 254
Lolium perenne
   as forage crop, 276
   root herbivory, 50
Longidorus, 22
Longidorus elongates, effect of elevated CO_2 concentrations, 225
Lotus corniculatus, soil fauna assemblages, 161
Lumbricidae, 37
Lumbricus terrestris
   as an ecosystem engineer, 4
   increased O_3 concentration, 240
   soil metabolism, 58
Lycosidae, 40

macroecology
   abundance-range relationships, 149
   altitudinal patterns, 139, 144
   distance-decay relationships, 137
   knowledge gaps, 286
   latitudinal patterns, 139
   local and regional richness patterns, 148
   species-area relationships, 135
macrofauna
   biogeography, 122
   definition, 14
   diversity and abundance, 34
   ecosystem function, 35, 59, 64, 65
   litter bag studies, 7
   management practices, 197
   organic farming, 199
   quantification, 90
   role in restoration ecology, 261
   successional patterns, 252, 253
   vegetation composition, 161, 164, 195
   vertical stratification, 180
Macrotermitinae, fungal farming termites, 37

Magicicada, life cycle, 39
Malaise trap. *See* pitfall trap
Mamestra brassica, aboveground-belowground linkages, 77
management practices
  assemblage structure, 196
  ecosystem function, contribution of soil fauna to, 195
  edaphic factors, effect on, 197
  homogenization of assemblages, 193
  legacies of, 193
Mastotermitidae, biogeography, 133
McMurdo Dry Valleys, ecosystem function, 81, 82
Medicago sativa, effect on mesostigmatid mite assemblages, 161
megafauna
  as ecosystem engineers, 34, 41
  diversity and abundance, 34
  ecosystem function, 59, 65
Megascolecidae, 37
Megascolides australis, 37
Meloidogyne, 20, 22, 23
  negative biotic interactions, 73
Meloidogyne hapla, suppression of, 282
Meloidogyne incognita
  biotic interaction, 283
  increased O_3 concentration, 240
  rhizodeposition, effect on, 49
  root development, effect on, 49
  suppression of, 200
Meloidogynidae, biogeography, 127
mesofauna
  altered rainfall regime, 234
  biogeography, 122, 131
  chlorine, 206
  definition, 14
  diversity and abundance, 27
  ecosystem function, 28, 55, 59, 65
  elevated CO_2 concentration, 224
  habitat, 28
  land use, 158
  litter bag studies, 7
  organic farming, 199
  quantification, 89
Mesostigmata. *See* mesostigmatid mites
mesostigmatid mites
  as biocontrol agents, 281
  climatic influences, 155
  DNA barcoding, 96
  edaphic influences, 158, 173, 178
  feeding activities, 29

freeze-thaw cycles, 230
land use, 158
management practices, 197
nitrogen deposition, 205
predators, effect as, 54, 184
restoration, 255
spatial patterns, 171, 173, 189
vegetation composition, 158
vertical stratification, 181
metabolic processes, effect of warming, 226
meta-community dynamics, assemblage structure, 188
Metarhizium, role in biocontrol, 280, 282
microarthropods
  as bioindicators, 209
  biogeography, 132
  climatic influences, 159
  density dependency, 184
  ecosystem function, 65
  edaphic influences, 177
  fertilizer application, 204
  global change, 227
  global change, interaction among drivers, 234, 244
  increased O_3 concentration, 240
  management practices, 201
  nitrogen deposition, 205
  pesticides, 195, 208
  predators, effect as, 201
  spatial patterns, 163, 169
  successional patterns, 249
  vegetation composition, 164
  vertical stratification, 180, 181
microbial biomass, effect of microbial grazing, 52
microcosms, use in soil ecology, 7
microfauna
  biogeography, 6, 122
  definition, 14
  diversity and abundance, 17
  ecosystem function, 18, 51
  elevated CO_2 concentration, 224
  habitat, 17
  microbial grazers, quantifying effect of, 18
microhabitat diversity, effect on soil fauna diversity, 176
microscope, development of, 4
millipedes
  agroforestry, 202
  calcium carbonate, 169
  defense, 40

Index

millipedes (cont.)
  diversity and abundance, 40
  ecosystem function, 65, 67
  feeding activities, 40
  restoration, 259
  role in restoration ecology, 261
  successional patterns, 253
minimum-tillage, influence of, 201
mining, effect of, 208
mites
  aboveground-belowground linkages, 239
  agroforestry, 202
  altered rainfall regime, 234
  as biocontrol agents, 281
  biotic interactions, 186
  calcium carbonate, 169
  climatic influences, 153
  diversity and abundance, 28
  ecosystem function, 55, 58
  elevated CO_2 concentration, 224
  feeding guilds, 30
  fertilizer application, 206
  increased O_3 concentration, 240
  land use, 199
  life cycle, 28, 29
  management practices, 198, 201
  nitrogen deposition, 205
  pesticides, 208
  restoration, 258, 259
  species-area relationships, 137
  successional patterns, 248, 249, 250, 253
  trophic cascades, 71
  vegetation composition, 161, 163
  warming, 228, 229, 231
  water potential, 12, 29
moder, definition, 12
molecular sequencing approaches, use in soil ecology, 8
Monogononta, 25
Mononchoidea, edaphic influences, 157
mor, definition, 13
mulching, effect of, 200
mull, definition, 12
Muscidae, 39
Mycetophilidae, 39
Mycotozoa, RNA approaches, 94
Myriapoda, 34
  diversity and abundance, 40
Myrmicinae, biogeography, 133
Myzus persica, effect of soil fauna, 77

N-acetylglucosaminidase, effect of fungal grazing, 66
nano sensors, soil fauna distribution, 96
naphthalene
  criticisms, 102
  use in soil ecology, 101, 102, 109
natural enemies
  escape from, 79
  role in agroecosystems, 274
  soil amendments, 201
natural habitat, contribution to soil biodiversity, 275
nematodes, 17
  aboveground herbivory, 76, 165
  aboveground-belowground linkages, 239
  abundance-range relationships, 150
  agroforestry, 202
  altered rainfall regime, 233, 234, 236
  altitudinal patterns, 146
  as biocontrol agents, 20
  as bioindicators, 20, 111
  bacterial feeders, 23
  biogeography, 127, 128
  channel index, 112
  chemoreceptors, 20
  climatic influences, 153
  colonizer – persister scale, 111
  competition for resources, 186
  cover crop, 276
  dauer larvae, 21
  distance-decay relationships, 139
  disturbance, influence of, 187
  diversity and abundance, 20
  ecosystem function, 45, 48, 101, 109
  edaphic influences, 159, 160, 178
  effect of root feeders on aphids, 76
  elevated CO_2 concentration, 224, 225, 242
  enrichment index, 112
  entomopathogenic, 24
  feeding types, 21
  fertilizer application, 203, 204, 206
  forage crop, 276
  freeze-thaw cycles, 231
  fungal feeders, 23
  global change, interaction among drivers, 234
  heavy metals, 207, 208, 209
  increased O_3 concentration, 240
  intracellular freezing, 21
  land use, 199
  latitudinal patterns, 140

life cycle, 20
local and regional species richness relationships, 148
Maturity index, 111
microbial assemblages, effect on, 49
omnivores, 24
organic farming, 200
phylogenetic clustering, 190
plant parasite index, 111
plant parasites, 21
predators, effect of, 184
predatory, 23
quantification, 87, 88
quantitative PCR, applications, 113
restoration, 254, 259
rhizosphere, 176
soil amendments, 200
species-area relationships, 137
structure index, 112
successional patterns, 248, 250, 254
sulfur dioxide, 206
survival strategies, 21
trophic cascades, 71
vegetation composition, 156, 163, 164
vertical stratification, 180, 182
warming, 227, 228, 229
network analysis, application of, 118
Neuroptera, 39
neutral lipid fatty acids, as biomarkers, 108
neutral theory, use in soil ecology, 188
Nicodrilus caliginosus, effect of vegetation composition, 165
NINJA, use in nematology, 112
Nippostrongylus, molecular clock, 127
nitrogen, changes in biogeochemical cycles, 192, 203, 204, 205
novel assemblages, global change effects, 270

ocelli, springtail morphology, 97
Ocnerodrilidae, biogeography, 133
Octodrilus, effect on weathering, 61
Oniscus asellus, fungal grazing, 66, 69
Onychiuridae, 31
Orbiliomycete, as nematode trapping fungi, 282
organic farming, effect on soil fauna, 199
organic horizon, biological activity, 12
organic matter, 1
oribatid mites
 aboveground herbivory, 76, 165
 biogeography, 131

chlorine, 206
climatic influences, 155, 159
consumption of nematodes, 54
deterministic processes, 188
dispersal, 171, 188
diversity and abundance, 29
edaphic influences, 158, 173, 178
endemism, 131
feeding activities, 29
heavy metals, 208
land use, 158
latitudinal patterns, 140
litter quality, 163
management practices, 197
predators, effect of, 184
restoration, 254, 259
spatial patterns, 171, 173, 189
species-area relationships, 136
successional patterns, 249, 253, 254
trophic cascades, 71
vegetation composition, 158, 195
vertical stratification, 182
Oribatida. *See* oribatid mites
orographic cloud formation, influence on assemblage structure, 147
overdispersion
 earthworms, 189
 functional traits, 99
 springtail functional traits, 174

Panagrellus redivivus, fungal grazing, 66
Panagrolaimus davidi, intracellular freezing, 21
panphytophagous, 34
parasite genes, in nematodes, 22
Parasitiformes, 28
Paratylenchus, effect of soil water availability, 157
particle size, definitions, 9
Pasteuria penetrans, negative biotic interactions, 73
Pauropoda
 diversity and abundance, 34, 40
 ecosystem function, 40
 management practices, 198
permafrost, effect of warming, 243
pesticides, effect of, 206
pests and pathogens, suppression of, 200
Phasmarhabditis hermaphrodita, consumption of, 54
pheromones, contribution to aggregation, 170

Philonthus rubripennis, predator-prey
    interactions, 72
phosphatase, effect of microbial grazing,
    52, 66
phosphodiesterase, effect of fungal grazing, 66
phospholipid fatty acids, as biomarkers, 87,
    108
phosphorus, changes in biogeochemical
    cycles, 192, 203
Photorhabdus
    as microbial symbiont, 280
    suppression of plant pathogens, 282
photosynthetically derived carbon, fate of,
    10, 51, 105, 106
phytophagous, 32
Phytoseiidae, biogeography, 132
Picea abies, effect of Protozoa on growth, 47
Piloderma croceum, 50
pitfall trap extraction, 90
plant growth promoting fungi, role in
    agriculture, 282
plant growth promoting rhizobacteria, role
    in agriculture, 282
plant productivity, effect of microbial
    grazing, 52
Plantago lanceolata
    decomposer assemblages, 163
    earthworms, effect of, 62
    soil fauna assemblages, 161
plant-soil feedbacks
    contribution of soil fauna, 45, 78
    ecosystem structure, 79
    succession, 80
Plasmodiophorida, RNA approaches, 94
Platynothrus peltifer
    consumption of nematodes, 54
    heavy metals, 208
Plectidae, effect of altered rainfall regime,
    235
Plectus murrayi, feeding preference, 53
Pleuretra hystrix, biogeography, 129
Poa annua, aboveground-belowground
    linkages, 77
Poduromorpha, 30
    forage crop, 276
Poecilus versicolor, detection of prey in gut
    content, 108
Populus tremuloides, effect of increased O_3
    concentration, 240
porosphere, biological activity, 9
potworms, 28
    acid rain, 209
    agrochemicals, 208

altered rainfall regime, 234
as bioturbators, 58
as ecosystem engineers, 33
biogeography, 132
climatic influences, 153
diversity and abundance, 32
ecosystem function, 58, 59, 231
feeding activities, 33
heavy metals, 208, 209
increased O_3 concentration, 240
land use, 199
life cycle, 33
quantification, 89
soil aggregation, 59
spatial patterns, 169
successional patterns, 252
vegetation composition, 161, 163
vertical stratification, 182
warming, 227
Pratylenchinae, biogeography, 127
Pratylenchus, 22, 23
Pratylenchus penetrans
    plant growth, 50
Pratylenchus thornei, suppression of, 201
Pratylenchys penetrans
    negative biotic interactions, 73
predator-prey interactions, 72
    assemblage structure, 183
    warming, 231
predators
    ecosystem function, 68, 70
    trophic cascades, 71
predatory beetles, as biocontrol
    agents, 43
primary succession, definition, 246
principal coordinates of neighbouring
    matrices
    application in variance partitioning,
    116
Prionchulus punctatus, trophic
    cascades, 71
productivity, effect on soil fauna diversity,
    180
Prostigmata. *See* prostigmatid mites
prostigmatid mites, 28
    climatic influences, 159
    edaphic influences, 157
    freeze-thaw cycles, 230
Protaphorura armata
    plant growth, 50
    selective feeding, 31
Protorhabditis oxyuroides, effect on nitrogen
    cycling, 51

Protozoa, 17
  aboveground-belowground
    linkages, 76
  altered rainfall regime, 235
  as a resource, 47
  as bioindicators, 113
  as predators, 47
  biogeography, 124, 125
  biomass production, 46
  climatic influences, 153
  distance-decay relationships, 139
  diversity and abundance, 18
  ecosystem function, 19, 45,
    46, 101
  edaphic influences, 168
  feeding types, 18
  increased O_3 concentration,
    240
  latitudinal patterns, 140
  life cycles, 19
  limitations of activity, 19
  management practices, 196
  microbial assemblages, effect on, 46
  mycorrhizal forming fungi, effect
    on, 47
  presence in Antarctica, 126
  protistology, 5
  quantification, 87
  rhizosphere, 46, 176
  successional patterns, 248, 249
  survival strategies, 18
  vegetation composition, 164
Protura, 28
  diversity and abundance, 34
  management practices, 198
  restoration, 256
Pselliodudae, biogeography, 135
Pseudomonas chlororaphis, suppression of
    plant pathogens, 282
Pseudomonas protegens, suppression of plant
    pathogens, 282
pseudoscorpions, 28
  diversity and abundance, 33
  life cycle, 33
Pseudoterranova, molecular clock, 127
Pterostichus, effect of competition, 186

Qudsianematidae, effect of altered rainfall
    regime, 235
Quedius liangshanensis, predator-prey
    interactions, 72
Quercus robur, 50
Quercus rubra, litter decomposition, 104

radioisotopes, application of
  ^{14}carbon, 107
  ^{32}phosphorus, 107
  ^{65}zinc, 8
rarefaction curves
  assemblage structure, 91
  rotifers, 130
  springtails, 189
Reginaldia omodeoi, as a bioturbator, 38
residue addition, effect of, 200
Resinicium bicolor, preferential grazing on, 66
restoration
  invasive species impacts, 265
restoration
  soil fauna influences on, 254
restoration
  limitations, 266
Rhabditidae, effect of elevated CO_2
    concentration, 242
Rhabditis dolichura, predation by amoeba, 47
Rhabditis intermedia, effect on nitrogen
    cycling, 51
Rhabditis terricola, predation by amoeba, 47
Rhinotermitidae, biogeography, 133
rhizosphere
  biological activity, 9, 10
  biological hotspot, 176
  root exudation, 51
riparian zones, contribution to soil
    biodiversity, 275
root development, effect of Protozoa, 47
root exudation
  fate of photosynthetically derived
    carbon, 1, 106
  nematodes, effect of, 49
root herbivores
  aboveground-belowground linkages, 75
  abundances, 39
  ecosystem function, 43, 66, 67
  plant carbon allocation, 107
  role in succession, 262
  vegetation composition, effect on, 66
Rothamsted, 5, 47
Rotifera. *See* rotifers
rotifers, 17
  altitudinal patterns, 146
  biogeography, 129
  distance-decay relationships, 139
  diversity and abundance, 25
  endemism, 129, 130
  feeding activities, 25, 26
  life cycle, 26
  vegetation composition, 163

Sarcoptiformes, 28
Scarabaeidae, 43, 108
Scheloribates moestus, litter decomposition, 104
scorpions, as predators of soil fauna, 40
Scottnema lindsayae
    endemism, 127
Scottnema lindsayae, feeding preference, 53
Scutigerinidae, biogeography, 135
secondary succession, definition, 246
selective feeding, effect of, 43, 46
silicon cycling, effect of Protozoa, 19
Sinella curviseta, effect of increased O_3 concentration, 240
Sitona, influences on nitrogen cycling, 67
Sminthuridae, 32
Sminthurides malmgreni, succession, 248
snails
    calcium carbonate, 169
    feeding activities, 41
snow cover, effect on assemblage structure, 230
soil biodiversity
    cover crop, 276
    dilution experiments, 84
    ecosystem function, 8, 80, 81, 82, 83, 84, 272, 279
    ecosystem function, knowledge gaps, 286
    fine scale patterns, 175
    functional redundancy, 81
    hierarchical framework approaches, 85
    human wellbeing, importance to, 288
    identification gap, the, 14
    losses of, 3
    management of, 272
    multifunctionality, 83, 84
    pest and pathogen suppression, 280
    poor man's rainforest, the, 2
    reservoirs, management options, 275
    restoration, 265
    suppression of soil-transmitted diseases, 288
    vegetation composition, 195
soil ecology, development as a field of research, 2
soil fauna
    aggregation, 170
    as a resource, 3
    as bioindicators, 272
    biodiversity hotspots, 271
    conservation, 271
    diversity and abundance, 5
    ecosystem function, 2, 5, 7, 42, 43
    endemism, 286
    food web manipulations, 101
    invasive species, 214
    litter decomposition, 104
    microhabitat preferences, 177
    morphological classification, 14
    provision of services, 43
    role in moderating the success of alien species, 213
    role in restoration ecology, 260, 262
    the role of geothermal activity, 128
    threatened species, 271
    vegetation composition, 161
soil fauna biomass, global patterns, 121
soil food web models
    DayCent, biogeochemical cycling, 109
    ecosystem function, 74, 101, 109
    limitations, 109
soil food web structure
    agroecosystems, 283
    cover crop, 276
    ecosystem function, 67
    edaphic influences, 166
    elevated CO_2 concentration, 226
    functional redundancy, 109
    global change, 227, 242, 270
    management practices, 196
    restoration, 256
    role in agroecosystems, 274
    successional patterns, 250, 252
    superphosphate, effect of, 118
    vegetation composition, 161
soil formation, drivers, 1
soil health, importance to human wellbeing, 1
soil inoculants, role in restoration ecology, 263
soil organic matter, management of, 275
soil pores
    as habitat, 11
    definitions, 12
soil respiration
    microbial, 1
    warming, effect of, 231
soil sterilization, use in soil ecology, 8
soil structure, 9
soil texture, 9
soil-transmitted helminths, influence on human wellbeing, 288
Solenopsis invicta, distribution, 217
species co-existence – area relationship, definition, 136

species loss, effect of, 193
species richness, definitions, 92
Sphagnum magellanicum, amoeba assemblages, 114
spiders
 as biocontrol agents, 281
 as ecosystem engineers, 40
 as soil fauna, 40
 edaphic influences, 173
 management practices, 197
 soil amendments, 201
 spatial patterns, 173
 species-area relationships, 137
 successional patterns, 249
springtails
 aboveground-belowground linkages, 239
 agroforestry, 202
 altered rainfall regime, 234
 altitudinal patterns, 147
 biotic interactions, 186
 climatic influences, 153
 desiccation tolerance, 32
 dispersal, 188
 disturbance, influence of, 187
 diversity and abundance, 30
 ecosystem function, 32, 55, 57, 58
 edaphic influences, 157, 158
 elevated CO_2 concentration, 240
 extreme environments, 32
 feeding activities, 5, 31, 55
 fertilizer application, 204
 forage crop, 276
 freeze-thaw cycles, 230
 functional traits, 97
 habitat preferences, 32
 heavy metals, 208
 increased O_3 concentration, 240
 invasive species, 216
 land use, 158
 latitudinal patterns, 143
 life cycle, 30, 31
 management practices, 198, 201
 microbial assemblages, effect on, 56
 nitrogen deposition, 205
 predators, effect of, 184
 restoration, 258
 soil formation, contribution to, 31
 spatial patterns, 173, 174, 189
 species-area relationships, 136, 137
 successional patterns, 248, 249, 253, 254
 trophic cascades, 71

vegetation composition, 161, 195
vertical stratification, 181
warming, 228, 231
water potential, 12
stable isotope probing
 ^{13}carbon, 8, 47, 50, 56, 106, 109
 ^{13}C-labeled glucose, 105
 ^{15}nitrogen, 8, 48, 50, 109
 ^{18}oxygen, 8, 107
 application, 104
 constraints, 105
 use with biomarkers, 108
stable isotope ratios
 ^{13}carbon/^{12}carbon, 53, 105
 ^{15}nitrogen/^{14}nitrogen, 53, 56, 105
Staphylinidae, 39
Steganacarus magnus
 calcium carbonate content, 169
 consumption of nematodes, 54
Steinernema, 24, 25
 as biocontrol agents, 280
Steinernema feltiae
 consumption of, 54
 intracellular freezing, 21
Steinernematidae, 24
Stephensia brunnichella, aboveground-belowground linkages, 238
stoichiometry
 fertilizer application, influence of, 203
 use in soil ecology, 99
strategic tillage, effect of, 198
stress-response hypothesis, influence of herbivores, 219
Strongyloides stercoralis, management of, 288
structural equation models
 application, 116
 hypothesis testing, 116
 limitations, 118
 phosphorus fertilization, effect of, 118
 quantifying ecosystem function, 117
succession
 contribution of soil fauna, 43
 disturbance effects, 246
 ecosystem recovery, 246
 vegetation composition, 247, 258
sulfur dioxide, effect of, 206
sustainable management practices
 agroecosystems, 277, 279
 contribution of soil fauna, 270

Symphyla, 28
  diversity and abundance, 34, 40
  ecosystem function, 40
  restoration, 256
Symphypleona, 31
  forage crop, 276

Tabanidae, 39
tallgrass prairie, effect of nitrogen addition, 204
Taraxacum officinale, effect on mesostigmatid mite assemblages, 161
Tardigrada. *See* tardigrades
tardigrades, 17
  biogeography, 130
  diversity and abundance, 25, 26
  edaphic influences, 160
  feeding activities, 25, 26
  heavy metals, 208
  life cycle, 26
  survival strategies, 26
terminal restriction fragment length polymorphism, as a biomarker, 110
termites
  agroforestry, 202
  altitudinal patterns, 146
  as ecosystem engineers, 37, 64
  biogeography, 133
  breakdown of woody material, 63
  climatic influences, 156
  disturbance, influence of, 187
  diversity and abundance, 35
  ecosystem function, 63, 64, 65
  endemism, 133
  feeding activities, 37
  gut microbes, contributions of, 36
  invasive species, 217, 270
  land use change, 194
  latitudinal patterns, 142
  litter decomposition, effect on, 103
  nests, 37
  restoration, 258
  spatial patterns, 170
  substrate use, 107
  vegetation structure, effect on, 161
  warming, effect on distribution, 233
Termitidae, biogeography, 133
termitosphere, biological activity, 9, 11
Termopsidae, biogeography, 133
testate amoeba, 18, 47
  biogeography, 125

  distribution, 114
  heat waves, 230
  warming, 228
Tetracanthella bryura, succession, 248
Tetracanthella wahlgreni, succession, 248
thermal lethal limits, effect of warming, 226
Thysanoptera, effect of elevated CO_2 concentration, 224
Thysanura, effect of management practices, 198
tillage, use for pest control, 198
Tipulidae, 39
top-down control, 70, 71, 73
  assemblage structure, 184
  global change effects, 243
  pest and pathogen suppression, 280
  role in biocontrol, 201
trichobothria, springtail morphology, 97
Trichoderma viride, trophic cascades, 72
Trichodoridae, effect of elevated CO_2 concentration, 242
Trichostrongylus, molecular clock, 127
Trifolium pretense, as forage crop, 276
Trifolium repens
  aboveground-belowground linkages, 77
  decomposer assemblages, 163
  plant parasitic nematodes, 282
  role as forage crop, 276
  root herbivory, 50
Trombidiformes, 28
trophic cascades, 70, 71
  ecosystem function, 70
  elevated CO_2 concentration, 224
  invasive species, 211
  warming, 232
tropospheric ozone (O_3) concentration, effect of changes in, 239
Tullgren funnels, mesofauna extraction, 89
Tylenchorhynchus, 22
Tyleptus, biogeography, 127

UN Sustainable Development Goals, 289
underdispersion, of springtail functional traits, 174

variance partitioning, application, 114, 171
vertebrates, as soil fauna, 2
vertical stratification
  ground beetles, 171
  springtail functional traits, 98

warming
  ecosystem responses, 221
  soil fauna assemblages, 232
water bears. *See* tardigrades
water holding capacity, 9
water infiltration, 9
wire-worms, climatic influences, 156

Xenorhabdus, as microbial symbiont, 280
Xiphinema, 22
X-ray computed tomography, soil fauna distribution, 96

Zea mays, litter decomposition, 104

Printed in the United States
by Baker & Taylor Publisher Services